ROUTLEDGE LIBRARY EDITIONS: WW2

Volume 15

THE JAPAN/AMERICA FILM WARS

THE JAPAN/AMERICA FILM WARS
World War II Propaganda and its
Cultural Contexts

Edited by
ABÉ MARK NORNES AND FUKUSHIMA YUKIO

LONDON AND NEW YORK

First published in 1994 by Harwood Academic Publishers

This edition first published in 2022
by Routledge
2 Park Square, Milton Park, Abingdon, Oxon OX14 4RN

and by Routledge
605 Third Avenue, New York, NY 10158

Routledge is an imprint of the Taylor & Francis Group, an informa business

© 1994 Harwood Academic Publishers GmbH

All rights reserved. No part of this book may be reprinted or reproduced or utilised in any form or by any electronic, mechanical, or other means, now known or hereafter invented, including photocopying and recording, or in any information storage or retrieval system, without permission in writing from the publishers.

Trademark notice: Product or corporate names may be trademarks or registered trademarks, and are used only for identification and explanation without intent to infringe.

British Library Cataloguing in Publication Data
A catalogue record for this book is available from the British Library

ISBN: 978-1-03-201217-9 (Set)
ISBN: 978-1-00-319367-8 (Set) (ebk)
ISBN: 978-1-03-207014-8 (Volume 15) (hbk)
ISBN: 978-1-03-207087-2 (Volume 15) (pbk)
ISBN: 978-1-00-320528-9 (Volume 15) (ebk)

DOI: 10.4324/9781003205289

Publisher's Note
The publisher has gone to great lengths to ensure the quality of this reprint but points out that some imperfections in the original copies may be apparent.

Disclaimer
The publisher has made every effort to trace copyright holders and would welcome correspondence from those they have been unable to trace.

THE JAPAN/AMERICA FILM WARS

WORLD WAR II PROPAGANDA AND ITS CULTURAL CONTEXTS

Edited by

Abé Mark Nornes

and

Fukushima Yukio

Yamagata International Documentary Film Festival
Tokyo, Japan

harwood academic publishers
Switzerland • Australia • Belgium • France • Germany • Great Britain •
India • Japan • Malaysia • Netherlands • Russia • Singapore • USA

Copyright ©1994 by Harwood Academic Publishers GmbH, Poststrasse 22, 7000 Chur, Switzerland. All rights reserved.

Harwood Academic Publishers

Private Bag 8
Camberwell, Victoria 3124
Australia

12 Cour Saint-Eloi
75012 Paris
France

Christburger Str. 11
10405 Berlin
Germany

Post Office Box 90
Reading, Berkshire RG1 8JL
Great Britain

3-14-9, Okubo
Shinjuku-ku, Tokyo 169
Japan

Emmaplein 5
1075 AW Amsterdam
Netherlands

820 Town Center Drive
Langhorne, Pennsylvania 19047
United States of America

Originally published in Japanese and English in 1991 as *Nichibei eigasen / Media Wars: Then & Now* by Cinematrix Co. Ltd., Tokyo, Japan. Also published in 1991 as *Nichibei eigasen* by Seikyūsha Publishers, Tokyo, Japan.

Copyright © 1991 Cinematrix Co. Ltd., Tokyo, Japan; articles published with the permission of the authors.

No part of this book may be reproduced or utilized in any form or by any means, electronic or mechanical, including photocopying and recording, or by any information storage or retrieval system, without permission in writing from the publisher. Printed in the United States of America.

To the memory of
Ogawa Shinsuke
(1935–1992)

Contents

Introduction to the Series	ix
Preface	xi
PART I THE CALL TO CINEMATIC ARMS	1
Feeling in Tune — Perhaps Inspired... *John Grierson*	3
PART II THE JAPAN–AMERICA FILM WAR	5
War and Cinema in Japan *Shimizu Akira*	7
The United States Government and the Use of Motion Pictures during World War II *William T. Murphy*	59
PART III MANUFACTURING THE ENEMY	69
The Other and the Machine *Ueno Toshiya*	71
Warring Images: Stereotype and American Representations of the Japanese, 1941–1991 *Michael Renov*	95
PART IV VIOLENT IMAGES AND THEIR VARIOUS PLEASURES	119
Cinema / Nihilism / Freedom *Nibuya Takashi*	121
Cherry Trees and Corpses: Representations of Violence from WWII *Abé Mark Nornes*	147
PART V WHEN THE HUMAN BEINGS ARE GONE...	163
Tsurumi Shunsuke and *Kogawa Tetsuo* Discuss *The Effects of the Atomic Bomb on Hiroshima and Nagasaki*	165
Discussion Afterword *Abé Mark Nornes*	183

viii Contents

PART VI THE FILMS: FROM MUKDEN TO TOKYO BAY — 187

Films Essays by
  Yamane Sadao, Abé Mark Nornes and Komatsuzawa Hajime

PEARL HARBOR
Greater East Asia News #1 — Air Attacks over Hawaii, December 7, Momotaro's Sea Eagle — 189

JAPAN IN TIME OF CRISIS
Lifeline of the Sea, Japan in Time of Crisis, Picture Book 1936 (Momotaro vs. Mickey Mouse) — 197

CHINA
Diary of Boys Reclaiming the Land, China Incident, The Battle of China — 203

THE HOMEFRONT
Women of Steel, We Are Working So So Hard, Justice, Introduction to Our Weaponry Series: The Fighting Homefront, Topaz 1942–1945, Japanese Relocation, Fighting Young Citizens, Sending Off Our Students (Never to Return) — 209

MANUFACTURING THE ENEMY
The Educational System of Japan, Superman: Japoteurs, Private Snafu: Censored, Princess Iron Fan, Weapons of the Heart, Nippon Banzai, Let's Have a Drink, Dawn of Freedom — 221

VIOLENCE
Combat Film Report — No. 722, Jap Zero, Sacred Soldiers of the Sky, Kill or Be Killed, The Fleet That Came to Stay, Civilian Victims of Military Brutality — 243

BANNED CLASSICS
Let There be Light, Soldiers at the Front — 259

IN THE WAKE OF HIROSHIMA AND NAGASAKI
"Atomic Bombing" Interviews with Crews of "Enola Gay" and "The Great Artiste," The Effects of the Atomic Bomb on Hiroshima and Nagasaki, A Japanese Tragedy, History and Memory — 263

Bibliography — 271

Sources — 275

Index — 279

Contributors — 293

Introduction to the Series

Studies in Film and Video is a series of multi-authored volumes exploring, in some depth, particular topics in film, television, and video studies. As with *Quarterly Review of Film and Video,* the journal out of which the series emerged, the work published will focus on areas of research that are among the most pressing for the current study of culture: studies of gender, race and sexuality of representation; critical inquiries into postcolonial and cross-cultural media practices; explorations of new critical or theoretical dimensions in media studies; research on the function and effects of new technologies on global image cultures. The books of this series will enlarge and clarify current understandings of film and video culture during an era of their dramatic reconfiguration.

Preface

Recently, NHK broadcast a new Japanese version of the famous British documentary *7 Up*, in which a set of people are interviewed about their lives every seven years. The original is up to age 35, but this is the first effort for the Japanese. The most striking question of the program was, "If Japan goes to war, who would it fight?" Without hesitation, every child replied, "America." That seven-year-olds perceive the United States as a potential enemy says a lot about the state of US–Japan relations. It also suggests with some immediacy the continuing impact of our violent confrontation fifty years ago. The inertia of this period's violence and racial hatred is difficult to stop.

It should be noted, however, that none of the Japanese children felt a war would happen. They were quite positive that Japan is at peace and will stay that way. At the same time, the Liberal Democratic Party recently built a coalition to push a controversial bill through the Diet allowing Japan's Self-Defense Force (what the government calls the military) to participate in United Nations Peace Keeping Operations (what the UN calls war). This linguistic sleight of hand is, in fact, what this book is primarily concerned with: the recognition of the role of representation and its deployment, as it were, in the waging of war.

The origins of this book are rather unusual. Its first incarnation was as a retrospective catalog for a film festival in Japan. The Yamagata International Documentary Film Festival was the first festival in Asia dedicated exclusively to the documentary form. Flooded with tax monies, city and prefectural governments across Japan have erected beautiful art museums and cultural complexes. These facilities have one thing in common: they are empty. That is an exaggeration; however, people here often talk about a lack of "software" for their "hardware." As a result, film festivals of various sizes have popped up in the last five years. Not only do the festivals fill those halls, but they fulfill the governments' obligations to "internationalization" (whatever that means, no one is sure).

The Yamagata festival is part of this phenomenon; however, it has distinguished itself by its support for independent Asian filmmakers and its imaginative programming. Outside of a regular competition, the festival organizes a variety of sidebars. For the 1991 festival, these included Stephen Teo's program of independent Asian film and video, Yasui Yoshio's continuing survey of the history of Japanese documentary, a selection of new and unfinished Japanese films, and a retrospective of World War II documentaries that Fukushima Yukio and I curated. It was this last program from which this book arose.

Nineteen ninety-one was, of course, the fiftieth anniversary of Pearl Harbor. We anticipated not only a media blitz covering the anniversary, but also an intense period in Japan–America relations. For our part, we hoped to avoid hyperbole, showing these rare films and concentrating on what they have to teach us today. As the planning proceeded through the fall of 1990, it grew in both scope and gravity.

The decisive event occurred when Yukio and I travelled to the National Archives in Washington, DC, where most of the American and many of the Japanese films are preserved. Near the beginning of our stay, we flicked on our hotel's television and it wasn't long before a news anchor stopped in mid-report to announce reports of shooting in Iraq. That night, minds spinning with the violent images of the Pacific War, we watched the sky over Baghdad light up and the world go to war once again. Day after day, we would immerse ourselves in World War II images for nine hours, walk past the White House back to our hotel, and then watch more war on CNN. This experience fundamentally affected our approach to the retrospective, for we constantly found revealing similarities and differences between the way the two wars were represented. It may be long over now, but it is no less crucial to examine the intimate relationship of image-making to warfare, for the Gulf War was certainly not a war to end all wars.

A formidable obstacle to this goal is simply attaining enough intellectual distance to see that relationship at all. We tend to take it for granted, as is evidenced by the way journalists and spectators cling to their desire for "objectivity" in their reportage. With the distance afforded by the passing of time — fifty years in this case — it is much easier to see the weaknesses in our documentary images and soundtracks. For example, what were once considered "documentary" descriptions of the Japanese enemy can only be described as examples of the period's virulent racial hatred when we consider them now. Perhaps half a century from now we will find the demonization of Iraqis and Saddam Hussein just as disturbing. This is only one example of how we can foreground the culturally constructed nature of representations that seem so faithful to the reality we experience.

Far more effective than this temporal distance is the perspective created when we encounter other cultures, as anyone who has travelled overseas with an open mind can testify. If you remain in your cultural milieu and its hermetically sealed media environment, the world is an eminently benign place. However, when faced with a completely different way of living and thinking, one's own milieu suddenly seems far from natural. One's own culturally absorbed assumptions about the world become relativized, an experience that can be either thrilling or frightening.

We used this presumption to structure the retrospective. To literally force viewers out of their complacent spectator positions, we screened similar films from Japan and America back to back. For example, *We Are Working So So Hard*, about Japanese women in a uniform factory, was shown directly after the Rosie the Riveter film *Women of Steel*. By playing these two films off each other, many of their ideological underpinnings and the sexual politics of war suddenly became visible. To supplement this dialogical approach, we invited the authors of this book, as well as Bill Nichols and Shu Lea Cheang, to participate in nightly discussions. We were especially interested in encouraging people to connect these issues with their own media experience of war.

This was also a central reason for the catalog and its unusual depth. Yukio and I structured the book according to the same dialogical principles governing the screenings. We paired American and Japanese writers to discuss historical and theoretical aspects of the representation of World War II and of war in general. They discuss similar issues from differing perspectives, and reveal quite disparate approaches to film criticism.

THE CALL TO CINEMATIC ARMS

The book opens with a speech by the famous documentarist John Grierson. His comments at the Academy Awards dinner amounted to a call to cinematic arms. The very fact that a documentarist was invited to address the Academy sums up several important issues at the center of this project: the Hollywood film industry participated fervently in the war effort, and this resulted in a narrowing of the differences between documentary filmmaking and its fictional counterpart in Hollywood (an experience that continues to affect documentary in terms of conventions). From this jumping off point, the subsequent essays explain what happened and how we may think about this "film war."

THE JAPAN–AMERICA FILM WAR

The first pair of essays puts the historical period of Grierson's declaration of cinematic war into narrative form. Shimizu Akira offers a detailed history of the film bureaucracy during the war period, and how small changes in wording translated into a gradual co-option of the film industry into the war effort. Since Shimizu lived this history (he worked as a film journalist in the film industries of both Tokyo and Shanghai during the war), he crisscrosses a wealth of detail with personal anecdotes. As head of the United States National Archives' Motion Picture, Video and Sound section, William T. Murphy has spent more time around the American propaganda films than anyone. For this volume he summarizes the key films and events of the war.

MANUFACTURING THE ENEMY

Every war needs an enemy, and Ueno Toshiya and Michael Renov analyze how their respective governments formed public opinion and rallied their peoples around issues and enemies. Ueno looks at the complicity of film criticism of the period, and notes that the Asian enemy was in an ambiguous third position between Self and Other. This is an important critical intervention, for previous writers have always stressed the simple "absence" of enemy images. At the retrospective discussions, Renov suggested this analysis avoids the dubious binary constructions of Western criticism and may reveal a more Asian critical mode. As for his own essay, Renov theorizes various functions of stereotyping, including positive ones. He concentrates on the impact of the war's racism on Japanese Americans and gives welcome attention to the efforts of Asian American artists in constructing alternative histories. Both authors connect their thoughts to the war in the Persian Gulf.

VIOLENT IMAGES AND THEIR VARIOUS PLEASURES

The final pair of essays speculate on the pleasures and fascinations available in the violent images of conflict, as well as our responsibilities before them. Nibuya

Takashi's writing style builds on repetition and incremental variation, circulating around a wide variety of compelling issues concerning our obligations as spectators before images of death and destruction. Pivoting around acts of violence, he raises basic questions about the relationships between film and video, between technology and culture, and between the essence of the violent image and our accountability before it. In my essay, I attempt to identify several ways in which violence is represented, and how that representation functions within the culture it was produced. By describing the differences between Japanese and American reportage during World War II, it becomes clear that the Gulf War coverage holds much in common with that of Japanese propaganda of the thirties and forties.

WHEN THE HUMAN BEINGS ARE GONE...

One of the most important documentaries in film history is also one of the least seen: *The Effects of the Atomic Bomb on Hiroshima and Nagasaki* Nearly all of our black and white moving images of Hiroshima and Nagasaki come from this film, which came frighteningly close to total suppression. Had the American supervisor not ferreted away a 16mm print of the film in a midwestern depository, the world would be impoverished of some of its most important images of war. For various reasons, we were unsure a screening at Yamagata would be possible (it was in the end), so we arranged the next best thing. We asked two of the most interesting scholars in Japan, Tsurumi Shunsuke and Kogawa Tetsuo, to discuss the film in a *taidan*.

The taidan, or *zadan*, is a convention of Japanese magazines and books. While the regular interview places an interviewee at the mercy of a reporter who effaces his/her position of power and meaning, the zadan faces off two or more people of equal stature. This form of the interview goes way back; indeed, one of the first sound documentaries in Japan was a filmed zadan called *Victorious Japan (Kagayaku Nippon)*. Zadan often result in rather tame, predictable affairs; however, the wit and cutting criticism of Tsurumi and Kogawa result in an uncommonly fascinating discussion.

A word of warning: the production history of this film is extremely complicated, and many versions of its story are circulating in both Japanese and English. After Tsurumi and Kogawa met, Yukio and I obtained extensive production materials, including contracts and Strategic Bombing Survey memoranda. We also talked with two of the original people involved in the project, American supervisor Daniel McGovern and Japanese director Ito Sueo. It is important to read the discussion afterword, where we try to straighten out some points of misunderstanding in previous histories. It was somewhat embarrassing to learn new information that makes a few of the things Kogawa and Tsurumi say erroneous. At the same time, the attitudes that arise from the misinformation of previous accounts suggest some of the consequences involved in the simple writing of history.

THE FILMS: FROM MUKDEN TO TOKYO BAY

This section features short analyses of all the films screened at the Yamagata International Documentary Film Festival sidebar. They are grouped according to programs of the restropective, which may give readers a glimpse at what they missed. By nature, the essays lack a coherent line of argument; however, they contain valuable information, particularly since little has been published on Japanese documentary. Furthermore, while many of the American films have been treated in narrative histories, this is one of the few times they have come under close scrutiny.

Finally, I would like to make a comment or two on writing styles. Western readers will find the articles by Murphy, Renov and myself written in a "natural," familiar style. The Japanese writers offer some slightly different approaches, from Nibuya's roundabout approach, to Shimizu's painstaking lists and their raw data-like feel. We have also preserved original citation styles, for the difference is culturally based. Western criticism strives for a unified, standard style based on exhaustive detail. On the other hand, there are no standard styles for citation in Japan, which may come from very basic differences of thinking in regard to originality. Sometimes, as in Komatsuzawa's essay, it becomes difficult to tell what is original and what is extended quotation. At any rate, all sources mentioned in the text may be found in the final bibliography.

There are some people I would like to thank, beginning with Yano Kazuyuki who, as director of the Yamagata festival, went out of his way to make the retrospective and its catalog a reality. Kogawa Tetsuo led us to new writers. Saiki Tomonori of the Film Center and Yasui Yoshio of Planet Film Archives provided invaluable help for introducing us to films, photographs and written materials. Their knowledge of Japanese cinema came in handy while compiling the index and source list. We received needed practical support from Tomizuka Masaki, a citizen of Yamagata. We apologize that his essay on the role Yamagata intellectuals played in the promotion of the war had to be dropped from this volume. We are also grateful to our translators Susanne Sohermann, Maya Todeschini, Ronald Foster, and Hamaguchi Kōichi. This entire project would not have been possible without the cooperation and collaboration of William Murphy of the National Archives, Oba Matatoshi of the National Film Center of Japan, and Shimizu Akira of the Japan Film Library Council (Kawakita Memorial Film Institute). This brings me to my personal gratitude to Fukushima Yukio, with whom I enjoyed a true collaboration in every way. This partnership between Japanese and American programmers, between Japanese and American critics and film institutions, has been most exciting, and in my mind it is an example of the potential riches of Japan–America relations. I have experienced few things so pleasurable and meaningful. The readers of this volume missed the show, but at least there is the book.

Abé Mark Nornes

PART I
THE CALL TO CINEMATIC ARMS

Fig. 1.
(Credit: National Archives)

Feeling in Tune — Perhaps Inspired...

John Grierson

Long ago the documentary film set itself the not very popular task of talking about facts when people were more interested in illusions; of describing social problems which were embarrassing to some and ugly to many; of keeping men's consciences just a little closer to the dreadful grindstone of actuality.

At this time we are all, in one way or another, concerned in the high duty of creating and maintaining the morale which is necessary for a hard and absolute war. We are concerned with that most vital of all defenses in depth: the strong spirit of the people and their will to order and sacrifice. In that work it is not a question of which is lesser or greater: to lighten men's hearts with comedy or to hold them to the sticking point with films of more serious content. Both are necessary. I was reminded of this the other day by a story which came over from Mr. Brendon Bracken, the Minister of Information in England. It seems that when the Soviet War Delegation visited London, they asked Mr. Bracken if they might see a film; and Mr. Bracken said he would be very pleased, and he had some very nice documentaries to show them. The Soviet spokesman said, "Thank you very much — and he was sure the documentaries were very nice indeed, but, it Mr. Bracken didn't mind, the one film on earth his warriors wanted to see was Mr. Chaplin's *Dictator*.

Today's war tasks take us away from our peace-time concern with sociological problems. They are more immediate and more urgent. We are concerned with reporting the battle fronts. We have the duty of keeping the people in touch with their men on distant battlefields, on the high seas and in the air. Because authenticity has always been our watchword, we cannot avoid its more dangerous implications now. Already some of us know the responsibility of sending our camera-crews into danger and losing our people; and among the warring nations scores of cameramen have already died in the line of duty. In that record of bravery Germans, the Russians and the Australians have been particularly honorable. Wherever, in all the elements, there has been front-line fighting, their cameras have been up.

We have the more difficult duty — the most difficult of all from a mental point of view — of shaping from our war observations on every front — both military and civilian — the strategic pattern of highly complex events: of helping the people

---

JOHN GRIERSON *was a pioneer of documentary cinema, having initiated documentary movements in both England and Canada. During the war, he was the commissioner of the National Film Board of Canada. These are excerpts from a speech he presented to the movers and shakers of Hollywood concerning the duty of documentarists in Total War. The occasion was the 14th Annual Academy Awards banquet in 1942.*

to a broad and simple understanding of what is happening — of where they fit in — of what in duty is expected of them. Nothing is so certain as that men cannot give their best if they are bewildered, and particularly so in a democracy; and the greatest, perhaps, of all our film responsibilities is to give people, in simple dramatic patterns of thought and feeling, a sense of the true issues which lie behind the maze of events in this difficult moment of human history. Feeling themselves in tune — perhaps inspired — they will the more intensively give of their utmost and so will we.

In this field the best work today is being done, I think, by Louis de Rochemont and Stuart Legg.

It would be a poor business, however, if in following the hard and objective patterns of historic events, we forget the simple pattern of human reaction which persists in death and disaster, like seed in the scorched earth. None has kept the humanist record more nobly than Joris Ivens, Herbert Kline and Rey Scott in their war-time descriptions of Spain and Poland and China; and the English School is doing it brilliantly in films like *London Can Take It, Ordinary People, Letters from Home* and *Target for Tonight*. The cry of humanity is not, perhaps, the most potent motif in propaganda, nor the most useful, when the new forms of war are calling us hard and inexorable disciplines of all kinds. But we would be denying our democratic birthright if we ever became so hard that we could not hear it.

Lastly, there is a duty which falls on all of this industry alike. It is humble; it is deeply ordinary; it carries no honors with it. Theaters will not applaud it; like private soldiering, it will go completely unnoticed. But it is none-the-less vital. That is the simple duty of chores of war publicity and instruction. We can use the film to help the fighting services in their daily instruction; we can help the thousand and one Civilian Defense Services to a better understanding of their sometimes quite local duties; we can aid industrial morale and speed the organization of new skills in the service of our country. Mr. Disney has already given his great talent to such routine affairs as the teaching of gunnery and the encouragement of war savings; and nothing has honored Hollywood more than the willingness of men like Mr. Zanuck, Mr. Ford and Mr. Capra to step down from the grandiose preoccupations of major production to perform these simple but necessary jobs.

There will be much more of this to do in the future. There is a contribution which every kind of film and every kind of technician can make to help everyone — on military and civilian front alike — to do his job just a little bit better, and feel, however obscure he may be, a fighting force in the national effort. I hope you will not take it amiss if I say to an industry that has so often sought only the exciting, the meretricious and the spectacular, that this sober and humble and unselfish duty of helping the people, wherever they may be organized, to effective citizenship and good soldiering, will be the best evidence that we have, in all reality, aligned our art with the public purpose and have dedicated it, in all realism, to the pressing needs of our united cause.

PART II
THE JAPAN — AMERICA FILM WAR

War and Cinema in Japan

Shimizu Akira

I JAPANESE ATTITUDES TOWARD THE WAR

Japan's Invasion of China: The Absence of a Sense of Guilt

The Shōwa period officially began on 25 December 1926, but since the period's first year consisted of only one week, the true beginning of the era must be situated in 1927. In June of that year, Prime Minister Tanaka Gi'ichi, a former member of the army, organized the "Eastern Conference" (Tōhō Kaigi), only two months after taking office. The leaders of the Foreign Ministry, the Ministry of War, the Naval Department and the Kantō (Kwantung) Army all took part in the conference. The Kantō Army, an elite corps dispatched for the protection of Japan's interests in Manchuria, derived its name from the "Kantō-area" (*Kantō-shū*), the Japanese appellation of their newly leased territory located at the southern tip of the Liaotung Peninsula (including Lushun (Port Arthur) and Talien).

The purpose of the Eastern Conference was to decide upon Japan's basic policies toward China. While the former Cabinet had pursued a policy of cooperation with the United States and England, and of non-intervention in China, the new conference leaders set forth a more aggressive policy of "self-defense" for the protection of Japan's interests in Manchuria and Mongolia. This policy of "self-defense," which in actuality translated into military intervention, effectively furnished the pretext for Japan's invasion of China.

Immediately following the conference, Chinese newspapers published the text of the so-called "Tanaka Memorial," which begins with the words, "If you want to conquer China, you must first conquer Manchuria and Mongolia; if you want to conquer the world, you must first conquer China." The memorial was translated into English and achieved world-wide notoriety; after the war, it constituted a major issue in the Tokyo Trials. However, it was concluded that the memorandum was a sham. Be it as it may, as Kamei Fumio has pointed out in his 39-minute documentary (*A Japanese Tragedy* (*Nihon no higeki*, also *The Tragedy of Japan*, 1946)) the policies that were advocated in the memorial, which he showed in the opening part of the film, were actually those carried out by Japan until her disastrous defeat in World War II.

How did the Japanese public react to the prospect of an invasion of China? To the Japanese, whose government had taken every opportunity to intervene in China's internal affairs, often using military force, the invasion seemed nothing out of the ordinary; in fact, it seemed almost commonsensical. Therefore, there was no feeling of guilt or wrong-doing among the people, many of whom did not even associate Japanese politics with the term "invasion."

With the exception of a few intellectuals who habitually tried to gain insight into the future by connecting past and present events, to those who were blessed with the possibilities or occasions to look beyond national boundaries and outside into the world, and to those believers in leftist thought, the vast majority of the Japanese had taken their prewar education at face value. They did not feel any incongruity towards the emperor-system which was at the center of prewar ideology.

The ordinary Japanese at that time were not only unaware of the meaning of invasion, but also lacked any feeling of guilt toward the concept of war as such. This may seem incomprehensible to those who grew up after Japan's defeat in World War II, but unless we try to put ourselves into the mental framework of the Japanese of that time, we will never understand prewar Japan. In order to do so, it is also necessary to go back in history.

Two Successful Wars

The Meiji Restoration of 1868 brought an end to feudalism and transformed Japan into an unified state with the emperor system at its ideological center. The Meiji leaders, eager to catch up with the modern capitalist powers of Europe and the United States, embarked upon a policy of economic growth achieved by militarization, epitomized by the motto "rich country, strong army" (Fukokū kyōhei). The desire to modernize furnished the pretext for a typically imperialist policy, intent on increasing Japan's domination over its neighboring countries. For the leaders of a narrow island-country, imperialism was seen as the only way toward progress and material enrichment.

Japan's imperialist policy reached two climaxes in the Sino-Japanese War (1894-1895) in which Japan fought the Ch'ing Empire which controlled all China, and the Russo-Japanese War (1904-1905), waged against Imperial Russia. The Sino-Japanese War arose from the contestants' competing aspirations to the Korean peninsula; anxious not to fall behind its powerful neighbor, Japan embarked upon a "preventive war" to assert its claims upon Korea.

At the close of an eight-month long battle, Japan achieved complete victory over the Ch'ing Empire which turned out to be unexpectedly weak militarily. Besides crushing China's aspirations to Korea, Japan wrested the Liaotung Peninsula, Taiwan and the Penghu Islands from China, and also obtained an indemnity which was more than sufficient to compensate it for its military expenses.

However, not even a week after Japan's claim upon the Liaotung Peninsula was sealed, Russia, along with Germany and France, demanded the restitution of the territory in the so-called "Triple Intervention." Japan reluctantly gave in, but fostered a feeling of deep-seated resentment against Russia from then on.

Subsequently, Russia went on to build the Eastern Chinese Railway in the north-eastern part of China (Manchuria), and declared Lushun and Talien, both on the Liaotung Peninsula, leased territories. In addition, the Russians gave no indication of planning to withdraw the troops they had sent to China, ostensibly to help suppress the Boxer Rebellion of 1898. Russia also expanded its railroad network in

China by laying a railroad from the city of Harbin, located at the center of the Eastern Chinese Railway, to Lushun and Talien. To top it off, it also created a military stronghold in Lushun. Of course, this amounted to an outright colonization of Manchuria. If allowed to run their full course, these policies would not only threaten Korea's independence, but also prevent Japan from acquiring new territories. Out of this sense of crisis, staking everything on one card, Japan waged another "preventive war," this time by challenging one of the world's most powerful countries, Russia.

Although the Japanese troops had to stop the pursuit of the Russian ground forces at the city of Feng Tian (Mukden, today's Shenyang) because of a lack of ammunition, they were able to deal the Russian navy a deadly blow. Through the mediation of the United States, the contestants signed a peace agreement. The Kantō (Kwantung) region became Japan's leased territory. In the bargain Japan also acquired the Eastern Chinese Railway between Changchun and Lushun and related rights, as well as the southern area (from 50 degrees N. Lat. of Karafuto, or present-day Sakhalin). The South Manchurian Railway Company (Mantetsu), which was newly established for the management of the railway connecting the cities of Changchun and Lushun, became the main agency for the management of the related rights for Fushun coal mines and the iron works of Anshan, as well as for the development of the land along the railroad lines.

The term "preventive war" may seem less offensive to the ear than the term "war of aggression" or "invasion," but the difference lies only in terminology. Even a "preventive war" is a war fought essentially with the aim of preventing the enemy from snatching away what one desires for oneself, and is thus nothing but a imperialist quest for the acquisition of new power. In the final analysis, a "preventive war" is a "war of aggression." The Sino-Japanese War was a battle fought over the invasion of Korea, and the Russo-Japanese War was fought over the invasion of Manchuria. In both cases, it must be remembered that Japan attacked first, and declared war only later.

After the Sino-Japanese War, Japan completely isolated Korea from China and embarked upon an occupation program which assured increasing domination over Korea, and finally culminated in the whole-sale colonization of Korea by the bloodless annexation of the peninsula in 1910.

Casualties from the Sino-Japanese War numbered 17,000, those from the Russo-Japanese War 118,000 (Source: *Kindai Nihon sōgō nenpyō* [Chronology of Modern Japan], Iwanami Shoten). The casualties were comparatively few, and the two wars were extremely successful from a strategic point of view, having established Japan's control over both Korea and Manchuria. Satisfaction at having acquired new territories ran deep among the Japanese people. In conclusion, the Japanese were able to reap enormous benefits from these two wars. This fact is of great significance for the understanding of later developments.

The glaring military weakness of the Ch'ing Empire at the time of the Sino-Japanese War gave rise among many Japanese to a feeling of contempt toward the Chinese, leading to derogatory expressions like *"chankoro,"* which is comparable to the English "chink." Japan's newly-acquired arrogance effectively neutralized any pangs of conscience it might have felt with regard to her brutal attack upon the

Chinese people. Japan's surprise victory over the Russian Empire strengthened feelings of national unity and patriotism, rendering the Japanese immune to any feeling of wrong-doing in war.

Among the Meiji Japanese who experienced these two "successful" wars and fought under the rallying cry "rich country, strong army," a militaristic attitude became universal and all-pervasive.

At the beginning of World War I in 1914, Japan attacked China's Tsingtao (which was territory leased by Germany). This was an expedition based on the Anglo-Japanese Alliance concluded in 1902. In the same year, Japan occupied the South Sea Islands to the north of the equator heretofore under German control. These islands, of which Saipan is the main one, became Japan's mandated territories. These two battles put Japan on the side of the victor nations in World War I, although it was least important.

This battle was called *"Nichi-doku-sensō"* (Japanese-German War) in Japan. When considered within the general framework of World War I, the conflict seemed to be no more than a tiny local war, and the term "Japanese-German War" was not used outside Japan. However, the war had much significance from the point of view of the Japanese, who placed it on a continuum along with the Sino-Japanese and the Russo-Japanese Wars. When considered together, it became apparent that the respective time span separating each war from the next was exactly 10 years. This curious coincidence led many Japanese to indulge in the self-satisfied vision that by waging war every 10 years, Japan had gotten progressively bigger and more powerful.

In truth, not all of Japan's military endeavors had been crowned by success. One example is Japan's expedition to Siberia (1918), undertaken in concert with American, British and French forces in an effort to intervene in the civil war following the Russian revolution. By sending 73,000 men to Siberia, Japan violated an international agreement that limited the number of soldiers to be dispatched by each country to 7,000. Nevertheless, the Japanese army could not prevent the massacre of 122 Japanese prisoners (including civilians) by Russian partisans at Nikolaevsk-na-Amure (Nikō Incident, 1920). Able to obtain neither revenge nor compensation, the Japanese forces were forced to withdraw.

This tragic incident was promptly made into a film directed by Sakata Shigenori entitled *Nikō saigo no hi* (*The Last Day of Nikolaevsk*, Nikkatsu Mukōjima, 1920). Released barely three months after the massacre, this sleight of hand can be seen as one of the earliest examples of the sensationalist militaristic film. The picture aroused much righteous indignation and anger among the public, and set a new record by playing for three consecutive weeks at the Asakusa Opera Theater.

II THE BEGINNING OF JAPAN'S INVASION OF CHINA

Morale Booster in a Difficult Time: The Manchurian Incident

On the evening of 18 September 1931, there was a bombing attack on the South Manchurian Railway in the suburb of Feng Tian (Mukden) near Liutiaokou. Interpreting the attack as a provocation from the Chinese, the Kantō Army immediately began an all-round offensive against Chang Hsuehliang's army, the military clique in Feng Tian. On the following day, the Japanese occupied the castle of Feng Tian. It is a well-known fact today that the attack upon the railway was actually a plot contrived by the Japanese army. Moreover, the damage to the rails caused by the bombing attack amounted to a mere 1.64 yards in length (Source: *Shōwa-shi zenkiroku* [Complete Record of the Shōwa Era], Mainichi Shinbunsha), making Japan's retaliatory measures seem more than disproportionate. The Japanese government declared its non-expansion policy, but the local army ran alone, and the fighting soon spread over the whole of Manchuria. In Japan, the war is known as the Manchurian Incident; the Chinese simply term it the 9/18 Incident.

At that time, Chang Hsuehliang, who was in Peiping (present-day Beijing; at that time, the capital was Nanking), requested the aid of Chiang Chiehshi (Chiang Kaishek) in Nanking, but the latter did not send any reinforcements. Preoccupied by the rise of the Communist Party, Chiang Chiehshi was carrying out a policy of "assuring internal safety first, attacking the external enemy later," and was in no position to send his army off to battle with the Japanese military.

In January 1932, the Japanese occupied Chinchow, followed by Harbin in February, so that Manchuria's areas of strategic importance were under Japanese control. On March 1, Japan proclaimed the foundation of a new nation, Manchukuo. The former Shuantong emperor Pu Yi, who was chased from the Ch'ing emperor's throne when he was small, ascended to the position of regent, and Manchuria's capital Cheng Chun was renamed Shinking. All this happened just half a year after the Manchurian Incident.

Both the Japanese army and bureaucracy now concentrated their efforts on the development of Manchukuo, which was given the motto, "Harmony between five families, realm of peace and prosperity." "Five families" was meant to indicate the five peoples of Manchuria, Japan, Korea, Mongolia, and Han (China), but in reality Manchukuo was a puppet nation manipulated solely by the Japanese government. The whole of Manchuria was effectively reduced to the status of a Japanese colony.

In general, the Japanese were more than happy about these developments. The Manchurian Incident was welcomed with the chronic optimism that had prevailed ever since the Sino-Japanese War, epitomized by the expression "there's no way we're going to lose against the chankoro." The Japanese people were elated by the fact that it took less than half a year for their military to establish a new state once hostilities had broken out.

In 1929, Japan was suffering from an economic slump, caused by the shockwaves that followed the crash of the New York stock market and the worldwide panic that ensued. Despite two mass arrests of Communist Party members in 1928 and 1929, leftist thought penetrated the Japanese intelligentsia ever more deeply. To top if off, the Tohoku and Hokkaido regions suffered heavy crop losses in 1931 because of unusually cold weather; the famine was so severe that the practice of selling Japanese farm girls to brothels became commonplace in these areas.

In his films *I Graduated, But...(Daigaku wa deta keredo*, 1929) and *Tokyo Chorus (Tokyo no gassho*, 1931), director Ozu Yasujiro depicted the difficulties of finding a job during this dark time. "Tendency films," which showed the influence of leftist thought, appeared in close succession, for example: Uchida Tomu's *A Living Doll (Ikeru ningyō)*, Tsuji Kichirō's *Kasahari kenpō (An Umbrellamaker's Sword)*, Itō

Fig. 1. *I Graduated, But...*
(Credit: Japan Film Library Council)

Fig. 2. *Metropolitan Symphony.*
(Credit: Japan Film Library Council)

Daisuke's *The Sword Saving Many by Killing One (Issatsu tashoken)* and *Man-Slashing, Horse-Piercing Sword (Zanjin zanbaken)*, Mizoguchi Kenji's *Metropolitan Symphony (Tokai kōkyōgaku,* all made in 1929), Suzuki Jūkichi's *What Made Her Do It? (Nani ga kanojo o sō saseta ka,* 1930), and Kinugasa Teinosuke's *Before Dawn (Reimei izen,* 1931).

Those were hard times for the Japanese, and the birth of Manchukuo provided a tremendous boost to popular morale. To those who had grown weary of living on their narrow island, Manchuria seemed to be a kind of paradise, full of possibilities for the future. The fact that the "tendency films" that had been so popular completely disappeared after 1932 was due not only to government censorship, but to the popular enthusiasm and optimism that had been kindled by Japan's military successes.

The First Shanghai Incident and The Sensationalist Film

In January 1932, prior to the establishment of Manchukuo, the Japanese army engaged the Chinese in a battle at Shanghai, ostensibly in retaliation for the massacre of a group of Japanese monks at the hands of the Chinese. Today, it is a well-established fact that the massacre was part of a conspiracy devised and financed by the Japanese army's Special Service Agency. Claiming that Japan's national interest was at stake, a naval brigade of the Japanese navy stationed at Shanghai attacked the Chinese army (First Shanghai Incident). Unsuccessful at first, it obtained reinforcement from the ground forces and launched an all-out attack. Nevertheless, the war situation came to a deadlock.

In the midst of the bitter battle, three particularly brave soldiers sacrificed themselves by becoming "human bullets"; their heroism became the talk of the day and made headlines in Japan. The incident took place in a suburb of Shanghai, Miaohangchen, where the enemy had laid wire entanglements. The three men dashed into the enemy position carrying a 10-foot long bomb. It blew them to pieces, but opened a trench for a successful attack by the Japanese forces. The three heroes can be considered the forerunners of the notorious suicide-attack commandos of World War II, the special submarine units and *kamikaze* pilots.

However, in retrospect, this whole incident remains shrouded in much doubt. It appears that it should have been possible for the three men to return alive because the soldiers that immediately followed them emerged unscathed from the explosion; thus, it is likely that their deaths were due to a technical error or to an accident, and were not the result of a premeditated self-sacrificial act.

Nevertheless, it goes without saying that these investigations were shelved and that the former interpretation, much more apt to foster people's enthusiasm for the war, was promoted as the most valid one. The action by the three men was seen as a heroism without parallel in the world, and the three soldiers were exalted as paragons of heroism and loyalty. Naturally, the incident was brought immediately to the screen by Japan's major film companies. The first film, directed by Negishi Toichirō and five other directors from the Kawai Motion Picture Co., was titled *Chūkon nikudan sanyūshi (The Faithful Spirits of the Three Soldiers That Became Human Bullets)*. Five other companies followed suit, each producing their own version of the three heroes. The first film was released on 3 March 1932, the last on March 17,

Fig. 3. War's other casualty — Shanghai Under Japanese attack.
(Credit: National Archives)

not even a month after the incident occurred (on February 22). This fact is emblematic of the sensationalism and opportunism of the genre.

Another pet theme that was cinematized by many companies, among them Shōchiku Kamata, was the tale of Lieutenant-Commander Kuga. The "Kuga Series" was inaugurated with *Bujin no seika — Kuga shōsa (The Essence of the Warrior Spirit: Lieutenant-Commander Kuga)* by director Matsuishi Osamu of Shinkō Kinema. The tale runs as follows: Kuga Noboru, an infantry lieutenant and batallion commander in the battle at Chiangwanchen, was first reported killed in action. However, it turned out that he had been severely injured in the battle and taken prisoner by the Chinese. Upon negotiations with the Chinese, he regained his liberty, and joined the Japanese army at Shanghai. While receiving medical treatment, he could no longer bear the shame at having been taken prisoner and shot himself. The arrest of a batallion commander being an unusual incident with potentially far-reaching political implications, no information was released until the government completed a thorough investigation of the incident. The results of the investigation were publicly announced, with a comment by military minister Araki Sadao entitled, "The Honoring of Reputation and Responsibility — Manifestations of the Military Spirit."

The message issued by the government in its "War Instructions" of January 1941 that "a soldier should not accept the humiliation of being taken prisoner," can be seen as a direct continuation of the kind of suicidal heroism advocated by Lt. Kuga. This attitude, an expression of the ancient *bushidō* (way of the warrior), helped shape a peculiarly Japanese military ethic which is in contradiction with modern international law.

The cinematographic versions of the "Three Human Bullets" and Lt. Kuga, though hastily produced and shorter than one hour, were shown in every movie theater in Japan and exercised a tremendous fascination upon the Japanese public.

In reality, the general war situation did not look so favorable, despite the army's repeated large-scale dispatches of military reinforcements and the combined efforts of the ground forces, navy and air force. The 19th regiment, the strongest army under Chiang Chiehshi's command, was battling the Japanese ground forces, and known as the "Iron Army"; moreover, it gained the fervent support of the general population, with students and workers swelling its ranks as plain-clothes soldiers. The desperate fight put up by this army took the Japanese by surprise. Meanwhile, international public opinion also continued to exert pressure upon the Japanese government. Finally, reeling from the heavy losses and grappling with mounting international protest, the Japanese called for a cease-fire on March 3. The Japanese military power concentrated solely on Shanghai was now exceeding more than twice the military force that had been required to subdue the whole of Manchuria; and yet, a cease-fire, which would bring the Japanese no profit, became inevitable.

Once the Japanese military abandoned its attack upon Shanghai, it concentrated its efforts solely upon the construction and development of Manchukuo. On 1 March 1934, the eve of the second anniversary of the establishment of Manchukuo, Pu Yi (who until then had carried the title of regent) was made emperor, and the era name was changed from *Daidō* to *Kōtoku*. Meanwhile, upon a desperate appeal by the Chinese government, the League of Nations decided to send an investigative body to Manchuria. The latter concluded that the entire Manchurian Incident was a conspiracy devised by the Japanese, and put forth a proposal for the settlement of the dispute. However, the Japanese rejected the proposal and withdrew from the League.

In the cinema, in a break from the tradition of the hastily-made sensationalist film, first-rate filmmakers tried their hand at the topic. Mizoguchi Kenji's *The Dawn of the Founding of Manchukuo and Mongolia* (*Man-Mō kenkoku no reimei*, 1932) and Uchida Tomu's *Asia Calling* (*Sakebu Ajia*, 1933) were both made on a large scale, and shot on the original locations. Mizoguchi's film featured Irie Takako as a Matahari-like spy heroine, while Uchida's work, as one of the few talking pictures in Japan, seemed mainly intent on selling Fujiwara Yoshie's songs to the public. Both were mediocre.

The China Incident and "The 15-year War" — A Term Unknown In Japan

On 7 July 1937, there was a clash between the Japanese and Chinese armies in the Peiping suburb at Lukouch'iao (Marco Polo Bridge). The exact causes of the clash still remain in doubt, though it is fairly clear that the collision was not due to a stratagem devised by the Japanese army, as had been the case in the Manchurian Incident. According to the most common interpretation, the clash was the result of a misunderstanding or the accidental firing of a gun. In the middle of the night, the Japanese army was carrying out rifle practice (on territory not permitted by China), violating China's territorial rights. The Chinese forces stationed there took it as a provocation and fired back. The Japanese army immediately escalated the conflict into a full-scale military confrontation, in direct contradiction to the government's professed policy of non-expansion. Therefore, whatever the immediate causes of the incident were, there is no doubt that the Japanese turned a potentially harmless situation into a full-scale Japanese aggression by choosing to escalate the conflict.

Fig. 4. *The Dawn of the Founding of Manchukuo and Mangolia.*
(Credit: Japan Film Library Council)

Immediately following the clash, the Japanese went on to occupy Peiping and Tientsin. The battle was initially called the "North China Incident," but after the battle lines spread to other parts of China, it was officially renamed "China Incident."

On August 13, the war flames also spread to Shanghai. Prior to the outbreak of the battle, Captain Oyama Isao from the Japanese navy was killed by Chinese security forces while on an inspection round; anticipating the large-scale dispatch of Japanese ground forces in retaliation, the Chinese launched an attack on the Japanese naval brigades, aiming at its wholesale destruction (Second Shanghai Incident). At the close of a hard and bitter struggle, the numerically inferior Japanese naval brigades were just barely able to hold out until reinforcements arrived. However, just as the Japanese had been taken by surprise by the enemy's stubborn resistance in the First Shanghai Incident four years earlier, they were met again by a ferocious counter-attack by the Chinese, who feared for very existence of their native land.

Despite several reinforcements, there was no prospect of ending the battle even after two months had passed. Finally, some Japanese troops were dispatched to the north shore of Hangchow Bay; they launched a surprise attack on the enemy from the rear, thus enabling the Japanese to attack the Chinese from both sides. It took the Japanese a full three months to lead the battle to a conclusion and finally capture Shanghai.

Capitalizing on the momentum gained from this victory, the Japanese occupied Nanking, the capital of the People's Government, on December 13. However, Chiang Chiehshi had already transferred the capital to Chungking. The Nanking Massacre took place immediately after the Japanese army occupied the city. Despite the Japanese government's repeated attempts to camouflage the truth, it is now widely known that the casualties, which included many women and children, amounted to 200,000. Though the massacre was apparently prompted by Japanese resentment at the enemy's bitter resistance in Shanghai, the underlying motive must be sought in the contempt for the Chinese which had been festering among the Japanese ever since the Sino-Japanese war.

In truth of fact, the Japanese were waging a full-fledged war against the Chinese, though its Japanese government never officially declared war and persisted in using the euphemistic term "incident." The reason for this must be sought in the fact that the official use of the word "war" would have jeopardized the importation of arms from third powers which, in continuing to export weapons to a warring Japan, would have violated the law of neutrality.

Against the government's expectations, however, the China "Incident" had become a protracted war. Further magnified by the outbreak of hostilities against Great Britain and the United States, the conflict now turned into the "Greater East Asia War," the official appellation used by the Japanese government.

In the chronology of Japanese history, the Manchurian Incident took place in 1931, and was settled by the establishment of Manchukuo in 1932, followed by the China Incident in 1937. This conveyed the impression that the years between 1932 and 1937 were relatively uneventful ones. From the perspective of the Japanese, this five-year period between the establishment of the puppet state of Manchukuo and the China Incident seemed to be a peaceful one, filled with the activities of reconstruction and rebuilding.

However, in the historical perspective of the Chinese, there are no such subdivisions. The entire period from the 9/18 (i.e. Manchurian) Incident to Japan's surrender in 1945 is taken by the Chinese to be a seamless whole, referred to as the "15-Year War." This difference clearly reflects the perceptual and experiential gap which separates invader and victim. While the Japanese tend to boast the "successes" of their policies of invasion, the Chinese insist upon seeing this entire period as one of protracted victimization and suffering.

Of course, it is a gross distortion of historical facts to claim that the Manchukuo period was an uneventful and peaceful one. In fact, there were several "incidents," which were never reported by the Japanese press. For example, there was the Fushun coal mine rebellion (the so-called Yangpeipao Incident, 1932); the ensuing massacre by Japanese forces of an entire village which had given refuge to the Fushun rebels (Pingtingshan Incident, 1932); and an armed insurrection organized by farmers whose land was taken by colonial settlers (Tulongshan Incident, 1934). There were countless other rebellions and terrorist acts.

The Japanese military dismissed these uprisings as the politically insignificant acts of "bandits" and "marauders" scouring the countryside, and the military carried out repeated purges ostensibly to "subjugate the bandits." A Japanese officer who tried to intervene in the Tulongshan Incident was killed along with all his subordinates. Among the so-called "bandits," there was also a guerilla organization called the "Revolutionary Northeast Chinese People's Army," which at its height numbered some 300,000 members. At this time, there was not even a word for "guerilla" in Japanese. When Futoshi's army defeated the Japanese Kantō Army and the Inner Mongolian troops led by Te-wang in Suiyuan province (Suiyuan Incident, 1936) in just one week, news of the victory spread all over China and provided a boost to anti-Japanese resistance. The Japanese public was kept in complete ignorance about all these events, contrary to the Chinese, for whom they were part and parcel of the long "15-Year War."

III THE ESCALATION OF THE WAR AND THE REACTION OF THE CINEMA WORLD

A Drastic Change in the World Situation

My brother was employed by the South Manchurian Railway, and after entering university I decided to visit him in Manchuria during my summer vacation. Just before my departure, it was reported that Japanese and Chinese forces had collided at Lukouchiao (Marco Polo Bridge), but I decided to leave nevertheless. While I was travelling all over Manchuria, the conflict escalated, and by the time I returned home, the war flames had already spread to Shanghai.

When I returned, I was shocked to see how much the streets had changed in a mere 40 days. Women asking passersby to stitch one stitch on the *senninbari* (thousand-stitch belt, a charm for soldiers) could be seen everywhere. Today's young generation probably no longer knows what "thousand-stitch belts" are so an explanation is due. They were strips of white cotton cloth with a thousand round marks imprinted on them; after having asked a thousand women to painstakingly fill each mark with red thread, the women offered the belts to soldiers departing for the front. When fastened around the stomach, these lucky charms were said to prevent soldiers from being hit by bullets. The custom began during the Russo-Japanese war.

The draft call (*akagami*, "red paper") had been issued just days earlier and there were only several days remaining until the men would enter the army. It was no easy task for these women to produce the belts in such a short time, and they applied themselves wholeheartedly to this effort.

At the time of the Manchurian Incident, I had been a second-grade middle school student, but I never saw any woman sewing a senninbari in the streets. I had believed that this was because only soldiers in active service were in the war and no reserve or supplementary units were drafted. I knew later that by the time the First Shanghai Incident took place, a general draft was called and senninbari already existed, but the custom was not nearly as widespread.

Once the conflict escalated into the "China Incident," the city was overflowing with "senninbari girls," whose numbers increased by the day. More people were drafted daily, including neighbors and people I knew. Contrary to the Manchurian and First Shanghai Incidents, which were morale boosters in difficult times and had seemed very remote, this conflict hit close to home and involved us much more intimately.

Following Peiping, Tientsin, and Shanghai, finally China's capital, Nanking, was taken and the people celebrated the victory with lantern processions, basking in a self-complacent optimism. Since it had taken less than half a year to build Japan's puppet state Manchukuo, people were convinced that the war would end as soon as other puppet regimes were established in Northern and Central China. It is true that an interim government under the leadership of Wang Kemin (Wang Ching-wei) was set up in Peiping, and a restoration government was established in Nanking under Liang Hungchih; however, the war did not end.

The Birth of the Newsreel Theaters

In a period where Japanese men departed to the front in increasing numbers, the newsreel caught the people's special attention. Of course, this was a time before television, and films could provide the vivid coverage that newspapers and radio broadcasts could not. Families whose loved ones had departed to the front devoured these weekly newsreels, hoping to catch a glimpse of their husbands, fathers, brothers or sons. When someone was lucky enough to find a loved one on the newsreel, they could obtain a still photograph of that section of the movie from the company that had produced the film. They were aptly named "meetings on the screen" *(sukuriin-gotaimen)*, and sometimes the more dramatic episodes made headlines in the newspapers.

These newsreels were produced weekly by five companies, Asahi, Daimaitōnichi, Yomiuri, Dōmei and the Shinbun Renmei (an association of powerful local newspapers), but the families concerned naturally wanted to see all of them every week. To keep up with the public's ever-increasing demand for these films, newsreel-movie theaters — small theaters that charged low entrance fees — were opened successively all over Japan. Each session ran for about one hour or one hour and a half, combining the newsreel with short documentary clips and children's movies.

The War Depicted in Feature Films

At the time of the Manchurian and First Shanghai Incidents, the opportunistic sensationalist film still predominated. However, once the conflict became a full-fledged war involving the whole of China, more realistic films, which looked the face of war squarely in the eye and appealed to the people with some strong message, began to make their appearance. ·

Five Scouts
(*Gonin no sekkō-hei*, directed by Tasaka Tomotaka, Nikkatsu, 1938)

This depicts the mutual trust and affection between the platoon leader (played by Kosugi Isamu) worried about the safety of his five scouts, who return safely from their difficult mission. Though the movie was on a small scale and shot in only one location (the village occupied by the platoon), it won great acclaim as a war movie which emphasized the strength of human emotions.

The Road to Peace in the Orient
(*Tōyō heiwa no michi*, directed by Suzuki Jūkichi, Tōwa Shōji, 1938)

Produced by Kawakita Nagamasa (who had a strong interest in China), this was set against the grandiose background of North China in mid-winter, and featured some Chinese performers who had been recruited on the spot. It was the first Japanese-Chinese co-production. Tracing the long journey of a peasant couple that had left their war-ravaged hometown behind to join their relatives in Peking, the film took

Fig. 5. Newsreel theater program.

Fig. 6. Newsreel theater program.

Fig. 7. *The Road to Peace in the Orient.*
(Credit: Japan Film Library Council)

the opportunity to give a more humane portrayal of the Japanese armed forces. By emphasizing that the troops, called "Eastern Devils" by the Chinese, were decidedly not the cruel destroyers and pillagers they were made out to be, the filmmakers attempted to show ways in which Japanese and Chinese could work together.

Shanhai rikusentai
(*Shanghai Navy Brigades,* directed by Kumagai Hisatora, Tōhō, 1939)

The Second Shanghai Incident was the theme of Kumagai Hisatora's *Shanghai Navy Brigades* which vividly depicts the Japanese navy's desperate 11-day struggle against the Chinese until the arrival of reinforcement troops. Focusing on the fate of a particular squadron and its leader (played by Obinata Den), and shot on location, it is a powerful and emotionally stirring work. In fact, because of its faithfulness to historical and chronological detail and explanatory diagrams and maps, the film became the first example of the "semi-documentary" movie in Japan. A long way from the cinematographic eulogies to the "Japanese military spirit," it was a turning point in the genre of the war film.

Mud and Soldiers
(*Tsuchi to heitai*, directed by Tasaka Tomotaka, Nikkatsu, 1939)

Tasaka Tomotaka's *Mud and Soldiers* was the film version of Hino Ashihei's best seller. The film depicted the everyday life of a Japanese squadron stationed in China, consisting mainly of long marches interspersed with occasional battles and rare periods of rest. This monotonous lifestyle was thought to be emblematic of that of all Japanese troops stationed in China over long periods of time. The powerful film made a great impact on the Japanese public.

Flaming Sky
(*Moyuru ōzora*, directed by Abe Yutaka, Tōhō, 1940)

Abe Yutaka's *Flaming Sky* opens with a depiction of the hard training undergone by young pilots, and focuses on a fierce air battle. In its intensity and power, it was a ground-breaking work, rivaling the best of the American air force movies. Much of its success was due to the painstaking work of photographer Miyajima Yoshio and the special-effects specialist Tsubaraya Eiji.

The Story of Tank Commander Nishizumi
(*Nishizumi senshachō-den*, directed by Yoshimura Kimisaburō, Shōchiku, 1940)

Yoshimura Kimisaburō's *The Story of Tank Commander Nishizumi* is a typical war-hero movie, depicting the brave deeds of tank commander Nishizumi who was killed in the battle at Suchow. Morally upright and composed, but full of sympathy and affection for his superiors, the commander was the idea war-hero, especially because he was played by Uehara Ken.

General, Staff, and Soldiers
(*Shōgun to sanbō to hei*, directed by Taguchi Satoshi, Nikkatsu, 1942)

Taguchi Satoshi's *General, Staff, and Soldiers* was set against the magnificent natural background of Shansi province and produced with the help of the Japanese troops stationed there. It depicts the strategic tactics of more than 10,000 soldiers. A possible change in strategy which would necessitate the transfer of one of the battalions gives rise to much discussion among the staff, who are divided in their opinions as to whether the transfer should take place. Finally, the commanding officer, who up to now had listened silently to this discussion, is entrusted to make the decision. The film focuses on the theme of strategy as such, and as its title indicates, examines the respective roles played by the general, staff and soldiers as well as the organic relationships that bind them together. The film approached the war from a new angle, and on a much grander scale than other war movies had previously done. The author of the original novel, Ijiichi Susumu, was a military man as well as a novelist; otherwise, he would surely have been unable to depict so vividly the conflicts that could arise between strategic planners and the staff.

All these movies were made before the outbreak of the war against the United States and Great Britain, and they deal solely with China (*General, Staff, and Soldiers* was released after the beginning of the war against the Allied Forces, but the shooting started long before that). In these films, there was no fighting spirit or feeling of animosity toward the Chinese people; rather, they were meant to convince the Chinese of Japan's good intentions and benevolence. They typically featured examples of Chinese rebels themselves underwent a conversion, and were compelled to realize the futility and meaninglessness of their revolt. The normal Japanese attitude toward the Chinese was that of self-righteousness.

The Proliferation of Feature-length Documentary Films

When talking about the Japanese documentary film, one should not forget the achievements of the Yokohama Cinema Company, which was the first to produce documentary films of feature length. Feature-length documentaries inaugurated a new era in filmmaking, and since they could be shown in ordinary movie theaters, they played a decisive role in the popularization of the genre. The following are some of the Yokohama Cinema's representative works. Each featured general direction by Saeki Eisuke, the company director, photography by Ueno Yukikio, and editing and commentary by Aochi Chūzō.

Lifeline of the Sea
(*Umi no seimeisen*, also *Lifeline of the Ocean*, directed by Saeki Eisuke, Yokohama, 1933)

This film examined the meaning of national defense for the people of the South Sea Islands which had become Japan's mandated territories.

Japan Advancing to the North
(*Hokushin Nihon*, directed by Saeki Eisuke, Yokohama, 1934)

Depicting the situation of colonized Karafuto (Sakhalin) and the Chishima islands, this work emphasized the importance of defending the Northern Territories.

Minami jūjisei wa maneku
(*The Southern Cross Beckons*, directed by Saeki Eisuke, Yokohama, 1938)

This intended to promote Japanese emigration, and introduced the natural scenery of various South American countries.

Though these films all closely reflected Japan's national policy they cannot be dismissed as simple propaganda movies. Filmed on location, they introduced magnificent landscapes and unknown local cultures to the Japanese public. Following suit the Tōhō company established a "Culture Film Section" and produced feature length documentary movies such as the following:

Dotō o kette
(*In the Face of the High Seas*, also *Over the High Seas*, photography by Shirai Shigeru, Tōhō, 1937)

This was a record of the Japanese warship Ashigara's attendance of the King of England's coronation ceremony, followed by its visit to the military harbor of Kiel in Germany, Japan's Anti-Comintern Pact ally. Finally, it depicted the Japanese sailors' disciplined life-style on the warship, and the various landscapes that could be seen from the ship before it called on a port.

Gunkanki ni eikō are
(*Glory to the Colours!*, photography by Fujii Sei, Tōhō, 1937)

Fujii Sei's film was meant to be a record of the four-month long European visit of the two military training ships Yakumo and Iwate. However, during their trip the China Incident had spread to Shanghai and they returned to Japan in mid-journey.

Both documentaries were produced under the supervision of Japan's navy and thus the voice-over was strongly propagandistic in tone.

The full-scale war with China happened to break out just when the feature-length documentary was gaining momentum and enjoying a popularity among the public that put it on a par with dramatic films. Naturally, the war gave much impetus to the production of this genre.

At wartime, the public always wants to see the actual circumstances at the front. War gave not only the newsreel, but also the documentary feature film a prolific period. Eager not to miss out on the opportunities proffered by history, Tōhō's Culture Film Section produced documentaries which closely followed the war situation, such as the following:

Shanghai
(photography by Miki Shigeru, editing by Kamei Fumio, 1938)
Nanking
(photography by Shirai Shigeru, editing by Akimoto Ken, 1938)
Peking
(photography by Kawaguchi Sei'ichi, editing by Kamei Fumio, 1938)

These movies differed considerably in their mood and scope. *Shanghai* features a bullet-ridden iron helmet, a crushed trumpet and destroyed water bottle, suggesting the pathos of a war-raveged city. Kamei Fumio's editing earned much praise, and the film was even voted the fourth best film in the "best ten" list set up by *Kinema Junpō*. In contrast, *Nanking* focuses on more flashy battle scenes, from the first soldier climbing the city wall to the army's triumphal entry ceremony. *Peking* is different again, focusing on those parts of the ancient city which escaped the bloodshed and ravages of battle.

There were many other feature-length documentaries shot on location, for example:

Dawn
(*Sikuang*, directed by Tanaka Yoshitsugu, Dōmei, 1938)
Senyū no uta
(*Song for a War Comrade*, photographed and edited by Richard Angst (German), Tōhō, 1939)
Yōsukō kantai
(*Fleet on the Yangtze River*, photographed and edited by Kimura Sotoji, Tōhō, 1939)
Seisen
(*Holy War*, Daimai-tōnichi and Yokohama, 1939)
Shintairiku kensetsu no kiroku
(*Record of the Construction of a New Continent*, directed by Tanaka Yoshitsugu, Dōmei, 1940)

Kanton shingun shō
(*March on Canton*, supervised by Takagi Toshirō, Dai Nihon Bunka, 1940)
Yōsukō
(*Yangtze River*, supervised by Aochi Chūzō, Yokohama Cinema 1940)
Futsuin shinchū
(*Advancing Upon French Indo-China*, produced by Kitabayashi Atsushi, Shinseki, 1941)
Kōkū kichi
(*Navy Base*, supervised and directed by Takagi Toshirō, Daimai-tonichi, 1941)

A Phantom Movie: *Soldiers at the Front*

There were also "problem" films which did not see the light of the film theaters during wartime. The most famous is *Soldiers at the Front* (*Tatakau heitai*, also *Fighting Soldiers*, 1939) directed by Kamei Fumio. After the Japanese military's conquest of Nanking and Suchow, more than 300,000 men were mobilized for an expedition aimed at the conquest of the city of Hankou. The War Ministry entrusted Tōhō with the making of a documentary which would record the army's victorious march on Hankou. Tōhō's Kamei Fumio, who had made a name for himself with the editing of *Shanghai*, was given the task. Hankou, which formed metropolitan Wuhan together with the neighboring cities of Wuchang and Hanyang, was the most important city in the area. After Chiang Chiehshi had transferred the capital from Nanking to Chungking, many political organizations were moved to Hankou, making it China's *de facto* capital until the Japanese began their offensive on the city. On 27 October 1938, the Japanese occupied Wuhan. In Japan, news of the victory was celebrated with much enthusiasm and a wave of lantern processions similar to the time of Nanking's conquest. When the military entrusted Tōhō with the documentary's production, they naturally expected a film that would extol the Japanese army's brave struggle and depict its march toward another heroic victory.

However, Kamei's documentary turned out to be exactly the opposite. There were old peasants and children who had been burned out of their houses and who just stood there in blank amazement, as well as endless lines of refugees stretching over the countryside. The Japanese army seemed thoroughly exhausted and disgusted by their diet consisting solely of dried vegetables; sick army horses were left behind to die by the roadside. There were family letters and photographs of their children found on the bodies of Japanese soldiers who had been killed in action. When the army finally enters a ruined and empty Hankou, the predominant emotion is not one of triumph but of fatigue and exhaustion; some soldiers fall asleep right on the spot. Such were some of the scenes depicted in Kamei Fumio's *Soldiers at the Front*.

Of course, the film never made it through censorship and was not publicly shown, thus it became a "phantom movie" (*moboroshi no eiga*). At that time, the government could allow no truthful and honest depiction of the realities of war; only an aestheticized, heroicized view of the fighting designed to stir up enthusiasm among the people was permitted to reach the public.

Kamei's film still exists today and can now be seen by everyone. However, one scene, in which some soldiers cremate the corpses of their comrades in the darkness, is unaccountably missing. The moving shot of a single, sick army horse which is left behind by the troops and finally collapses was used by Kamei for a later film, *War and Peace* (*Sensō to heiwa*, co-directed by Yamamoto Satsuo).

The Chinese Continent as Japan's Dreamscape

After the conquest of Hankou, there were no more large-scale advances by the Japanese military. Realizing the futility of pursuing the stubbornly resisting Chinese army, the army concentrated its efforts on rebuilding the occupied territories. New governments were set up, and new policies aimed at confining Chiang Chiehshi's power to Chungking were carried out. In response to this, Wang Chaoming (Chingwei) left Chungking for Nanking and established a new government in March 1940, intending to absorb both the temporary government of Peking and Nanking's restoration government. Wang transferred the capital to Nanking with the aim of setting up a true national government capable of confronting the Japanese army as an independent power. However, Wang's ambitions remained unfulfilled and his administration became just another Japanese puppet. In Chungking, his government was mocked as a "sham government."

Be that as it may, to the Japanese the occupied territories were no longer battle arenas but a kind of promised land to rebuild and shape according to their designs. Movies reflect the endless fascination the Chinese continent exercised upon the Japanese mind:

> "The Manchurian star Li Hsianglan, a peerless beauty who has captured the heart of all of Manchuria, plays opposite [actor] Hasegawa Kazuo...A young lady of 20 years, she is the daughter of the illustrious mayor of Mukden, who has commanded the whole of Manchuria; having studied at the Japanese school in Peking for many years, her Japanese is flawless..."

This is an excerpt from a blurb in *Kinema Junpō* for the release of *Song of the White Orchid* (*Byakuran no uta*, directed by Watanabe Kunio, 1939), a film that inaugurated Tōhō's "continental series" which was to become the company's gold mine. In a later review, Shigeno Tatsuhiko went on to say that, "Li Hsianglan outshines Japanese actresses by her beautiful singing and perfect Japanese..." In fact, the actress, though born in Manchuria, was one-hundred percent Japanese; her real name was Yamaguchi Yoshiko and her father, Yamaguchi Fumio, was from Saga Prefecture, her mother Ai from Fukuoka Prefecture.

Fig. 8. *Song of the White Orchid.*
(Credit: Japan Film Library Council)

Under the pseudonym "Li Hsianglan" (also Ri Kō-ran), Yamaguchi became the Manchurian Motion Picture Association's (Manshū Eiga Kyōkai, also Man'ei) top star. Her box-office value, spurred by advertisements such as these, was so high that her real identity became a "top company secret," with much care taken not to divulge it to the public. Because *Song of the White Orchid* had become such as hit, Yamaguchi and her partner Hasegawa Kazuo (Tōhō's top star) co-starred in two more movies, *China Night* (*Shina no yoru*, directed by Fushimizu Osamu, 1940) and *Vow in the Desert* (*Nessa no chikai*, directed by Watanabe Kunio, 1940); their popularity skyrocketed. *Song of the White Orchid* was set in Manchuria, while *China Night* and *Vow in the Desert* were set in Shanghai and Peking respectively. Among the parts played by Hasegawa were that of a skillful engineer and a generous sailor on a freight ship, while Yamaguchi played a Shanghai orphan, or a daughter from a respectable family who was taking singing lessons. The plot always followed the same scheme: love would blossom between the two; meanwhile, anti-Japanese elements that were sowing unrest around them would be eradicated, and their love would come to symbolize the friendship and goodwill between Japan and Manchuria, or Japan and China. As it always happens when a nation tries to justify its invasion of another, the Japanese denounced the natural Chinese national consciousness as "anti-Japanese," and thus unconditionally bad. They constructed an ideal image of China to suit their own dreams and aspirations. With her seductive Chinese style, sweet rapturous voice and unbelievably good Japanese, Li Hsianglan became the object of yearning of many Japanese.

On 11 February 1941, National Foundation Day (formerly called Empire Day), there was a famous incident at the Nichigeki Theater. The theater had announced a special live-show featuring a famous star called "The Singing Li Hsianglan." From early morning on, people eager to hear the actress sing flocked to the theater; it is

Fig. 9. *10,000 Ri of Fertile Land.*
(Credit: Japan Film Library Council)

said that the queue formed by these people was so long that it encircled the large theater building by more than seven times. At 9:30 a.m., when the doors were supposed to open, over 5,000 people were crowding the entrance doors, with fights erupting here and there. Everyone rushed the ticket sales counter, and the resulting chaos caused the police to be mobilized. In the end, the entire show had to be called off. The undercurrent of Li Hsianglan's explosive popularity was provided by the "continental fever" wave which had swept Japan. Similar to Manchuria, which in reality was a Japanese colony, China was also to develop and prosper under Japanese occupation. This optimistic outlook made China an object of desire among the Japanese — an attitude that can be compared to the Japanese postwar passion for overseas travel. Li Hsianglan became the idol of her time.

Outside of the productions cited above, the following are among the films which depicted the Japanese colonization of Manchuria in positive terms:

10,000 Ri of Fertile Land [1 ri = approximately two and a half square miles]
(*Yokudo banri,* directed by Kurata Bunjin, Nikkatsu, 1940)
Ohinata Village
(*Ohinata mura,* directed by Toyoda Shirō, Tokyo Hassei, 1940)

IV THE MOTION PICTURE LAW AND ITS INFLUENCE

The Contents of the Motion Picture Law

By this time, the Motion Picture Law (*eigahō*) had already come into effect. In March 1939, the Motion Picture Law came before the 74th Diet, passed the Lower House and the House of Peers, and was officially announced on April 5. For about half a year, the Regulations for Enforcement were elaborated, and came into effect starting October 1.

This law followed the example of the Motion Picture Law established by the Nazi German government under Adolf Hitler, which made film a supporting instrument for the execution of Nazi policy; fascist Italy had also enacted similar laws. In November 1936, Japan had entered into an anti-communist treaty (officially called the Anti-Comintern Pact) with Germany, and in November 1937 Italy joined in what is now known as the Japanese German Italian Anti-Comintern Pact. In reality, this reacted to a menace to the Soviet Union, but these regulations cannot be separated from the quick and resolute actions of Germany as it steadily sped up its preparations for the Second World War; in wartime Japan, this was very much sympathized with. After this treaty, the word "allies" (*meikō*) came into preferential use to designate Germany and Italy.

The trend to put film under direct governmental control without being dependent on the interests of private profit-pursuing enterprises had precedent in the Proposition Concerning the Creation of National Policy Films, laid before the 64th Diet in February 1933. Conforming to this legislation, a Motion Pictures Control Committee was formed in March 1934. However, while there was still no subsequent concrete development, the convenient opportunity to establish the Motion Picture Law suddenly occurred around 1937, and the fact that it was realized in no time at all is certainly related to Japan's approach to Germany at that time.

The Motion Picture Law consists of 26 articles. Five days before the enforcement, on 27 September 1939, 58 more articles concerning Regulations for the Enforcement of the Motion Picture Law were officially announced by ministerial ordinance of the Home Affairs Ministry, the Ministry of Education, and the Ministry of Welfare.

The Motion Picture Law starts with the following text:

> "This law intends to urge the qualitative improvement of motion pictures and to plan the healthy development of the film industry in order to contribute to the progress of the national culture." (First Article)

Let us summarize the contents of this law in due order, as follows ("Law" stands for "Motion Picture Law," and "regulations" for "Regulations for the Enforcement of the Motion Pictures Law"; the subsequent number indicates the number of the article, e.g. 2 for the "second article."):

1) License system for film production and film distribution (law 2-4, regulation 1-5).
2) Registration system for film directors, actors and photographers (law 5-7, regulation 6-12).
3) Restrictions of late-night work for minors and women (law 8, regulation 13).
4) Permission of the scenarios for fiction films before shooting (law 8, regulation 14-15).
5) Recommendation of films contributing to the improvement of the national culture (law 10, regulation 16-17).
6) Legal deposit of films recognized as necessary for preservation at the Ministry of Education (law 11, regulation 18).
7) Restriction of the distribution of foreign films (law 12, regulation 19-23).
8) Censorship of exported films and films shown in Japan (law 12, regulation 24-34).
9) Compulsory screening of culture films (law 15, regulation 35-41).
10) Restriction of the number of projections for foreign films (law 16, regulation 42).
11) Time restrictions on the duration of one showing, age restrictions for the audiences, license system for projectionists (law 17, regulation 43-49).
12) Authority of command especially concerning indispensable film producers, distributors and exhibitors (law 18).
13) Establishment of the Motion Pictures Committee as consultative organ (law 19). This part was cancelled on 6 March 1941.
14) Visits of inspection at film production sets and in film theaters (law 20).
15) Penal regulations for violations (law 21-26, regulation 50-52).
16) Additional rules for the enforcement (regulation 53-58).

Item (9) indicates "culture films" (*bunka eiga*), as documentaries were usually designated, but the original text of regulation 35 reads only: "Films (excluding fiction films) that contribute to the cultivation of the national spirit or the development of the national intellectual faculties, recognized as such by the Minister of Education." In the revision of 9 September 1940, the term "culture films" was the official word, but in the text only the expression "excluding fiction films" was changed into "non-fiction films." The rest remained the same. In this same revision, "current-events films" (newsreels) were added to the compulsory screenings.

The Reaction of the Film World

The mass media at that time continually used the expression "our country's first cultural legislation" to describe the Motion Picture Law. Depending on the way of thinking, two possible interpretations can be made. There is general agreement that because the government recognized the importance of cinema, a special law concerning film was enacted before similar proceedings in other fields of art and entertainment. However, opinions differ if this signified protection or interference for the movie industry.

However, the mechanical comments like "a bad law legally suppressing the freedom of cultural activities," suddenly made by everybody after the war, were never heard at the time of the law's enactment. Rather, it was expected that the law would "correct the balance between the limping cultural side of film as compared to the business side," as one critic concluded from the very text of the first article: "The law intends to urge the qualitative improvement of the motion pictures" (Togawa Naosuke (now Togawa Naoki). "Eigahō no yobikentō" [Preliminary Examination of the Motion Picture Law], *Eiga Hyōron*, October 1939).

Businessmen in related fields also welcomed the law. The license system for film production and distribution (v. 1) was seen by big companies as a protection policy. Since the large companies were continuously afflicted by the time bomb-like danger of dissatisfied staff members who had left the company and started their own independent production business, they thought that under the license system such troubles would not occur anymore and that the dangers of rivalry would be avoided. Nowadays, independent production and independent film-showing enjoy great popularity in strict contrast to the 1930s, but then the Japanese people were forced to believe that free competition cannot exist in wartime.

The directors, the actors, the photographers all had to be registered, and an ability certificate was required (v. 2). People who had already shown their talents could easily get this certificate by simply following the prescribed procedure, but from then on, a proficiency examination had to be taken. The sudden interruption of the limitless appearance of new faces was a kind of life security for people who were already qualified. In particular, actors in supporting roles, who had angrily seen how beautiful faces scouted in the streets became stars in no time at all, could finally be proud of their status and their rights.

However, they had to pay for it. Some actors were refused registration because of inappropriate stage names, and were compelled to change their names. Since the name of the actor Fujiwara Kamatari could be misunderstood as that of a highborn historical person, it had to be changed into Fujiwara Keita; people who were arrested for being members of left-wing theater groups were forced to use their real names when appearing in films.

The permission of scenarios before shooting commonly called preproduction censorship (v. 4), was required under the pretext to avoid countless financial losses and wasted effort, as was common with films that had not passed censorship (after shooting). Only Iwasaki Akira, a notoriously progressive film critic, directly dissented: "That [law] strikes out the creativity and spontaneity of film authors, limits the themes and contents of films, and atrophies, even kills, the film" ("Jizen kenetsu no hei" [The Corrupt Practice of Preproduction Censorship], *Asahi Shinbun*, 4 April 1939). The periodical *Kinema Junpō* can be considered as a kind of party in power in the film journalism of that time, for it was closely connected with the industry. The appointed opposition was *Eiga Hyōron*. This magazine published the previously mentioned article, "Eigahō no yobikentō," by Togawa Naosuke. In the course of 19 pages, he develops a detailed discussion without a trace of opposition, characterizing the censorship of public morals before shooting as simply prevention of financial waste, even adding the hope to expel morally or artistically low productions.

Judging from the main postwar attitudes, an opinion opposing censorship before shooting as restriction of the freedom of expression can be considered a natural reaction. However, at that time, with the exception of Iwasaki, no opposite opinion was expressed, giving proof enough of the mood concerning the Motion Picture Law. However, Iwasaki needed courage for this utterance. On 24 January 1940, just three months after the enforcement of the Motion Picture Law, Iwasaki was arrested and finally, after an unbelievable eight months in a custody camp, prosecuted. He then spent half a year in a detention house as an "unconvicted prisoner." The official charge was "Violation of the Maintenance of Public Order Act." This law, originally established to control associations trying to change the constitution of the nation or circumvent the private property system, was then loosely interpreted, and is one example among many of the robbery of freedom of thought and knowledge. Iwasaki reported that during the investigations, he was told by a policeman: "It is your own fault. You are in here because you opposed the Motion Picture Law, as you always do" (Iwasaki Akira. *Nihon eiga shishi* [A Private History of Japanese Cinema]).

Iwasaki's assertion was certainly not a groundless one. The movie industry was under incredibly strict control. Among many others, the scenario for a film *The Flavor of Green Tea Over Rice (Ochazuke no aji)* by Ozu Yasujirō and Ikeda Tadao did not pass censorship before shooting. The simple farewell of a couple eating a plain rice meal on the eve of the husband's departure for the war was considered unpleasant, at least that was the reason for the script's refusal. According to convention, relatives and friends should assemble on the eve of the departure and celebrate the "glorious call" on a grand scale.

Recommendation (v. 5) and preservation by legal deposit (v. 6) of films are potentially good intentions, however, that did not concern "masterpieces," but "films contributing to the improvement of national culture." Using this expression clearly shows the guiding conscience of the persons concerned.

The censorship of films shown in Japan (v. 8) was equally strict. In the beginning, the following seven articles were the guiding principles. None of the mentioned items could appear in films shown in Japan.

1) That which may profane the dignity of the Imperial House or injure the dignity of the Empire.
2) That which may inculcate ideas which offend national laws.

3) That which may obstruct general politics, military affairs, foreign politics, economics and other public interests.
4) That which may corrupt good morals or demoralize public moral principles.
5) That which may strikingly injure the purity of the Japanese language.
6) Remarkably awkward technical production.
7) That which may hinder the development of the national culture.

With the revision of the law starting 21 December 1940, the following new item was added as number (4), and (4) to (7) were renumbered as (5) to (8):

4) That which may obstruct the enlightening propagation of the basics of the execution of national policy.

In other words, this item aimed to ostracize anti-war films.

Concerning the exportation of films, the initial articles (1) and (6) were the same; in (3), only the terms "obstruct" and "public interests" were modified to "injure" and "profits of the empire" respectively. The meaning of the original articles (2), (4), (5), and (7) was rendered in the following items: "That which may provoke misunderstandings of the national culture" and "That which may argue against exportation"; all together five articles regulated the export of Japanese films. In the revision, the same article governing showing within Japan was added: "That which may obstruct the unenlightening propagation of the basic items regarding the execution of national policy."

The Activation of the Culture Film

The point now in question is the compulsory screening of culture films (v. 9). To be honest, the term "compulsory screening" (*gimu jōei*) was coined by myself; at the time, it was called the "forced screening" (*kyōsei jōei*) of culture films. The text of the Motion Picture Law indicates that "the responsible minister can arrange by decree for the screening by film exhibitors of a specified kind of films that benefits public education." Resuming this part, the term would be "decree screening" (*meirei jōei*), but this expression as well as "forced screening" sounds overly aggressive to today's readers, so I chose "compulsory screenings," because at the time it was received as such. In the film business world itself, the term "forced screening" was used. Nowadays, a strong resistance would be felt towards this word, and from the fact that it was calmly used in that time, the numbness of the normal citizen against decrees and constraints can be vividly imagined.

The definition of the culture film mentioned above was as follows: "Films (excluding fiction films) that contribute to the cultivation of the national spirit or the development of the national intellectual faculties, recognized as such by the Minister of Education." The word "cultivation" (*kanyō*) means literally "educating like soaking into nature" (source: *Iwanami kokugo jiten* [Iwanami Japanese Dictionary]). "National Spirit" (*kokumin seishin*) indicates the desirable spirit the normal citizen was supposed to possess; the same idea was expressed by the popular phrase "loyalty to the emperor, love for the country" (*chūkun aikoku*), contributing to warfare and submitting to the absolute rule of the emperor, which was above any criticism. "Intellectual faculties" (*chinō*) means the function of the brain, and the literal meaning of "development" *(keibai)* is "enlightening cultivation *(keihatsu baiyō);* thus a film had to provide knowledge to render the citizens intelligent. Since the word "or" is used, one of the above conditions was sufficient for a film to attain the precious label "culture film." However, a basic condition was that only "non-fiction films," that is documentary films, could apply. Along with the Motion Picture Law, a new official was appointed at the Ministry of Education who had to acknowledge documentaries as culture films according to these conditions.

This kind of film is generally called "educational film," *(kyōiku eiga)* in the United States (for this reason, the term "documentary films" *(kiroku eiga)*. However in those days they were always called "culture films," without any doubt or resistance. There is a special reason for this.

The president of Tōwa Shōji (now Tōhō Tōwa), Kawakita Nagamasa, dominated the film business world before the war by importing and distributing many excellent European films. He also presented *"kulturfilm,"* made by Germany's biggest film production company UFA (which also produced feature films). Among these pictures were many gem-like shorts supervised by Dr. Nikolas Kaufmann. *Natur als Shützerin im Kampf ums Dasein (Nature as Protector in the Struggle for Survival), Der Ameisenstaat (The State of the Ants), Vom Uhu und anderen Gseichtern der nacht (About the Eagle-Owl and Other Faces in the Night), Nimrod mit der Kamera (Nimrod with the Camera), Die Wunderwelt des Teichs (The Phantastic World of a Pond), Bienenstaat (The State of the Bees),* or *Kamerajagd auf Seehunde (Chasing Seals with a Camera)* are faithful ecological descriptions of the lives of animals, made with hidden cameras and recorded with an omnidirectional microphone. The process of the blooming or sprouting of plants, which in reality takes many hours or even days, becomes visible to the eye by pixillation, taking one frame every couple minutes or even several hours. The strong impact of the mystical vital power of plants shown by the strenuous shooting can be felt in film such as *Grüne Vagabunden (Green Vagabonds), Kraftleistungen der Pflanzen (The Powerful Achievements of Plants), The Evolution of Sex in Plants,* or *Sinnerleben der Pflanzen (The Sensory Life of Plants).* There are also interesting scientific educational films, which use the many possibilities of film, especially microscopy and fast motion, as in *Rain, Thunder and Lightning, Röntgenstrahlen (X-rays), Kalt, kälter, am kältersten (Cold, Colder, the Coldest), Unsichtbare Hindernisse (Invisible Obstacles),* and *Lotsen der Luft (Pilots of the Air).*

As mentioned before, long documentary films were made one after another in wartime, but short documentaries did not profit by the special circumstances. In general, there were few chances to show short films in theaters, thus the receipts were not at all insured. However, the Motion Picture Law obliged all film theaters with a feature film screening program to show culture films and newsreels *("nyūsueiga,"* an English loan word; in the law text, the term "current events" film was used, since words of foreign origin were banned). In a standard program consisting of one feature film, one short culture film and one newsreel, even a culture film of about 10 minutes length would garner at least 10 percent of the general distribution revenue received from the theaters; therefore, the culture film boomed unexpectedly.

At first, producers could not supply the sudden and unanimous demand of theater owners for more and more culture films; on top of that, since these films

Fig. 10. *The Beach at Ebb Tide on One Day.*
(Credit: Japan Film Library Council)

promised constant revenues, everybody embarked on the production of them. A boom occurred. Some directors who had not been successful within feature filmmaking converted to culture films. The most superior model for all these films was the German kulturfilm.

The Beach At Ebb Tide on One Day (*Aru hi no higata*, Riken, 1940) by director Shimomura Kenji depicts the life of small animals and birds at the seaside in early spring. Patiently shot with a long-focus lens, it is a representative work for today's "watching picture." Subsequently, Shimomura made similar films, such as *Fujisan-roku no tori* (*The Birds at the Foot of Mount Fuji*, Riken, 1940), *Jihi shinchō* (*The Cuckoo*, Riken, 1942). Because the director left so many films with superior ecological observation, he was called "Shimomura of the birds."

Other masterpieces of this genre include *Snow Country* (*Yukiguni*, Geijutsu, 1939) by director Ishimoto Tōkichi, which describes the urgent protection measures against snow taken by the people during the long winter in the northern region, and the damage they suffer from snow. *Tsuchi ni ikiru* (*Living by the Earth*, Tōhō, 1939) by the director Miki Shigeru, scrupulously documents farmers involved in the hard process of cultivating rice over the span of one year. *Aru hobo no kiroku* (*Record of a Nursery*, Geijutsu, 1942) by the director Mizuki Sōya, shows everyday life in a day-care center in an industrial area in natural-feeling shots. The filmmakers were successful in their efforts to get the children used to the camera by always placing it in front of them so that they lose any interest and even any consciousness of it being there.

Another film, *Young Soldiers of the Sky* (*Sora no shōnenhei*, Geijutsu,1942), depicted the severe training process of young navy pilots and was directed by Inoue Kan. It was selected as best culture film of the year because it was a kind of "bible" for the boys' education at the time.

War and Cinema in Japan 35

Fig. 11. *Record of Nursery.*
(Credit: Japan Film Library Council)

The war situation in China entered into a deadlock, and during the search for peace measures many long documentaries (all made in 1941) directed the public's attention to Southeast Asia. Some examples are *Ranryō Indo* (*Indonesia*, Saneisha, supervised by Atsumi Teruo and Satō Hirokazu), *Ran'in tanbōki* (*Report on Indonesia*, Daimai-tōnichi, supervised by Hirakida Sei'ichi), *Taikoku no zenbō* (*The Complete Thailand*, Yomiuri, planned by Sagimiya Fumihiko), and *Tachiagaru Tai* (*Thailand Rising*, Daimai-tōnichi, directed by Hirakida Sei'ichi).

After the suppression of *Soldiers at the Front*, Kamei Fumio made *Kobayashi Issa* (Tōhō, 1941). Using the *haiku* of Kobayashi Issa as pretext, this short film ironically contrasts the difficult life of the farmers in Nagano Prefecture, Issa's birthplace, with a summer resort in the area; the view of a temple where the offertories from the blind devotees pour in like rain, and forms an unique, essay-like work. This film did not pass the examination for culture films prescribed by the Motion Picture Law. The constant, sarcastic social criticism of this film did not serve "the cultivation of the national spirit," and since it also could not "develop the intellectual faculties," it did not become part of the compulsory screenings in film theaters. This kind of film was rather strangely called "other film," in contrast to the branches feature film, culture films, and current-events film. These "other films" covered popular documentaries from the *sumō* tournaments, or the series *Asahi hōmu gurafu* (Asahi Home Graph) which was published every other week; they were shown in places comparable to the film theaters specializing in newsreels.

Like Iwasaki, Kamei was arrested under the charge of "having violated the maintenance of public order" in October 1941, and spent almost two years in custody camps and detention houses; he was released on probation in August 1943. Of course, his name had already been erased from the list of available directors, which existed according to the regulations of the Motion Picture Law.

36 Shimizu A.

Fig. 12. *Kobayashi Issa.*
(Credit: Japan Film Library Council)

The Centralization of the Newsreel

The four companies competing in the production of newsreels (Asahi, Daimai-tōnichi, Yomiuri, and Dōmei; *Shinbun Dōmei nyūsu* (*United Newspapers Dōmei News*, ceased to be published at the end of June 1939) disappeared all together after the edition of the second week of May 1940, and from then on the newly-formed Nihon Motion Picture Co. (Nichiei) was solely responsible for the production of newsreels. The official reason was to avoid wasting materials since different companies all pursued the same events, but of course the real intention was the central control of the flow of information during wartime. The best staff of all companies was selected to form Nichiei.

The Asahi Motion Picture Co. commemorated the announcement of the closing down of its *Asahi sekai nyūsu* (*Asahi World News*) with the production of the film *Nyūsu eiga hattatsu shi — yakushin no ato* (*History of the Development of the Newsreel — Traces of Rapid Progress*). This film reassembled the important scenes of the previous six years' issues of the *Asahi sekai nyūsu* combined with fragments of the history of the documentary since the pioneer days of film, beginning with the documentary of the kabuki play *Maple Viewing (Momijigari)*, shot in 1899. Therefore, this film is of greatest value as historical material.

The Second World War started in September 1939, when Germny overran Poland in the blitz, then forced France to admit defeat in June 1940. Impressed by these glorious results, Italy participated in the war on the German side, and the Tripartite Pact between Japan, Germany, and Italy was concluded in September of that year. Contrary to the former anti-communist agreement which bore the Soviet Union in mind, this pact between the three countries aimed at the military restraint of the United States.

In October, the Imperial Rule Assistance Association was organized, replacing the political parties by unification. This state-controlled organ of the government "conveyed the will of the superior to the normal citizen" *(jōi katatsu)*. Criticism of the government completely disappeared from then on.

On 11 November 1940, a splendid ceremony was held to celebrate the 2,600 year of the Imperial Reign on a grand scale. Counting from the year of the accession to the throne of the first emperor Jimmu, this was a kind of Imperial Calendar, opposing a so-called "Emperor's Era" to the Christian Era. This term was of no significance at all on an international level and served only the self-complacency of nationalism.

In this way, Japan tightened her system steadily to finally become a totalitarian state.

V THE FILM WORLD IN THE TIME OF THE GREAT EAST ASIA WAR

The Bombshell Declaration of the Cabinet Information Board

At the time of the China Incident, the Japanese army also went into action on the territories other than China: in September 1940, it advanced into the northern part of today's Vietnam. This action was intended to cut the supply route for war materials for China from the south; after France had been defeated on the European battlefront, an agreement was comparatively easily concluded, which did not even cause noticeable troubles internationally.

However, when moving further into the southern part of Indochina in July of the following year, international protests followed almost instantly. The reason for this is quite simple. Considered from today's aviation techniques, the bombers at the time had the unbelievably short action radius of less than 2,000 kilometers (1,250 miles). At that time, around the beginning of the China Incident, unprecedented heroic attempts like flight of bombing raids across the sea from Kyūshū in southern Japan to Nanking in China caused great excitement. Under these conditions, Singapore (then a British possession) and even the petroleum treasury of Indonesia were within the reach of bombing planes starting from Indochina, while they had been unattainable from the northern part of that country. Japan had been vacillating a long time between the choice of the northern policy, intending to advance into Siberia with the enemy being Soviet Russia, and the southern policy, chasing after the key commodities of Southeast Asia, which led to expected friction with England, the United States and the Netherlands. Finally, advancing into southern Indochina was the first step of the fulfillment of the southern policy.

The march in occurred without bloodshed because of the previously concluded agreement with France, but immediately after the beginning of the treaty negotiations with France, the United States froze all Japanese assets in the States. England and the Netherlands followed this example quickly. Moreover, the Netherlands and the United States forbid the export of petroleum to Japan. All this happened within one week from the negotiations, immediately after the Japanese army had advanced into southern Indochina. The condition for the cancelation of the embargo

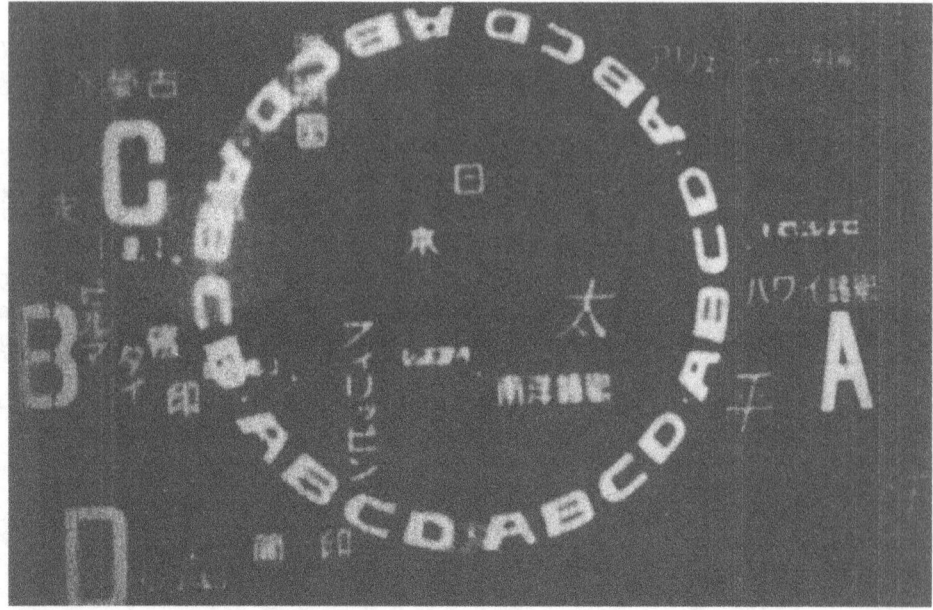

Fig. 13. Paranoic map of the ABCD enemies (Americans, British, Chinese, Dutch) surrounding Japan. From *Nippon Banzai*.
(Credit: Komatsuzawa Hajime)

was the withdrawal of the Japanese troops from China. This quick and decisive measure gives enough account of how much these countries had previously taken precautions for the Japanese aggression, and how much they abhorred it.

The Japanese mass media at that time glorified the China Incident with the completely illogical word "holy war," and carefully covered up the cold wing of the international public opinion. Although the actual facts about the advance into southern Indochina were published in the news, the background for this was kept top secret; only the retaliation measures of each country were reported without a moment's delay. The term "ABCD siege" ("A" standing for America, "B" for Britain, "C" for China, and "D" for Dutch) was coined, the position of Japan as the victim was adopted, and a feeling of danger inflamed. Already economic isolation could not be avoided, and the shortage in commodities became critical, especially the embargo on oil represented a problem of vital importance for Japan.

Under these existing circumstances, the Cabinet Information Board issued the following bombshell declaration on 16 August 1941, to the address of the chief executives of the film world. "Since raw film stock is a war material, not even one inch can be made available for private use, according to the current mobilization of goods for war preparations. The film world is required to take proper measures." The completely shocked chief executives understood this declaration as a reprimand directed at film associations for non-cooperation in view of the situation, and proposed the establishment of a film control commission conforming to the existing control commissions for important industries. However, the intentions of the governmental authorities concerned was a more severe one, out of a more realistic reason. Since the import of raw film stock from the United States could no longer be expected, and one could not rely on an increased production of film in Japan to replace this gap, and also the demand for war stock for military and information use increased, the shortage of raw film stock for film use had attained a serious stage. However, "not even one inch can be made available for private use" did not mean to shut up the business when the company's stock of raw film material had reached the ground. It was simply a broad hint to extort from the business world a system of allotments graced to private users, after having counted backward and deducted this share from the whole production of raw film material. Having waited for the reaction from the industry, the government put forward a new plan on August 25.

According to this plan, the production of feature films should be concentrated in the hands of two commercial corporations. The total production was limited to four films a month for both companies together, and there were to be 50 distribution prints per film. The production of culture films would be made by one commercial corporation and by Nichiei, which was to be reorganized as an incorporated association. The number of the produced films and prints would be the same as for the feature film. Nichiei also had to produce enlightening propaganda films according to the intentions of the government and current-events films, and the distribution was to be unified in one public service corporation by investment of the formerly mentioned four companies, which also had to take care of the distribution of foreign films. This severe unification program was beyond all imagination, and threw the business world into utter confusion; conferences between the chief executives of the business world and representatives of the Cabinet Information Board were held almost every other day. At that time, 10 production companies had received the accreditation according to the Motion Picture Law. Finally, it was concluded that they should be merged not into two, but three companies, and to compensate for the increased production of six films per month, it was agreed that the number of release prints per film should be reduced to 30, in order not to exceed the original consumption volume of film stock in the government plan.

One company was Shōchiku, united with Kōa; the second was Tōhō, formed by its union with Tokyo Hassei, Nan'o, Takarazuka, and Daihō; the third was a newly-formed company uniting Shinkō and Daitō, and Nikkatsu made an investment in kind in the form of its production structure (film studios).

The mass media at that time called these measures the "ready-for-war attitude of the film industry."

The big enterprises, who had believed that the Motion Picture Law would protect them, were clearly demonstrated within just two years since its enforcement, that this law held the power of life and death over them. The continuation of independent productions like the Tokyo Hassei, which had left beautiful literary films such as *Young People* (*Wakai hito*, 1937) and *Spring on Leper's Island* (*Kojima no haru*, 1940), both directed by Toyoda Shirō, was already a dream of the past.

In the middle of these preparations for the change to a ready-for-war attitude by the entire industry, Japan finally declared war on the United States and Great Britain on 8 December 1941. From that day on, the film distribution permissions for American companies were revoked, and film from the States and Great Britain suddenly became "enemy's films," their screening being forbidden for all movie theaters in Japan. The government decided to call all events including the battles in China, "The Greater East Asian War," the term "Pacific War" being used only after the end of the war, following the American practice.

In the beginning of the war, glorious war results were published without fail. The film industry changed completely. The third film company was named Dai-Nihon Eiga Seisaku Kabushikigaisha (Greater Japan Film Production Corporation), Daiei for short. In January of the following year, the inaugural meeting was held. Nikkatsu, which had given its studios as investment in kind, kept its own film theater chain together with its formerly produced films, and continued as a performance company. The unification of the distribution structures went on smoothly, absorbing business staff members of each company, and in February the incorporated association for film distribution was established.

The number of authorized culture film production amounted to far over 200, reflecting the boom in this branch caused by the Motion Picture Law. The incorporated association Nichiei absorbed several other film producers: the culture film sections of Tōhō and Shōchiku, Daimai-tōnichi, Yomiuri, Jūjiya, Fuji Studio, and Tokyo Bunka Eiga (a part of Shinkō Kinema); therefore, it became very powerful, but the final unification into just one commercial corporation turned out to be extremely difficult, and suggestions for more than two companies were made. With this point still unresolved, the film industry entered in a new era on 1 April 1942, according to the "ready-for-war attitude "

With six films allowed per month, each company was assigned two films. The nationwide distribution was re-organized by splitting the film theaters into two chains, one called the red chain, the other the white one. With an invariable 30 prints per film, the numbering of the theaters was an easy task; every theater got its number in the ranking of one chain, thus the distribution becoming automatic. Production according to the plan was the basis for this new era of ready-made distribution.

The unification of the culture film world was finally settled; Riken Kagaku Motion Picture Co. absorbed 10 minor companies, Asahi merged with Geijutsu, together absorbing eight minor companies, and Dentsū Motion Picture Section (Dentsū Eigabu) swallowed up four companies and was renamed Dentsū Motion Picture Co. (Dentsū Eigasha). With these three companies, the problem concerning the unification of culture film producers was solved, but two whole years had been necessary. Yokohama Cinema and Tōa Hassei did not take part in the unification, but withdrew from film production, relying on their film processing facilities and their recording studios.

Soliciting "National Films"

In May 1941, three months before the propagation of the ready-for-war attitude, the Cabinet Information Board announced a plan to request "national films" *(kokumin eiga)* and scenarios. In a definition by the Board, national films "originate from national life, manifest the high-minded ideas, have great artistic value, and finally contribute to the accomplishment of national policy and to enlightening propaganda."

Regarding the request for national films, the participation of the main film production companies was asked for. First, a conference concerning the main subject chosen by the company was held, and at the next stage the scenario writer and the director directly received a subsidy beforehand for the writing of the script. This scenario had to be examined by a jury, then a subsidy was granted for the shooting. Among the completed films, the Special Prize of the President of the Cabinet Information Board was to be awarded to excellent works. Compared to former competitions, the subsidy beforehand during the production process and the direct allotment to the designed scenario writers and directors were outstanding characteristics. The jury members were to be selected among civilian film critics and the intelligentsia.

In the first year of this plan, 1941, seven companies out of 10 (excluding Nan'o, Takarazuka, and Daiho) were entrusted with film production, and among the films of the five remaining companies, Shōchiku, Tōhō, Nikkatsu, Shinkō, and Kōa (absorbed by Shōchiku), no work was applicable for the Special Prize of the President of the Cabinet Information Board. However, a Prize of the Cabinet Information Board was shared between *There Was a Father (Chichi ariki)*, which was directed by Ozu Yasujirō for Shōchiku, and *Generals, Staff, and Soldiers*, directed by Taguchi Satoshi for Nikkatsu.

In 1942, during the Greater East Asian War, the production request was revised into a production encouragement, and to the production process assistance regulation, the text "Meeting the necessities, guidance by the authorities concerned will be received" was added. After the unification as preparation for war, the remaining three companies were urged to participate with two films each, but finally just three films from two companies participated. Among them, *The War at Sea from Hawaii to Malaya (Hawai Marē okikaisen)*, directed by Yamamoto Kajirō for Tōhō, was selected for the Special Prize of the Cabinet Information Board. *All-out Attack on Singapore (Shingaporu sōkōgeki)*, directed by Shima Kōji for Daiei, had been the recipient of assistance, but failed to be finished within the time limit and was thus disqualified.

In spite of the Cabinet Information Board's active plan regarding subsidies during the production process, the film industry fostered no special enthusiasm in the production of national films. Therefore, the system was widely changed in 1943. The individual promotion of specific participating productions was cancelled, and all scenarios of each company were to be examined by a jury; among these, enlightening propaganda films and especially brilliant works were selected to be national films. The films completed by the end of the year were nominated for the prize. In 1943, six films were nominated: *Flying South in His Plane (Aiki minami e tobu,* Shōchiku), *Navy (Kaigun,* directed by Tasaka Tomotaka, Shōchiku), *Toward the Decisive Battle in the Sky (Kessen no ōzora e), Hot Wind (Neppū,* Tōhō), *Himetaru kakugo (Hidden Preparedness,* Tōhō), and *Shussei mae jūnijikan (Twelve Hours before Going to the Front,* Daiei). However, no film was awarded the Special Prize of the President of the Cabinet Information Board, and *Navy, Toward the Decisive Battle in the Sky,* and *Flying South in His Plane* obtained the Prize of the Cabinet Information Board.

In this way, the selection of national films became a kind of preliminary contest for the Cabinet Information Board competition. As a result, of the total production number in 1944 of only 45 films for all three companies combined, 26 works, that is more than half of the productions received the "National Film of the Cabinet Information Board" stamp; no authority was associated with it any longer. Some of these films not selected even at the scenario stage, but thanks to the guidance and corrections received, the completed work was chosen. This extremely indulgent proceeding no longer promoted the best as expected in the initial subsidy plan, but became a form of leverage for the lowest strata of film production.

In September of this year, the Cabinet Information Board required the incorporated association Dai-Nihon Eiga Kyōkai (Greater Japan Film Association) to examine national films. Furthermore, the definition was modified to "films contributing to the reinforcement of military power together with the uplifting of the national spirit in wartime" and "films recognized as suitable for showing to the whole population as enlightening propaganda"; the initial phrase "great artistic value" being blown to the winds.

The application for scenarios for national films was now made publicly, and a jury formed of scenario writers, directors and film critics decided upon them. In spite of this new system, the Prize of the Cabinet Information Board was never awarded to one of these scenarios. Quite a few professionals from the studios participated, as well. Kurosawa Akira received the first Cabinet Information Board Prize. Shindō Kaneto received the first prize for a work of merits and the second Cabinet Information Board Prize, and Tabata Tsuneo was awarded the third Cabinet Information Board Prize. It served as a gateway to success for a director's career. Among the selected scenarios, some were actually made into films, such as *Mother-and-Child Grass (Hahako-gusa)* from the first competition, and *Yasen gungakutai (Military Musical Band and the Front)* from the third.

The Transition to National Policy as seen in Cinema

The model type for Japanese films desired by the Cabinet Information Board is explained in the definition of national films made in May 1941: "Films originating from the national ideal, manifesting the high-minded national ideal, having great artistic value, and finally contributing to the accomplishment of national policy and to enlightening propaganda." It is of profound significance that these words were changed after three years to: "Films contributing to the reinforcement of military power together with the uplifting of the national spirit in wartime" and "films recognized as suitable for showing to the whole population as enlightening propaganda."

The former version originated from the times of the China Incident, the euphemistic term for the war operations concerning solely China. This was a time when nobody thought of fighting Great Britain and the United States. The latter definition was created in the middle of long desperate fights against America during the Greater East Asia War.

During the China Incident, at least until the time of the lantern processions celebrating the attack on Hankou, the great majority of Japanese were convinced that this incident would quickly be settled by the installation of pro-Japanese political powers centered in Peking and Shanghai. Thus China would become in reality a Japanese colony, a second Manchukuo. However, even after the establishment of the new government under Wang Chaoming in Nanking, the administration in Chungking took no account of this "sham government," and the bitter resistance under Chiang Chiehshi against it did not shake at all. Japan was very eager to find a clue to end this unexpectedly long war, but no feeling of defeat existed among the Japanese people. Air raids to the Japanese mainland were not expected at all, and local defeats were carefully excluded from the information routes, much less the battles with communist guerillas. Without the knowledge of all that, the despise for the Chinese that had existed since the Sino-Japanese War was still deeply rooted in the mind of the ordinary Japanese.

The films also condemned any attack against Japan without reservation, adopting the slogan "holy war" as being above any criticism and in the name of the Emperor. At the same time, Chinese masses cooperating with Japan were treated as close friends. These were the big fundamental principles for the representation of Chinese people in film. The glory of the draft call; the remaining family members being helped by their neighbors; the brave fighting of the soldiers at the front and their difficulties; all of this was transmitted. Since a soldier had to undergo these hardships the population at home also has to endure all hardships and privations. In the pattern above, the spirit of sacrificing oneself for the Empire was taught to the public. Firmly believing in the ultimate victory, being killed in action was considered a noble sacrifice. Many efforts were made to support the surviving families. These were the necessary and sufficient conditions for the national policy required from the film industry at the time of the China Incident.

However, since war flames had spread to the Greater East Asia War facing the United States and England, the situation changed entirely. Beginning with the attack on Pearl Harbor, the elaborated first attacks by the Japanese in some fights allowed brilliant war results exceeding all expectations and throwing the general public into ecstasy. Hong Kong, Indochina (Vietnam), Malaysia, Singapore, Dutch-India (Indonesia), the Philippines, Burma (Myanmar) were occupied one after the other. In the end, the Japanese army even marched into New Guinea. In exchange for mainland China, dreams were sprouting new in the direction of Southeast Asia. The general opinion was that the Asian nations were now liberated from the colonization by European and American countries, and instead of the simple "holy war," the somewhat more reasonable argument about a "troublesome moral duty" was preferred. Moreover, instead of slogans like "Everything and Everybody under One Universe," which expressed the leadership of the Japanese Emperor for all nations and gave the impression of mental training (and was hardly understood by the addressees), the term "Greater East Asia Co-Prosperity Sphere" was — without considering the possibilities of realization — slightly more convincing.

However, considering the long front line across the western part of the Pacific Ocean and the material resources of the United States, the war situation became disadvantageous for Japan day by day. In the naval battle at Midway in June 1942, the Japanese navy lost its dominant position over the Pacific, a mere six months after the attack on Pearl Harbor. In the naval battle at Leyte in October 1944, the Japanese combined fleet was downright annihilated. These disastrous defeats were not transmitted to the Japanese public. Saipan, at that time under Japanese rule, was attacked. From this strategically important island, big formations of American long-distance bombers raided the Japanese mainland almost every other day, without the Japanese side being able to strike back. After many cities were reduced to ashes, after the dropping of atomic bombs on Hiroshima and Nagasaki, Japan finally capitulated. Together with this development in the war situation, the national policy required in films also changed quite quickly.

The concrete progress will be clear when studying the actual films of that time.

Demonstrations of War Results

The first months of war seethed with brilliant battle results, and these results were promptly arranged into documentary films or reproduced in fiction films. They were shown not only all over Japan, but also in the territories occupied by the Japanese army. These films intended to uplift morale, and attached great importance to the demonstration of Japan's military might. Among the fiction films, the following deserve attention. Each made with the support of the Army Information Office, they are laborious works produced with much effort.

The Day England Fell
(*Eikoku kuzururu no hi*, directed by Tanaka Shigeo, Daiei, 1942)
The War at Sea from Hawaii to Malaya
(*Hawai Marē okikaisen*, directed by Yamamoto Kajirō, Tōhō, 1942)

The special-effects staff of Tōhō, with Tsuburaya Eiji as leader, used many elaborate miniatures of Pearl Harbor to create forceful scenes with special effects photography. The first half deals with the period before the attack on Pearl Harbor and the process of forging young naval officers through severe training. The latter half is set in the Malayan Sea and shows how a British ship is sent to the bottom.

All-out Attack on Singapore
(*Shingaporu sōkōgeki*, directed by Shima Kōji, Daiei, 1943)
Fire On That Flag!
(*Ano hata o ute*, Philippine release title: *Dawn of Freedom*, directed by Abe Yutaka, Tōhō, 1944)

The scene is set on the Philippines war front. The film shows how the Japanese army occupies Manila, suppresses the Bataan Peninsula, and attacks Corregidor Island until the American army is driven away from the Philippines. An extremely large staff went to the actual locations, Filipino actors were appointed in large numbers, speaking English, and other things made this a great and very dense work, never seen in war films before. However, there is a very heavy smack of propaganda intended to plant an anti-American consciousness into the Filipinos, as well as inspire pro-Japanese feelings.

After *Fire On That Flag!*, there were no other feature films demonstrating the war results on such a grand scale. The reason for this change lies in the fact that unfortunately, war results to be proud of no longer existed, and the tide of war turned from attack to defense and finally to gradual decline. However, the documentary film closely followed each military operation in long films like those described below. These were the unrivaled territory of Nichiei, which had many cameramen following the army to the front and thus became machinery for the production of enlightening propaganda of the state.

Malayan War Front — A Record of the March Onward
(*Marē senki — shingeki no kiroku*, supervised by Iida Shinmi, Nichiei, 1942)

This is a record of the army's march south on the Malayan peninsula and their attack on Singapore. During the cease-fire negotiations, an extremely effective scene was shot in fast-motion by a quick-witted cameraman, showing a shocked and alarmed commander of the British army, Percival, reacting to the demands of Japanese commander Yamashita for unconditional surrender.

Malayan War Front — The Birth of Shonan Island
(*Marē senki — Shōnan-tō tanjō*, directed by Miki Shigeru, Nichiei, 1942)

"Shōnan" was the new name for Singapore, created by the occupying Japanese army.

War Report from Burma
(*Biruma senki*, the names of the staff members are unknown)
Oriental Song of Victory
(*Tōyō no gaika*, supervised by Sawamura Tsutomu, Philippines Special Information Group, 1942)

This covers the suppression of the Bataan Peninsula and the attack on Corregidor. It is the only film made without the help of Nichiei. The Philippine Special Information Group controlled the whole production from the first plans to the completion. Since all scenes were especially shot for this film, it was quite different from the newsreels, and distinguished itself further by the editing and development that was made in laboratories on location.

Tairiku shinsenjō
(*New Battlefield on the Continent*, Nichiei and Chūka Den'ei, 1943)

Since the beginning of the Greater East Asian War, the front line in China was prone to be forgotten. This is record of the successful war operations in Chekan, where the American air force in China was annihilated, and mineral resources acquired.

Gochin
(*Attack to Sink*, supervised by Watanabe Yoshimi, Nichiei, 1944)

The word "gochin" was frequently used during the war in the General Headquarters' statements, and literally means a fast attack to sink ships, which finally submerge after a certain time. This term was used to make a distinction from the normal "sending to the bottom." Three photography teams were sent with three submarines respectively, sallying forth to the Indian Ocean. They recorded the sinking of an enemy ship by torpedoes, the questioning of rescued prisoners, the rise to the surface at night for the bombardment of an enemy oil tanker that had not been completely sunk by torpedoes, the successful attack and sinking of an incidentally discovered enemy transport fleet by torpedoes, the thrill of avoiding the dangerous torpedo counterattack of the escorting enemy destroyer by submerging again and again to deeper waters, and the alternate use of the single periscope by the commander of the submarine and the camera. All these events, performed without the possibility of rehearsals, form an excellent documentary film unparalleled in the world.

It is interesting that not a single news cameraman was taken along at the time of the attack of Pearl Harbor. The maintenance of the secret that the operation started from an aircraft carrier may have been a motive, but probably the real reason was that they would have regretted sparing a single plane for the cameraman in this extremely daring war operation. For the confirmation of the battle's results, some still photographs shot by the navy itself were officially published; these were also used frequently in films, together with a talkative voice-over narration that was not terribly interesting. In sharp contrast to this, it was an idea of the navy itself to board a whole camera crew in a narrow submarine for *Attack to Sink*; it is clear that the military authorities gradually recognized the propagandistic power of film.

The air raid on Hawaii was also transformed into Japan's first feature-length animation film. The story of *Momotarō's Sea Eagle* (*Momotarō no umiwashi*, directed by Seo Mitsuyo, Geijutsu, 1943) is modeled after the hero of an old Japanese tale, *Momotarō*, and his conquest of the enemy.

Commemorative Screenings for The Beginning of The War and Exalting of The Fighting Spirit

Within a month following the beginning of the war, it was already decided that the eighth day of each month was to be "The Day of Humbly Receiving the Emperor's Orders." On that day, an Imperial edict was respectfully read in every school or working place, and everybody prayed for victory. I remember that one of these days, I was refused *sake* when I ordered it in a hot springs up in the Japanese alps.

December 8 became the memorial day for the beginning of the war, and the film world — in its ready-for-war attitude — arranged for special films suitable to the occasion.

Commemorative Screening for The First Anniversary of The Beginning of The War (1942):

> RED CHAIN: *The War at Sea from Hawaii to Malaya*
> WHITE CHAIN: *Oriental Song of Victory*

Commemorative Screening for The Second Anniversary of The Beginning of The War (1943):

> BOTH CHAINS: *Navy*

Iwata Tōyō's original novel for *Navy* was published serially in the *Asahi Shinbun*. The son of a merchant in Kagoshima receives strict training at a naval academy, and then participates as a commissioned naval officer in the attack on Pearl Harbor as a member of a submarine special attack corps.

Commemorative Screening for The Third Anniversary of The Beginning of The War (1944):

RED CHAIN: *Attendance in a Torpedo Squad*
(*Raigekitai shutsudō*, also *Torpedo Squadrons Move Out*, directed by Yamamoto Kajirō, Tōhō)

On an air base in the central part of the Pacific Ocean, naval officers fight with torpedoes against a powerful enemy mobile fleet, however, one after the other loses his life. It was more touching than heroic.

WHITE CHAIN: *Army*
(*Rikugun*, directed by Kinoshita Keisuke, Shōchiku).

The original novel by Hino Ashihei was published serially in the Asahi Newspaper. From the end of the Tokugawa *bakufu* through the Sino-Japanese and Russo-Japanese wars to the Shanghai Incidents, the life of four generations of the old Kokura family in Kyūshū and their commitments in war is depicted, showing the sense of duty of Japanese men as soldiers. In the last scene the mother follows her son as he marches off to the front; this scene's extremely long travelling shot became famous.

On December 8 of each year, these national policy films, some of excellent quality, were shown. They reflect clearly and honestly the changing war situation. The two films of the first year, *The War at Sea from Hawaii to Malaya* and *Oriental Song of Victory*, reflect the victorious feeling after battles and praise the excellent war results.

In the second year, *Navy* does not show off war results, but depicts the growth of a navy officer, an elite among the elite, in a dignified and solemn way. This film conveys a deep and grave exaltation of the war spirit, rousing a yearning for enlistment in the navy in the hearts of the spectators.

In the third year, in spite of the firm control of the press and the information media, no bright future is shown. *Attendance in a Torpedo Squad* incites a serious feeling of crisis, and *Army* centers on the sorrow of the mother who accompanies her son on his way to the front. The last scene, with the long moving shot conveying their reluctance to part, appears in the scenario in just one line: "The mother accompanies him to the station." The scenario passed the censorship before shooting, but at the time of the shooting, this line became a scene full of emotion in the typical style of the director Kinoshita Keisuke; it almost gives rise to anti-war feelings. The bulletin of the Dai-Nihon Eiga Kyōkai, *Nihon Eiga* (Japanese Film), wrote the following about this film: "The figure of the mother, ecstatic, half crazy, who elbows her way through the crowd to follow Shintarō [her son], is not a woman seeing her son off, but in its exaggeration and lack of common sense a highly deplorable and unnecessary stain on an otherwise fine film." The author is not indicated, but this is a typical example of the official reviews of that time.

The "war hero film" can be cited as one example of films that exalted the fighting spirit. The previously mentioned *Navy* is one of these; although based on an actual event, the real names of the two soldiers depicted in this film are avoided, since there were nine war heros at that time (normally, there are two crew members in a submarine for special attacks so there should be ten, but one member dropped out because of an accident).

General Katō's Falcon Fighters (*Katō hayabusa sentōtai*, directed by Yamamoto Kajirō, Tōhō, 1944) depicts Lt. Col. Katō Tateo (after his death, he received a double promotion of rank to major general) and his distinguished military services. As commander of the new fighter plane Hayabusa (falcon), the pride of the army, he achieved the honor of shooting down or destroying over 200 enemy planes. Like *The Story of Tank Commander Nishizumi*, made at the time of the China Incident, this work features the matchless star of war-hero films, Fujita Susumu. The actor was highly appraised for his rousing performance in the leading role, and won great fame. His bright smile, which does not really fit his angular face, made it easy for the audience to feel an intimacy with the personality of the hero, and he was friendly to his subordinates. Furthermore, in this film, the special effects department, the pride of Tōhō, created scenes of heroic aerial combat.

Captain Wakabayashi started his career as private, and became famous for his bravery at the China front and the attack of Hong Kong. At Guadalcanal, he endured hardships and privations, and finally died in a suicide attack against an enemy with overwhelming material superiority. The film depicting his life in this way, *Ato ni tsuzuku o shinzu* (*They Will Continue After Me*, directed by Watanabe Kunio, Tōhō, 1945), probably belongs to the war hero films as well, but since it was released on March 8, one day before the big air raids on Tokyo started, I could not see it.

The film based on the life of Dr. Hiraga Yuzuru, *The Angry Sea* (*Ikari no umi*, directed by Imai Tadashi, Tōhō, 1944), is also a film that uplifts the fighting spirit, although Hiraga cannot be considered a war hero. As an authority in the field of ship construction studies, he ensured that the Japanese navy held the first place in the world concerning capacities after a ratio of 5 : 5 : 3 (United States : Great Britain : Japan) for total tonnage of ships was forced on Japan in the 1921 Washington Conference. The way he devoted his life to the design of battleships is depicted. In his late years, he became president of Tokyo Imperial University (today Tokyo University), and died the year before the completion of this film.

The confidence in an energetic and powerful army, highly trained by severe drilling and discipline, was another element intended to exalt the fighting spirit; the following two culture films are outstanding examples.

The Basics of Victory (*Shōri no kiso*, also *The Foundation of Victory*, directed by Nakagawa Norio, Riken, 1942) offers a record of the training of students in the naval academy in Edajima, extending over three and a half years.

Sacred Soldiers of the Sky (*Sora no shinpei*, also *Divine Soldiers of the Sky*, directed by Watanabe Yoshimi, Nichiei, 1942) shows the intense ground training of army parachute troops up to their first jump. In February of this same year, a parachute troop landed in the region of Indonesia's biggest oil fields, Palembang in Sumatra, and occupied an airport and an oil refinery. Therefore, the public's attention concentrated on this new strategy for surprise attack.

In face of a war situation turning more severe day by day, students (whose military draft had been postponed) were called to arms. On 21 October 1943, a great celebration for the drafting of tens of thousands of students from 77 schools took place in the Meiji Jingu Athletic Stadium in Tokyo. Under the title *Sending Off Our Students (Never to Return)* (*Gakuto shutsujin*, also *Students Going to the Battle*), the newsreel *Nihon News* (*Nihon nyūsu*) spent over six minutes on this event in its 177th issue. I had graduated from university two years before, and I could not help but cry when I saw the parade advancing by firm steps in the drizzling rain, marching through puddles, with my alma mater taking the lead.

The intentions of the feature films listed below can be easily imagined by just reading the titles. The training of pilots was an urgent need for national policy.

Toward the Decisive Battle in the Sky (*Kessen no ōzora e*, directed by Watanabe Kunio, Tōhō, 1943)
Flying South in His Plane (*Aiki minami e tobu*, directed by Sasaki Yasushi, Shōchiku, 1943)
Hinawashi no haha (*The Mother of Little Eagle*, directed by Yoshimura Ren, Daiei, 1944)
Kimi koso tsugi no arawashi da (*You Are the Next Wild Eagle*, directed by Hozumi Toshimasa, Shōchiku, 1944)

These three companies competed in the production of these films, all of which were national films for the Cabinet Information Board. The last of them, *Kimi koso tsugi no arawashi da*, was released on 14 September 1944. In the sea battle at Leyte in the Philippines, the last hope for Japan as a strategic turning point, kamikaze suicide attack squads loaded with bombs were determined to deliver one plane to every American ship, starting on 25 October 1944. As one might expect, with regular pilots turning into members of these special attack groups, no films to recruit pilots were made from then on.

Increase of Production as an Imposed Theme

The induction order of the army was called *akagami* ("red paper"). Needless to say, the paper was red to facilitate its quick identification. There was also an induction order on *shirogami* ("white paper"). The National Draft Order was proclaimed, based on the fourth article of the National Mobilization Law, and accordingly, a shirogami compelled the recipient to work for the nation, regardless of personal priorities or predilections. Receiving the shirogami did not in the least mean that the red one was avoided, for the akagami had priority under any circumstances. This was proclaimed in July 1939. In the beginning, it was limited to persons with some technical experience, but with the Greater East-Asia War, the number of these workers increased rapidly. Technical experience ceased to be the decisive factor. In February 1944, it was decided, under the title "Extraordinary Measures for Decisive Battles," that all students from the senior high school level on were sent to factories, and that unmarried women from the ages of 14 to 25 were to be mobilized as female volunteer corps for munitions factories.

The fiction film was forced to cooperate in this loud cry for increased production. The following films belong in this group. Until the middle of 1943, this kind of project had not been seen. However, with the release of *Hot Wind* (*Neppū*) in October of that year, this theme became suddenly popular, reflecting the tide of war. All

Fig. 14. *Hot Wind.*
(Credit: Japan Film Library Council)

these films follow the same pattern: a rigorous production increase target is impeded by an obstacle, there are discussions on how to find a way out, a small love story is integrated, and finally the assigned norm is perfectly fulfilled.

Hot Wind
(*Neppū*, directed by Yamamoto Satsuo, Tōhō, 1943)

The production increase of iron and steel is the theme for this film. A smelting furnace is apt to go wrong, and finally stops. In the climactic scene, they venture to use dynamite as a dangerous method to make it work again.

Kessen
(*Decisive Battle*, directed by Hagiyama Teruo, Shōchiku, 1944)

In the confrontation between the shipbuilding department and the bridge construction department in a heavy industry company, the importance of shipbuilding in the present situation is explained. Yoshimura Kimisaburō was supposed to direct this film, but he was drafted; his chief assistant director Hagiyama Teruo replaced him.

Sinking of the Unsinkable Warship
(*Fuchinkan gekichin*, directed by Makino Masahiro, Shōchiku, 1944)

A factory produced parts for torpedoes just before the Greater East-Asia War. The efforts to fulfill the norm are connected in this film with the great war results in Hawaii and the sinking of an unsinkable warship in the Malayan Sea.

The Most Beautiful
(*Ichiban utsukushiku*, also *Most Beautifully*, directed by Kurosawa Akira, Tōhō 1944)

This film depicted a female worker charged to polish lenses in an optic ordnance factory. Different from the usual pattern of discussions about problems, it tells the story of a female worker who thoughtlessly mislays one uncorrected lens among the finished lenses because of overwork and mental stress. In the climactic scene, she searches all by herself throughout the night for this lens, manifesting her sense of responsibility.

Chi no tsume moji
(*Written with Bloody Nails*, directed by Chiba Yasuki, Daiei, 1944)

A factory produces aluminum, the main material for aircraft. The delivery of the source material bauxite, won in Indonesia, is prone to be interrupted. Therefore, the development of a new production method for making aluminum from indigenous materials becomes important.

Inochi no minato
(*Port of Life*, directed by Watanabe Kunio, Tōhō, 1944)

An exception, the scene for this film is not set in a factory. It depicts longshoremen (*okinakashi*), called harbor laborers (*kōwan romusha*) at that time, who insure the nation's fighting strength, although their importance is almost unknown

Santarō ganbaru
(*Santarō Giving His Best*, directed by Nomura Hiromasa, Shōchiku, 1944)

This film, set in an aircraft factory with boy workers, was supposed to promote increased production, but it was severely criticized for its lack of enthusiasm and vigor.

Torrent
(*Gekiryū*, directed by Ieki Miyoji, Shōchiku, 1944)

The theme is the increased production of coal. Since the appointed director Shibuya Minoru was drafted, his best pupil Ieki took over. This film represents an exception because the increase of production is not directly praised. Instead it deals mainly with family problems and the human relations between the workers there.

Shōchiku, Tōhō and Daiei exerted themselves without exception to make these films on increased production, just as they had with movies depicting the training of pilots. This was not a spontaneous idea. The project was allotted in the following way. Among the three most important heavy industries, iron and steel were assigned to Tōhō, and aluminum (the basic material for the aircraft industry) to Daiei. Shōchiku took care of coal.

At that time, censorship did not solely concern the scenario, but an examination at the first stage of the project itself also became customary. Before even starting to write the scenario, the production plan, the story, the staff members, and the cast had to be submitted to the Cabinet Information Board for approval. Of course, special attention was given to the fundamentals of how the theme was dealt with, but also to the description of characters and their personalities. It was also not unusual for the projects to be rejected out of hand. There were in fact three stages of censorship: one for the project, one for the scenario, and one for the completed film

At the end of 1943, the Dai-Nihon Eiga Kyōkai, which had outgrown its existence as the Imperial Rule Assistance Association of the film business, changed its monthly magazine *Nihon Eiga*. This had been available on the market, but now became an official bulletin distributed only to people in the industry; it had no cover, in the style of an official gazette, and was published twice a month. Self-complacent critics of film projects even appeared, clearly showing the guiding conscience of this journal.

REPAINTING THE MAP OF FILM EXHIBITION

In February 1944, measures for the organization of the entertainment business were published. This included a concrete plan for the suspension of high-class entertainment, the evacuation and dispersion of areas crowded with entertainment facilities, as well as essential points for the enforcement of this reform of the entertainment industry. These reforms were based on the "Essential Points Concerning Special Measures for Decisive Battles" decided by the Cabinet.

Concerning the suspension of high-class entertainment, the theaters (stage and film) listed below were shut down starting March 5 for a year's period, and entertainment charging more than five yen including tax (today's value: 10,000 yen or about US $100) were forbidden. The theaters with an asterisk (*) are film theaters.

TOKYO
Kabukiza (Kabuki Theater), Tokyo Gekijō (Tokyo Theater), Shinbashi Enbujō (Shinbashi Playhouse), Yūrakuza (Yūraku Theater), Tokyo Takarazuka Gekijō (Tokyo Takarazuka Theater), Teikoku Gekijō (Imperial Theater), Meijiza (Meiji Theater), Kokusai Gekijō (International Theater), *Nihon Gekijō (Japan Theater).

OSAKA
Osaka Kabukiza (Osaka Kabuki Theater), Nakaza (Naka Theater), Kadoza (Kado Theater), Kitano Gekijō (Kitano Theater), *Osaka Gekijō (Osaka Theater), *Umeda Eiga Gekijō (Umeda Film Theater).

KYOTO
Minamiza (Minami Theater).

KOBE
Shōchiku Gekijō (Shōchiku Theater).

NAGOYA
Misonoza (Misono Theater).

HYŌGO PREFECTURE
Takarazuka Dai-Gekijō (Takarazuka Main Theater).

In the first announcement, the Shinbashi Enbujō, the Meijiza, the Osaka Gekijō, the Umeda Eiga Gekijō, the Minamiza, and the Misonoza were to be transformed into movie theaters or theaters for mass entertainment such as popular plays or variety shows. The others were to be transformed into public halls or places of refuge in case of emergency, but reality proved different. The Cabinet Information Board moved into the Teikoku Gekijō, with the lobby minutely divided into offices, and the auditorium becoming a film preview room. On the other hand, the spectators' seats in the Nihon Gekijō were removed, and female volunteer corps manufactured balloon bombs in the big circular space. After one year, when closing time as projected in the initial plan had passed, these measures were extended and finally lasted until the end of the war.

Balloon bombs are incendiary bombs or small explosives suspended on a paper balloon of about 10 meters (11 yards) in diameter; they were entrusted to the wind over the Pacific Ocean, which normally blows from west to east, and by the time they reached America, they deflated, came down, and exploded. Of course, the success rate was quite low, and even exploding, they were just sporadic blind bombings. However, the American magazine *Time* reported that Japanese balloon bombs had come down in the state of Montana, near Kalispell. Moreover, some articles entitled "Mysterious Bombs from the Sky," or "Mountain Fires of Unknown Origin" appeared in newspapers. In total, 9,300 balloon bombs were set free, and at most 10 percent arrived. A mere child's play, these operations had to "rely on God's help"; Japan's military power had become very weak to fall back on such projects.

Concerning the dispersion and evacuation of areas with many entertainment facilities, such as Asakusa, Yūrakuchō, or Ginza, it was ordered that theaters annexed to big theaters that had been closed down should adapt to the situation and strive for other utilizations, and that some constructions in these parts, mainly wooden buildings, should be demolished. Film theaters also fell under these conditions: two in Asakusa, two in Shinjuku, four in Yūrakuchō/Ginza, two in Osaka, one in Kyoto, two in Kōbe, two in Nagoya (four other places were closed voluntarily), two in Yokohama, all together 21. The vacant lots caused by these demolitions were used for air defense.

The reform of entertainment was decided by the Home Ministry as follows.

First of all, the reforms concerned the content of entertainment. Based on the premise that everything must contribute to the uplifting of national morale, the following items were suitable:

1) Entertainment that contributes to the enhancement of the Japanese spiritual culture.
2) Entertainment that is simple, sturdy, cheerful, and generous.
3) Entertainment that encourages the construction of a new order of national life, in view of the accomplishments of the war.
4) Entertainment that avoids that which is isolated from the national life in wartime, or things that are gorgeous, frivolous, or unhealthy.

Secondly, the actual conditions for entertainment were revised.

1) One film screening should last about 100 minutes. Exceptions will be granted in special cases. The length of one feature film should not exceed 2,000 meters (that means 73 minutes projection time). The compulsory screening of culture films was cancelled; if shown, they were not to exceed two reels. The production of long culture films was to be considered.
2) The number of showings should increase as much as possible.
3) The location of entertainment should be gradually re-organized to cope with requirements concerning air defense and transport, and in sites where audiences needing encouragement are concentrated.
4) The number of first-run theaters should be increased, and the organization of the program should be made according to the directions of authorities to insure an appropriate distribution.

The number of screenings was also fixed with three on weekdays (one starting at noon, the two others after 6 p.m.), and four showing on Sundays and holidays, applicable from April 1. The limitation for a feature film to 73 minutes shocked film directors considerably. However, Mizoguchi Kenji's *Three Generations of Danjurō (Danjurō sandai)* lasts just 65 minutes, and was praised by the Dai-Nihon Eiga Kyōkai for its excellent artistic contribution.

Together with these measures, according to the policy that film was after all a form of acknowledgement of the services of the laborers in the war industry (at that time, they were called industrial warriors), first-run theaters were changed from the busiest quarters to important dwelling areas for laborers; this program started for the whole of Japan on April 13, under the title "Appropriate Re-arrangement According to Region." According to this program, first-run theaters increased from 122 houses to almost 200, and their distribution was completely revised. The re-organization of first-run theaters in Tokyo took place as follows:

RED CHAIN: Hibiya Eigeki, Ningyōchō Shōchiku, Hongō Shōchiku, Tatsumi Shōchiku, Senjū Kinbi, Ōhashi Tōhō, Ōji Rekodo, Shinjuku Teitoza, Totsuka Tōhō, Shibuya Shōchiku, Ōi Shōei, Ōmori Tōhō, Tachikawa Kinema, Hachiōji Tōhō

WHITE CHAIN: Asakusa Fujikan, Honjō Eia, Kōto Gekijō, Mukōjima Tōhō, Gonohashi Denki, Shibazonokan, Ebara Daiei, Gotanda Gekijō, Ushigome Tōhō, Ikebukuro Nissho, Nakano Eiga, Inokashira Kaikan, Kamata Jōsetsu, Kamata Denki, Ōmori Shōchiku.

The level of facilities these film theaters possessed was completely ignored in this arrangement. Since the program was reformed with the laborers in mind, film theaters that were — for the common sense of that time — sin the outskirts, where only one door separated the auditorium from the lavatories, were suddenly promoted to first-run theaters; on the other hand, first-class theaters in entertainment districts, such as the Asakusa Taishōkan or the Shibuya Tōhō, were degraded to third-run or even lower theaters. This situation was the result of the reform.

At the end of 1944, the shortage of raw film stock became even more serious. The number of release prints per film was reduced from 36 to 18. To adapt to this, the distribution company changed its programming again starting December 7, and was forced to stop distribution to 731 film theaters, about 40 percent of all film theaters in Japan.

TOWARDS DEFEAT

On 11 June 1944, the American army attacked Saipan. Japanese soldiers, army and navy united, offered desperate and fierce resistance, but all in vain; by July 7, all members of the garrison, 30,000 men, were killed in action. Also, over 10,000 civilians lost their lives. Until then, only Kyushu had been bombed on a small scale by the American air force, which came flying from bases in China. However, with Saipan as a base for the air force, the center of Japan, the Kanto and the Kansai regions, entered into the bombing radius of the enemy. This fear was realized on November 24, when about 70 long-distance bombers, type B-29, made an air raid on Tokyo.

When remembering the year 1945, I cannot imagine it as a continuation of 1944. I suppose that the aftermath of Saipan's loss suddenly started to take effect. February was still quite good, but from March on, everything became miserable. Starting from the evening of March 9 until March 10 before daybreak, a big formation of 325 B-29s planes (source: *Shōwa-shi zenkiroku* [Complete Record of the Shōwa Era], Mainichi Shinbunsha), attacked Tokyo, burning down 230,000 houses. Casualties amounted to 120,000. On March 14, Osaka was bombed, 130,000 houses lost. On March 17, the garrison of 23,000 men at Iwojima died in the defeat of the island. Situated more or less half-way between Saipan and the Japanese mainland, Iwojima served as a relay base for the B-29 bombers, allowing the air attacks to reach even the farthest northern parts of Japan. From this point, Japan also entered into

Fig. 15. Hirohito's seal affixed to the document directing the Japanese government to surrender. (Credit: National Archives)

the action bounds of the American P-51 fighter planes, adding the threat of shootings.

The attacks on Tokyo were repeated from April 13 to April 14 with 170 planes, on May 24 with 562 planes, and from May 25 to May 26 with 502 planes (ibid.). The Imperial Palace was also afflicted. According to American investigations, 50.8 percent of the city area in Tokyo was burned down. In this period, the enemy came almost every other day, obstinately bombing even minor cities in the countryside. One night was sufficient to annihilate a city with a population of 200,000 or 300,000 people.

Even after the disembarkation of the American army on Okinawa on April 1, the garrison continued to resist, and all 90,000 men were wiped out by June 23. Civilian victims amounted to 100,000. Under these circumstances, the government tried everything to find a policy to end the war, but the army insisted on decisive fighting on the mainland without making any concessions.

Even under these conditions, films were produced and screened in one way or another. When the air defense alarm rang, the screening was immediately stopped. In June, the film distribution companies merged with the Dai-Nihon Eiga Kyōkai to become Eiga Kōsha. It was still designed to intensify the unification of control and the leading role of the Cabinet Information Board, and the steady change of the structures continued.

Fig. 16. The Emperor's surrender address broadcast in a POW camp.
(Credit: National Archives)

The film *We are Working So So Hard* (*Watashitachi wa konna ni hataraite iru*, directed by Mizuki Sōya, Asahi) was made in 1945. It was not a feature film, just a short film providing a record of young women working in a factory for navy garments. In order to emphasize the desperate work of the girls, careless for never a minute, not even one second, the film was shot in fast motion. The speedy work of the girls, without looking aside, is really amazing; this is precisely wholehearted devotion. The title is impressive as well: "Although we work so so much, why, just why does Japan not win?" That is its meaning. This film was released on 28 June 1945. Within only six weeks, the atomic bomb was dropped on Nagasaki, and Japan surrendered.

On a journey in search of an evacuation place for my then pregnant wife, I heard the radio broadcast when the emperor announced the end of the war on August 15 in a train station in northern Japan. At the time I was 28, and for some unknown reason, I got away without receiving the akagami.

— Translated by *Susanne Shermann*
Maya Todeschini

The United States Government and the Use of Motion Pictures During World War II

William T. Murphy

The extensive use of the motion picture medium as an official means for documenting and waging war was a unique feature of World War II. To be sure, all of the major warring nations used films if for no other reason than as a means of propaganda to achieve their military and diplomatic objectives. The United States was no exception. It even enlisted Hollywood filmmakers to produce powerful and effective films that attempted to characterize the enemies and provide a moral and political basis for waging war.

To dismiss official films produced during the war due to their propagandistic content would be a serious error in historical judgment. The films as a whole are unique evidence of a critical period in the history of the modern era. They provide audiovisual documentation of how the filmmakers wished to portray their leaders, their institutions, their country, their allies, and above all, their enemies. In response to changes in the war situation, they describe shifting strategies for winning the war. Sometimes the most telling features were the intentional omissions, such as no references to Jews in films about the German concentration camps or to communism in films about Russian and Chinese allies. Finally, to depict the enemies, the films not only describe acts of aggression but resort to racial stereotyping that diminishes their humanity, leading to devastating criticism of the very nature of Axis internal political and social structure and the leaders they produced. The fact that these films were made by groups through a collective and bureaucratic process further attests to their research value as audiovisual documents of the war.

The careful viewer, however, will distinguish between the message value and the factual value of each film. Both have their place in historical studies and in documentary film production that draws upon archival film. The German film *Campaign in Poland* (1940), though an outrageous propaganda film on the German invasion of Poland, shows the effectiveness of the coordinated attack in considerable detail. Although the Russian attack on eastern Poland took place simultaneously, there is no comparable Russian film on the initial seizure of Polish territory. The Germans were proud of their dubious accomplishment.

The United States produced numerous films that have considerable value for the study of World War II. They are remarkable for their breadth and scope and their level of detail. When the unedited record films are taken into account, it can be

Fig. 1. The Signal Corps gathering images in South-East Asia.
(Credit: National Archives)

safely said that this war was the most visually documented war ever to have taken place. In the limited space of this article, we can only survey some of the most important items.

The use of motion pictures during World War I provided a precedent. The United States Army Signal Corps established a motion picture unit whose work has resulted in the preservation of approximately 1,000,000 feet of 35mm black-and-white silent film from the years 1917-1920, footage which serves as a visual record of the war. This collection, now in the National Archives in Washington, shows the domestic activities, recruitment, military training, and combat operations with the AEF in the fields and towns of France. It even contains fairly extensive footage of the Allied invasion of Siberia and Northern Russia. The Signal Corps produced several films such as *America's Answer* and *Pershing's Crusaders* that were used to promote the war effort. Nonetheless, these films together with those produced by the Committee on Public Information, the first media propaganda agency of the U.S. Government, failed to take real advantage of the power of film as a means of persuasion. Their static long shots, contrived portraiture, and deadening editorial pace reflected few of the cinematic skills that had already been used by directors like D.W. Griffith. Unlike the experience of World War II, the motion picture industry greats did not take charge of military filmmaking.

During the years between the wars military filmmaking entered into a moribund state, though films continued to be used for study and training. Outside the military, however, the documentary movement experienced steady growth, but not in a way that would help the military to make better films. During the 1930s the documentary film became identified as a means of support for leftist causes, that is, pro-labor and anti-fascist. Though some of the skilled documentary filmmakers, for example, Willard Van Dyke, from this movement went on to make films for the U.S. Office of War Information, none had a major production role in the military. Even Pare Lorentz, the great director of *The Plow That Broke the Plains* (1936) and *The River* (1937), produced by the U.S. Department of Agriculture, was not given a major film production during the war. (Instead, he made pilot training films for the Air Transport Command.) On the eve of World War II, the Congress abolished the U.S. Film Service, which Lorentz headed, criticizing his pro-New Deal films and raising the specter of domestic propaganda. Thus, when war finally came, the War Department did not look to skilled documentary filmmakers but to Hollywood writers and directors.

One of the first places the Government turned to was the Disney Studios, which did a number of aircraft and warship identification training films as well as special effects and animation on many other films. Disney also entered into an arrangement with the Coordinator of Inter-American Affairs for a series of anti-Nazi shorts and animated films. These included *Reason and Emotion, Education for Death, Chicken Little,* and *Der Fuehrer's Face,* also known as *Donald Duck in Nutzi Land,* which won an Academy Award as the best animated short of 1942. What these films have in common is an anti-totalitarian theme brilliantly expressed through Disney's inimitable and irreverent cartoon characters.

The first major Navy film of the war was the *The Battle of Midway* (1942), photographed, written and directed by John Ford, then a commander in the Navy. Ford shot the film in 16mm Kodachrome, which was later blown up to 35mm Technicolor for theatrical release. The film depicts a confined microcosm of what actually was an enormous battle at sea. The American forces seem to achieve victory because of their moral strength expressed in Ford's folksy style, not because of their superior tactics or armaments. Strict censorship made a more informative film unlikely at that time.

Subsequently, Ford's photographic detachment was assigned to the Office of Strategic Services, better known as the OSS. Few realize that this relatively small agency made extensive use of motion pictures for their training, research,

Fig. 2. John Ford.
(Credit: Japan Film Library Council)

and clandestine activities. Several films analyzed the people and geography of Japan; these included *Japanese Behavior, Geography of Japan, Natural Resources of Japan,* and *Japanese Coast Line.* Indeed the majority of OSS films relate to the war against Japan, especially activities in the China-Burma-India (CBI) theater of operations. *Mission to Yenan* shows the visit of an American military and diplomatic delegation to the Chinese communist headquarters; and numerous films were made about operations in Thailand and Burma.

The OSS's most important film in retrospect is *December 7th* (1943), though it is usually associated with the Navy because of Ford's involvement and because the short version won an Academy Award as a Navy film. Col. William B. Donavan, head of the OSS, proposed the making of a film about the Japanese attack on Pearl Harbor to the Secretary of the Navy. The film was made under John Ford's supervision while he was still attached to the OSS. Lt. Gregg Toland, cameraman on the feature film *Grapes of Wrath*, directed most of the original shooting. The long version, 83-minutes, though completed, was never released owing to criticism by the Secretary of the Navy and by Admiral Harold Stark, Chief of Naval Operations, who objected to its portrayal of the Navy as being unprepared. Otherwise, the film follows classic propaganda lines: an idyllic island paradise is savagely violated, provoking our indignation. The film questions the loyalty of persons of Japanese ancestry who live in Hawaii. The film bluntly suggests that their loyalty through their religion, language, and culture lies more with the emperor than with the president. Using actors, sets, scripts, and studio lighting, the film tries to illustrate how Japanese in all walks of life gleaned information from all over the island to facilitate the attack's planning and execution. The short version, 20-minutes, that won the award concentrates exclusively on the attack. It too consists of studio shots, re-enactments, and process shots with models together with some actuality footage, more predominant in the aftermath of the attack. Just as the United States naval forces were unprepared for the attack, so were the military and newsreel cameramen. Re-creating it on film required fabrication and poetic license. It incorporates some captured film, but very little was available due to Japan's military success. It still seems astonishing that the Japanese forces did not create more photographic documentation of the attack.

From a cinematic standpoint, one of the most important naval films was *The Fighting Lady* (1944), produced by Louis de Rochemont

Fig. 3. Frank Capra.
(Credit: Japan Film Library Council)

and photographed under the supervision of Edward Steichen, the famous photographer. It succeeded because of its evocation of routine life aboard an aircraft carrier in the Pacific. The Navy documented the island campaign strategy in a number of combat documentary films. *With the Marines at Tarawa* (1944) and *To The Shores of Iwo Jima* (1945) are grim portrayals of the heavy cost in lives of invading and wrenching each island from its Japanese defenders. *Fury in the Pacific* (1944), *Battle for the Marianas* (1944), and *The Fleet That Came to Stay* (1945) remain enduring visual documents of the ferocity of the war in the Pacific.

The most ideological films among the American documentaries were those produced by the Signal Corps for the War Department. Of these the most important are the *Why We Fight* series and other orientation films produced under the general supervision of Frank Capra, the highly successful director of Hollywood comedies. As a major and lieutenant-colonel, Capra recruited Hollywood talent such as Walter Huston, Anthony Veiller, and Anatole Litvak and together they formed a production unit that for the most part worked outside the normal Signal Corps chain of command. According to Capra's autobiography, none other than Chief of Staff George C. Marshall ordered the production of the orientation series. "To win this war," Marshall told Capra, "we must win the battle for men's minds." These films would become a required part of military training.

The filmmakers assumed that the average American soldier had relatively little formal education, and hence little understanding of how events in far off lands affected him. In addition, the films were meant to eradicate any vestiges of isolationist sentiment so prevalent before the attack on Pearl Harbor.

There are seven films in the well-known *Why We Fight* series: *Prelude to War* (1943), *The Nazis Strike* (1943), *Divide and Conquer* (1943), *The Battle of Britain* (1943), *The Battle of Russia* (1943), *The Battle of China* (1943), *War Comes to America* (1945). Each film runs about one hour, except for the one on Russia which is closer to 90-minutes.

In many respects they are simple and emotional history lessons, and effectiveness studies questioned their ultimate usefulness. Nevertheless, they represented the most ambitious effort to teach history with film, and in terms of production values may still hold that claim despite all the television histories of recent years.

They are still important for study for several reasons. They provide a visual and mental framework for understanding the mass psychology of an era. In *Prelude to War* the world is divided between democracy and fascism, between good and evil. In the fascist countries of Germany, Italy, and Japan, ruled by dictators and military cliques, the people have surrendered their free will. Decisions are made for them, leading to a series of aggressive acts against other countries like China, Ethiopia, and Poland. *War Comes to America*, tries to define Americans and American life, their heritage and institutions, all of which appear threatened by fascist aggression. Through a dazzling display of rapid-paced imagery expertly cut to a synchronized music score the *Why We Fight* series stands as the most enduring monument to the American films of World War II.

As a motion picture executive, Capra controlled or influenced many of the Army's most important productions. He accomplished this through the initiation and review of projects, assignment of personnel, control of production facilities, and when necessary rescue of uncompleted projects that ran into trouble.

Capra also took a leading role in the production of *The Negro Soldier* (1944), directed by Stuart Heisler and written by Carleton Moss. Despite the hypocrisy of officially sanctioned segregation of troops, this film aimed at promoting racial harmony by detailing the contributions of black persons to American history and culture and by showing their role in the war effort. The Navy made a similar film called *The Negro Sailor*, which was less effective in it presentation.

Again under Capra's firm hand, the Signal Corps collaborated with their British allies to produce *Tunisian Victory* (1944), a film documenting the invasion of North Africa and the coordinated British and American campaigns that resulted in a massive capitulation of the German army.

Toward the latter part of the war in Europe as the defeat of Germany seemed inevitable, the Capra unit turned more and more toward Japan. There was a genuine fear that the victories in Europe might have weakened American resolve to bring about Japan's total defeat. This is the underlying theme of *Two Down and One To Go* (1945) and *On To Tokyo* (1945) which argue against such complacency and describe the gargantuan military effort presumably needed to defeat Japan.

Capra also served as the producer for *The Stilwell Road* (1945), a joint production of the War Department and British film units. It tells the story of the construction of the "Burma Road." Named after General Joseph Stilwell who commanded Chinese troops, the film describes the enormous difficulties of fighting Japanese forces while building and securing a supply route to China. *The Stilwell Road* tells an adventurous story utilizing some of the most dramatic war footage ever shot.

The Capra unit planned a *Know Your Ally* series but only one was made, *Know Your Ally: Britain* (1945). They also planned a *Know Your Enemy* series. However, only one film was made using that title, *Know Your Enemy: Japan* (1945). The companion film, *Here is Germany* (1945), meant to serve the same purpose.

During its one-hour running time, *Know Your Enemy: Japan* attempts to present an historical and sociological account of Japanese society from the beginning of its recorded history, through its opening to the west, to its acts of international aggression in the 1930s and 1940s. The film portrays a monolithic society whose religion, unquestioning obedience to authority, militarism, including its samurai warrior code, have led it on a destructive path. *Know Your Enemy: Japan* is the most notorious of the Capra films because it is a totally unmitigated work of propaganda although masterfully made with slick and powerful images moved quickly along by the rapid editorial pacing so characteristic of Capra's work. The film had an unusual provenance in that Joris Ivens, the Dutch documentarian who made, among many others, *The Four Hundred Million* (1939), worked on the script but left in a disagreement. In the end, the film was released only a short period of time due to the war's cessation in August 1945.

Here is Germany (1945) discusses the history and character of the German people who were responsible for such unspeakable atrocities. Tracing the history of Germany from Frederick the Great to Adolf Hitler, it finds patterns of militarism, aggressive behavior, and crack pot theories about a master race. *Your Job in Germany* (1945), aimed essentially at the occupation troops, carries this theme further by encouraging distrust of the German character and by warning against fraternization with the populace, a policy that quickly succumbed to the exigencies of the Cold War between the United States and the Soviet Union. *Our Job in Japan* (1946), supervised by Theodor Geisel ("Dr. Suess") and co-written by Carl Foreman, was sympathetic to the Japanese people, blaming the war on its leaders.

Frank Capra and the other directors, writers, and editors who worked with him have left an enormous legacy of documentaries that historians will perpetually analyze, debate and interpret for each generation. However brilliantly made, the films had only a limited educational usefulness according to the military's own effectiveness studies. In the final analysis, they have little value for studying the war's causes and events. What they offered wittingly and unwittingly, was a moral and psychological spectrum in which Americans could identify with national values — individualism, respect for basic freedoms, a sense of fair play, and so on — and formulate in their minds a set of criteria to compare the Allied nations and the Axis. Above all, the devastating portrayals of the fascist governments and societies as shown in these films was generally unique to American productions. The enemy was not some distant threat on the horizon but odious societies whose continued existence threatened international peace and ultimately the security of the United States itself.

The Capra films have become artifacts or museum pieces that lose much of their power outside their historical context. Captain John Huston, another Hollywood director, made three films while he was in the Army that have transcended the confines of Capra's historicism. The films are *Report from the Aleutians* (1943), *The Battle of San Pietro* (1943), and *Let There Be Light* (1946). They continue as enduring works of cinematic art because they elucidate universal themes: the behavior of men in battle and the emotional effects of war, any war. Huston's trilogy of films have lasting credibility because the people in them seem real and they attract our sympathy and understanding. This subject matter, combined with Huston's sensitive direction, distinguished his films from all the rest. *Report from the Aleutians*, shot in color, tells story of the fight against the Japanese in the Aleutian chain. *The Battle of San Pietro* was cut to a length much shorter than Huston would have preferred. Even so, it shows the tremendous difficulties in the Liri Valley campaign in Italy as illustrated by the fighting for the small village of San Pietro, which resulted in the deaths of many Americans who tried to dislodge Germans from their well defended positions. Finally, *Let There Be Light* dramatizes the clinical treatment of veterans who suffered psychological trauma as a result of their experiences in combat. The film promoted the acceptance and the re-entry of veterans into the mainstream of American life; it meant to show that trauma victims could be rehabilitated and could resume their normal lives as civilians. Unfortunately it never reached its intended audience; for many years the film was only available to professional medical personnel.

The last great military campaign film of the war in Europe was *The True Glory* (1945), jointly produced by the British Ministry of Information and the U.S. Signal Corps and co-directed by Carol Reed and Garson Kanin. Almost 90-minutes, this stirring documentary drew upon spectacular combat film in order to portray Allied operations from the invasion of Normandy to the definitive defeat of the Third

Reich. Stylistically, the film liberated documentary from the constrictions of the studio-recorded narration by using the vernacular of servicemen and passages of blank verse as well as General Eisenhower's voice. Above all the film was a tribute to the soldiers, and as such it was honored with an Academy Award.

The most important film activity on the civilian side of the U.S. Government during the war took place in the Office of War Information (OWI), which for a time had both a domestic branch and an overseas branch for motion picture production. In general, the OWI worked independently from the Hollywood talent that was so readily available to the military. On the other hand, the OWI had the advantage of drawing upon many skilled documentary filmmakers who had learned their craft during the 1930s when the documentary was used to bring attention to the pervasive social and economic crisis of the Depression and to the aggressive nature of fascism. The somewhat controversial background of its production staff may help to explain why they were limited in what they could accomplish. As a group the films were well made but ultimately unexciting and noncontroversial.

The films of the domestic branch tried to make the problems that the war brought to the homefront a little more understandable and palatable, such as the housing shortage, transportation restrictions, rationing, employment shortages, and so on, exemplified by such films as *Women Wanted* and *Send Your Tin Cans to War*. Nevertheless, the domestic branch embroiled itself in conflicts with the Hollywood industry over the review of scripts and what film might be good or not good for the war effort. This dichotomy, exacerbated by the motion picture industry's stiff opposition to OWI domestic film production, found sympathetic voices in the U.S. Congress which controlled the OWI appropriation. OWI's funding for domestic film was virtually eliminated at the height of the war.

Congressional opinion even affected the content of motion pictures intended for overseas distribution. Congressional opponents to the President Roosevelt's New Deal did not want the OWI to become a propaganda mill for his administration to be used as a means to help guarantee his election. The fear that the use of official motion pictures might play a role in domestic politics was so real that in 1948 Congress passed the U.S. Information and Educational Exchange Act which banned films intended for overseas from domestic dissemination.

The motion pictures from OWI's overseas program dealt less with the enemy than with the projection of United States as a nation, its institutions, its land, and its people. Its problems on virtually every level were deliberately excluded. Produced to combat Axis propaganda about American life, the films aimed at audiences in Allied countries and neutral ones as well as the people newly liberated from occupation.

Films like *Cowboy* (1943) and *Northwest USA* (1944), both directed by Willard Van Dyke, presented appealing regional portraits of America. Similarly, *The Town*, made by Josef von Sternberg, and exception to the rule about feature film directors in OWI, describes the significance of small towns in American society, with their mixed immigrant lineage, eclectic architecture, and their easy going, tolerant way of living together. *Swedes in America* further pursued the theme of the assimilation of immigrants into American life. And *The Cummington Story* (1945) depicted the successful integration of European refugees into a small New England town.

Toscanini: Hymn of the Nations (1944) made by Irving Lerner and Alexander Hackenschmied (Hammid), exploited not only the talent but the Italian ancestry of the maestro Arturo Toscanini to celebrate the liberation of Italy.

The Autobiography of a Jeep (1943), made by Joseph Krumgold, and *The Window Cleaner* (1945), made by Jules Bucher, tried to offer some tongue-in-cheek insight into the American character marked by strong individualism, ingenuity, and a sense of humour in even in the most dangerous situations.

One OWI film that seemed anomalous to the others was *Japanese Relocation* (1944), an awkward and unconvincing attempt to explain the military necessity for the forced relocation of Americans of Japanese ancestry to relocation centers. The film's pathetic images belie the narrator's talk about fairness, education, and employment skills for the internees. The War Relocation Authority produced a similar film, *Challenge to Democracy*, which attempted to present the relocation policy in as positive a light as possible, yet it encountered the same structural problem matching image and sound in constant contradiction.

This survey endeavors to include many historically important American films made during the war years not because of the well known or obscure filmmakers who made them, but because they contain unique audiovisual documentation of the war. On one level, especially the military campaign films, they contain pictorially factual information which no amount of written description can replace. On another level entirely, using the military orientation films as an example, they are evidence of a conceptual framework the filmmakers tried to impart to their viewers for understanding the real or imagined issues of the conflict. Thus, they give witting and perhaps unwitting testimony to a whole range of ideas and attitudes that are essential for understanding the tragic drama of a war that destroyed so many lives.

There are many other titles worthy of study. In addition, there are millions of feet of unedited combat record film which enhances the visual documentation of the war. The Army Signal Corps documentation includes the footage of the liberation of the German concentration camps. The Army Air Forces files include extensive color footage of ground and aerial operations in Europe from D-Day, 6 June 1944, to the defeat and occupation of Germany. The files of the U.S. Strategic Bombing Survey include extensive unedited color footage of the effects of the atomic bombing of Hiroshima and Nagasaki. And then there are films about World War II that are important for the study of the postwar period and the impact of the incipient Cold War in the occupied countries.

The most complete collection of the motion pictures discussed in this survey is preserved in the National Archives in Washington, in the custody of the Motion Picture, Sound, and Video Branch. All have been copied from the dangerous nitrate-based film onto modern safety copies. Films from this era are well catalogued and are available for study in the Branch's research room.

PART III
MANUFACTURING
THE ENEMY

The Other and the Machine

Ueno Toshiya

I "FILM WAR"

"War is film; film is war." This claim, put forth by theorists such as Paul Virilio and popularized during the last few years, is not really such an unconventional expression, nor does it represent a particularly eccentric or novel point of view. As we have discovered recently, the term *"eigasen"* (literally: film war — the Japanese title of this book and retrospective) was already in vogue in Japan during World War II and has been used in the same context, a fact which compels us to reconsider the tactics and history contained in the structure of the argument "film = war."

During the more than 40 years since the end of World War II, terms such as "media war," "information war," and recently in the case of the Gulf War, "Nintendo war," have been used with great enthusiasm. Likewise, as we try to cope with the electronic informatization of the post-Cold War world, we have come to be haunted by an image of war which itself is completely controlled by such technology. While the images of war produced by film and video are not "propaganda" in a narrow sense, various studies have shown that many of these images duplicate the propagandistic image in both form and structure. This phenomenon is not limited to film; it applies to graphic visual representations such as photos and posters as well.

Clearly, if we are allowed to rephrase von Clausewitz' famous formula: "film is the continuation of war by other means." The empirical and theoretical conditions which support this thesis can be grouped into four major points.

To begin with, there is the linkage between cameras as "visual machines," and weapons as "high-speed machines." It has often been pointed out that the technology required for cameras is very similar to that needed for guns. The principle used in the Gatling gun, for example, is the same as that used in the rotary camera. Likewise, Etienne Jules Marey's famous machine was literally a "photographic gun."

Second are the methods used in the manufacturing of an image. In 1917, Edward Steichen, who served as a war photographer during the World War I, in a seeming anticipation of the aesthetics of the machine age, arranged and produced a large volume of war photos using a division of labor similar to that employed in factories. This project, which was carried out by a staff of more than 1,000 and relied on Fordian assembly-line production techniques, suggests the structural similarity between the processes used in military production and those required for the

Fig. 1.

completion of an image. Needless to say, the "organic link" (solidarity) between image and combat, manufacture and production, has been expanded and diversified to an even greater degree by the electronic technology of today.

Third, the semantic and graphic structure of an image has priority over the ideology which motivates it (i.e., form is more important than content). For example, the graphics and design of the well-known propaganda magazine *FRONT*, published in Japan during World War II, conform in many ways to the visual codes of Russian formalism. These compositions make the most of close-ups and dynamic perspective, and though they are graphics which support a totalitarian system, they bear a striking resemblance to the visual language employed in "revolutionary graphics." No matter how much the "telos" of the respective ideologies differs, the narrative and the visual schemes — in other words, the forms of expression — which structure both descriptive accounts and fiction, unwittingly resemble each other at an unconscious level, an irony which allows us to perceive the special nature of the language of images of war.

Finally, what should be emphasized above all is the fact that Sergei Eisenstein's *Battleship Potemkin*, which even today serves as one of the most important paradigms of film technique, was nothing other than a war film, focused as it was on the depiction of civil war. But that is not all. Through his montage technique, Eisenstein consistently demonstrates that the clash of images on the screen could itself be taken to represent battle and conflict. There is a reason why war thus becomes from the very beginning the object of visual media (literally: image media). Among the numerous events in which humankind finds itself embroiled, nothing seems to contribute so greatly to drastic changes in perception as does war. The close symbiotic relationship between film and war, image and war, can thus be traced to the very "origin" of film (i.e., Eisenstein's *Potemkin*). In analyzing any image of war, irrespective of whether it is a document, propaganda or fiction, we must examine and unmask the various meanings of war which have been reduced through informatization and examine them as "indicative objects" *(shiji — taishō)*. In other words, an individual who comes across an image of war encounters "the origin of the image the image of the origin" which can already be perceived in the "war = film" framework. However, we should not fix this "origin" at too remote a point. An "origin" which can be narrated in the abstract would do no more than open the way toward metaphysical speculation, and thus end up concealing the problematic surrounding film and war. In fact, in Japan at least, the framework for the argument "film = war" outlined to date has been premised on the discursive situation of the postmodern period (the 1980s up to the Gulf War?), and has become a kind of cliché. On the other hand, it is also clear that this type of discourse has tended to be extremely anti-historical. For these reasons, it is necessary that we examine exactly how and when the notion that "war is film; film is war" was constructed, by looking at individual cases.

While it is clear that the term "film war" *(eigasen)* was already in use in Japan during the war, we must now consider whether the term was used in the same context/logic as in the examples outlined above, or whether its meanings were entirely different. This is an important problem because at first sight, the term "film war" may seem no different semantically from terms like "intelligence war" or "psychological warfare," used in conventional military terminology.

In his book *Eigasen* (Film War), Tsumura Hideo makes the following observation:

> "War is always ultimately settled by armed force. But in order to generate and preserve the military power necessary for the kind of continuous and tenacious 'ability to destroy' characteristic of long-term modern warfare, it is necessary to bring together all of the accumulated power of a nation's people. The wars of the 20th century have seen the emergence of this kind of military power, but the various elements that brought it forth, as well as the process of its generation, are exceedingly complicated.
>
> "...In the broadest sense, this means that every war film must have some sort of 'philosophy' (ideology). To date, the war films in our country have been simple depictions of tactical operations, but from now on, we must clarify, through film, the way of thinking of the Japanese people who are pressing on in their crusade for the construction of a Greater East Asia. In accordance with this aim it is necessary to have war films which depict conquest and war strategies" (page 37).

Needless to say, in a system of total war, the activities of the entire community are centered around the war, and citizens' contribution to the war effort is emphasized. It must not be forgotten that throughout history, many cultural and ideological endeavors have been utilized for information management and the general intelligence required for spy activities. The kind of intelligence warfare carried out for the obtaining of "cultural territory" is of course very different from the "action" depicted in spy films which depict the battle as taking place at a very simplistic level. The sudden rise to power and development of mass communications and the various media, have contributed greatly to the institutionalization of "war" in realms other than that of military power. Recognizing this, Tsumura places emphasis on the role played by film in the following passage:

> "It is during this period of two decades of peace that ideological war *(shisōsen)* has been carried to its utmost extreme. The weapons of this war include newspapers, the wire services and the high speed radio waves of the powerful radio networks. Film, too, has been newly employed, along with the various forms of artistic expression found in music and literature, the political and military commentary, and strategic cultural enterprises. No doubt, peacetime provides the ultimate arena for ideological warfare. Through a continuous long-term offensive it becomes possible to encroach

upon the national ideology of one's opponents, and to control their attitudes and customs."

In a passage from *Sekai eigasensō* (World Film Wars) written in 1944, author Shibata Yoshio, after having suggested in a rather fanatical manner that the film industry is controlled by Jewish capitalists, continues with the following observation:

> "During peacetime, it is possible to penetrate deeply into the core of one's opponent and to exert one's power by wearing the masks of 'art' and 'entertainment.' It is the 'film war' which makes this possible" (page 4).

When the literature, music and film of one culture are introduced into another cultural sphere, a kind of "cultural invasion" occurs, even if there is no desire or ideology for domination at work. This is something which can be seen frequently under modern cultural conditions (it is possible to assume the existence of an omnipresent "pure war" that lies dormant during peacetime, but we will discuss this at a later point).

What was the attitude of people in the film industry not directly involved in propaganda activities or intelligence for political or military purposes toward the "film war," in terms of its necessity and special properties? Let's pick a few examples from the essays and symposiums published in the magazine *Eiga Junpō*. Although we can only obtain a somewhat fragmentary picture from these quotations, it is possible to get a sense of the prevalent mood during the time that the term "film war" began to emerge.

To begin with the simplest example, some people saw film as a metaphor for war and weaponry. In an article entitled "Eigajin no kakushin" (A Revolution Among Cinematographers) published in *Eiga Junpō* in 1943, this usage is readily apparent. Here we find comments such as "film is the weapon of ideological war," and the suggestion that the portrayal and reportage of war in film is a process no different from the distribution of a commodity. In fact, in numerous issues of the magazine published in 1943, we can find variations on this theme of film as a "bullet."

Again, in *Sekai eigasensō* Shibata Yoshio includes the following quote from Heinrich Edvard Jacob's *Blood and Celluloid*: "Film has played an extremely powerful role as a weapon in world war. This weapon should be feared in the same way that we fear tanks, submarines, artillery, airplanes and poison gas. Like other war industries, the film industry is immersed in a kind of continuous war situation even in peacetime." These quotes would seem to suggest that the argument that film as a weapon was not an uncommon notion at all in the world at that time.

On the other hand, it is clear that the Japanese were keenly aware of the fact that the technology for this important ideological weapon belonged mainly to their enemies in Europe and America. Nothing brought this fact home more closely than the beautiful color cinematography of *Gone with the Wind*, which painfully illustrated the superiority and power of the enemy, at least as far as the "film war" was concerned. Over and over again, Japanese writers lamented the fact that Japanese films could only be made in black and white and that production and distribution lagged far behind that of the enemy. For example, Imamura Taihei, in his essay "Sensō to eiga" (War and Film) complained bitterly about this point. He writes: "All of our motion picture cameras are American, and we do not have the means to restock any of them. This dependence on the enemy for the greatest weapon of ideological war indicates just how far behind Japan is lagging in the Greater East Asia War" (1941).

Allow me to mention a visual example. In the 11 July 1942 issue of *Eiga Junpo*, there is an entry entitled "Rakkasan butai no satsueisha" (Photographers of the Airborne Infantry). The reality of the "film war" is subtly revealed to us in this photo of cinematographer Honma Kinsuke, from the Navy press corps. With the airplane canopy as background, the cameraman is wearing a tattered flight helmet and glasses. Looking downward, he grasps his film camera as though it were a rifle. Nothing presents more accurately the realities of the "film war" than this single photograph. But equally interesting is the caption which accompanies the photo :

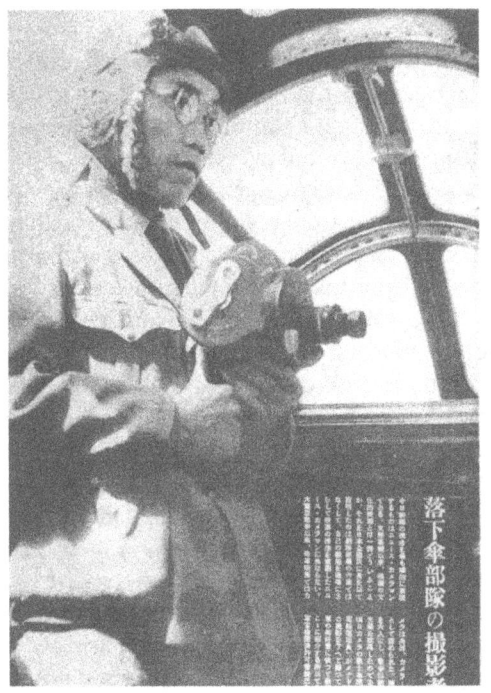

"It is the news cameraman who most straight-forwardly expresses the mission of film today. Ever since the China Incident, we have asked ourselves what the cultural function of film should be. The Japanese people have been given a satisfactory answer not by the writers in dramatic film departments, but by news cameramen whose aim is the advancement of film as part of their job on the scene. Since the Greater East Asian War, the camera has been the weapon in news film, and cameramen have been recognized as civilian employees of the army. Film methods have brought about the maturation of film, and war has bestowed a great honor on cinema."

Anyone will certainly recognize here that within this framework, news cameramen who risked their lives came to be viewed as heroes, and films which portrayed the war were excessively aestheticized.

Walter Benjamin already recognized that the aestheticization of art was a well-worn device of fascist aesthetics. But there is still much debate as to whether the "film wars" waged by the Allied nations really escaped this same framework "war = film," or if this framework has truly been abandoned in the post-Cold War world.

If we limit the meaning of "cultural war" *(bunkasen)* and "ideological war" *(shisōsen)* to the simple notion that culture is an instrument of war, then "film war" can only be put in the narrow category of "psychological" *(shinrisen)* or propaganda warfare *(sendensen)*. But even if "film war" is an important element in cultural or ideological warfare, it is uniquely distinguished by the fact that it has the same formal structure — the same "schematic diagram for perception and practice" — as war and combat.

Victory in war does not limit itself to the expansion of economic hegemony and the acquisition of new territory. Rather, war plays an important role in the domination and control of the "immaterial" loci of schemes of perception and sensation. Perhaps this is the essence of the meaning of "film war." This of course means that a "real war film" does not necessarily need any battle scenes. It seems that from the moment that film was capable of violently shocking the viewers through the medium of technology, it was classified in the same category as arms and weapons. In other words, what we have to examine is not only the meaning (psychological, ideological and other) of "war = film," but rather its form and processes of operation. What we must clarify is the aesthetics peculiar to the "film war," an aesthetics which has already been materialized by the "machine."

II THE DISCIPLINE OF THE MACHINE

In watching some of the war films produced in Japan during World War II, one is immediately struck by the uniformity of not only the soldiers but the general population depicted there. It would seem natural that the standardization of people should be one of the ideals of a totalitarian system, but we cannot help but be shocked by the depiction of almost "android-like" individuals and groups. It was not without reason that the film *Know your Enemy: Japan* (1945) made by the Allies during the war, should begin with the lines: "the Japanese all bear a striking resemblance to each other; they are like photographs taken from the same negative."

Let us concentrate on the bodies and faces depicted in the films of wartime Japan, a time during which the group was given overriding importance in everyday life and schooling. It is extremely ironical that the figure of the "Nō mask-like face," which has been consistently embraced by Westerners as a paranoid image of "the (Oriental) Other," should be the very image of the self constructed by the Japanese themselves.

When seen with hindsight, or if you will, from a post-modernist position, one can easily interpret this stereotyped image of "the Japanese" — or rather, the stereotyping of their self-image by the Japanese themselves — as a metaphor for "the machine" or for "androids," but this facile analysis is likely to invite misunderstanding. In seeing films such as *The War at Sea from Hawaii to Malaya* (*Hawai Marē okikaisen*, 1942), or *Young Soldiers of the Sky* (*Sora no shōnenhei*, 1942), we inevitably encounter depictions of "machine-like" soldiers' bodies and groups, regardless of whether the film was documentary or fiction. There is a strange beauty to these soldiers, whose bodies merge completely with their airplanes, which are at once weapons and means of transport, and the soldiers shown exercising in unison in a school yard (granted you can also see this kind of behavior today, among people who have absolutely no interest in "stirring up fighting spirit").

In the context of the "machine," it is necessary to consider two processes. First are cases in which the camera lens, and the documentary method itself, are distinguished by a machine-like nature. Second are cases in which individual bodies and groups are depicted just like machines. In film, these two processes usually overlap.

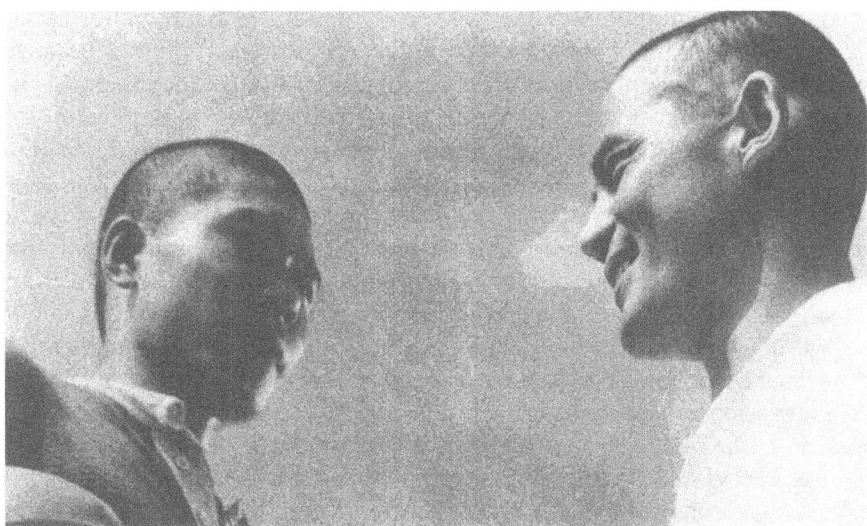

Fig. 3. *War at sea from Hawaii to Malaya.*
(Credit: Japan Film Library Council)

Incidentally, the idea of reducing the meaning of a war situation to a sense of thrill or "speed," and to a machine-like positioning of both people and objects, is not foreign to futuristic aesthetics.

Let us now consider the problem of the machine in the "film war" a machine which becomes not only an instrument or technique but the very principle of the group.

The philosopher and scholar of aesthetics Nakai Masakazu, in an analysis which subtly recalls the aesthetic theories from pre-World War I to the futurists and the Bauhaus movement, skillfully articulated the drastic changes in human perception brought about by the machine and technology. The term "kino-eye" ("camera eye") was no longer unusual by the 1930s, but Nakai anticipated that the film, as "camera eye," would bring about a great change in the human perceptual map, and he already speculated on the "logic" permeating film in connection with the processes of control exercised by the group (in war?) and institutions.

What was the peculiarity of the film camera, as "camera eye," according to Nakai? First, the events fixed on film were not merely reports or depictions of facts. The shooting itself had been predetermined ("edited") according to a particular point of view, so that a raw depiction of "reality" was impossible from the start. As early as in the beginning of the 1930s, Nakai was aware of the "physical group nature" (*butsuriteki shūdanteki seikaku*) contained within the operation of images and brought about by technology. In his book *Kikai no me* (The Eye of the Machine), Nakai makes the following observation:

> "It is not only the manufacturing process of a film which is collective (*shūdanteki*), but the very form of a film is itself collective. This process of collectivization points to its thoroughly social (group-) nature. Its machine-like nature signifies the combination of the machine and humans. In other words, this is the 'physical group nature' [of film]."

This sounds very complicated, but Nakai's main thesis is that the information (*jōhō*, "intelligence") brought about by the production of images differs fundamentally from the information diffused by literature or paintings. Intelligence is no simple transmittal of information. As Heidegger said, to "inform" is to "in-form" (i.e. "putting-into-form" as much as transmitting a message), and information thus becomes institutionalized. Now, what does institutionalization mean in this case? Naturally, the elements (content) of the message are institutionalized, but it is also the perspective or angle of the receiver of the message which becomes institutionalized. This is where the essence of the meaning of informatization brought about by the new media lies, cinema playing an important role in this great change. In fact, the "eye of the machine" which we encountered during wartime is emblematic for the much larger struggle between the medium of film itself and the conventional forms of expressions of the past.

Just as an individual's experiences, passing through his/her eyes and ears, become that individual's personal memories, the same kind of memorization process occurs within groups and organizations, passing through the "eye of the machine" of the camera lenses. In reportage and documentaries based on images, the subject becomes anonymous and depersonalized to the point of non-existence. The problem is not, "who took these pictures," but through what process these pictures were "constructed" into a coherent image. The subject is no longer an individual but the group itself. Coming close to espousing a fascist aesthetics, Nakai makes the following comment:

> "In this context, documents or records (*kiroku*), rather than being the expression of an individual artistic specialist, express the desirable effects of collective (literally: committee-like) responsibility and collective editing of all popular information. The documentary film has a future only as a collective structure, and in this sense, its possibilities are great.
>
> "...Because of the transition from an individualistic structure to a totalitarian one, mind-and-body techniques become institutionalized technology, which in turn causes the memorization function to turn into a recording function" (*Shisōteki kiki ni okeru geijutsu narabi ni sono dōkō* [Arts and Their Tendencies in Ideological Crisis], 1932).

During the 10 years or so separating Nakai's pronouncements from the beginning of the war, such notions were not avant-garde; they were deeply etched into the consciousness of the persons concerned in Japan's "film war." For example, Takagi Toshirō from the cultural film department of Nichiei, stated that wartime newsreels were not simply information, and argued that the films depicting the Greater East Asia War had to be "developed into documentaries and histories based on the image."

It is not only the image that can be taken as a "machine." Just as soldiers' bodies are depicted like machines in film, the entire group, the entire nation, is taken to be a single organic structure. This concept appears clearly in statements such as the following:

> "At present, Japanese history is progressing by the hour, accumulating its achievements and continuing its development toward a world history more magnificent and brilliant than mankind has ever seen. This heroic history continues to be made by we

fellow countrymen, brothers tied together by the same flesh and the same blood. At the same time, what sublime pleasure it is to continue living in the same place, while history is continuing to advance by the hour" (Takagi Toshirō. *Rekishi e no jōnetsu* [The Passion for History]).

"...Because films give the occasion for diverse pleasures, all concentrated in one place, we should not watch them as individuals; we must emphasize the notion that we are indeed a group of Japanese...In case the black-out continues for a long period of time, we must make efforts to show films all over Japan, making it no longer necessary for the public to flock to amusement centers [where they enjoy more frivolous entertainment]. We must ensure a country-wide distribution of films, so that there will be no waste both timewise and from the point of view of traffic. At the same time, we must make provisions against emergencies [in case of aerial attacks, etc.]" (Fuwa Suketoshi. *Kessenka ni shosuru eigakai* [The Film World During the Decisive Stage of the War]).

Though it is the ironclad rule of all mass communication to try to achieve quick reporting, it is also true that in a real time situation, this kind of reporting aims at nothing less but at driving the whole of a group or a nation into a "center" of frenzy and feverish excitement, and at "constructing" it into a coherent unity with a specific communal identity (there is a type of hidden "power" there, its manifestations ranging from the Nazi's "Zeppelin Vert" to today's "media freak").

The subject is not the individual but the group, the entire collective body as a "machine." The frenzied enthusiasm for technology led to the depersonalization of the subject of individual labor and manufacture, of living and fighting. Worse yet, the technology craze gave rise to the glorification of this entire situation. This perversion was not just a pathology limited to the Italian futurists, but became the basic ideological support for people's life-world during the Second World War.

In his article, "Kyonen no bunka eiga" [Last Year's Culture Films], *Eiga Junpō*, 11 March 1942), Imamura Taihei makes the following observation, with regard to the film *Young Soldiers of the Sky* (though somewhat lengthy, it is worth quoting in its entirety):

"The film...is meaningful because of its success in taking footage from the air, but this success is still merely limited to the technical aspect...The air planes as such are not sufficiently depicted yet. And there is no sufficient grasp of the sense of speed in mid-air. In the culture film of today, the various sensations experienced by the pilots are not well transmitted to the viewers. In the case of the somersault, for example, the viewer is deprived from the visual experience of the pilot's perception of the plane's movement. As the depictions of airplanes in film will increase from now on, the expression of particular 'on-airplane' sensations will certainly became a major theme of the documentary film...Perhaps, the near future will see the emergence of 'mechanical tales' *(rikigakuteki na monogatari)* which feature airplanes, cars, locomotives and ships, as well as industrial machines — for example all the machinery of a factory — as heroes. In old times, people attributed human characteristics to animals and plants, and thus created fables and allegories; nowadays, we attribute human characteristics to the machine, and will perhaps create allegories on the machine. This kind of allegorization is already present in Walt Disney's *Donald Duck and the Robot*, but it appears that the documentary film will potentiality take this one step further. The roots for the dissatisfaction we feel toward depictions of the machine in today's culture films lies in the fact that the filmmakers have treated the machine as something cold and fearful. But people who deal with machines everyday see them with a different, more affectionate eye, the same way they might look at their pet dog or pet horse. I think that once you start looking at them in such a light, machines will come to life, and blood will start flowing through them. Such living machines will begin to sing a new song. A fresh, original perception of the life of the machine; a poetic originality with regard to the machine; a new yearning for the machine *(kikai ni taisuru atarashii yume)* — all these things are sorely lacking in the depictions of today's culture films."

The feature film *Attendence in a Torpedo Squad (Raigekitai shutsudō*, also *Torpedo Squadrons Move Out*, 1943), made in the final stages of the war and focusing on aerial battle, depicted pilots heartbroken at the loss of their beloved planes to enemy fire, and soldiers trying to protect their burning air craft at the risk of their lives. In this film, there may be no positive, admiring attitude toward the "beauty of the machine," but it could be argued that the depiction, if unintentionally, comes close to Imamura's suggestion of the machine permeated by life blood. Today, we might feel that we have no relationship whatsoever to this kind of fanatical "sympathy" or "yearning" for the machine, but in reality this perception is only superficial. Even if the political and ideological "telos" might differ, we cannot extract ourselves from the same kind of gravitational field, constituted as it is by the "discipline" of the collectivity.

For example, let us consider the comments of "film war" theorists on the film *The War at Sea from Hawaii to Malaya*. Some emphasize the special filming technique with which this film was made, pointing out that real events were transformed into fabrications once they were put into images. At the same time, many others argued that this film must be taken as a "real" documentary film. This kind of mixture, or combination, between fiction and historical document, the "real thing" and its imitation, is a phenomenon which already existed at a much earlier time than we like to believe (Incidentally, the special effects used in the film were created by Tsuburaya Eiji who later created Godzilla and Ultraman).

Within the paradigm of the "film war," image (film), group, and the machine mutually implicate each other, thus constructing a particular kind of discipline *(kiritsu)* and ethos. The identities of the individuals depicted in these films are supported by their institutional position, controlled by their symbiotic relationship to the machine, and hierarchically shaped by the accumulation of their historical past (tradition, ancestors, "the imperial way," and so on). It was this very task of constructing and reproducing the coupling between individual and group, which was taken on by the films made in the "film war," and the discursive space constructed around them. Now, the problem which must be considered is whether this self/subjecthood constructed by the discipline of the machine, was conceived in opposition to a certain type of enemy, a certain type of "Other."

III THE "OTHER" AND THE ENEMY

The Tiger of Malaya (Marai no tora, 1943) is a war propaganda film based on the famous legend of Harimao. The hero, Tani Yutaka, who had fallen into a trap staged by British Imperialists and saw his child murdered by them, assumes the leadership of a group of bandits and rampages about the Malayan peninsula in revenge. There is a striking scene in which the bandits, sitting around a camp fire, sing a popular

The Otherness and the Machine 81

Fig. 4. *Attendance in a Torpedo Squad.*
(Credit: Japan Film Library Council)

Fig. 5. *Attendance in a Torpedo Squad.*
(Credit: Japan Film Library Council)

Fig. 6. Magazine ad for *The Tiger of Malaya*.

song in unison. A few years ago, this song, called "Rusa Sayan," became a hit melody sung by Singapore's singer Dick Lee, riding on the "world music" [ethnic music] boom. Dick Lee repeatedly told his Japanese audience that "Asia is One," and that "We are all brothers," but as a "yuppie" born to a Chinese business family in Singapore, he naturally did not harbor any militant intentions ["Asia is One" was a slogan the Japanese used to justify their invasion policy in the Greater East Asia War]. But we for one have suppressed the bitter history and suffering expressed in this melody, using the convenient catchword "world music," and merely enjoying the harmony of the sounds. Would it be an exaggeration to claim that there is a "world music war" just a there is a "film war?" We obliterate the question of melody's past — how it came to be, and in what context it was sung — and can thus accept and enjoy it as a harmless song. In reality, if there is no "Asia" here, there is no "other" either.

Are we really able to "accept" a foreign culture? Whether an alien culture (the "other") appears in the form of an enemy, an ally, or a people subjugated by the self, can a true encounter with this "other" really take place? Though we might live in an urbanized culture which is made up of a patchwork of different ethnicities, this does not mean that we can exempt ourselves from such questioning. How was the situation in the past, during the war? In discussing the problem of the "film war," we must ask: how did Japan meet with "the other," and how did she try to evade or suppress such encounters? This problem also has a direct bearing on our gaze on the "present."

In talking about "the other" in films produced during wartime Japan, we must first consider the problem of the war "enemy." How did Japanese World War II films depict the "enemy?" Thus far, many people have examined this question, and come up with the same answer: namely, they find the image of the "enemy" is startlingly absent in these films. It is certain that there are very few depictions of American and British soldiers, and among these few, the latter are usually not depicted as hateful enemies. By bringing to mind a few such works, this fact becomes readily apparent.

For example, in the documentary film *Oriental Song of Victory (Tōyō no gaika)*, there are depictions of GIs who had been taken prisoner following the fall of Corregidor in the Philippines to the Japanese. Though prisoners, they don't look particularly gloomy, enjoying themselves at the beach, chatting with their friends and smiling. According to the voice-over narration, these scenes express the pathos of the "corrupted" American way of life, but there is no attempt to whip up strong war sentiment. There is a scene in which the enemy captain seeks to surrender, with the Japanese commander intimidating and threatening him, but even so, there is no attempt to depict the "enemy" as strong "other" who must be defeated; rather, he is portrayed as pitiful weakling.

The situation is practically the same in feature films. The captured spy pilots in *Attendance in a Torpedo Squad* are depicted solely as powerless, helplessly smiling beings, wanting in decorum and discipline. In *The War at Sea from Hawaii to Malaya*, the existence of the "enemy" is merely hinted at by the American jazz and dance music from Hawaiian radio stations, transmitted by radios in Japanese aircraft carriers and bombers.

In European and American war films, the "enemy" is treated more stereotypically, as someone who is clearly bad and who must be hated. Even if this is not the case — as in films like *Know Your Enemy*, for example — the special characteristics, appearance, life-style, psychology and morality of the "enemy" are depicted to the minutest detail. Though the "enemy" must be annihilated, he is also seen as a kind of "other." In order to defeat the "enemy," it is necessary to know the "enemy," and the "other" who constitutes this enemy. In other words, in thinking about an alien culture, one's own culture — even for just one moment — becomes relativized, one begins to think about one's own "self." The "enemy = other" becomes truly an object for self-reflection, a mirror image.

It was only natural that many theorists should have focused on the peculiarity of the Japanese war film which does not depict the "enemy" or "other" in this fashion. "What 'enemy' should we fight?" "Why should we fight?" The Japanese war film did not ask such questions but focused mainly on the question, "How should we fight?" This is an issue which has been debated by many postwar film critics. Western war propaganda films usually exaggerate and caricaturize the enemy's cruelty and inhumanity, but the Japanese model institutionalized in the

Fig. 7. A site of struggle in the Japan-America film war—the Times Theater in Manila.

"film war" was different: the biggest problem was how soldiers and citizens could make themselves stronger, and construct themselves into strong subjects able to endure to the end, however great their suffering and pain. To come to the point, the psychology of the Japanese war film was motivated by a sense of indebtedness toward a transcendental entity, the emperor — and the attendant desire to "repay" the emperor for his kindness *(ongaeshi)* — as well as by an ascetic impulse ("discipline?") toward the enduring of suffering and pursuit of human perfection. In this context, the ideal was a self which had renounced itself completely, a "self-less" self.

All this being said, is it really true that the Japanese did not encounter the "other" in places other than the battlefield? Can we really claim that the "enemy" did not become an issue in the "film war?" It rather seems that the "other," or the "enemy," is treated in ways different from ordinary propaganda, ways which are also expressed — if not conspicuously — in the Japanese war film.

Was the "other" depicted in the "film war" simply and merely an "enemy?" This is the first problem that needs to be considered. For example, in *Oriental Song of Victory* and *Malayan War Front — A Record of the March Onward (Marē senki — shingeki no kiroku*, 1942), what was the position of the natives who had just been liberated from American-English domination through Japanese victory? Were they to be considered enemies or allies? The "other" in war was not simply an enemy that had to be annihilated; he/she was also constituted by the people who were to be subjugated or assimilated racially and economically.

The Japanese "film war" during the Second World War was strongly aware of the existence of an "other." This "other" were the natives, who were not enemies to be slaughtered but rather objects to be assimilated, persuaded and even seduced, and who were both potential enemies and friends. The front lines of the "film war" were aware of this problem.

There were subtle differences between Manchuria and the South Seas, as far as the position of the "other" was concerned — a fact which is brought home by witness accounts such as the following:

> "The majority of the social class in the South Seas which is in a position to see films has been superficially Westernized [literally: is covered by a thin veneer of English and American influence]. The lower class barbarians never see films. I think that it would be good policy to strip [the upper classes] of their veneer." (Tada Reikichi. "Kessen-ki eigakai no shinro" [The Path of the Film World During the Decisive Stage of the War], *Eiga Junpō*, 21 March 1943.)

To the people of the South Seas, who had been immersed in Western values and customs, the Japanese film must have seemed quite unaccomplished in terms of narration, tempo, and degree of perfection. It was only natural that the Japanese should have realized that it was necessary for them to revise their techniques and construct a format different from the one used previously. At the same time, it was the duty of the "film war" to enlighten the lower classes (barbarians!) who never saw films. In other words, the people who made and distributed the films were clearly aware of the "other" positioned outside the Japanese community, even if there was no "other" or "enemy" depicted in the films themselves.

For example, people like Amakasu Masahiko, who was one of the string-pullers of the Kwantung Army and the person in charge of the Manshū Eiga Kyōkai

(Manchurian Film Association), clearly recognized the existence of an "other" who differed from the Japanese both in values and perception.

"The films of the Manchurian Film Association are primarily targeted at the uncultured masses, especially the masses of the Manchurians who comprise more than half of the population; it is essential that our films be accepted by them. We must treat and educate them like children, and explain things gradually in plain language to them." (Amakasu Masahiko, "Kessenka no Man'ei" [The Manchurian Film Association During the Decisive Stage of the War], *Eiga Junpō*, 1 March 1943.)

"It is more than sufficient to make films which please the Manchurians, and there is absolutely no necessity to make films which intrigue the Japanese. The Japanese often go into the wrong direction because they tend to make films on the exotic sides of Manchuria that they are so fascinated with. We must not forget that the object [viewers] are the Manchurians themselves." ("Manjin no tame ni eiga o tsukuru" [Making Films for Manchurians], *Eiga Junpō*, 1 August 1942.)

However, it would be a mistake to claim that Amakasu's assertions were widely accepted. For example, in a symposium titled, *Nanpō eiga kōsaku* (The Production of South Seas Films), Suda Shōta made the following comment:

"Ideally, I am opposed to dividing up films into ones made for a domestic audience and others made for an outside audience. First, such a division is out of the question from a logistic point of view (materials, money, etc.). Moreover, I don't think there can be films which are useful only abroad and are of no interest for those within Japan. If a film should be truly useful abroad, it must also interest the Japanese themselves."

Be that as it may, what must be emphasized is that even though the position of the "other" became an issue in the Japanese "film war," the problem was only considered from the point of view of Japanese interest. That is, the "other" was not really considered as a real problem, and thus treated in a very limited fashion.

Let us take the animated film *Momotarō — Divine Troops of the Ocean* (*Momotarō —umi no shinpei*) as an example which does not overtly aim at a depiction of the "other," but nevertheless unwittingly outlines a "topology" (*isō*) of the difference of the "other." The story line, which deals with animals that become personified and unite in order to defeat the enemy demons, is extremely interesting in its positing of the relationship between self and other. Strangely, in this film, it is only Momotarō — who gives orders to the animals — who is considered "human," and the animals are all "sub-humans"; moreover, the enemy is a non-human monstrous demon — a caricature of the English and Americans. In this allegorical depiction, there lies concealed a curious politics of the other.

For example, if we take Momotarō to be representing the Japanese, the fighting animals would be the natives living on the territories subjugated by Japanese imperialism, the "non-Japanese" supposed to be enlightened by the "film war" and other information activities. However, this same structure, composed by the human "subject" and the sub-human "other," also applies to the situation within Japan, the inside of the Japanese communal body. To the Japanese people, who are the "children," the emperor represents a transcendental "other," albeit different from the "other" constituted by the enemy. The relationship between Momotarō and the animals can be said to symbolize the relationship between the emperor and the Japanese people. This problem can be represented in the following diagram:

Momotarō / Animals / Demon
Japanese / People under Japanese / Enemy people
Emperor / Common Japanese / Enemy people

If we extract a common structure out of these three relationships between self and other, we get the following:

Transcendental existence / Self and Community / Aliens

It is precisely because of this underlying structure that the depiction of the "other" in Japanese war film was so complicated. The "other" who exists outside the customs and culture of the Japanese community is put in an ambiguous position — as the alien *(ijin)*, demon, monster, and so on — and the transcendental entity which supports the entire communal body becomes an "other" who can never be attained, as much as the members of the community might try to unite themselves with him. Thus, the "other" in Japanese war films is not absent, but rather in a position of omnipresence. Placed as he/she is at various, contradictory levels, he/she remains in a position of unresolved ambiguity.

Now, how should we approach the problem of the transcendental entity which supports our national community? Let us consider this issue from a theoretical point of view.

In attempting to analyze the "enemy" of a particular national community, we must consider what constitutes the basis for the latter's identity and unity. For support, let us draw on the theories of Slaboj Žižek, a Slovenian philosopher who boldly applied Lacanian psychoanalytical theory to political science, in particular the problem of nationality.

Žižek repeatedly brings up the term "nation-thing" in his writings (for example, in his *Eastern Europe's Republic of Gilead* and *Formal Democracy and Its Discontents*).Though the translation of the term "nation-thing" is very difficult and no fixed equivalent exists, let us provisionally translate it with "national thing" *(minzokuteki na mono)* or "nation = thing" *(minzoku = mono)*. This "national thing" or "nation = thing" is the root or principle which motivates the entire community. It is the principle which constructs the "nation state." As a driving force (a "motivation"), it normally remains invisible. Just as Kant, in his epistemology, suggested the existence of a "Thing-in-itself" *(Ding an sich)*, an "object without an object" which lies at the borderlines as well as the basis of perception, and which the subject can never grasp or comprehend, so does the "nation-thing" exist as a phenomenon which constructs the community as a community, without the community's being conscious of what exactly the "nation-thing" is.

To the members of the community, the "nation-thing" is simultaneously the "Self" (with a capital S), and the "other." It is precisely because this dimension was at stake in the depiction of the "other" in the Japanese war cinema, that the films lacked a clear image of the "other" as "enemy."

In this sense, it could be argued that the national bond is a common relationship oriented toward a specifically embodied form of pleasure and enjoyment. Though national unity and identity does not itself become an object, it is sustained by a relationship with a "thing" which preserves absolute enjoyment. According to Žižek, this "thing" is exposed when the threat to our way of life by an "other" becomes institutionalized. This is because the community must always institutionalize enjoyment. In Žižek's words:

> "A nation exists only as long as its specific enjoyment continues to be materialized in certain social practices, and transmitted in national myths that structure these practices."

In other words, the "nation-thing" exists only as long as the members of the community continue to believe in it. This "nation-thing" has nothing to do with biological origin or a supra-historical basis. It is a kind of special situation which occurs with the social appropriation and construction of pleasure and desire. The establishment of the nation state is thus intimately related to the desires and various enjoyments of the members of the community.

Now, the fact that these pleasures are collectively affirmed by all inevitably implies the existence of another (or others) who do not share them. To the persons involved in the Japanese "film war," it was inevitable that the natives of the South Seas and Manchuria should becomes such "others." Here, we can see an example of a "special" situation, in which the "other" becomes not an enemy to be battled and

Fig. 8. Filipino kids with a souvenir from the war.

defeated, but an "other" — whether he/she be considered as an "other" community, or as an "other" within a larger community (ie., Greater East Asia) — who does not share the transcendental "nation-thing" of the Japanese community.

IV FROM FILM-WAR TO MEDIA-WAR

It is hardly necessary to mention that there is an extremely intimate relationship between war and the visual media. This is not only true for the information activities surrounding the recording of, and reporting on, the war; it is the very structure underlying the various phenomenon of war, especially the forms of the representations (of war), which are intricately related to the various visual media. To say nothing of the relationship between the camera and fire arms, the make-up of the pillbox resembles the structure of a "camera obscura": to shoot the enemy means to illuminate him. Consequently, a soldier becomes the player (performer as well as contestant) in an absurd game called war, while at the same time also being a spectator to it.

As Clausewitz points out in his *On War*, a soldier who newly arrives at the front ends up looking at the battlefield "as if he was looking at a show," and is thrust into a kind of shock situation. To be specific, Clausewitz argues, "once a certain limit has been passed, the light of reason begins to become active in another medium, changing their pathways."

Naturally, the utilization of various battle techniques based on perception — beginning with visual perception — is a time-honored tradition, expressed for example in the trap or booby trap. Information operations which are used as strategies to deceive the human eye lend themselves very well to the recording of war and the gathering of information on the scene. Paul Virilio has accurately analyzed this problem in the following observation:

> "War can never break free from the magical spectacle because its very purpose is to *produce* that spectacle: to fell the enemy is not so much to capture as to 'captivate' him, to instil the fear of death before he actually dies." *(War and Cinema)*

The fact that people like Virilio were so aware of this problem at a time when visual media were not very developed or popularized, should lead us to suspect that the "show"-aspect of war has increased drastically in 20th century wars which have seen the transition from the "machine-eye" of photography and film to the "electronic eye" of video.

For example, the intricate links between the visual metaphors appearing in witness accounts and descriptions of the Vietnam War and film technology are well documented. Many soldiers who had just been drafted said that they were "going to see a movie" before departing to the dangerous front lines, or complained that they "hated this kind of Movie" when faced with an unexpectedly dangerous situation. Michael Herr, who was involved as a script writer and editorial supervisor in many Vietnam War films accompanied American soldiers on their missions as a journalist and wrote an extremely interesting, non-fictional series of accounts, published as *Dispatches*, in which he repeatedly suggests that the Vietnam War was a "media freak" war. He comments on the irony of the fact that the rock music, drugs and films used to keep the soldiers' emotions and perceptions in check, were used in the same way by the American anti-war counter-culture, so that the latter's "perceptual map" resembled that of the soldiers on the battlefield. When the psychological after-effects among repatriated soldiers became a social problem, the term used to characterize phenomena like sudden mental derangement or speeding among these soldiers, was "flashback," again a term borrowed from film technology.

Of course, since ancient times, all wars have comprised an element of "intelligence war," but the Vietnam War differs fundamentally from former wars in the fact that it was carried out with the use of mass reproduction techniques and a great number of media. It can be said that it was here that the transition from the "film war" as narrowly defined (the ideological propaganda-information operations typical for World War II) to the "media war" (information operations which regulate communication and a totalized unconscious with regard to the Vietnam and Cold wars), took place. In other words, the various elements of the "film war" have changed their shape, but they have most certainly been appropriated by the "media war."

If the fact that the persons most concerned with the war, the soldiers, were simultaneously the players as well as spectators — if this is indeed one aspect of war — then how much more must war seem like a "show" to the civilians, to whom war is accessible only through records and the media, and who thus remain idle spectators [literally: those who see the war as a "fire on the opposite shore"].

Kamei Katsuichirō, in an essay on *Kindai no chōkoku* (Overcoming the Modern [a July 1942 symposium featuring famous literary scholars and philosophers, such as Kobayashi Hideo, Nishitani Keiji, and Hayashi Fusao, who felt their debate would mean the end of "modern civilization" in Japan and open a "glorious new age." — ed.]), already commented on the violence lurking in information and documentation:

> "[This problem] is obvious when we consider cases in which the sublime deeds committed in war become the objects of journalism, or are made into radio programs, films, and *"naniwa-bushi"* [the musical recital of ancient tales]. I for one am amazed at how swiftly such things are propagated. — There is a lofty deed — A team of photographers rushed to the site — The deed is broadcast by the radio — It is published in newspapers — It is made into a film — And then forgotten. This whole process occurs very rapidly, and ends up completely denying all the gloom and sophisticated lyricism inherent in the sublime deed. It is only at a superficial level that all kinds of meaningless details are explored and endlessly reiterated" (*Gendai seishin ni kan suru oboegaki* [A Memorandum on Today's Spirit], 1942).

There is a kind of "power" (*chikara*) which is imposed on the spectators who are experiencing war through their gaze. This power points to another kind of war, concealed in the depths of every war.

The transition from the "film war" (as a subgenre of the "intelligence" or "cultural war") to the "media war," can also be considered from a different angle: the change in the spectator's position and perspective. Let us consider this issue by taking the world events which took place in the last few years — China's Tienanmen Square Incident, the fall of the Berlin Wall, the Gulf War, the coup d'état in the Soviet Union, and the like — as examples.

I wish to draw attention to the fact that the attempt to construct a "political science of the gaze" (shisen no seijigaku) using the term "spectator," had been made surprisingly long ago. The 19th century philosopher Kant analyzed the relationship between a historical incident, the French Revolution, and the intellectuals in the following terms:

> "This revolution has elicited such a favorable reaction among the entirety of the spectators (those who were not directly involved in the performance of game), that their enthusiasm touches on fanatic frenzy.
>
> "The important thing here is the mode of thinking commonly expressed by the spectators with regard to the "performance" (game) constituted by this great political change. This mode of thinking expresses an universal, unselfish sympathy for the performers on one side of the game, while it opposes those on the other side. Though such thinking runs the danger of being extremely disadvantageous to the spectators themselves, it is made into something public and communal." *(Struggle of the Departments)*

From the perspective of today, Kant, who lived in an age where there were practically no visual media, correctly analyzed the position of the "spectators of history." Whether it be in the past or the present, the problem remains very much the same. For example, we who are in a position of spectators, and to whom war is no more than a historical event appearing in television, radio or film, face the same issue. First, it is possible that when confronted with a great historical incident, spectators or observers can become just as frenzied or agitated by the event as the players, or even more so. Moreover, Kant argues that it is possible that the judgement pronounced by those spectators "outside," who have no direct relationship to the incident and no special interests in it, be a fair and universal one expressing the opinion of "world citizens."

Setting aside the question of whether Kant's last assertion is right or wrong, it is clear that our position vis-a-vis an event or incident is truly that of a spectator/observer (as enthusiast). For instance, we were outraged by the People's Army's oppression of the demonstrators in Beijing, profoundly moved by the destruction of the Berlin Wall, struck by the exchange of missiles during the Gulf War which we took as "TV games," felt sympathy toward the citizens of Moscow who resisted by confronting military tanks on the street. All these situations were instances of the spectator's "gaze" (chūshi) which occurred within the media, beginning with television. Just as the 18th century spectators in Kant's analysis were controlled by the media of the written word and hearsay, 20th century spectators are constructed solely by photographs, films, and the communication media.

It is not only that all wars comprise an element of "show"; like the people chained inside the dark recesses of "Plato's Cave," we are shackled inside the "Plato's Caves" of revolutions and wars. Actually, Plato's famous metaphor somewhat resembles the camera obscura or the setup of the theater or movie theater.

Whatever the historical period, the spectators are shackled to media's "chains." Are they thus really able to escape from these chains and contemplate the situation freely, as Kant's citizens and intellectuals seem to have done? To consider this problem, we must emphasize that the situation of the "tele-spectator" which emerged so clearly during the violent historical events of the past few years, is different from that of a "conventional" spectator.

Though the Tienanmen Square Incident and the coup d'état in the Soviet Union are often considered to be similar, there are many differences between the two as far as media-theory is concerned. When the confrontation between the military and the people took place in front of the government office of the Russian Republic, and the coup leaders' incompetence became more and more obvious, the images and news concerning these events were ironically transmitted world-wide in real time. There was surprisingly little censorship exercised by the Russians on the Western mass media, and the information that was transmitted was quite faithful to reality) of course, a completely accurate description of reality is really impossible, and now we know that the information was biased toward the Americans and Yeltsin's supporters). On the other hand, in the Chinese case there were strong press restrictions, and the information that was communicated was intentionally distorted. It was not transmitted in real time, but with an intentional delay.

The time difference between the recording and transmitting of information is very important. This is another reason why we must make a distinction between "film war" and "media war." Photographs and films, extremely powerful weapons in the "cultural war"/"intelligence warfare" from World War II to the Vietnam War, both necessitate a minimum of time for the chemical processing of the image, so that transmission is deferred. However, today's electronic technology — as anyone will have noticed who has followed the coup d'état and the Gulf War on television — aims at a completely simultaneous, real time transmission of the event. The temporal nature of real time is such that it conveys the illusion that the absolute distance which separates spectators from actors is dissolved, for however brief a moment. The effects of this illusion are far more serious than the ideological effects brought about by the propaganda of photographs, graphic designs, and film. In going from "film war" to "media war," "information operations" do not undergo a qualitative change, but rather multiply their power.

It is interesting to note that in both China and the Soviet Union, the popular desire for democratization chose public spaces such as large squares, or streets in front of government offices, as its "space of resistance" *(teikō no basho)*. In doing so, it is certain that the protesters have retraced the Western march toward modernization, which has constructed urban centers by focusing on public spaces and public domains. (It has been suggested that in Hong Kong, another "place of resistance" was established in front of a building with a giant screen onto which images of Tienanmen were projected. One could argue that this is one of the positive aspects of telecommunications.)

It is true that these images of popular resistance in public spaces stirred up enthusiasm and sympathy in we telespectators, but it must be emphasized that the space we participated in by means of telecommunication, was not a "physical" public space, but only a "information space" *(jōhō no hiroba)*, a "public image," as it were. Ironically, this "public image" lurks in the background of the rose-colored visions of oppositional media theorists who foresee an utopian model of a new society, called "network society" or "teletopia."

Recently, some thinkers and critics here and abroad have sought to justify, or judge, the Gulf War as a "post-modern war." Their discourse bears a striking resemblance to that of intellectuals who discussed "overcoming the modern" during World War II. Past or present, a way of thinking which is forgetful of history habitually privileges its own "present." "Now, it is different from before"; "X has ended, from now on it will be Y"; these are some of the catchphrases of this philosophy. (In this context, let us recall that is was on the basis of such thinking that specialists in futurist aesthetics lent aesthetic support to the war.)

There is no doubt that the Gulf War was the most thoroughly "informatized" war in history, in the sense that it attempted to completely eliminate what was not in the "present." The issue is not so much the record-breaking amount of high tech and electronic technology that had been utilized for this war. Rather, the war exercised a yet unprecedented degree of (symbolic) violence in uniformly arousing the same kinds of impressions and feelings — a kind of "sober enthusiasm?" — among a great number of people. Granted, we who watch (or are made to watch) the Gulf War as a game in the true sense of the word, might well be expressing a certain kind of "enthusiasm" or "sympathy" toward it; however, we are not the kind of spectators who run risks in backing one side or the other. Believe as we might that we have the luxury of all kinds of perspectives, in reality these have become codified into an unitary type, a stereotypical spectator. The enormous amount of real time information has merely led to the institutionalization of a kind of "remote" participation in the opinion of "world citizens" — the public opinion of a "New World Order"!? "This war is really like a game": when the Pentagon succeeded in conveying this impression to a large number of people in the world, it achieved a definite success in the Gulf War, given its undisguised attempts to expunge all images of physical and bodily destruction from the media. Likewise, with the diffusion of images of water birds covered with oil to convey the destruction of oil fields by the Iraqis, the Americans achieved a great success in the "media war" — what convinced the viewers was the sheer power of the image; whether the information itself was accurate was not at issue. In a "real time war," neither soldiers nor citizens have any time to make their own judgements.

In the depths of so-called "normal" warfare, there lies concealed another kind of war. It varies both in nature and terminology, ranging from intelligence war, cultural war, film war, to media war and so on. In each of these wars, there is a confrontation between the continuous stream of "information operations," and we spectators. As the receivers of information, we are already involved in the war, and become inescapably embroiled in it.

Now, is it possible for the telespectator to pursue a more active strategy? How can we cast doubt on established information methods, "rescan" and rearrange the information available, by using different, alternative pathways? Of course, these are extremely difficult choices, and there are no easy answers. Perhaps Nakai Masakazu's comment might be helpful:

> "...In the cinema, time is depicted by the transitions between one picture and the other, the continuation from cut to cut. In the world of linguistics, symbols are connected to each other by copulas. Critics use copulas to express their intentions, and to convince their readers.

"However, in film there is no attempt to link different pictures by 'copulas,' and the cuts are left to be seen by the viewers just as they are. The viewers make their own connections between the cuts, according to their own desires and intentions. Even if the filmmakers might be unhappy about it, the spectators will make up their own minds, and come up with their own connections" (*Eiga no motsu bunpō* [The Grammar of Film], 1950).

Considered from today's perspective, Nakai's view of the passive spectator who nevertheless holds the decisive key to the interpretation of the image, may seem all to optimistic. However, this does not change the fact that the final process of creation and production in information exchange is entrusted to the unconsciousness of the general public. Though the "space" (*ma*) between cut and cut is much more hidden than it was at the time of the "film war," high-resolution information is enforcing a unidimensional grammar and code, however diversified it might have become on the surface.

Nakai had already recognized the strategic importance of the "copula" at the time of the "film war"; how will our world, dominated as it is by the electronic technology of the "media wars," discover and assess it? Our own battle lines will certainly emerge out of such questioning.

— Translated by *Maya Todeschini*

Warring Images: Stereotype and American Representations of the Japanese, 1941-1991

Michael Renov

> "Stereotypes can assume a life of their own, rooted not in reality but in the myth-making made necessary by our need to control our world."
>
> —Sander L. Gilman, Difference and Pathology

> "I was drinking about a fifth and a half of whiskey every day. Sometimes homemade, sometimes what I could buy. It was the only way I could kill. I had friends who were Japanese and I kept thinking every time I pulled a trigger on a man or pushed a flamethrower down into a hole: What is this person's family gonna say when he doesn't come back? He's got a wife, he's got children, somebody".

> "They would show us movies. Japanese women didn't cry. They would accept the ashes stoically. I knew different. They went home and cried."
>
> —John Garcia, from Studs Terkel's The Good War: An Oral History of World War II

What follows is an attempt to think through several difficult and somewhat disparate questions, all of which bear upon the history of American representations of the Japanese a half-century ago. In doing so, I will focus upon the notion of "otherness" — defined as a categorical, hierarchical and, in this instance, racially motivated separation between self and outsider — and the ways in which it can be exploited or countervailed in a contemporary media environment. towards that end, a number of World War II American tracts — of propaganda and war aims promotion — will be examined, including posters, Hollywood films and documentaries produced by the War Department. Alongside this material, I propose to consider the more recent work of independent Asian American artists who, in rewriting their own histories, have begun to recover a lost history for all Japanese Americans, domestic victims of America's wartime racism.

Finally, I will discuss one more instance of independent documentary production from the U.S., a collaboratively authored series of videotapes entitled the Gulf Crisis TV Project. Broadcast at the height of anti-Arab hysteria during the recent Gulf War amidst the monolithic cheerleading of CNN and other mainstream "news" entities, the Gulf Crisis TV Project articulated a position critical of the war and its unspoken ideological foundations. A sequence in one of the programs (*Manufactur-

ing the Enemy) is particularly relevant to this discussion for the parallels it draws between recent expressions of racially based hostility toward Arab-Americans and the climate of feeling which resulted in the internment of Japanese Americans a half-century earlier.

On the basis of these three historical sites of media production — American World War II propaganda, Asian American independent work since 1970 and the Gulf Crisis TV Project of 1991 — I will conclude by arguing for the social necessity of alternative media enterprises capable of countering the streamlined and state managed images which trade on stereotype, mould prevailing public images to their own ends and move millions to violence against a perceived "other." There was no such venue for public contestation in the 1940s; we have, through the screenings of this festival, ample evidence of the dire result.

I return, then, to a series of questions — and thus to a range of texts and their analysis — which I shall use to frame the discussion. Though fraught with political and ideological complexity, these questions emerge as crucial to heightened historical understanding between Japan and the United States, to the future health of all cross-cultural representations and to the potential role of documentary film and video in the establishment and assessment of public policy goals, including those of war and peace. Among the questions to be explored are these:

- What is the character and function of stereotyping, particularly in the ideological pressure cooker of wartime?

- What is the "reality effect" of documentary film and video and what role can these media forms play in the construction or dissolution of stereotypical discourse?

- On what historical grounds can we account for the virulence of the anti-Japanese rhetoric of World War II America and in what specific ways was it manifest?

- How can the seizure of property and incarceration of 120,000 Japanese Americans during those years be understood in terms of stereotypical discourse and how have recent Asian American artists sought to recoup their losses through a reinscription of personal memory and public history?

- Is it possible to employ documentary techniques within a mass media context to resist the effects of government-sponsored, racially-based stereotyping during wartime? What is the political importance of alternative mediamaking in the current media environment?

RACE AND STEREOTYPE

"Know Your Enemy — Japan followed Capra's rule of thumb (Let the enemy speak for himself) in an exceptionally evocative manner...Beneath its dazzling surface imagery...the message was simple, conveyed in a stark metaphor and a striking visual image. The audience was told that the Japanese resembled "photographic prints off the same negative." Visually, this was reinforced by repeated scenes of a steel bar being hammered in a forge."
— John W. Dower, War Without Mercy: Race & Power in the Pacific War

"Once a Jap, always a Jap...you cannot regenerate a Jap, convert him and make him the same as a white man any more than you can reverse the laws of nature."
— John Rankin, U.S. Congressman, Mississippi

"Here's a very personal question: Have you killed a Jap soldier today?"
— Opening narration from Justice

It is here within the domain of wartime stereotypes that we encounter the most disturbing and dehumanizing instances of cross-cultural representation, the images and rhetoric which must be confronted if we are to ridiculous determine their cause and avoid their recurrence. Rather than devote myself to simply reproducing the virulently racist constructions endemic to America's waging of war in the Pacific (John W. Dower's *War Without Mercy* offers an exhaustive account of the savagery of the conflict as fought and represented by both sides), it seems to me crucial to dig further in order to theorize an underlying dynamic of the stereotype which can account for all obsessively vilifying characterizations of "others." Japanese and American wartime excesses can thus be placed in a broader conceptual framework that engenders understanding in addition to strong emotional response.

Despite this concern for root causes, the concrete features of the wartime encounter between Japan and the United States deserve careful study. Dower is at pains to historicize the race hates and war hates which typified the Pacific conflict and thus offer explanation for the actions on both sides. He argues persuasively that the number of casualties sustained by the principal combatant nations (and by other Asian peoples such as the Chinese, Filipinos and Indonesians) as well as the sheer intensity of hatred expressed toward the enemy — civilian and soldier alike — are incomprehensible without a grounding in both Japanese and American social

Fig. 1. The not too suble conclusion of *Let's Have a Drink*.

history. On the American side — to which I shall confine myself — Dower narrates the historical matrix that prepares the way for wartime excesses: the legacy of 19th century evolutionism and its presumptions of racial superiority; a century of "Yellow Peril" rhetoric in response to Chinese and Japanese immigration; Oriental exclusion laws and enforced segregation by the mid-1920s; limitations on land ownership by alien Japanese; and, at the level of popular culture, an intransigent strain of nativism resulting in a series of books and films warning of Japanese aggression at home and abroad.[1] These are just a few of the significant forces or events which were historically determining (creating a climate of social pressures and limits within which subsequent racist manifestations arose). Any search for the basis of stereotyping must, however, move beyond such a historicizing account.

We might begin this search for the fundamental source and recurrent psycho-social functions of stereotyping with the crawl that introduces the Gulf Crisis TV Project's *Manufacturing the Enemy*. There the producers offer a series of definitions of the stereotype, pieces of a diagnosis which might serve to explain the actions and behaviors which are the subject of what follows.

> "A stereotype is a projective device used to make it easy to behave toward people in socially functional ways...
>
> "You call a people 'barbarians'...or you call a group 'criminals' if you want to suspend just laws of decency and behave towards them in an otherwise criminal way.
>
> "This is a function for coping with threats for it justifies both dismissing and brutalizing these groups."

Two important points deserve some discussion: first, the notion of "projective device"; second, the assumption of a "social function" for the stereotype. Projection is a psychological term for the attribution of internal states to an externalized object; traits attached to the stereotyped "other" are said to originate within the psyche of the self. The "other" is thus a kind of screen or mirror for one's internalized idealizations, both "good" and "bad." This feature of the definition lies firmly within the realm of psychoanalysis and will be discussed further below.

The second point — the social utility of the stereotype — suggests that stereotyping can serve destructive social ends when "managed" by a political party, nation-state or subculture. The hatred mobilized through recourse to stereotype can fuel violent or discriminatory acts by one group against another on the basis of the latter's (putatively) shared characteristics or physical traits. While the above definition leaves unstated the question of intention (is this social function circumstantial or the product of a conspiracy?), it does at least begin to comprehend the critical features of stereotypical discourse within a framework of cause and effect. It is worthwhile examining the phenomenon of stereotyping in even finer detail.

We might return to Dower's book to pursue our search for a deeper understanding of the stereotype in the context of the Pacific War. There the author expresses some puzzlement as to the speed and forcefulness of "the easy transition from antagonistic to congenial images on all sides," the way in which "[t]he demonic Westerners could suddenly become transformed into their tutelary guise" during the postwar Occupation.[2] Conversely, in their own studies on the subject of racial stereotyping, scholars such as Sander L. Gilman and Homi K. Bhabha have emphasized the underlying structures of mind and thought that can account for the deep-seatedness and volatility of stereotypical discourse (what Gilman calls its "protean" character). It seems to me entirely necessary to understand stereotyping as a dynamic rooted in psychical as well as historical processes if we are to succeed in educating ourselves towards its control.[3]

Gilman believes that "stereotyping is a universal means of coping with anxieties "engendered by our inability to control the world."[4] He proposes that we require certain "immutable structures" that can assure us of our power to grasp the play of difference that surrounds us at the level of thought, object or person. Homi Bhabha offers a similar assessment, arguing that "[t]he stereotype is not a simplification because it is a false representation of a given reality. It is a simplification because it is an arrested, fixated form of representation that...[denies] the play of difference."[5] In a response to our inability to control an ever-changing environment, we limit the threat that otherness poses through the creation of fixed images. Bhabha goes on to claim that such an arrest of difference facilitates a sense of clear-cut opposition between the self — more or less fluid in its identifications and idealizations — and the stereotyped "other" — fixed, immutable and available for appropriation.

The radical split between self and "other" helps to uphold a racial fantasy discernible in both Japanese and American contexts: "the fantasy that dramatizes the impossible desire for a pure, undifferentiated origin."[6] The racial "other" as stereotype emerges as both the grounds for anxiety and the source of its relief. As an image, arrested and controlled, it serves as an inverted mirror of identity. In racial terms, the "other" is the support of a defining hierarchy; mongrelized or fallen from grace, the "other" defines the purity of one's own lineage.

Gilman traces the origins of stereotyping to childhood development, arguing that the self is itself split into "good" and "bad" components. The "bad" self comes to be identified with the mental representation of the "bad" object (that which, in the infantile world, causes pain or anxiety); the "bad" that we perceive within us thus becomes projected or cast out onto external objects. Stereotypes are thus "a crude set of mental representations of the world"; the Manichean domains that have dominated global history during this century — East and West, Axis Powers and Allies, Communists and the Free World — correspond to this most primitive (but powerful and deeply rooted) dichotimization.[7] We are said to be equally capable of projecting idealized self-images (the "good" self) onto an "other" with a dramatic vacillation between the two remaining psychologically viable.[8] Gilman's discussion of the volatility of shifting stereotypical valences offers substantial explanation for the variability of Japanese/American stereotypes that appears to puzzle Dower.

But the line between "good" and "bad" responds to stresses occurring within the psyche. Thus paradigm shifts in our mental representations of the world can and do occur. We can move from fearing to glorifying the Other. We can move from loving to hating. The most negative stereotype always has an overtly positive counterweight. As any image is shifted, all stereotypes shift. Thus stereotypes are inherently protean rather than rigid.[9]

If we accept this account of the psychic basis of stereotyping, we should not be surprised to discover its ubiquity or even its virulence. Both the Anglo-Saxon and Japanese traditions were notable for deeply rooted racial pride bolstered in the former instance by centuries of colonial occupation around the world and in the latter by a culturally shared conviction as to the racial purity of the Yamato race and its 2,600 year history as an unconquered people. As strongly held as these ideas of racial supremacy might have been in both cases, the culture's potential for projection onto its evil "other" wielded an equal force. The Japanese were diminutive, childlike in temperament, simian in appearance (scientific proof of their debased evolutionary station) and never to be trusted; the Americans were overgrown and devilish, ill-smelling and licentious.

But the Japanese/American confrontation was not a unique case; indeed, Dower writes of the way in which the Japanese were "saddled with racial stereotypes that Europeans and Americans had applied to nonwhites for centuries: during the conquest of the New World, the slave trade, the Indian wars in the United States, the agitation against Chinese immigrants in America, the colonization of Asia and Africa, the U.S. conquest of the Philippines at the turn of the century."[10] One need only consult Edward Said's classic text, *Orientalism*, for an extended discussion of the ways in which Europeans have constructed a non-Western "other" whose chief characteristics remain intact across centuries and major geographic boundaries.

It is crucial that we consider the ways in which a wartime climate can fuel the intensity of racial hatred through a hardening of boundaries along the dichotomous split between "us" and "them." A pressure or ideologically produced and sustained urgency is created culture-wide that reinforces consensual behavior through positive rewards (the approbation of top-down propaganda campaigns, peer group support and traditions of filial piety or team play) as well as negative ones (the death of community members, fearfulness and a constantly renewed loathing towards those whose actions appear to challenge accepted values). What's more, the intensity aroused through this identification of the enemy as the embodiment of evil and the source of all conflict spirals upward as it confronts its mirror self in the attitudes and behaviors of its "other." For the underlying dynamic of projection and stereotype which fuels the enemy's hatred is identical to one's own. Certainly, all the governing societal conditions outlined above can be applied equally to Japan and to the United States during the Pacific War. Dower notes that many of the stereotypical traits claimed by one combatant nation for the other (e.g., bestiality or barbarianism) were mutually attributed.

If, as Gilman states, "stereotypes arise when self-integration is threatened," it becomes possible to see wartime stereotyping as the manifestation of a shared and heavily reinforced perception of a threat to national integrity.

Fig. 2.

A crucial distinction — that between the pathological and non-pathological personality — is equally pertinent to our discussion; the former (person or state) remains "consistently aggressive toward the real people and objects to which the stereotypical representations correspond...[while] the latter is able to repress the aggression and deal with people as individuals."[11] A state of war evinces a kind of cultural pathology, a general inability (or unwillingness) to treat people of an "other" designation as individuals.

The blindness caused by this stereotyping dynamic can be extended to "others" who may share one's own state citizenship, a fact discovered by the two-thirds of the interned Japanese Americans who were born in the United States. In the words of General John L. DeWitt, head of the West Coast Defense Command: "A Jap's a Jap...It makes no difference whether he is an American citizen or not...I don't want any of them...There is no way to determine their loyalty."[12] For what is at stake is the control of one's world, this time understood not at the level of infantile personality formation but of global politics. That which is identified as the source of threat — namely, the enemy — becomes the wellspring of all that is evil, the object of culturally shared projection. It is into this setting of deeply rooted emotion that we must now place the documentary film, without doubt the most effective tool for mass projection ever devised.

DOCUMENTARY FILM: TOOL FOR MASS PROJECTION

> "The photographic image is the object itself, the object freed from the conditions of time and space that govern it. No matter how fuzzy, distorted, or discolored, no matter how lacking in documentary value the image may be, it shares, by virtue of the very process of its becoming, the being of the model of which it is the reproduction; it is the model."
> — André Bazin, "The Ontology of the Photographic Image"

> "[T]he photograph...becomes meaningful in certain transactions and has real effects, but — cannot refer or be referred to a pre-photographic reality as to a truth...[W]e have to see that every photograph is the result of specific and, in every sense, significant distortions which render its relation to any prior reality deeply problematic and raise the question of the determining level of the material apparatus and of the social practices within which photography takes place."
> — John Tagg, The Burden of Representation

In his autobiography, *The Name Above the Title*, Frank Capra describes his reaction to a first viewing of Leni Riefenstahl's *Triumph of the Will*. In his words, "Satan couldn't have devised a more blood-chilling superspectacle — I sat alone and pondered. How could I mount a counterattack against *Triumph of the Will*?"[13] It should come as no surprise that three terms coalesce in this prelude to Capra's discussion of his own strategies for wartime documentary film production — the demonic, spectacle and war. It was he, noted American populist and one of Hollywood's premier storytellers, who was tapped by General George C. Marshall to explain to American soldiers, citizens and allies *Why We Fight* in a series of seven feature-length documentary films. In his effort to make "the best damned documentary films ever made" (his promise to Marshall), Capra seems to have intuited John Tagg's pronouncement: "Every photograph is the result of specific and, in every sense, significant distortions."

We might extrapolate upon Tagg's dictum to say that every documentary film or videotape is the result of a lengthy series of selections (instances of the maker's interventions which are constitutive) — from the choice of lens, film stock, camera position and distance to choices surrounding sound recording and mixing techniques, editing strategies, and musical and/or narrational accompaniment.[14] No documentary image is innocent; it is mistaken for its referent (that which existed before the lens at some other time and place) at our collective peril. Capra knew about the malleability of the image and even more about editing, the power of association. He gave proof of his acumen in *The Battle of China* as he joined newsreel images of Japanese planes firing on an American gunboat to a narrated description of the attack of "the blood-crazed Japs." These images of an air attack — indistinguishable from so many others — instantly evoke, on account of the narration which blankets them, both bestiality and madness (two of the archetypal attributes of America's wartime "other").

Time and again, Capra mobilizes words and images to reinforce prevailing stereotypes, both "good" and "bad." The Chinese allies, "spontaneously driven by an epic impulse" embark on "a Homeric journey...30 million people moving westward...westward to freedom" in an effort to evade Japanese coastal encroachment, evoking the westward expansionism of America itself. When the Chinese blow up the dikes which hold back the Yellow River, the Japanese invaders are shown beating a watery retreat, thus calling to Western minds a Biblical referent and an act of divine retribution — the drowning of the Egyptian Pharaoh and his men as they pursued Moses and the Children of Israel across the Red Sea. Images of Chinese labor processes are characteristically collective and patiently painstaking (pulling a barge upstream by hand, children breaking down rocks with tiny hammers) while the archival images chosen to represent the Japanese show them to be vicious and aggressive (shouting their celebrant "banzai," beating or bayonetting the helpless). Even the Disney animation which provides graphic representation of troop movements bears a stereotypical charge; Chinese activity is denoted by white arrows, the Japanese by black. Through these various acts of appropriation, the Asian allies temporarily become "white."

The case of the Disney graphics in the Capra films offers apt illustration of the potential for ideological inflection for even the most benign filmic elements. What could be more empirically documentary than a chart of troop movement? And yet opportunities for coloring and connotation abound. In a manner to which the history of the African American experience bears tragic witness, blackness in Western culture has been freighted with notions of evil and moral turpitude. On the basis of a near-subliminal color contrast, Capra is able to cast the Chinese and Japanese as instant hero and villain. Such moments of graphic illustration can be colored in a number of other ways as well, for example through the use of musical accompaniment, festive or foreboding according to the desired emotional impact. What appears to be a straightforward presentation of factual material can, in fact, be strongly if subtly inflected by authorial choices calculated to sway audiences.

At a time of consensual action, when the enemy is clearly demarcated and the lines drawn, films which rally statistics towards an argument or recontextualize documentary footage retrieved from many sources (including the enemy) can mobilize a persuasive force of staggering proportion. If we, as individuals or nations, believe that the newsreel image is always neutral, that the document cannot lie, or even if we receive no encouragement within our culture to question the status of every image as truth, we become subject to a persuasive force capable of overturning some of our most basic ethical principles.

I have written elsewhere about the several functions which define the documentary film — the preservational, the persuasive, the expressive and the analytical.[15] At certain moments and in the hands of particular practitioners, one or the other of these functions may be decisively foregrounded. For the historical and ideological reasons discussed above, wartime documentary films produced by combatant nations were heavily weighted in the direction of persuasion. The specific character of that persuasiveness — its goals and methods — varied. The Japanese and American documents featured in these festival screenings offer ample evidence of that variability. Certain British war films exemplify an approach to persuasion unlike those of either the Japanese or Americans.

The bulk of British wartime documentary films feature persuasive tactics quite at odds with their American ally's interest in defining the enemy, focusing instead on producing wartime paeans to English stoicism and resilience. Films such as *Listen To Britain* (1942) or *Fires Were Started* (1943) — two remarkable works by Humphrey Jennings — celebrate the common culture and cohesiveness of Britain at war. In *Listen To Britain*, compositional choices (one memorable image — soldiers, silhouetted against the evening sky, guarding the British coastline), picture editing and the creation of sound bridges all help to orchestrate a vision of a nation, unmarked by class or gendered divisions, fighting as one. There are almost no direct references to the German menace although it is the unimaged Luftwaffe — for the moment held at bay by the RAF — which prompts repeated glances skyward. Instead the film celebrates Britain's proud past and its sheer indomitability, echoed in the title of another wartime documentary, *London Can Take It*. Big Ben, the BBC blanketing the globe with its war coverage, the dome of St. Paul's — these are the audio-visual icons around which Jennings rallies mass support.

No matter the concrete manifestation of the national imperative toward wartime persuasion, however, cinema — and the documentary film form most of all — remains a tool of great potency. This was known to the nations at war in World War II; it was also known some years before to V.I. Lenin whose maxim — "the cinema is for us the most important of all the arts" — is a statement about the power of the motion picture to solidify national identity and move great numbers of people toward state goals. All of the filmmaking practices alluded to above — the Soviet efforts of the twenties, the German, British, Japanese and American propaganda films of the thirties and forties — are inconceivable outside of state authority and guidance. These social visions projected to millions by cinematic means are, in every case, cut to the cloth of government policy. They explain, they celebrate, they predict, they inculpate. And they do so in a manner that maximizes their persuasive force while leaving little space for counter-instances or dissent.

The wartime documentary film can thus be seen as an ideal domain of stereotypical discourse. These are the films which, in their appropriation of apparently evidentiary images (archival footage, newsreels, shots of the recognizable and the everyday), can rally mass support and inspire joint action. Sounds and images projected in the dark can tap popular memory through Biblical references or a musical phrase; the most treasured values of American culture, instantly evoked by shots of children at play or the Washington Monument, can be made to seem the direct targets of enemy attack. Responses — elicited on the spot, frequently by recourse to "real" images — can be shaped and intensified by the canny filmmaker then harnessed to wartime aims. Wartime consensus only fuels the fire which burns against the debased "other." It is worth exploring some representations of the Japanese produced in wartime America in greater detail.

"THIS IS THE ENEMY"

In the autumn of 1942, the Museum of Modern Art in New York exhibited 200 war posters from among the thousands submitted to a campaign drive spearheaded by "Artists for Victory," a coalition of 26 arts organizations dedicated to patriotic service. The images were meant to illustrate one of several war slogans, among them "Deliver Us From Evil," "Buy More War Bonds," "Loose Talk Sinks Ships," "Victory Starts Here," and — the most salient of all for our purposes —"This Is the Enemy." Of the handful of posters featured in *Life* magazine's coverage of the exhibition (21 December 1942), there is a notable difference between the character of the representations of the European as against the Asian enemy. Four of the six "This Is the Enemy" images depict Nazi violence and sacrilege: a daggered hand smashing through the stained glass of a church window or desecrating an American flag. In the most horrific of them, the superimposed face of Hitler oversees a ravaged landscape. In the background, flames lick over a church spire; the foreground is littered with corpses. Chief among the dead is a woman, pierced through the heart, her body resting against a plaque which reads "God Bless Our Home." Her lifeless hand is held by a hysterically-crying child who sits up to his waist in a pool of blood. The evils associated with the Nazi enemy are forcefully invoked: cruelty, antagonism to cherished values of church and family, mass homicide.

The two examples of Japanese "This Is the Enemy" posters provide, however, a considerable contrast to the German; they are both more explicit in their depiction of enemy atrocities and clearly racially-driven. While the European nemesis may be figured as a defiler of the sacred, the Japanese are "othered" with far greater vehemence.[16] In one poster, a Japanese soldier, swarthy and simian of posture, stands half erect, with a naked woman slung over his shoulder; the alabaster of her exposed skin contrasts hyperbolically with that of her captor. In yet another instance, a dagger-wielding Japanese soldier, his yellow face drawn wide in a snarl, reaches for a horror-stricken white woman fleeing from the lower left edge of the frame. The grotesquerie of the image results from two excessive elements: the teeth and nails (now fangs and claws) of the Asian man are hyperbolized in the direction of the bestial while a low-key, low-angle lighting effect transforms the painted image into nightmare. While the threat of the "other" is in all cases figured as the brutalization of the woman, the most fundamental assault within the patriarchal order because it annihilates the medium of exchange and reproduction, the savagery and bestiality of the Asian is crucially foregrounded. Such images are calcu-

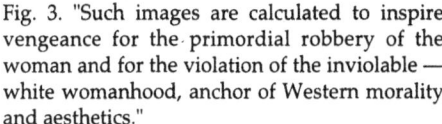

Fig. 3. "Such images are calculated to inspire vengeance for the primordial robbery of the woman and for the violation of the inviolable — white womanhood, anchor of Western morality and aesthetics."

Fig. 4. "...The teeth and nails (now fangs and claws) of the Asian man are hyperbolized in the direction of the bestial while a low-key, low-angle lighting effect transforms the painted image into nightmare."

lated to inspire vengeance for the primordial robbery of the woman and for the violation of the inviolable — white womanhood, anchor of Western morality and aesthetics.

The 29 April 1944 cover of *Liberty* magazine is equally explicit in its projection of animality upon the Japanese. Three uniformed soldiers of the Empire — one bedecked in medals, all buck-toothed and bespectacled — are shown perched upon a fallen tree trunk as bombs rain down from behind and above. The gestured pose of this figure group — hands placed over ears, eyes, and mouth respectively — enact the "hear no evil, see no evil, speak no evil" adage (with "Japanese-ness" functioning as the visible shorthand for evil). But the cover illustrates far more than a hackneyed moral injunction, for once again these enemy soldiers are imaged as apelike, their dark, fur-covered hands and feet inhumanly outsized and grasping. Such dehumanizing representations as these can, in the end, be said to have a cumulative effect. The atomic resolution to the war could be faced without remorse by a society assured of the enemy's subhumanity.

In wartime Hollywood films such as *The Purple Heart* (1944) and *Guadalcanal Diary* (1943), visual as well as cultural codes were mobilized in the service of stereotype. In the latter film, the enemy was depicted in camouflage, capable of merging with the jungle flora, much as the Vietnamese were in *Platoon* (1986). This is clearly not a Rousseauian reference (the Asian "other" as idyllically close to nature) — the enemy is "of nature" to be sure, but in a manner suggestive of the

Fig. 5. The cover of *Liberty Magazine* de-humanizes (or more appropriately, sub-humanizes) the enemy with a variation of the adage of "hear no evil, see no evil, speak no evil," itself modeled after a famous temple carving in

simian reference of the *Liberty* cover. He is simply meant to occupy a lower rung on the evolutionary ladder. When, in *Guadalcanal Diary*, a patrol discovers an enemy encampment only recently abandoned, one American soldier cannot conceal his distaste for the alien look and smell of the "other's" cuisine. His face a mask of disgust, the G.I. sniffs gingerly at what look to be the remnants of a rice cake and some raw fish, foods now much in demand by Western sophisticates.

In *The Purple Heart*, Japanese linguistic characters are described as "chicken scratch"; the enemy's most elemental powers of symbolization are devalued at the same moment that the figure of animality recurs. Low-angle placement of camera and light source reinforces the sense of threat and grotesquerie attached to the Japanese characters throughout *The Purple Heart*, a film based upon the trial and sentencing of eight pilots (led by Colonel James Doolittle) who had been shot down over China following a Tokyo bombing raid in 1942. By the time of the making of the film, it was widely known that three of the American flyers had been executed (October 1934). Dower's discussion of the case in *War Without Mercy* is instructive. The denunciations spurred by the incident were nearly identical on both sides; the acts of the enemy (bombing civilians on the one hand or executing captured combatants on the other) were "barbarous," "uncivilized," "inhuman," "depraved."[17] In Lewis Milestone's film version, the Japanese soldiers and jurists are leering, buck-toothed aggressors who possess no code of justice. In a "detail" of casting both fitting and ironic, none of the "enemy" roles were played by Japanese American actors who, even had they agreed to play the parts, could not have done so. It was they who were the prisoners — in camps not so very far away from the backlots of 20th Century Fox. It is unlikely that American audiences would have known the difference in any case.

Indeed, the inability to distinguish among Asians — betraying a kind of smug indifference recently parodied in Valerie Soe's tape, *All Orientals Look the Same* — came to be a problem when dealing with the Chinese allies during World War II, a problem to which I have alluded earlier in my discussion of Capra's *The Battle of China*. In yet another instance of popular culture's dispatch to war service, cartoonist Milton Caniff contributed his familiar illustrative style to the U.S. Army's *Pocket Guide to China*, a pamphlet for American forces fighting in the Pacific. Using the figure of his fictional character Steve Canyon as the soldier's guide, Caniff provided the pictures that could tell the story.

The task was a challenging one: how to split one stereotype into two. For indeed, Caniff and company were charged with educating the American fighting man to a degree sufficient to distinguish between two racial groups while remaining entirely within the domain of stereotypical speech. Always the connotative meanings of the text had to express praise for the ally while disparaging the enemy. For example, the Chinese are said to be "dull bronze" in color while the Japanese are "more on the lemon-yellow side"; a precious metal is opposed to a bitter fruit.[18] The pamphlet continues: "Look at their profiles and teeth...C usually has evenly set choppers — J has buck teeth...the Chinese smiles easily — the Jap usually expects to be shot." The physical characteristics of the two are typically contrasted through some reference to the

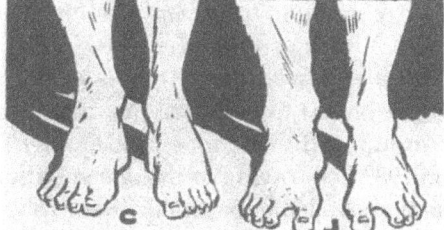

Fig. 6. Steve Canyon.

relative similarity of the Chinese physical type to the Euro-American: "C's eyes are set like any European's or American's — but have a marked *squint*...J has eyes slanted toward his nose." The Chinese "and other Asiatics" have "fairly normal feet" while the Japanese soldiers will usually have a "wide space between the first and second toes" from wearing wooden sandals or *geta*.

The message is clear: the Chinese are more like us, only we never noticed it before. Their eyes and feet are really like ours; they are a cheerful and attractive people with a ready, even-toothed smile. The Japanese are distinctively "othered" by comparison. There is a kind of grotesque confusion in the very placement of their facial features; their eyes slant down to where their noses should be. They have bad teeth, misshapen feet and are paranoid — if paranoia is the appropriate term for what is everywhere reinforced as just reward for being a lesser species.

Such racially-based disparagement as this would, by necessity, apply equally to Japanese people who happened also to be citizens of the United States. Stereotyping tactics such as these that placed the human integrity of an entire race in jeopardy would have as their historical correlative an unapologetic assault upon the rights of many thousands of American citizens and alien residents. It is to the internment camp experience of the 120,000 Japanese Americans of the first- and second-generation — the Issei and Nisei — that we now turn, with particular regard for the active reinvestigation of that history by artists of the Sansei generation.

THE RETURN TO MANZANAR

> *FRAMED*
> *"It was a bum rap. We were FRAMED."*
> *FRAME*
> *FRAME of reference*
> *ReFRAMED*
> — Bruce and Norman Yonemoto, from
> FRAMED, *a video installation*

> *"I don't know where this came from, but I just had this fragment, this picture that's always been in my mind. My mother, she's standing at a faucet and it's really hot outside. And she's filling this canteen and the water's really cold and it feels really good. And outside the sun's just so hot, it's just beating down. And there's this dust that gets in everywhere and they're always sweeping the floors."*
>
> — Rea Tajiri, History and Memory

According to the *Asian American Media Reference Guide*, second edition (1990), a source book of more than 1,000 films and videotapes made by Asian American artists, no fewer than 15 media works have been made since the early 1970s which focus on the topic of the Japanese American relocation camp experience during World War II.[19] The Yonemoto brother's *Framed*, a video installation twice exhibited in 1989 is — owing to the site specific nature of all installation pieces — unlisted and unavailable for rental. These 16 works share a common interest in the radical reexamination of a historical occurrence crucial to the understanding of American stereotyping of the Japanese during World War II. For it is only through consideration of the internment experience — the uprooting and imprisonment of all Japa-

Fig. 7. Americans under the gun — "We are setting a standard for the rest of the world in the treatment of the people who may have loyalties to an enemy nation. We are protecting ourselves without violating the principles of Christian decency." From the narration of *Japanese Relocation*.
(Credit: National Archives)

nese Americans living on the West Coast with inestimable damage done to the health, economic fortunes and self-esteem of two generations of Americans — that we can assess the domestic as well as global effects of wartime racism in the United States.[20]

One element of the incarceration procedure is particularly significant to this discussion. When the Japanese residents reported to the camps, federal officials confiscated cameras as "dangerous contraband," an action that effectively robbed the internees of their most powerful tool for the documentation and potential redefinition of their lives. It was clear that those who committed the Japanese Americans to these desert camps would represent them and their history in ways that would serve the state's best interests rather than any experiential "truth."

According to the government-produced film, *Japanese Relocation*, the internees, in an act of patriotic good faith, are said to have "cooperated wholeheartedly" in their imprisonment. In a scene that echoes the pioneer (and All-American) spirit alluded to in Capra's description of the Chinese people's great westward migration in *The Battle of China*, these thousands of dispossessed Americans are shown being shipped off by truck and train to lands "full of opportunity." There, anonymously bunkered in the desolate locales of 10 states, they are to be given the opportunity to make the desert flower. Milton Eisenhower, brother of the great general, is the spokesperson for the enactment of Executive Order 9066 whose job it is to whitewash wholesale imprisonment on the basis of racial origin. The arrogance and self-serving logic of his explanation is rarely lost on contemporary audiences. The film concludes with the following narration:

"We are setting a standard for the rest of the world in the treatment of people who *may* [my emphasis] have loyalties to an enemy nation. We are protecting ourselves without violating the principles of Christian decency [no mention made of Buddhist decency]. And we won't change this fundamental decency no matter what our enemies do. But of course we hope most earnestly that our example will influence the Axis powers in their treatment of Americans who fall into their hands."

It has frequently been repeated that no act of subversion or espionage was ever proved against a Japanese American during the war years. This is significant given the equation that the above statement makes between Americans of Japanese descent and the wartime enemy. For of course the harm was entirely one-sided. Generations of Americans were, through the internment experience, inculcated with a sense of guilt and shame that proved indelible for many. But if the majority of the Issei and Nisei found personal expiation a difficult task given their culturally reinforced sense of loyalty to authority — governmental or familial — members of the next generation have remained obsessed with the active reinscription of Japanese American history. The media works which they have produced — from oral histories with internees to meditations on memory — move far beyond apologia. Through the aggressive reinvestigation of the past effected in these pieces, history itself becomes the object of investigation. It used to be a commonplace that history was the story of great public deeds and, by extension, of great (white) men — as told by other great (white) men. Recent trends in the field have recognized that the distinction between public and private histories is suspect on intellectual as well as ideological grounds. Women, non-Western peoples, and all those who, by virtue of their race, gender or sexual orientation, have been officially dispossessed of a history have begun to fight back. They have done so by means of the written word as well as by the constructions of sound and image. The seizure of cameras at the relocation camps can now be redefined as a failed attempt on the part of government authorities to rob the interned of any future access to their own past. If the visible evidence is lacking, the intrepid media historiographer can rewrite history through recourse to interview, present-tense footage of past campsites or by the sheer force of creative imagination.

One of the truly trailblazing efforts of this sort is Robert Nakamura's *Manzanar* (1971), a short super-8 film shot by a former internee who, as a UCLA film school student some years later, made a solitary (and aesthetically triumphant) return to the past. It is a viscerally felt meditation on Nakamura's own experience which nonetheless pays homage to two generations of kinsmen. Using a mix of traditional Japanese vocal and instrumental elements as audio accompaniment to the handheld images, Nakamura focuses upon the ravaged landscape and the few remaining markers of what took place there. Little is left to testify other than the discards — broken dishes, pieces of a wall — but what remains visible is rendered all the more poignant. An insect crawls slowly across an inscription of a name carved in stone ("Tom Fujisaki 10/7/43"). That deeply-etched reminder becomes a hieroglyph bearing witness to a past — and to a person — that can never be erased so long as memory and imagination survive. The film's emotional climax occurs in a flurry of music and hand-held images as the filmmaker charges (in a blind rage?) across the desert landscape. It is as though Nakamura's lurching camera is exorcising a past officially buried and mastering it in an act of memorial reconstruction. One feels the unleashing of three decades of anger and frustration through the camera's eye.

In the 1980s, two other Asian American independent filmmakers, Loni Ding and Steven Okazaki, produced significant works on aspects of the wartime Japanese American experience. Ding's *Nisei Soldier: Standard Bearer for an Exiled People* (1984) is a sensitive treatment of the young men who chose to leave the camps to enter military service and in so doing became the most decorated unit in American history. While any film about the storied 442nd Infantry Regiment must tell the tales of struggle and survival endemic to men at war, *Nisei Soldier* is equally intent upon asking anew — and for these hero/internees — "Why We Fight." The ironies are bitter and layered. With the unit's casualties running at 300% over 20 months, there were many gold stars (denoting a fallen son) hanging on concentration camps doors. Was the bravery of these men a sign of super-patriotism at odds with their treatment? They were, after all, segregated and perhaps too frequently assigned the most dangerous missions. Or was their soldiering the sole legitimate outlet for the fury they felt but could never channel to its proper source? Ding provides no answers but instead offers a gentle tribute; she is the chronicler of men who spoke their history only on the battlefield.

Ding's more recent film, *The Color of Honor* (1987) returns to the submerged history of the Japanese American GI, in this case focusing on the duties they performed for the U.S. Military Intelligence. The ironies were compounded for these men who fought the invisible war of Special Services — cracking codes, translating and interrogating the captured Japanese soldiers — while continuing to experience the racial prejudice responsible for their people's mass incarceration at home. But more than that, *Honor* returns to the men themselves. One man's recounting of his return stateside provides a particularly instructive insight into the power of these films to rekindle latent passions. Rudy Tanaka, now partially disabled, tells of the confrontation with his former high school principal, the man responsible for expelling Tanaka and his brother on racial grounds in the days after Pearl Harbor. Finding him before the assembled students, Tanaka demands an apology on the spot or he will "wipe the stage with him, I don't care which." The principal apologizes.

Ding has said that this moment, of all the film's 100 minutes, never fails to inspire the most heated debates during post-screening discussions. Some in the Japanese American audience decry Tanaka's threat as a mere reflection of violence absorbed while others applaud it as a gesture of self-determination of a sort all too lacking in the generation as a whole. Ding, a Chinese American aware of the moral compromise of the "good Chinese" role decreed by wartime policy, remains devoted to a kind of historical excavation of the Japanese American experience through the making of her films. They bring a people and their stories to the attention of millions while continuing to inspire controversy and renewed self-awareness within the Japanese American community.

Steven Okazaki's *Unfinished Business: The Japanese American Internment Cases* (1984) is a product of the militancy of the 1980s, the time during which the battle for reparations for internees reached its peak. Okazaki, who consciously uses the term "concentration camp," takes as his focus three men who resisted Executive Order 9066 and challenged government policy. These were the men who chose the public degradation and imprisonment accorded them as conscientious objectors but who continued to struggle for their dignity. That struggle became, by the 1980s, a legal battle fought in courtrooms across the land. Okazaki celebrates the resolve of 40 years which kept the challenge to the constitutionality of internment alive and the inner strength of those who, in resisting the most popular war of the century, chose prison stripes instead of khaki.

Days of Waiting (1989) is another film about conscious choices. In it, Okazaki mines yet another source of historical irony through the life story of a white woman who chose to share the wartime incarceration of her Japanese American husband and there in the camps discovered for the first time a sense of social identity. As told by the filmmaker, Estelle Ishigo was a kind of artistic waif of *fin de siecle* San Francisco who found her romantic match in Arthur Ichigo. After more than a decade of marriage, Ishigo was fired from her art school teaching job on the basis of her interracial marriage. She was soon sharing the indignities and small triumphs of the more than 12,000 internees confined to a single square mile of land near Heart Mountain, Wyoming.

The strength of the film lies in the way in which the figure of Estelle Ishigo subverts the expected categorizations of insider and outsider that so animated the period. Ishigo's experience proves that race can be a matter of choice as well as birth, that race can be functionally determined through conscious alliances and identifications. If the Caucasian American can begin to see the drama of internment from Ishigo's hybrid position, new sources of empathy may be tapped. And stereotype can thus be deposed.

It is this overturning of the dynamic of the stereotype that binds together these works and establishes their pertinence to this discussion. If we look and listen, the racially-grounded generalizations which dictated public policy become untenable. For these films give the lie to the top-down, government-sanctioned pronouncements which were the unchallenged public images of an era. Japanese Americans are accorded the complexity and variability unavailable to them during the 1940s through the appropriation of the means of reproduction by a group of Asian American independent artists. And this means of reproduction amounts to a franchise on history and its active re-writing.

Fig. 8. *History and Memory*.
(Credit: Rea Tajiri)

I have saved to the end of my discussion the most recent

and perhaps most ambitious of these works. In a manner reminiscent of Robert Nakamura's *Manzanar*, Rea Tajiri's *History and Memory* mixes historical reinscription with autobiography, but with a far more complex weave of image sources and temporalities. Tajiri's address to memory is also a kind of gift; the tape attempts to supply images of her mother's life in the Poston, Arizona relocation camp. And yet, though the mother's recollection of the camps is uneven, it is the artist herself who

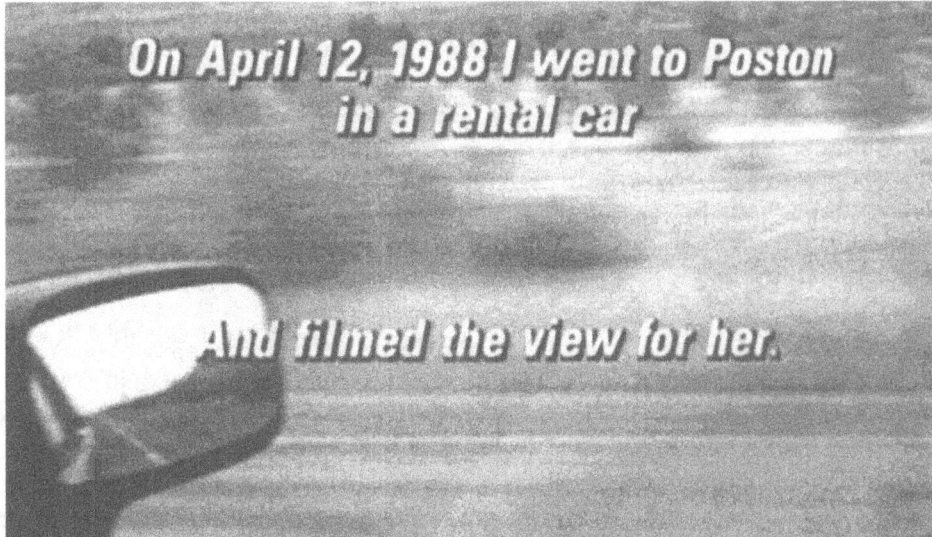

Fig. 9 & 10. *History and Memory*.
(Credit: Rea Tajiri)

most requires the act of visual reconstruction. She narrates her desire very near the tape's beginning:

> "I don't know where this came from, but I just had this fragment, this picture that's always been in my mind. My mother, she's filling this canteen and the water's really cold and it feels really good. And outside the sun's just so hot, it's just beating down. And there's this dust that gets in everywhere and they're always sweeping the floors."

Like a child of a Holocaust survivor, Tajiri is obsessed with the pain suffered by family members before her birth, manifest in her case by "the search for an ever-absent image." This is a particularly telling image for its overlay of water, life-giving and beneficent, and the recurring historical motif of resentment at the successes of the Japanese American small farmer. For indeed these farmers "brought water to the land and made things grow" — according to stereotype but in affirmation of life. And now, in 1991, Tajiri searches for a memory which is personal, familial and cultural all at once.

> "I remember having this feeling growing up that I was haunted by something, that I was living within a family full of ghosts. There was this place that they knew about. I had never been there, yet I had a memory for it. I could remember a time of great sadness before I was born."

The tone of the tape is confessional in its plumbing of the depths of obsession, testimonial in its expression of the emotional linkage of mother and daughter. Tajiri claims in a crawl that accompanies spoken narration (there are frequently multiple channels of information which compete for our attention) that she was able to intuit the exact location of her mother's barracks when visiting the Poston campsite.

In a strategy of disjunctive layering of image sources, anecdotes or historical markers that recurs throughout, the theme of obsession with identity is played out in a comic vein through the story of Tajiri's sister. She collects pictures of movie stars or cute boys she follows in the park. Most of them are white. The artist's preoccupations, on the other hand, are historically rooted: "There are things that have happened in the world while there were cameras watching, things we have image for." She sets out to transform memory into history and thus depose from hegemonic power the false histories of imagemakers from Hollywood or Washington. Examples of both types of the latter abound, from wartime propaganda tracts such as *Japanese Relocation* or *December 7th* to the glossier but still potent fictions — *Bad Day at Black Rock* (1954), *From Here to Eternity* (1954) or *Come See the Paradise* (1990).

We know through Nietzsche of "creative forgetfulness," the removal from consciousness of that which denies rather than affirms life. And yet, like a time-traveller in a Chris Marker film, Tajiri wishes to retrieve an image of particular intensity from her mother's past: her hands filling a canteen with cold water in the middle of the desert. Of course that retrieval is, more than anything, a gift the artist gives to herself and her generation. For the tape culminates in a victory which is shared by all the Asian American independent artists through whom the stereotypes — rarefied, abstract, and dehumanized — have been supplanted by the sounds and images of experience, memory, counterhistory. Tajiri concludes: "But now I found I could connect the picture to the story. I could forgive my mother her loss of memory and could make this image for her."

The tape's resolution signals more than personal achievement. It sounds but the most recent note in a rich chorus of contemporary voices engaged in a political act combining creative imagination and the will to document. History has been rewritten.

MEDIA ACTIVISM AS COUNTER-STEREOTYPE

> "Between American TV and the American print media, the war has been presented as if it was a finely engineered piece of art or a high-tech tea party. American troops were uniformly professional, courteous and kind, even toward captured Iraqi weaklings. And anyone who was wounded or died just vanished."
> — Carol Squiers, "Screening the War: Filmmakers & Critics on the Images that Made History"

> "The point is to encourage people to take control of their own lives, their own images, to begin representing their own struggles without a high degree of technical expertise, to become speaking subjects, makers of meaning, active participants instead of passive consumers."
> — Sherry Millner, "All That Glitters..."

Up until the moment that the bombs began to fall on Iraq and the Gulf War began in earnest (mid-January 1991), American mass media coverage of the debates surrounding proposed military intervention in the Middle East presented the image of a nation divided. Within hours of the first air attacks, a veil of self-censorship began to descend upon the land so that few who tuned into CNN's non-stop coverage might have guessed that organized acts of resistance to the war continued unabated and in some cases intensified. As Carol Squiers observed, the American news media were transformed into cheerleaders and propagandists: "What happened was a war; what we saw was military promotion. Few in the United States seem to notice a distinction."[21]

There were those who did notice. And some of them, banding together to form the Gulf Crisis TV Project, acted upon their political analysis, producing a series of 30-minute programs that focused upon a range of issues related to the war. In the expose style of another, earlier cultural manifestation — the guerrilla television movement of the early 1970s — these programs provided extensive documentation of anti-war activities as well as political analysis of the motives and methods of government planners. Two decades earlier, collectives such as the Ant Farm, Global Village, Videofreex and Top Value Television had begun to show Americans electronic versions of themselves never before seen on the *CBS Evening News*. TVTV's *Four More Years* (1972) provided unique coverage of the 1972 Republican National Convention, spending more time with the anti-war protesters in the streets and the news gatherers on the floor of the convention center — themselves media celebrities such as Walter Cronkite, Dan Rather and Mike Wallace — than with the party chieftains or their chosen candidates (Nixon-Agnew).

The Gulf Crisis TV Project's immediate predecessors were Paper Tiger TV and Deep Dish TV Network, both products of the 1980s. Originally formed in New York in 1981 as a cable TV-based platform for media criticism, Paper Tiger has created more than 200 half-hour programs devoted to countering the prevailing mythologies of American popular culture in a cheaply-produced, no-holds-barred format. From attacks on tabloid journalism and TV soap operas *(Joan Does Dynasty)* to diatribes against American TV news *(Brian Winston Reads the TV News)*, Paper Tiger has provided scholars, artists and political activists with the opportunity to share television space with Ted Turner or Arsenio Hall. The Deep Dish TV Network simply expanded on the Paper Tiger insight by renting satellite time and beaming their programs to hundreds of downlinks across America.

With the Gulf Crisis TV Project, media activists took on a very concrete challenge to produce a political counterdiscourse on the same tight schedule as the "big boys." It took 30 years for Japanese American artists to recreate their histories; those dying beneath a hail of missiles could not afford the wait. More than 300 public-access cable stations across the country took the "feed" from the Project; 30 PBS stations broadcast the series, often with multiple repeats. It is estimated to have reached 40% of the total audience for public broadcasting (itself an admittedly small slice of the TV pie). Canada's Vision, TV Channel Four in the U.K., SPC Australian TV and national television in Dubai all broadcast the Gulf Crisis programs. It is necessary to say that, despite these broadcasts, the war was still fought, thousands still died. But every program that casts doubt upon the wisdom of this and every war, every expose of ignorance or complacency, affects the fragile balance of support for the deployment of billion-dollar missiles and the endangerment of human lives.

I won't have much to say about the programs themselves, although the episode entitled *Manufacturing the Enemy* made clear that the racism against Arab Americans in the 1990s had its regrettable antecedents in the Japanese American internment camps 50 years before. It is my contention that the most important thing about the Gulf Crisis TV Project is the fact of its existence. In the media-charged global environment we now share, alternative voices and visions are our best insurance for survival. And the price of that insurance is the creation and support of media groups devoted to the critique and thorough-going inquiry of public policy. This means that no national television culture can afford to exist solely for profit or state-guided education. If we accept Louis Althusser's notion that any cultural or educational institution functions within late capitalism as a kind of "ideological state apparatus," we might then say that a minimum of television channel time and space must be systematically devoted to programming which functions with a degree of autonomy — outside of if not entirely beyond the sway of state control. Such an initiative can never of course be mandated from above; it requires the collaborative efforts of independent makers. But these artists and cultural workers cannot hope to succeed in the tedious, frequently unrewarding task of networking and downscale production without a degree of public support.

And therein lies the internal contradiction. Alternative visions and social critiques can maintain their integrity only if they are allowed to exist apart, but no capital-intensive operation such as television production can survive without access to the tools or the airwaves. The initiative which will allow alternative media to flourish in market-driven economies from the U.S. to Europe, Asia and Africa must begin with public awareness. For the establishment and safeguarding of a culture of dissent in any nation is the surest hedge against the violation of human dignity or the wholesale condemnation of a people on the basis of race or class or gender. Fifty years have been required to begin the healing of hatreds that raged across the Pacific, binding American and Japanese alike in a corrosive dynamic of racial stereotype. Atonement for all the deaths and all the liberties lost begins by guarding against any future reenactments. Alternative cultural vehicles might have allowed the thousands of Japanese Americans interned to speak rather than be spoken for; certainly, more cross-cultural trafficking in the days before the war would have narrowed the gulf that separated the Issei and Nisei from their neighbors.

What I am calling for is nothing less than the systematic implementation of *counter-stereotyping*, the un-fixing of images, the embrace of rather than recoiling from difference. Although we indeed stereotype as a means to confirm our control of the world, we need not do so in a pathological manner, unable to differentiate in any meaningful way among the men and women who share our planet. We need not spend another 50 years recovering from the next onslaught of "warring images."

My thanks to Loni Ding, Linda Mabalot, Steven Okazaki, Rea Tajiri and Bruce Yonemoto for access to and discussion of their work.

NOTES

1. I am grateful to Gregory Waller for his useful study of American film treatments of the Japanese in the period between 1909 and 1915. While there has been extensive scholarship on works of popular fiction such as Homer Lea's *The Valor of Ignorance* (1909) — which predicted the successful invasion of the U.S. west coast by the Japanese and was reprinted in 1942 as a prophetic work — far less is known about the more than 100 films from 40 different companies which conditioned American response to Japan and the Japanese during this period. [Gregory A. Waller, "Historicizing, a Test Cast: Japan on American Screens, 1909-1915," an unpublished paper delivered at the Society for Cinema Studies conference, Los Angeles, CA May 1991.]
2. John W. Dower, *War Without Mercy: Race & Power in the Pacific War* (New York: Pantheon Books, 1986), 308. In fairness, it should be noted that Dower amply historicizes the shifting stereotypes of Japanese and Americans during and after the war, noting "the malleable and double-faceted nature of the dominant wartime stereotypes." (308) The antecedents and points of reference to which Dower turns for explanation of the radically shifting stereotype — e.g., the demonic outsider of Japanese folk culture — are surely useful historical markers. There is no effort made, however, to locate the dynamic of stereotyping at the level of psychic operations, another crucial dimension for historical understanding.
3. Gilman describes the long term social utility of his analytic endeavor in this way: "The need for stereotypes runs so deep that I do not think it will ever be thwarted; nor do I think that it will ever be converted to purely harmless expression. But I believe that education and study can expose the ideologies with which we structure our world, and perhaps help put us in the habit of self-reflection." [Sander L. Gilman, *Difference and Pathology: Stereotypes of Sexuality, Race and Madness* (Ithaca: Cornell University Press, 1985), 12.]
4. Gilman, 12.
5. Homi K. Bhabha, "The Other Question — the Stereotype and Colonial Discourse," *Screen* XXIV/6 (November-December 1983): 27.
6. Bhabha, 33.
7. For a clear but extended account of the psychic origins of the stereotype, see Gilman's introductory essay in *Difference and Pathology*: "Introduction: What Are Stereotypes and Why Use Texts to Study Them?," 15-35.
8. I have pursued the logic of the idealized "other" in my "Imaging the Other: Representations of Vietnam in Sixties Political Documentary" in *From Hanoi to Hollywood*, Linda Dittmar and Gene Machaud, ed. (New Brunswick, NJ: Rutgers University Press, 1990), 255-268.
9. Gilman, 18.
10. Dower, 10.
11. Gilman, 18.

12. John Morton Blum, *V Was For Victory: Politics and American Culture During World War II* (New York: Harcourt Brace Jovanovich, 1976), 159.
13. Frank Capra, *The Name Above the Title* (New York: The Macmillan Company, 1971), 328-329.
14. For more discussion on the range and effects of the filmmaker's creative choices, see my "Re-Thinking Documentary: Toward a Taxonomy of Mediation," *Wide Angle* VIII/3 & 4 (1986): 71-77.
15. See my "Towards a Documentary Poetics" in *Documentary Film: Essays Critical and Theoretical*, Michael Renov, ed. (New York: Routledge), 1993.
16. I undertake a similar analysis of the racist depiction of the Japanese enemy during World War II, this time as the historical context for representations of the Vietnamese two decades later, in "Imaging the Other: Representations of Vietnam in Sixties Political Documentary."
17. Dower, 49.
18. This description is taken from a *Life* story on Caniff's wartime contribution, "Speaking of Pictures," *Life* (1 March 1943): 12.
19. Copies of this media reference guide can be obtained from Asian CineVision at 32 East Broadway, New York, NY 10002; phone number (212) 925-8685; FAX (212) 925-8157.
20. It was not until 1988 that the U.S. Congress conceded to the award of financial compensation or the offering of an official apology to those who lost their liberty behind barbed wire.
21. Carol Squiers, "Screening the War: Filmmakers & Critics on the Images that Made History," *International Documentary: The Journal of Non-Fiction Film and Video 8* (Spring 1991): 21.

FILMOGRAPHY: A LISTING OF WORKS ON THE INTERNMENT CAMP EXPERIENCE BY ASIAN AMERICAN INDEPENDENT ARTISTS

Bitter Memory: America's Concentration Camps, The. Video, 30 min., b&w. Source: Chinese for Affirmative Action.

Color of Honor, The. Loni Ding, 1987, 16mm, 100 min., color. Source: Vox Productions.

Concentrated Americans. Michael Yoshida and Jenni Morozumi, documentary audiocassette, 30 min. Source: CrossCurrent Media.

Conversations: Before the War/After the War. Karen Ishizuka and Robert Nakamura, 1986, 16mm, 30 min., b&w. Source: Generation Films.

Days of Waiting. Steven Okazaki, 1989, 16mm, 28 min., color. Source: Mouchette Films.

Emi. Michael Toshiyuki Uno, 1978, 16mm, 28 min., color. Source: GPN.

Family Gathering. Lise Yasui and Ann Tegnell, 16mm, color. Source: Lise Yasui.

Framed. Bruce and Norman Yonemoto, video installation, 1989.

History and Memory. Rea Tajiri, 1991, video, color. Source: Video Data Bank.

Invisible Citizens: Japanese Americans. Keiko Tsuno, 1983, video, 58 min., color. Source: Downtown Community Television.

Japanese Americans in Concentration Camps (Boston). Asian American Resource Workshop, 1981, video, 360 min., color. Source Asian American Resource Workshop.

Japanese Americans in Concentration Camps (Los Angeles). Visual Communications, 1981, video, 120 min., color. Source: Visual Communications.

Manzanar. Robert Nakamura, 1971, 16mm, color. Source: Visual Communications.

Nisei Soldier: Standard Bearer for an Exiled People. Loni Ding, 1984, 16mm, 30 min., color. Source: Vox Productions.

Perceptions: Japanese American Redress. Sandra Yep, 1982, video, 25 min., color. Source: Sandra Yep.

Unfinished Business. Steven Okazaki, 1984, 16mm, 60 min., color. Source: Mouchette Films.

PART IV
VIOLENT IMAGES AND THEIR VARIOUS PLEASURES

Cinema/Nihilism/Freedom

Nibuya Takashi

> "The man with a good memory does not remember anything because he does not forget anything."
>
> —*Samuel Beckett*, Proust

Cinema, or the image as a medium of film and video, is generally, essentially "immoral." Therefore, no matter the kind of film, those who watch them and those who make them must be required to bear that essential "immorality" of the movies. Or they have to be required to *enjoy and endure* it, although it sounds the same.

The "immorality" of movies ··· For example, we know that we can *enjoy* moving images no matter how impending and cruel they may be (There are various phases in pleasure; in the case of moving images, sympathy, fear and the like may be enjoyable, even intoxicating ···). As a matter of fact, everybody knows that documentary videos about the victims of wars, accidents and crimes are the least-known, longest-selling items at video shops. Or, there must be quite a few people who went through the intoxicating experience of the "beauty" of the nighttime image of Baghdad under air-attack at the beginning of the so-called "Gulf War." Surely, we can sense something indecent about these immoralities in front of images, and it is not comfortable to imagine the intoxicating viewing of videos of people dying. But it is useless to criticize or denounce such attitudes on account of moral senselessness, decadence, or indecent abnormality. Rather, we must begin by looking directly at that immorality included in movies and video images, and consider it their essence.

The immorality *essentially* included in movies or video images ··· Should we consider it, we first must recognize the qualitative differences between film images and video images. Because those qualitative differences must be surface in each image's immorality, as well.

First, let us begin with video images, for their immorality probably has a more simple structure than that of cinema.

Everyone knows that filmic images (*firumueizō*) have no so-to-speak "present tense." Between shooting and screening, however, there exist several technical *odd jobs* such as development and the like, so when we look at the images the actual "incidents" have already gone and disappeared. Filmic images are essentially anachronic and are able to possess only "past tense" (Here we may face more complex questions, but for the time being, let's pass them by). On the other hand, what about video images? It could be said that when the function of recording becomes a reality, situations come to resemble the images of film. Incidents which have passed will be repeated over and over again as images · · · . But it needs to be recognized that the essence upon which video technology is primarily based is the *simultaneousness* between those who watch and that which is watched. "Live coverage," the broadcasting of incidents in real-time, determines the qualitative character of video images.

Since the early stages of television broadcasting, the video image's greatest strength was its ability to report incidents occurring in remote places in real time, simultaneously, particularly since the establishment of live, world-wide coverage with the symbolic and sensational worldwide *simultaneous* broadcasting of the "major incident" of President Kennedy's assassination. That is to say, video images are essentially "present tense"-like, and they are different from filmic images in this regard. Since the establishment of recording functions, video images also possessed "past tense," but that *past character* is qualitatively different from filmic images. "Past" is the essence of filmic images; it is only *accompanying* for video images. For example, with any news image, if there is no indication that "this was previously recorded," it is difficult to tell present tense from past tense only from the image. In other words, the past tense of a video image is the *result of repeating a real-time image*, and does not belong to the essence of that image. The essences of video images are simultaneousness and present tense.

Needless to say, because of this actuality, video images become much more powerful reporting apparatuses than film images. In the case of the Gulf War, or the recent confusion of the Soviet Federations, the power of real-time reporting has been confirmed. Video images *directly* connect those who watch and that which is watched through their simultaneousness. · · · Here we also find the "immorality" included in video images.

The essences of video images are present tense and simultaneousness between those who watch and that which is watched. To repeat again, these situations do not change with the repeated broadcasting of past incidents; those images are different from film images and always are repeated and *re*-broadcast as "present." Video images are simultaneous · · · In other words, by drawing on a metaphor, it could be said that video images bring forth between those who watch and that which is watched what resembles the relationship between passengers of moving trains and the spectacle beyond the windows. Passengers of trains look through the glass of windows, and television audiences look through the glass of Braun tubes, both watch "external incidents" which are happening simultaneously with their own time. · · · Yet here the relationship of irresponsibility inevitably surfaces. For example, let's imagine a single murder is happening beyond the windows of the passing train. Passengers become real-time witnesses. However, they instantly move to another real-time incident = spectacle along with the moving train, and the ongoing incident also retreats. "What became of that later?" is the only thing those who watch video images can say, and summarizes the relationship between the external incidents and the spectators. Video images *directly* connect those who watch and that which is watched, making them meet due to their simultaneousness. But this directness essentially lacks a responsible relationship. Excited by baseball coverage, excited by war coverage, excited by the eruption of a volcano, excited by coverage of a coup d'état ··· "What became of that later?" ··· And among these series of thrills, among thrills of perhaps each a different nature, there exists one common character, namely, irresponsibility. Of course, according to the position of those who watch, this irresponsibility has various levels. For those who have relatives at the "scenes" of the war, the coup d'état, the eruption of the volcano, it will become a sense of powerlessness at being separated by glass. In any case, the simultaneousness of incidents *and* the sense of irresponsibility/powerlessness at being separated by glass ··· There can be no doubt that these secretly characterize video images.

Directness *and* irresponsibility filling video images ··· These constitute the basis of "immorality" in video. Simultaneous events directly thrill audiences ··· However, audiences know they will not be engulfed in that "reality," for that "reality" is decidedly unreal, a hyper-reality if you will. At any rate, there exists an "immorality" essentially included in video images. We who watch video images are disturbed by those spectacles, but are *allowed* to irresponsibly "enjoy" them while suspending our relationship with them, like passengers in passing trains.

Then what about the "immorality" in the filmic image? At least, according to the "theory of evolution" the filmic image is a more primitive apparatus than the video image. However, what filmic images draw is more complex than what video images do. The irresponsibility which separates lens and film — this is different from that of video. As mentioned above, the filmic image is essentially anachronic and time differences exist between incidents occurring in front of the lens and the audiences who watch them. When they are watched, regardless of whether they occurred several decades ago or only the other day, incidents are regarded as past things or vanished things. They can be only watched in past tense, as *happened*. Therefore, rather than being irresponsible, spectators watch incidents in a situation where they cannot bear responsibility. How can we take responsibility for incidents which are already over? If we can talk about the irresponsibility in filmic images, this is all that can be said. That is to say, we cannot take responsibility before the fact.

"Immorality" in filmic images ··· If we speak prematurely, it will be a kind of "emptiness" included in filmic image or exists in the "nihilism" of the filmic image. However, these are too vague. We must make a detour for a short while.

The filmic image essentially pregnant with "emptiness" ··· In a sense, this is simple. The filmic image has only past tense. Those who appear, the happenings, the spectacles, are expressed only as "what has already gone." It might be said that the situation is the same in the case of video images in terms of function. However, let me repeat that the video image's essence is its "present tense." It is seen as something already gone, which is not an inevitable situation based on that image's nature but only an accompanying result. Or it could be called "already gone" in the same sense as our immediate present, but there can be no mistake that the essential

Fig. 1 & 2. *"Here exist paradoxes of weird time and twisted tense"*— A soldier who sacrificed his life carried these photographs to the war to remind him of his village and his family (both alive and dead); an American brought them home as a memento of the war in which he risked his life; we look at them to...

"already gone" occurring in filmic images is different in nature. (Perhaps, at this point this explanation sounds too sophistical).

To repeat again, the filmic image has only "past tense" and "that which happened in the past" is included in its essence. Those people, accidents, spectacles, which are filmed, developed and screened, appear only as "what has disappeared" or "what has gone." In this sense, the filmic image has always attached to it a faint "smell of death." Film says "this man has vanished" or "*this* world has vanished." This is to say, "reality" always appears late and with that delay, that "reality" is always slightly rancid. That "reality" is always already anachronic, "out-of-date." The world and all those people shot by film will always appear as something always already slightly "dead" and "deceased." In other words, here an "emptiness of death" is *essentially* included. What is shot on film is just slightly "dead" ··· Conversely, it could be said that filmmakers slightly resemble "murderers." I am not sure to what degree the legend that savages are fearful of cameras because "they will steal their life-spirit" is true. But even if it is true, we cannot laugh at such naive fears. Of course, one's life-spirit cannot be sucked out by film. But at least, on film, on the developed print, we are actually slightly "dead." Or we are slightly "killed" by photographers.

··· The filmic image is anachronic and includes the "emptiness of death." The "reality" reflected in it always already emits a slight rancidness, that is, appears only as something that has always already "retreated into emptiness." In a sense, it could be said that this anachronism and "emptiness" constitute the mysterious dazzle of filmic images, for here exist paradoxes of weird time and twisted tense. When the filmic image is screened, "what has already gone" *appears* there. What has gone appears *here and now* ··· Or it would be good to remember the paradox of a heavenly body. As you know well, the stars we watch, even the closest moon, are

Fig. 3. A photograph of the photographer's own death during a kamikaze attack.
(Credit: National Archives)

not simultaneous with us. Depending on their arrival at the speed of light, they are delayed appearances; we regard the moon's appearances of a few minutes past as the immediately *present* one, but time *differences* of several light years or tens of thousands of light years become astoundingly huge. A heavenly body is absolutely anachronic. There are stars with various time differences ranging from a few minutes to hundreds of thousand years, and due to such differences the form of stars "which have already gone" appear before us as what can now be seen. Something in film resembles the dazzle of anachronic heavenly bodies. (Thus, calling movie actors "stars" is strangely accurate.) And, therefore, filmic images must include the somewhat perverse fragrance of a *vice*-like necrophilia.

In any case, filmic images essentially include an "emptiness" resulting from the anachronism technologically and essentially contained in them.

"Nihilism" of the filmic image · · · Precisely speaking, this is not a quality belonging purely to the filmic image. It is similarly included in the video image, but it can be said that it is unavoidably exposed in the filmic image. Because video equipment fixes images by way of electrical signs resembling the optic nerves of humans, the video image can be *personified* with relative ease, but it will be difficult in the case of the filmic image which quite differently fixes the image by way of chemical reactions. In other words, in spite of its complex mechanism, the video image is always personified as "somebody's look" or it can be humanized; but in the case of the filmic image, in spite of its simplicity or because of its simplicity, its mechanics, its chemical aspects, its optics are prominent, and personification is difficult. That is to say, the look of filmic image is always "nobody's look" rather than "somebody's look" so it always includes an *inhuman* touch.

Nihilism · · · This is neither an ideological situation nor a metaphysical situation for filmic images; it is included as a simple attribute. That is to say, if nihilism means that there are no values, no meanings, no concerns and no passions, these are nothing more than simple attributes of mechanical/optical/chemical equipment, like camera and film, which bring the filmic image into existence. The filmic image simply sensitizes and records what is shot by the camera. Regardless of the object, corpses, flowers, cats, accidents, the camera itself shoots everything indiscriminately, in the same manner, *equal* in every way. In other words, it indiscriminately records everything as if interchangeable with anything. The camera itself does not make selections. On sensitizers (*kankōzai*), it indifferently, unemotionally, indiscriminately, meaninglessly fixes whole shadows of things which passed through the lens · · · In this way, what can be called absolute nihilism devoid of ideology is included in the essence of the filmic image.

· · · And here occurs a kind of conflict among cameraman, director, and editor. This is because they must change the "nobody's look" of camera/film *(kamera — firumu)* into "somebody's point-of-view," controlling and dominating it in particular concerns, directions of meaning, and "narrative" selections. But it cannot be completely successful. To repeat again, indifference, indiscriminateness · · · Namely nihilism, is an essential attribute of camera and film, and it is impossible to wipe it out perfectly. Therefore, *camera/film* nihilism always invades the filmic image. For example, when a battlefield and piles of dead bodies are filmed, cameraman and editor try to give it a signification of misery, passion, fear, emptiness of the battlefield, all in accordance to particular themes. But at the same time, the essential indifference of camera/film is also expressed. Between disturbed cameraman and the fear of the turbulent battlefield, camera/film continues operating mechanically, and its *inhuman* indifference (or it may be thought of as objectivity · · ·) is recorded in the basis of the image without being wiped off. This *inhuman* indifference of the filmic image may be hidden or complemented by inserting music, voice-over narration, or editing, but cannot itself be removed. That indifference or meaninglessness continues operating outside the thickness of "meaning" which voice-over narration, editing, mise-en-scene try to formulate, and secretly continues to demolish that thickness of "meaning."

A certain "emptiness" and "nihilism," these are included as essences in the filmic image. If the video image includes the "immorality" of irresponsibility in simultaneity, and film the "immorality" of "perversion and indifference," then "vice" must also be included. "Perversion"— because the filmic image, which is concerned with "reality" only in a way that "everything has been lost," always includes the perversity of a game with "death," and camera/film's nihilism includes a perverse game with "meaninglessness." Then, the absolute indifference regarding incidents and objects, the violent "zero-degree" of an indifference that can never be personified, these are always included in its basis (The reason why one of the documentary films about the atomic bomb on Hiroshima, filmed by a medical group, is prohibited

Fig. 4. A woman from Hiroshima exposes her wounds for the Strategic Bombing Survey. (Credit: Daniel McGovern Collection)

Fig. 5. (Credit: National Archives)

from general showing by the Ministry of Education may be found here; it is because in this film, which was earnestly made as a medical report, the absolute indifference of camera/film is violently exposed, nullifying the good will or passions of the photographers).

Simultaneousness and irresponsibility in the video image; "past tense" and indifference/meaninglessness in the filmic image. To repeat again, these are essential attributes of each apparatus and it is impossible to wipe them off. Therefore, it is also impossible to wipe off the *hidden* immorality originating in them. Despite any appeal to morality, there is no denying being intoxicated by the "beauty" of night air raids; there is no wiping off of the abnormality which plays with indifference, either. To repeat once again, this is a part of the attributes essentially included in those images. Therefore, our "duty" is not to wipe off, nullify, or hide them (hiding is only a hypocrisy) but to take part in that "immorality" *actively*. Needless to say, to actively take part does not mean to treat them negatively, either. Those are given conditions, and to negate them is only a irresponsible gesture. Irresponsibility, emptiness, nihilism, indifference, abnormality ··· to stand them, to endure them *while enjoying* them, only this attitude can mean accepting them actively.

The meaninglessness, indiscriminateness, indifference of camera/film ··· That is to say, to take part in "nihilism" actively. In the case of movies, this is not an ideological or metaphysical question at all. Simply put, it is the same as taking part in camera/film actively. To repeat again, "nihilism" is an attribute of camera/film. Although the same thing can be said about the video image, this question becomes unavoidable in movies due to their primitiveness as an apparatus. It is valuable to remember the simple fact that for a long time movie film was only available in the *inhuman* black-and-white image. That is, in the case of the movies, the look of

Fig. 6.
(Credit: National Archives)

camera/film continued being exposed in the surface of images as a different look which could not be personified, as a different eye which could not be reduced to the cameraman's eye, nor audiences' eye, nor as a "third eye" unable to be concealed.

Based on a theory that dogs perceive the world in black-and-white, there were people who claimed that the eye of cinema was a dog's eye. In any case, the look of movies is different from that of video images, as the latter has, from early stages, been devoted to imitating the human look in terms of simultaneousness and directness. From the very beginning, due to its anachronism, black-and-white imagery and its roughness of motion at 24 frames per second (18 fps at an earlier stage), the look of movies took active part in a different look, one which could not be reduced to a human look. In other words, a positive concern with the look of camera/film arose, a concern with camera/film's "nihilism" as a characteristic and a question.

Movies are different from the video images which try to imitate the human eye, and their inhuman and different look was one of their features from the beginning. So, when the Lumiére Brothers set up the first public screening, it is not strange that that screening was an enthusiastic success, even though the film was only showing workers entering into or going out of a factory from a fixed camera. People must have gone, not to see "interesting stories" as they do now, but to view the world seen through eyes other than human, a kind of "eternal recurrence" of the world viewed by the look of camera/film's "nihilism" (I wonder if the Lumiére Brothers knew about Nietzsche? ···).

During the classical period of the movies, that is from the 1920s to the 1940s which parallels the rapid technological innovations of camera/film, it can be said that the experiments of the movies actively took part in the look's different character, namely "nihilism."

For example, camera/film's nihilistic features such as indiscriminateness, indifference (objectivity), meaninglessness, utter lack of emotion, would be accepted as a "revolutionary look" in the Soviet Union, and go through remarkable development with the enthusiasm of revolution. For the indiscriminateness, indifference, meaninglessness of camera/film would have embodied the *materialistic* look that would destroy selectiveness, subjectivity and the meaningfulness of the bourgeois or petit-bourgeois worlds. Camera/film would provide an adequate look for the revolution of the proletariat/working class, and become the look embodying absolute equality of proletariat dictatorship where class selection, class meanings, class subjectivity would evaporate. For example, the work of Dziga Vertov, who established the methodology of the documentary ··· .

Still, however, the candid exposure of camera/film's rawness includes dangers, even for the look of the proletariat dictatorship. If that "nihilism" was applied unrestrictedly, there was a danger of destroying even proletariat community within that meaninglessness. Therefore, it would be necessary to invent a way of managing and controlling the unrestrictive character of camera-filmic nihilism. For example, the so-called "montage" technique of Sergei Eisenstein was invented, a technique polished to an almost *philosophical* level. In a sense, to scoop up the

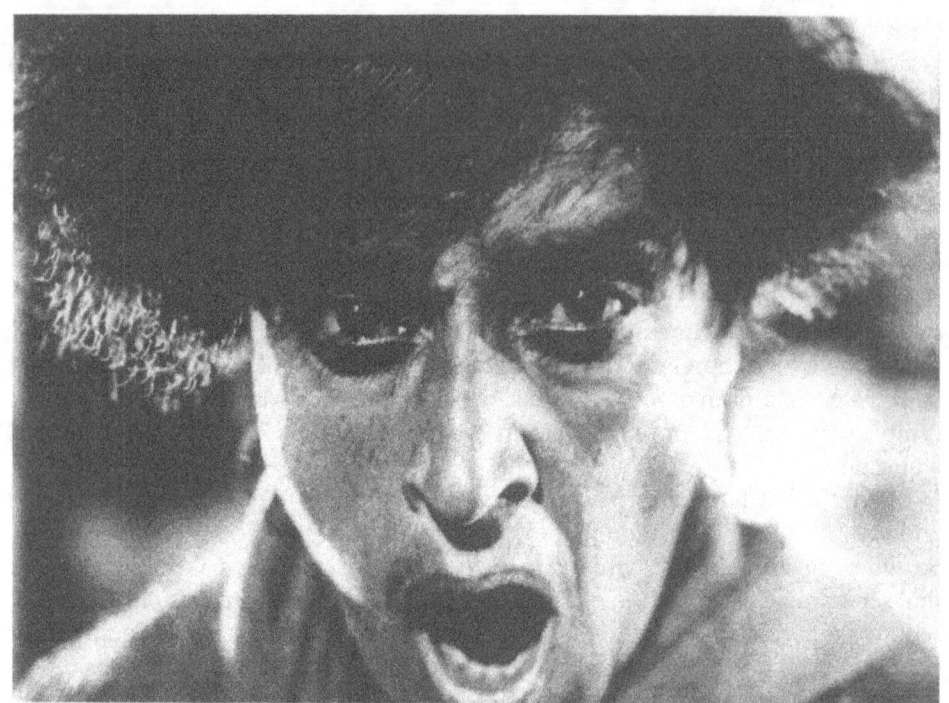

Fig. 7 & 8. *Battleship Potemkin*.
(Credit: Japan Film Library Council)

Cinema/Nihilism/Freedom 131

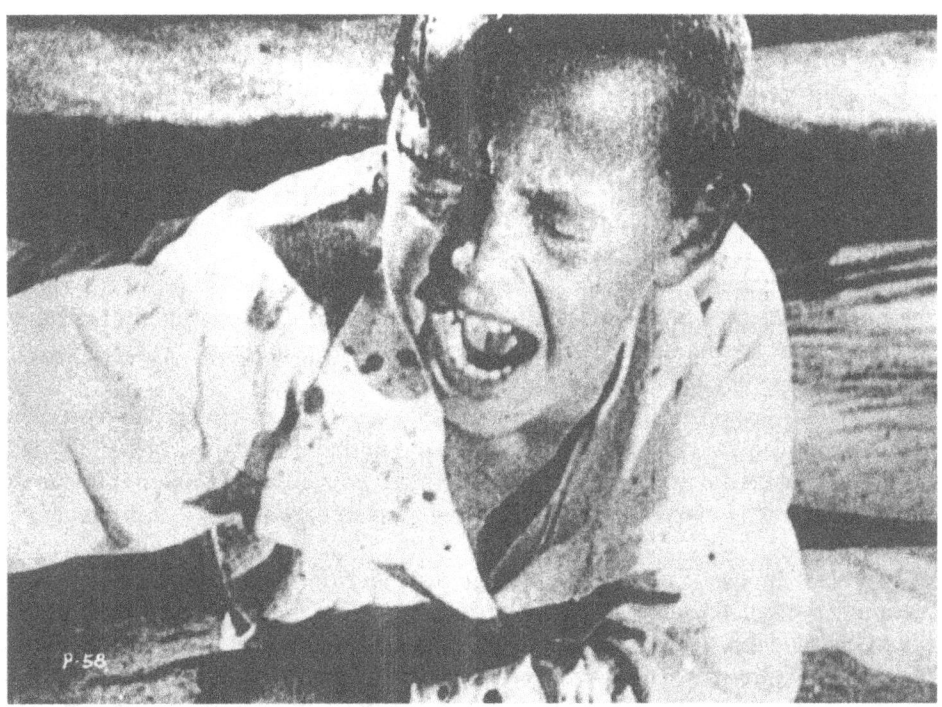

Fig. 9 & 10. *Battleship Potemkin*.
(Credit: Japan Film Library Council)

materialistic level, which is composed of the meaninglessness and indiscriminateness opened by camera/film, from the descending nihilism, and to polish it into a materialistic dialectical world figure — it can be said that this was an experiment of Eisenstein's montage.

Contemporaneously, for example, in America Griffith invented his own techniques of montage, or a little later in France, Robert Bresson also invented his peculiar montage. Although they are respectively heterogeneous, what is common among them is that they seek to introduce techniques to "manage" the nature of camera/film, namely "nihilism," *while actively taking part in it*. Or, in the sense that the ontological meaninglessness and the meaning of existence in the world of nihilism were questioned, it may be said that a certain "ontological" trial was sought (I wonder if Heidegger ever saw movies?).

In any case, from primitive cinema to the classical period, "cinema" accepted the "nihilism" of camera/film wholeheartedly. And *in* that acceptance, "image *in* camera/film," "meaning in camera/film," in other words, a method of "image in nihilism" or a way of existence for "meaning in meaninglessness" continued being invented.

To invent images in nihilism, to *manage* or decide the place of meanings in meaninglessness, these are the basis of "cinema." This is the reason why philosopher Gilles Deleuze could talk about "cinema" as accepting a question of philosophy and metaphysics at another level of camera in his massive book, *Cinema*. If it can be said that philosophy and metaphysics, especially after Nietzsche, polished themselves as creations and responses to concepts in a question of "meaninglessness," it could also be said that "cinema" polished itself as a creation of images in a question of nihilism opened by a thing called the camera. It is, so to speak, direct nihilism in a *materialistic* sense.

"Cinema," it could be said, is a *performance of images which continues to move in nihilism*. To repeat again, in this case "nihilism" belongs not to the ideological and metaphysical level, but to the experience of *a thing* called camera/film, and continues to take part in it, becoming a performance.

To take part in nihilism (that is, in camera) directly — this is an unavoidable, given experience. And here appear the fascinations of the "cinematic" image, or rather the abnormal intoxication. Although "cinematic" images present various images *against* nihilism, the *substance* of those images consists of film's anachronism ("all that is gone" appears ···), meaninglessness, indifference. Therefore, those images simultaneously appear only as ones already eroded and weakened by indifference and meaninglessness. And anachronism always

Fig. 11. The face of Ryū Chishū.
(Credit: Japan Film Library Council)

Fig. 12. "Everyone knows that *Tokyo Story* is by Ozu Yasujirō is enveloped with astounding intoxication and incomparable and trembling uncanniness."

spreads the "smell of death" and rancidness of "reality" in those images. It follows that the "cinematic" image (for example, Dietrich's face or the face of Ryū Chishū in the films of Ozu · · ·) continues to emit the destruction of species, meaninglessness, thinning, the atmosphere of death, and rancidness *at the same time* it appears. In this sense, it is abnormal, and its intoxication may be dizziness out of the essence of the image, where those things such as "meanings" *and* "meaninglessness," concentration and disruption, condensation and dispersion cannot help but appear as the *same things*. And these will constitute intoxication, fascination, and some uncanniness, which envelop the "cinematic" image · · · .

· · · Intoxication and uncanniness, for example, everyone knows that *Tokyo Story* by Ozu Yasujirō is enveloped with astounding intoxication and incomparable and trembling uncanniness. The "story" of this film is only a *nonsensical* sketch of "lower middle-class everyday life," like most of Ozu's films. One old married couple, who live in Onomichi, come to Tokyo to meet their eldest son, the bride of their dead second son, and other acquaintances. Although they are kept somewhat at a respectful distance, they spend a few days without any serious incidents, and on their way back to Onomichi, the old wife falls sick and after a short while, dies at home. Sons and daughters gather at Onomichi and soon disperse · · · The film ends with an old man left alone in a room and a shot of the bride (Hara Setsuko) leaving in a train, seemingly holding the determination for a new life = incident. This is the entire "story." But what covers this film with sometimes astounding intoxication is the "smell of death" which literally "slices" such a "story" vertically. It is not restricted to the "death" intertwined into the "story," like the communication between the bride who lost her husband at war and her old mother-in-law who will soon pass away with the "smell of death." Ozu's famous, peculiar long takes of empty rooms, corridors where characters appear and go out, groups of chimneys which are *symbolically* inserted repetitively, empty graveyards, roads, the sea and the like, are framed in inorganic quadrilaterals and let a certain "non-existence" steal into the film. I dare say "that something has gone" or "that everything has gone" is always exposed. And they sneak in, not as something like emotional lamentations, but as gestures which expose the neutrality of "nobody's look." In other words, touches of *inorganic* unemotionally, meaninglessness, and indiscriminateness themselves are exposed. Perhaps this is the reason why the impression just after watching this film is far from "beloved sorrow," rather it's close to trembling uncanniness, or the uncanny impression of "the dead" which is more uncanny than any other "ghost film." At the same time, this film captures the details of minute pleasure and sorrow of "lower middle-class everyday life" with a remarkable sensitivity, it also shows that such minimal "meanings" "values," "emotions" in our lives are exposed to the neutral look of nobody, to what can be called the secret, unemotional "look of death," with director Ozu's peculiar look; almost no one gazes at anyone in this film, and when one has to gaze, a camera comes in front of that person. Thus, looks toward the spectator which are gazes toward the "empty space" are frequently used. Audiences are also involved in that look of the camera, and the anxiety of the look which became an empty, desolate one.

For example, as in the look of Hara Setsuko, all of the characters begin talking by turning toward the camera, namely toward "nothing" where nobody is. And when screened, that "nothing" becomes the position of the spectators · · · That is to say, in a movie house, the gaze of Hara Setsuko is turned to us, without focusing on us, and at this moment, when we notice that what that gaze is looking at is a camera/"emptiness," we feel the fear and uncanniness that the audience might evaporate into "cinematic" emptiness.

Therefore, the "sense of uncertainty" felt just after watching *Tokyo Story* is not ideological at all, but materialistic in a *camera-related sense*. The camera-like look's worthlessness, indiscriminateness, unemotionality · · · In other words, *absolute* "nihilism" surfaces as this movie's "theme," or *hidden* "theme," in the manner in which it has been organized as a whole.

Fig. 13. The face of Hara Setsuko.
(Credit: Japan Film Library Council)

One Japanese film director, who appears dull-headed, said that the popularity of director Ozu Yasujirō in Europe and America, if there was any, was groundless and that it only comes from fraudulent intelligentsia's exoticism regarding Japanese feelings. Even though that claim may not be totally wrong, that surprise can be felt by anybody when the films of director Ozu are simply watched. That is to say, the popularity of director Ozu Yasujirō exists undoubtedly in the amazement toward astounding exposure of *camera-like non-existence (kamerateki fuzai)*. In other words, people recognize the amazement and intoxication regarding the fact that "nihilism," in the true sense of the word which includes no sentimentality or ideology, that the "nihilism" belonging to the essence of the camera is exposed through every procedure of concealment.

At any rate, in this manner, "cinema" succeeded in presenting a field of extremely peculiar images and opening its own place in relation to camera/film, namely active participation in "nihilism" and anachronic "emptiness." Peculiar, because as in the presentation of the face of "Hara Setsuko," "meaningfulness" and "meaninglessness" are not opposed but united as "identical things," as are "indifference" and "interest," and also indiscriminateness and selectiveness ··· Just as the "emptiness" of the screen and the image on it cannot be separated and opposed, they are presented as "identical things." In a manner of speaking, we encounter the birth of meaning in "cinema," but in the same place, we also witness the evaporation. "Cinematic" intoxication caused by film images and uncanniness are presented there ····.

*

In an interview, Jean-Luc Godard said, "Television is culture, but cinema is not." Needless to say, culture may be in the realm of "human things" (*ningenteki naru mono*) and their expressions. Therefore, to adapt the words of Godard frankly, television belongs to *human things*, but "cinema" does not.

As mentioned repeatedly, as long as video has the *inhuman* mechanical eye of the camera, "the third eye" as its medium, it is inhuman. In other words it includes the non-cultural. But the video camera makes it easy to be personified on account of its essential simultaneousness and its having an image system similar to that of human eyesight (visualization by electrical signs, much more minute frame continuity than "cinema" ··· and so on). More than that, it was developed in the direction of easy personification by emphasizing its function as "information equipment" as opposed to image equipment. Here, the inhuman character of the camera becomes transparent with humanized information, and it is rarely exposed as itself. In television, we watch "information," and rarely watch the picture *itself*, except for some accidents (some accidents ··· for example, when a cameraman who is simply shooting is shot to death and the camera falls onto the ground, continues operating, and indifferently goes on filming the dead body of the cameraman who was its "master," we momentarily notice that the camera is the eye

Fig. 14. Jean-Luc Godard.
(Credit: Japan Film Library Council)

composed of perfectly inhuman indifference). The television camera is easily transformed into transparent equipment through the function of human and cultural "information." The camera functions as transparent media.

On the other hand, the "movie" camera cannot become totally transparent inside the "narrative" or the "information" through which it *speaks* its essential anachronism and indifference. As mentioned above, it always includes a certain time difference between the image and its objects as its premise. There is a simultaneousness between the video image and its objects, and even in the case of recordings, it will continue to be latent as a certain premise of the video image. In the case of "cinematic" image, anachronism is an inevitable premise. Due to its simultaneousness, it is recognized as a *mental agreement* that "someone is there" beyond the video image. Compared to this, the "cinematic" image inevitably includes a certain time-lag between the image and its objects, that is, a strange deserted zone always expands, an emptiness separated by the "time" between the image and its objects. "There is no one beyond this image": this is the confusion and intoxication included in the "cinematic" image. In other words, in "cinematic" images, objects appear only with the intoxication that "they are already gone" (For example, the works of Jonas Mekas, a filmmaking genius who was born in Lithuania and continues to work in America, earnestly sticks to this nature of the "cinematic" image as something "already gone" or "all has gone." In Mekas' images, which continue showing relatives and friends, there exists a painful *ontological* sentimentalism toward "the time which keeps being lost" and an *ontological* shiver that those who are filmed in movies are always slightly dead · · · In this connection, the Lumière Brothers also called "cinema" "chronophotographe," that is, "time photography" · · ·).

In the inevitable anachronism and time-lag, something always sneaks into the "cinematic" image, something different from screened "information," a strange *excess* so to speak, which could be called "ontological emptiness." Something different from information, strange excess · · · something which belongs neither to the humanity of those who film nor to the humanity of those who are filmed, excess which cannot be reduced to "story" — "information" developing there, namely the naked touch of camera/film's *stupid otherness* which always continues to be exposed. That which does not hide no one's look, absolute indifference, indiscriminateness, and meaninglessness — it could be said camera/film as "nobody's eye" always and *secretly* continues to be exposed.

And because of this, "cinema" includes excess irreducible to "culture" as its inevitable thing. Alien substance which does not belong to culture, namely humanity, is necessarily included there.

Fig. 15. Sergei Eisenstein.
(Credit: Japan Film Library Council)

Because it does not belong to "culture" it brings about a certain kind of "suffering" in the "cinema." The human world, which requires "cultural" control of its signs toward every expression, has sensitively reacted to the *inhumanity* and the *aculturality* exposed by "cinema." That is to say, it continued to devote itself to hiding that exposure as effectively as possible. For example, Sergei Eisenstein began to be oppressed by the Stalin administration and its "cultural" policy of "social realism" from a certain period on, and although he escaped the purge, he was almost perfectly kept from filmmaking. However, the work of Eisenstein, who did not hide his absolute faith in materialistic dialectic, could not help but include "cinema"'s attributes such as inhumanity, aculturality, and nihilism, as unavoidable elements in his images because he was a true filmmaker. Precisely speaking, his films were shot as *conflicts* with them, and because of that, on the contrary, appearances of "enemies" could not help being exposed in his images. And "social realism," which requires "proletariat culture" for its educational nature and propaganda, prefers hiding that exposure to conflict. That is, it chooses a kind of "movie exile" and would totally remove the inclinations which would play with such exposures. Or, the same thing can be said about Hollywood pictures, especially after the 1950s. It became impossible for many filmmakers to continue making films in the so-called "red-purge" (It is indeed a strange irony this "cinema" that was mixed with inhumanity and aculturality was thought to conceal "Communist" ideology in America, and at the same time thought to hide "capitalistic bourgeois nihilism" in the Soviet Union ··· What ironic metaphors regarding the *same thing* ···).

From a certain period on, "cinema" is primarily required to belong to the "cultural" and continues to be required to revert to "the human," and in such "educational" requirements a huge number of filmmakers were denied (Needless to say, in the case of "cinema," which needs enormous capital, it is easier to deny authors compared to other expressive skills such as "literature," "painting," or "music." If funding is stopped, use of studios is prohibited, and screening is made difficult; a denial is easily completed. This is a hidden denial still carried out in Japanese cinema.).

The *inhumanity* and aculturality belonging to "Cinema" ··· That is, cinema has lived a history of suffering due to the exposure of indifference, indiscriminateness, meaninglessness inevitably required by camera/film. That exposure was minutely managed and removed ··· The "world of 'cinema' gave up the camera's miraculous nature," Robert Bresson would say with grave pain. Conversely, however,

Fig. 16. Robert Bresson.
(Credit: Japan Film Library Council)

it could be said that this fact indicates how gravely that which "cinema" essentially includes, at least latently, menaces and trembles "the organization." In a word, it is as if any "organization" or managing system such as a cultural "institution" were predicting the destruction of themselves when exposed to the essence of "cinema." What human organizations can cope with or win over are only those "enemies" which belong to the human. When confronted with the absolute indifference, when confronted with the stupid indifference of the inhuman or "*super*human" which have no interest in the human or the cultural, institutions and organizations face their absolute powerlessness. Who on earth could win against the stupidity of a cat sleeping on the coffin of its master, attracted by the delicate smell of rancidness. This *unimportant* powerlessness, however, continues to menace the organizations, authorities, and constitutions at their very bases. It must be imagined that "authority" fears being destroyed not in violent terrorism, but in a kind of fading of power at its absolute powerlessness in *relation to "cinema."*

When Godard says, "Television is culture, but cinema is not," what exists there is never a resentment about "cinema" being excluded from the cultural. Rather, it is decadence and only spells defeat for "cinema" to be cultural and human. Therefore, this is a declaration of war by Godard, an ingeniously sensuous militant, or it could even be a declaration of victory in advance. "Cinema" does not destroy culture, nor does it disintegrate humanity; it lets them self-destruct in an unusual collapse of power. In "cinema," every organization, authority, and administration must be exposed to their own determining powerlessness. That is to say, isn't film the power itself, which is opened in a different place from the humanistic horizon, the power which shows the *concrete* "freedom," "freedom" of being inhuman, "freedom" of being acultural, or could you say a Nietzschian "freedom" in an absolutely concrete place with no connection to metaphysics or ideology? What Godard is saying is nothing less than a premonition for a dazzling "victory" with a certain stupidity.

*

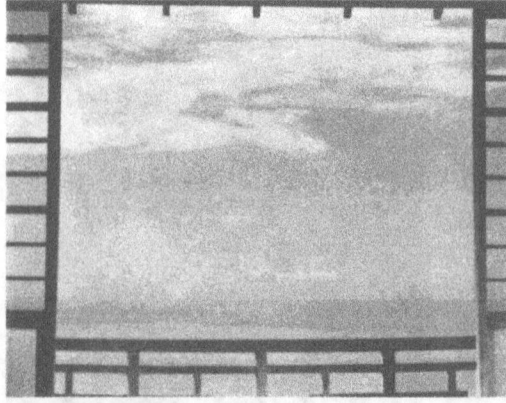

Fig. 17. *Tokyo Story.*
(Credit: Japan Film Library Council)

It's only a movie, this is true. The cat intoxicated by hazy rancidness on the coffin of its master is just a cat, in the same sense that it's only a movie (Let's abandon the sentimental, humanistic/cultural, hypocritical thinking that has the cat remaining on the coffin for love of its master ···).

However, in this word "only," there is an amazement and fear about humanity and the power of "cinema." Or it could be that absolute nonchalance, a premonition of self-destruction and freedom in the cruel indifference are what is included. At that *place* on the surface of "cinema," the "human world" composed of meanings and values which we have been relying on, continues to self-destruct while becoming grains of sand. It continues presenting the fading of power, the slipping away of power until it is totally removed. A world without humans ··· This was only an unhealthy vision pictured by the ideological, metaphysical, or mystical theory of eschatology before "cinema." While clinging to such a *human* unhealthiness, it might be said that we have been playing with empty visions of utopia. But "cinema" made the world without humans *materialistically* visible, not an ideological vision. The nobody's look of camera/film, the look of an absolute other, made it possible to reveal that the world is not made of chaos, flames, and tragedy, rather it is made of downright indifference, stupid indifference with no fear of lack. It exposes the simple but amazing spectacle in full-scale, showing with no sentiments that the world can do without human beings. In other words, it dislocates the excessively humanistic vision of an apocalyptic world, and presents a truly materialistic world devoid of humans in all its stupidity.

Here is the uncanniness of "cinema," the uncanniness which the films of director Ozu always emit, for example. Death, emptiness, deserted ··· Indifference, lack of intertwined human looks, desiccated boughs as the sound of film ···. However, here is a certain incomparable intoxication, the intoxication brought about by "absolute freedom." Every human thing, politics, religion, love, hatred, mercy, despair, hope, memory, culture ··· Intoxication of dry "freedom" presented in the place where all are perfectly evaporated, the place where no verb works except the empty "to be." Empty, because "to be" is the absolute verb, as Aristotle said; it includes no signification nor indiscriminateness. This *impartial* verb *(fuhenteki na dōshi)*, meaningless though it is, is nothing other than a universal verb *(fuhenteki na dōshi)*.

The uncanniness of "cinema," perhaps this originates in the simple but amazing (or, to imitate Bresson, miraculous ···) ability of camera/film to directly present the *fact* that we and the world including us ultimately have nothing except an empty verb "to be," using no ideological channels. But the appearance of "absolute freedom," which we dissolve in ideological visions in spite of our premonitions, deviates from every human institution and is made visible by that uncanniness. "Cinema" suggests that we might have been simply waiting for absolute freedom, that is, the "freedom" which we can only find in a thin, dry, sandy beach, where we ourselves have no meaning nor values except "to be," and have been only waiting for unusual pleasures in relation to "to be."

*

"Cinematic" freedom, in other words, "absolute freedom". ··· Here perhaps lies an unrivaled cruelty. Therefore, the history of film and the history of authority and institutions *kindly* tamed and concealed that cruelty *"for us,"* managed it and controlled it in the direction of "meaning," entertainment," "culture," "education," and "sentiment" (The "authority" is also a *kind guardian*. Like a welfare society. Or the "authority" protects its people in order to protect itself · · ·). But we have a *duty* to face "cinema" and its *cruelty*. To face "cinema" — I dare say this may be the *last ethics*.

I use the world *last* because we will surely experience *this* transparent cosmic indifference with absolute concreteness, which is different from the tragic ideology of Pascal in the surface of "cinema." And, although misery and cruelty unfold there and are surely fearful, it must also promise untold pleasures. It does not mean that there are no unusual pleasures "to be" in absolute meaninglessness, pleasures resembling mourning in which any sentiment are included.

Needless to say, in this case *ethics* does not mean morals, rather it resembles absolute immorality. This is because, frankly, it has something to do only with "the limit of possibility," with the edge of a certain competence. "No more than this" is its limit; there is no moral order to "not do." And although the cruelty of "absolute freedom" exists there (although it holds no meaning in and of itself), that cruelty also belongs to ethics and we have a *duty* to accept it. To repeat again, there is no lack of pleasure and fascination.

It may be said that in "cinema" there is the pleasure taught by the simple and desiccated fact of "being," a pleasure exactly like despair, the pleasure, which is *finally* handed over.

To continue watching "cinema." But our inert and controlled sensibility might be losing the power to find the cruelty of dehydrated fascination, or to endure it. It is clear that the faces of those who continue watching "cinema" are not those of *miserable supreme bliss* but invariably of musical *indulgence* eroded by sweet oblivion and the play of memory. Or it is perceived by paying attention to the flood of moralistic words seeking "culture" in "cinema." Or it is only an avoiding gesture mirroring overt praise of *the common and the vulgar*, sticking to the "street performance" anarchy of "cinema" while hating morals.

Therefore, even though this could be thought to be of bad taste, to continue to pay attention to the concrete cruelty of so-called "documentary films" may have a certain "educational" meaning. Spectacles of executions by firing squad, spectacles of miserable battlefields · · · To continue watching these scenes can include a certain unbearable immorality and abnormally bad taste. At the same time, however, by facing such spectacle, or more precisely by continuing to experience the exposure of the miserable indifference of camera/film which keeps on shooting such spectacles, we might be *deeply impressed* by the "freedom," another side of the cruelty included in the "cinema," our "last expressive equipment." Here, "cinema" would teach us, in ultimate forms, the world without humans, the transparent dryness in which the world will progress even without human beings, and finally the pleasure of the abnormal "freedom" that comes from the fact that we still exist in *that world*.

*

Broadcast on television a few years back, a short — perhaps less than five-minute film.

It was the spectacle of two Soviet soldiers' execution by gunshot, which was sent to news agencies all over the world by Afghan guerrillas. It might have been filmed in 8mm or recorded in inferior video; the picture is poor in quality and the faces of those who are there cannot be perceived. They have faded into anonymity. There is no sound. A man with a machine-gun forces two young soldiers to stand in front of a wall of what appears to be a hidden fortress in a wild mountain area. The faces of those two men, who begin taking off their clothes in confusion, are in strong sunshine within the vague picture frame, and seem to be laughing with embarrassment. The film is then momentarily discontinued. Then those three men are walking in a desert land with many rocks and scant weeds. The trembling of the grass suggests a stiff wind is blowing, and the half-naked soldiers walk side by side looking chilly. On the whole, there is no intense atmosphere. It looks like the scene of a strange stroll, which is neither normal nor abnormal in an image of fading color. It even seems that these two men are chatting and laughing. Suddenly, one man falls down in the weeds. No sound. White smoke is visible around the rifle of the accompanying soldier. With gestures of incomprehension, the other one tries to pull up the fallen man in his arms and looks back. Then he also drops like a rock. Again, white smoke can be seen around the rifle. The appearance of two half-naked men piled in the sunlight of a plateau in the blowing wind, and the vaguely colored figure of the man carelessly holding a rifle at his side are shown for a moment. And before long, the colors mix and the film stops.

I was stunned watching this film, and although it may be *unforgivable*, I fell into a certain kind of intoxication. This miserable death totally lacks relief. If there had been voices of hatred and people being wildly excited by the executions, at least various "meanings" could have been born, such as endless misery or hatred of war. But this totally lacked such elements. Simply put, three persons walk in a deserted, mountainous area, and then comes death. Of course, a camera existed that filmed the scene, and naturally there was more than one person behind it, or there might have been spectators rejoicing with hatred. But the image shows three persons, and there exists only a camera which indifferently records the images, functioning as an inhuman "third person." These are the impressions of this film. What covers this film is not the misery of the execution by gunfire, nor the cruelty of war, but the extraordinary uncanniness and absurdity of being deserted and the absolute powerlessness of "meaning." This powerlessness is different from the moralistic powerlessness opposing unreasonable violence, yet it may literally deprive us of physical strength, give us a feeling of helplessness which is sensed as something evaporating from one's skin. Here lies only an astounding sense of helplessness that there is no meaning, and that is all.

This film left a lingering *impression*. Here, impression means a physical "impression," like a pressure mark literally pushed on my body. Of course, initially there was a gloomy impression brought about by the spectacle of violent death without relief. But the astounding indifference that blankets this film, the expanding, absurd indifference due to the lack of elements such as sound, commentary, or music, leaves shivers which are different from fear or fury, and resembles the fading away of power before the endless barrenness. Even now, when I am watching a film or looking at the spectacle through a train window, this film starts to be projected almost visually in my memory. I lose my strength.

The world has no meaning ··· This kind of ideological nihilism or cynicism is, as a *conception*, only an easy childishness. Reaching adolescence, every child thinks of things at this level. As a matter of fact, this childish nihilism is not the experience of meaninglessness in a true sense; it's no less than the tiny, human and mostly temporal distraction of little people who cannot adjust themselves in the flood of various "meanings." It is only a *human* nihilism which everybody falls into for a few days. Being unable to select and control meaning, a nihilism caused by a kind of bad condition, a so to speak "disease of meaning."

However, the nihilism of camera/film is for the most part *absolutely* direct. In advance, camera/film itself does not seek "meaning" in any sense. It tries neither to film the meaningful nor film the meaningless; it is through a look which operates in a tautological and absolute indifference that it films what is filmed. Mechanical and mineral indifference ··· Or is it better to call it the absolute, barren look, or the look of zero degree? "Meaning" does not exist in advance, and therefore there can be no dispersion of "meaning," no "disease of meaning," nor "meaning of meaninglessness."

Bergson said that "meaninglessness" is the opposite concept of "meaning" after all, that is to say, he said that a negative form of "non-sense" is created as an opposite concept due to the existence of "meaning." This may be right at the level of humans, but it is not correct at the level of camera/film. From the very beginning, camera/film lacks a horizon of "meaning," so its "meaninglessness" is not a relative opposite concept but an absolute one. Namely, its nihilism is absolute.

Perhaps it's a simple accident that the time when Nietzsche began to open the horizons made of "*superhuman* absolute nihilism" against "human nihilism made up of resentment and jealousy" perfectly overlaps with the beginning of the "film industry" by the Lumiére brothers (Had Nietzsche ever watched a movie?). In any case, it can be said that "cinema" is the apparatus which materially presents Nietzsche's so-called "eternal recurrence," due to the fact that it includes absolute nihilism in its essence and can repeat the same image endlessly. It may be going too far to say that "cinema" is a visualization of Nietzsche's philosophy and commentary. But, if it can be said that the philosophy of the 20th century is a long and entangled commentary, it also may be said that our world has been a long and entangled commentary on "cinema."

It has already been a while since the phrase "death of cinema" began to be used half-rhetorically. In fact, the decline of the film industry world-wide is undeniable, and even if it has recovered recently, it can be thought of as only a temporal success of "transformation toward entertainment" in an attempt to compete with television and video. In addition, in the minute descriptions of "film history," "cinema" is already being "converted into history." Needless to say, "conversion into history" is the indication of a certain death. In many cases, historians begin to chatteringly talk about the dead.

Probably, cinema has begun to be truly dead; it may be possible to say this. But it is not certain whether we have truly experienced the horizon of unheard and cruel nihilism which "cinema" brought about, or if we already consumed and exhausted the barrenness of "the world" and its intoxication, or *intoxication in barrenness*, which continues to appear and to be presented in that horizon. In other words, it is not certain whether the cruel but not unpleasant touch of the horizon of "absolute freedom" *secretly* opened by "cinema" in its nihilism was completely experienced, or whether it can be said that since "cinema" completed its *mission*, so to speak, it begins to die a natural death.

··· In any case, perhaps it is probably true that *now* "cinema" is dying. Perhaps Godard's remark that "cinema is not culture" can be thought of as a daring premonition of its death, that is, a premonition of "cinema's death" from conversion into "culture." However, this "death" is not a result of the total consumption of its strength. To repeat again, it must be, so to speak, the *death of resentment in weakness* after a long, secret denial.

However, even in that premonition of "death," we are still not forbidden to be impressed by a certain violent touch included in the "cinema," the violent touch of the absolute indifference of camera/film squeezed out from concealment. It is latent in "cinema," no matter how *foolish* it may be, and this must be the reason why even "cinephiles" who talk especially about morals or entertainment have the "immoral" intoxication and shadows of "nihilism" somewhere in their faces, in the way fatigue from lack of sleep is secretly marked. Therefore, perhaps it is our "final service to cinema" to take active part in the true "immorality" of "cinema" by wiping off every oppression for "mourning" before "cinema's death" which is *near at hand*. The immorality of "cinema," that is, its absolute indifference, indiscriminateness, meaninglessness ··· To attempt to actively take part in the *cruel intoxication* or "miserable dullness" originating in it.

*

··· Once again, for example, to watch a film which records a war in various phases — here lies the certain "cruel educational character" of "cinema." Indeed, they teach us that violent inclinations or miserable deaths exist in the heart of human lives, and lead us to appeals to humanity or vows against war. However, "educational" includes not only this, but it also *more (ijō no mono)*. Those are inclined to be concealed or removed in "dramatic film," that is, what the rude form of "cinema" exposes as absolute indifference and absolute nihilism belonging to camera/film. And in those films we are taught not only the misery of war or the cruelty latent in humanity, but also "the fate of our century of cinema" and our "miserable fate" for having witnessed the emergence of a world which can operate without human beings.

Miserable fate ··· But it may not be a negative experience, just as Nietzsche tried to talk about a certain flaming "affirmation" there. In a sense, it also shows a cruel, open, wild horizon where we are "free" from "the disgrace of being human beings."

Fig. 18. A winner's view of the loser — with lives in the balance.
(Credit: National Archives)

At any rate, these films teach us the following things in their rudeness and cruelty: "cinema" might be dying (As "Communism" as *an organization* is dying). At the same time, we may not have consumed the *experiences* opened by "cinema" (Just as the *experiences* of "Communism" have not yet been exhausted.).

*

To repeat again, Robert Bresson, one of the "last filmmakers," called the camera a machine of miracles. When Bresson says miracle, it is really in a religious sense. It absolutely does not mean a machine showing the world of dreams and fantasies which cannot exist in reality. Bresson, a serious Catholic filmmaker, rigorously tries to separate "cinema" from the circus of looks. For him, the camera is a machine which strips the world and human beings to their zero degree, makes them nameless, and exposes them until they cease to exist, until meaninglessness and indifference, that is, until the edge of nonexistence. The camera means equipment that strips everything in a shadowless, cruel light. It opens an absolutely inhuman look and light ··· In other words, the look of angels in a true sense, and in the same sense that Catholics call angels miracles, he calls the camera a miracle (In the religious court of *The Trial of Joan of Arc*, one of his representative works, the argument developed there about the appearances of "angels" may be directly converted to the argument about the appearances of cameras in "cinema.").

The camera makes the absolute meaninglessness of the world and human beings visible in its "nihilism." However, only cruel meaninglessness exists here, devoid of ideology or sentiment. This cruelty of non-sense astounds us. As a Catholic filmmaker, Bresson would try to recognize the agency of "God" in this cruelty. Doesn't this "God," which exists as absolutely transcendent, attempt to appear or become an agency for the world in it's cruelty? Therefore, for Bresson, the camera is the look of angels, and at the same time it should be *worshiped* as an "apparatus of miracle" which makes the agency of "God" visible in its helpless cruelty.

··· It may no longer be possible for us to be impressed by the camera or "cinema" with the *religious piousness* of Bresson, or with his serious simplicity. In the first place, the recognition of the agency of "God" in the expanse of meaninglessness opened by the camera is made possible only by Bresson's own religious sensibility, and it is difficult for us to share it directly. So what is important here is not whether the camera is equipment bringing about the agency of "God" but the *fact* that at least it *might* be equipment which would latently open a space in which only "God" or absolutely "wild beasts" can survive, or the horizon which deviates from every human framework or becomes "free" from it, the cruel horizon.

To repeat again, it is impossible for us to watch "cinema" or be impressed with the camera's look with the serious simplicity of Bresson. Perhaps it is also useless to lament over this, for such a seriousness may even be ludicrous. The time of "cinema"'s *wild nature*, or to use Bresson's phrase, the time of the "cinematographe," is already past. Sophistication and mannerism covers "cinema"'s wild nature, and we may grieve over what we call "*Cinema* that has stopped being cinematograph." For him, "cinema" is the same thing as "Sodom." In any case, it is certain that "cinema" still has certain deviations, even in unhealthy, abnormal forms which could be called either angel-like or "Sodom"-like. It is still possible to live such reservations.

Aristotle confirms in a dignified tone that the wilderness freed from commandments is an attribute of "God" or of "wild beasts," and does not belong to human beings. How wonderful it would be turning this into a parody, if it could be confirmed that the fields of "cinema" still belong to "God" or "wild beasts," and not to human beings or culture! ··· And it may be possible. At least for the time being, we still have time to experience "such a simple pleasure" as "cinema," or rather, we should do this as *our duty*.

The camera remembers nothing. It is too indifferent to form memory. But it does not forget anything. It is pure memory equipment. But his memory equipment has no place which promises the recurrence of memory. That memory is empty memory devoid of promise.

> *"He cannot remember yesterday any more that he can remember to-morrow..."*
>
> — Samuel Beckett, Proust

— Translated by *Hamaguchi Kōichi*
with *Abé Mark Nornes*

Fig. 1.
(Credit: National Archives)

Cherry Trees and Corpses: Representations of Violence from WWII

Abé Mark Nornes

As a given, the violence of war is all too easily taken for granted. No where is this more true than in the documentary. While the violence of fiction film is erroneously blamed for inspiring the psychopaths of society, the violence of documentary is naively thought of as a mere recording or reflection. Both approaches fail to take into account the fact that violence in cinema is always represented. That is to say, the image of violence stands in for the real thing, and it is never a mere record, nor is it innocent. Every image of violence is produced within a culture which depicts the violence according to the complex needs and conventions of society. Depending on their culture and historical moment, all filmmakers will tweak their representations of violence differently, using all the cinematic tools at their disposal from editing to camera work to special effects. This is as true for documentary film as it is fiction.

It follows that by looking closely at the strategies at play in filmed violence, we can peek at the underpinnings of society in times of stress and contradiction. Japan and America are home to two of the most violent national cinemas in the world. This essay focusses on a wide variety of unusual documentary films from these two countries at a critical time when cinematic violence intersected with the very real violence of war. We should consider the violence of these documentaries in terms of quality not quantity, as representations not sober records. As a focal point for discussing the Japanese and American documentaries of World War II, I will describe four ways in which violence was represented. These four kinds of violence — professional, just, sacrifice, and massacre — promise to reveal as much about the prevailing attitudes of yesterday as today.

PROFESSIONAL VIOLENCE

> "This little girl of four was 500 meters from the epicenter. For about 14 days she was as lively as she could be, but gradually she lost vitality and got edema."
> — Narration from The Effects of the Atomic Bomb on Hiroshima and Nagasaki

> "As if about to die, this child cries, 'Mommy' but there is no mother to respond to the child's voice."
>
> — Narration for the same image from the TV Tokyo special, Confiscated Atomic Bomb Film (Bosshū sareta genbaku firumu)

The closest we can come to a sober documentation of brutality is professional violence.[1] These are images meant for a specific, limited audience. They are generally produced by professionals for professionals, whether they be doctors, police, or soldiers. In the case of World War II documentaries, they were classified and circulated only in the highest reaches of the government. Freed of the needs of propaganda, they are calm, matter-of-fact documents.

Civilian Victims of Military Brutality (1938, also known as the "Magee Nanking Massacre film"), for example, presents a bed-to-bed tour of a hospital in China. The violence is after the fact, bodily traces of Japanese soldiers' misbehavior. The film's lack of sound, haphazard editing, and amateur photography actually heighten the visceral impact of seeing the marks on Chinese bodies of radical, horrific violence. The intertitles (simple, white characters on a plain, gray background) also maintain this banal description of the unimaginable: "Pregnant with her first child, this 19-year old woman was bayoneted when she sought to resist raping at the hands of a Japanese soldier. When admitted to a refugee hospital she was found to have no less than 29 wounds." There is no anger in these images and texts, no indignation or horror or sadness. It is the mundane tone of a conversation between professionals.

In like manner, *The Effects of the Atomic Bomb on Hiroshimà and Nagasaki* (1946) was made with one overriding purpose: to have experts record the effects of the bomb before people and nature rework the surfaces of the land and human bodies. The atomic blast was an event beyond human experience, and the impulse towards preservation and observation resulted in detail of interest only to professionals. When Erik Barnouw came across the film in the late 1960s, he was disappointed by the film's seeming lack of compassion and attention to human suffering.[2] But Barnouw's expectations were driven by a humanistic perspective which profes-

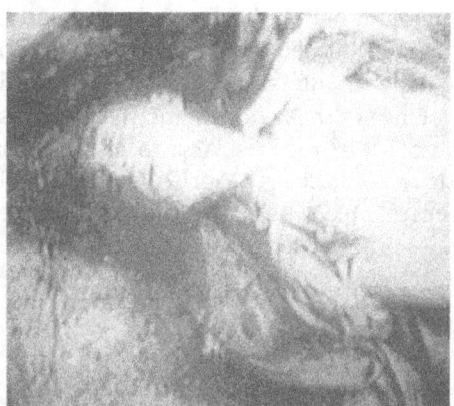 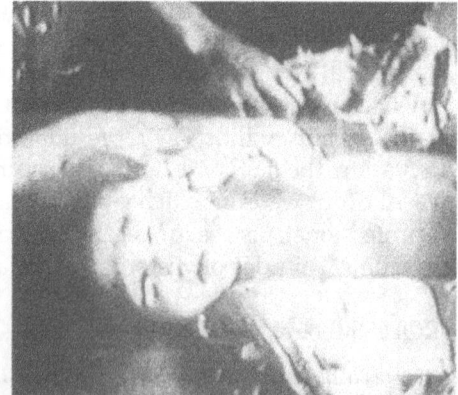

Fig. 2 & 3 Mirror images of the human body, but embedded in dramatically incongruous contexts — left: the subject of *Let's Have a Drink*'s biography; right: a child cries for mother in *The Effects of the Atomic Bomb* and *Confiscated Atomic Bomb Film*.

sional violence does not allow room for. *The Effects of the Atomic Bomb* is crammed with detail and couched in the scientific language of specialists. It guarantees to bore or frustrate the non-professional. TV Tokyo made a special on the film with the same expectations as Barnouw. They injected a note of melodrama foreign to the original film by repeating, in slow motion, a child mouthing the words, "*Okaasan, okaasan* (mommy see photo)." Combined with much different narration (see the epigraph above) and music in minor mode, it created an excess nowhere to be found in the professional violence of the original film.

It would be a mistake to confuse professional violence with objectivity and value-free observation. For one thing, the filmmakers of *The Effects of the Atomic Bomb* and *Civilian Victims* felt compelled to commit these past-tense images of violence to film before they faded into memory or oblivion. More importantly, the example of *Combat Film Report — CF722* (1944) shows how professional violence is still couched in cultural terms. This silent, unaffected "film memo" details the processing of soldiers through a field hospital somewhere in the Pacific theater. Wounded soldiers arrive on ox carts and undergo surgery that results in one of two outcomes: evacuation or burial. In the latter case, the soldier's transition from life to death is marked by a priest's last rites; his body is not simply left in the jungle, but is buried with a funeral service. The last shot is a close-up of a make-shift bamboo cross. The entire ending is infused with religious imagery, and evokes notions of Christian sacrifice. Restraint must not be identified with objectivity.

As texts, these films reign in their violence and attempt to defuse its power, but we must not forget the viewer. For some people, these films are unwatchable. This professional violence is for them a violence of excess which by nature defies naming. It's a violence that refuses to be tamed through textualization — uncontainable, ever-expanding.

I remember pulling a book out of a friend's bookshelf once. The title was *The Dead Speak of War*, and nothing — even this title — could have prepared me for what I found inside. You could call this a hidden history of warfare in the age of photography. Divided by conflict and starting from the American Civil War, this book simply contained photographs of war's impact on the human body. These are the images that war journalists and photographers have always taken, but from which we are "protected" from. Have you ever seen what happens to a human being's body when run over by a tank? After flipping through a few pages, I closed this book, slipped it back into its slot in the book case, and ever since then it has occassionally haunted my memory. Devoid of any text, outside of the title, this was the purest representation of the professional violence of our world's soldiers. These images expand beyond meaning, and people gasp before them — or at least they should. We have recently seen, however, that this reaction depends largely upon a triangular relationship between the spectator the image and the Law, for the jury of the Rodney King case proved that with repetition, close analysis, and guidance, one can become a professional viewer, and the most excessive images can be judged as just.

AMERICA'S JUST VIOLENCE

> "We shall wreak the vengeance of justice on these violators of peace, these assassins who attack without warning and these betrayers of treaty obligations and responsibilities of international law. Let the Japanese Ambassador go back to his masters and tell them that the United States answers Japan's challenge with steel-throated cannon and a sharp sword of retribution."
> — U.S. Senator Connally, head of the Foreign Relations Committee,
> New York Times, 8 December 1941.

Trenches filled with Japanese corpses; American bodies half buried in the sands of South Pacific beaches; Chinese civilians being systematically shot in the head; close-ups of dead Japanese crawling with flies; limp, emaciated bodies being loaded on a truck; Chinese being buried alive; dead infants...today's audiences would be shocked to discover how truly violent American WWII documentary was. The skillful editing, music and narration elicit visceral reactions in the most jaded of contemporary viewers. Emotional responses are natural, but the violence is not. It is represented and I call it "just."

This is not to say that the violence was justified. Rather, I name it "just" with a note of irony, taking my cue from the (absolutely serious) theatrical trailer *Justice*, which provides the definitive example. Produced to encourage Americans at the homefront to apply for war jobs, this film begins in a factory, where the narrator asks workers (on screen and in the theater), "Have you killed a Jap soldier today?" Images of Japanese atrocities accompany the fire and brimstone narration, which calls for "Justice for the soldiers of Japan, who tossed Chinese babies on their bayonets. Justice for the soldiers of Japan, who buried Chinese men and women alive. Justice for the soldiers of Japan, who ravaged and slaughtered the Chinese

Fig. 4. Tawara.
(Credit: National Archives)

people. Justice for the soldiers of Japan, who tortured, starved and murdered American prisoners of war. Justice for the soldiers of Japan, who would be committing these same crimes today in San Francisco, Chicago, Pittsburgh, New York, or any town." The ending tells audiences how they can help dole out the justice themselves; cross-cutting between factory floors and battlefields littered with Japanese corpses, the narrator booms, "Every forging...Kills a Jap. Every tank...Kills a Jap. Every truck...Kills a Jap. Every plane...Kills a Jap. Every shell...Kills a Jap. Every gun...Kills a Jap." This pounding repetition, combined with a body count approaching 100 people (dead or dying), makes *Justice* look like a snuff film if not a call to genocide. The shock of Pearl Harbor lies behind a simple logic here: the Japanese dragged us into a war through their savagery and treachery; with freedom and individual liberty on the American side, any degree of violence is a just response.

Nowhere is this more forcefully argued than in the unflinching brutality of *Kill or Be Killed*. With images of sports and worn cliches like "give the guy an even break" and "don't hit a man when he's down," the voice of God tells us that fair play is the very spirit of America. Needless to say, the enemies are a "gang of bandits with as much sense of fair play as a scorpion." Thus, the film catalogs the various methods soldiers are justified to deploy: slitting throats, bludgeoning skulls, bayoneting bellies, kicking testicles, among other techniques. *Kill or Be Killed* was designed to prepare soldiers for the reality of the battlefield, but films for civilians were no less brutal. The *Why We Fight* series, for example, recycled many of the images used in *Justice*. The series' *Battle of China* inserts the banal images of Rev. Magee into Capra's notorious hyperbole to produce quite a different effect. *Let's Have a Drink* features the biography of a fly-ridden Japanese corpse, from boyhood to his supposed participation in the Nanking Massacre, to the moment he was killed by American soldiers. The film then generalizes this dead Japanese' life to the entire military, reminding audiences that "there are still 6,000,000 Japanese soldiers left alive. Get the Jap and get it over!"

Fig. 5. American GI snapshot. A caption is written on the back: "Jap conquerer of Manila."

Although it's hard to imagine more extreme (documentary) violence than I've already described, there was a line filmmakers could not cross. The immediacy of documentary film was apparently too powerful to show Americans battlefield trophy hunting and the more hateful violence of their soldiers. However, still photography and the written word could. It was widely reported that Roosevelt received a letter opener made from a Japanese femur (he refused). A bizarre example may be found in a 1944 *Life* magazine, whose "Picture of the Week" showed a beautiful, young woman gazing almost lovingly at a Japanese skull on the table before her. The caption is disturbing — even surreal — for its casual tone:

> "When he said goodbye two years ago to Natalie Nickerson, 20, a war worker of Phoenix, Arizona, a big, handsome Navy lieutenant promised her a Jap. Last week Natalie received a human skull, autographed by her lieutenant and 13 friends, and inscribed 'This is a good Jap: a dead one picked up on the New Guinea beach.' Natalie, surprised at the gift, named it Tōjō. The armed forces disapprove strongly of this sort of thing."[3]

Charles Lindbergh described the shooting of surrendering Japanese, and the collection of Japanese teeth and ears. He found that trophy hunting was so widespread that a customs official in Hawaii once asked him if he was packing any bones.[4] While wartime and postwar writing contained accounts of this violence, it remained unrepresented in the cinema.[5]

Fig. 6. An American soldier brought this photograph back as a trophy from the battle on Tinian. Attached was a postcard: "Thank you for your letter. I thought I'd reply right away, but I had a test. Shimokawa-san is here and if I say 'Hi' I'm sure she'll smile and write you, too. I'll be coming to see you in August, so wait at the dock. I'm looking forward to seeing your face. Sayonara."

Though there was a line filmmakers could not cross, the violence gracing civilian movie screens was extreme by any measure. What can and cannot be shown is of crucial importance here, and during World War II it was very nearly a free for all. Violence we find excessive and gruesome in 1991 could be shown in 1944 precisely because it was just violence. Whether it was in fact "just" is another matter entirely. I use the term to refer not to its nature, but to the attitude with which it was dealt. What is most pertinent here is that Americans were supremely confident in their cause (and its violence). The depth of their confidence allowed them to look directly at their deeds with no remorse. The line marking out the un-representable constantly shifts from time to time and culture to culture. We'll find that what can and cannot be depicted is a crucial issue in considering the representation of violence in Japan and in the Gulf War.

JAPAN'S SACRIFICE VIOLENCE / MASSACRE VIOLENCE

If we go to the ocean
Corpses immersed in water
If we go to the mountains
Corpses enveloped in grass
We will die for the Emperor
Without looking back[6]
    — Lyrics by from a song used in countless wartime films
    (Originally from Ōtomono Yakamochi's Manyōshū)

    "I wonder what made him so sure that the Nanking Massacre is a historical fact...not a single veteran has ever come out with details in which he was directly or indirectly involved."
    — Letter to the editor, Japan Times, 10 February 1991.

The violence of Japanese soldiers (and its representation in cinema) can be divided into two modes, sacrifice and massacre. The former makes a spectacle of society's power over its members, while the latter threatens to reveal its essential contradictions and weaknesses; in cinema, sacrifice violence is aestheticized, while massacre violence must remain hidden from the screens. Tzvetan Todorov first identified these two types of violence in his study of Spain's conquest of the Americas. He used them to distinguish the violence of the Inquisition from the genocide of some 70,000,000 Native Americans. Marsha Kinder has recently argued for the relevance of the two terms for the Spanish cinema (particularly the fascist cinema under Franco). I would suggest that Todorov's definition rings uncannily true for those familiar with Japanese wartime cinema:

    "Sacrifice, [the prime example being the kamikaze — AMN] is a religious murder: It is performed in the name of the official ideology and will be perpetrated in public places, in sight of all...The victim's identity is determined by strict rules..., the sacrificial victim also counts by his personal qualities, the sacrifice of brave warriors is more highly appreciated than that of just anyone...The sacrifice...testifies to the power of the social fabric, to its mastery over the individual.

    "Massacre, on the other hand, reveals the weakness of this same social fabric...; hence it should be performed in some remote place [like China or the Philippines — AMN] where the law is only vaguely acknowledged...The more remote and alien the victims, the better: they are exterminated without remorse, more or less identified with animals. The individual identity of the massacre victim is by definition irrelevant (otherwise his death would be a murder)...Unlike sacrifices, massacres are generally not acknowledged or proclaimed, their very existence is kept secret and denied. This is because their social function is not recognized...

    "Far from the central government, far from royal law, all prohibitions give way,...revealing not a primitive nature, the beast sleeping in each of us, but a modern being...restrained by no morality and inflicting death because and when he pleases. The 'barbarity' of the Spaniards [as well as the Japanese — AMN] has nothing atavistic or bestial about it; it is quite human and heralds the advent of modern times."[7]

Japan demonstrated both kinds of violence during its exploits in the "Greater East Asian Co-Prosperity Sphere." While rallying its people around personal sacrifice and the ultimate desire for a beautiful death for the emperor and in defense of

Fig. 7. Filipino victims of Japanese military brutality.
(Credit: National Archives)

the homeland, the troops were off in various parts of Asia massacring soldiers and civilians alike. Examples of sacrificial violence abound in the wartime cinema, but massacre violence was beyond representation. It's not that they couldn't have recorded it; Shirai Shigeru, for example, was shooting *Nanking* (*Nankin*, 1938) during the massacre. In his biography, he describes mass machinegunnings next to the Yangtze, but he did not shoot the executions with his camera. Indeed, he tells the readers he saw much more but cannot continue writing.[8] Unlike their American colleagues, the line Japanese filmmakers could not cross was very close indeed.

There are no Japanese counterparts to *Justice, Kill or Be Killed, The Fleet That Came to Stay* (1945), or *With the Marines at Tarawa* (1945). In the famous Japanese combat films like *Malayan War Front — A Record of the March Onward* (*Marē senki — shingeki no kiroku*, 1942), *Oriental Song of Victory* (*Tōyō no gaika*, 1942), and *War Report from Burma* (*Biruma senki*, 1942) the real fighting is elided through gaps in time or maps with animated arrows representing each side. Combat photography is usually reduced to views of Japanese shooting heavy artillery and rifles. The ferocity of the battles is only obliquely suggested with long scenes displaying metonymic substitutes: helmets, guns, fallen airplanes, burned out trucks and tanks, and devastated bunkers strewn with abandoned belongings. The enemy makes on-screen appearances only in the sorry position of the POW. Violence against soldiers or civilians

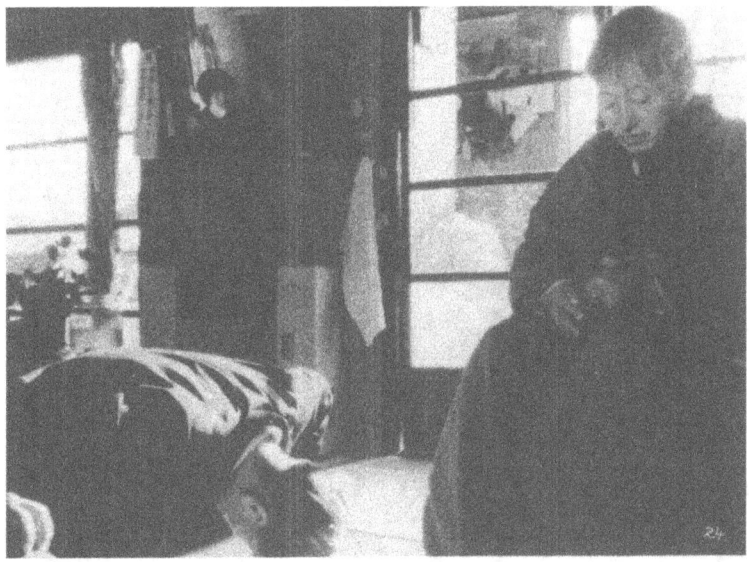

Fig. 8. Okazaki apologizing for beating the story out of a sick veteran — *The Emperor's Naked Army Marches On*.
(Credit: Hara Kazuo)

was written about, or even shown in still photos, but only in the context of individualized, ritual executions (often by sword). This context made the massacre violence appear legitimate rather than threatening...in other words, safely sacrificial.

The massacre violence of the Japanese military troubles Japanese to this day. In a knee-jerk reaction, the Japanese distributor of *The Last Emperor* (1987) tried to cut the newsreel footage of the Nanking Massacre. Denials of this event in guest editorials and letters to the editor pop up regularly. More generally, countries who fell victim to this brutality continue to be frustrated by the vagueness of text book accounts of the war. Documentaries like Hara Kazuo's account of Japanese cannibalism in *The Emperor's Naked Army Marches On* (*Yuki yukite shingun*, 1987) and Sekiguchi Noriko's history of forced prostitution of Japanese and Korean women in *Sensō Daughters* (*Senjō no onnatachi*, 1990) testify to the continuing threat of the war's massacre violence. Both filmmakers met resistance in their attempts to bring massacre violence into the light of the projector, and the central character of Hara's film even resorts to beating war stories out of veterans.

While massacre violence rarely made it to the screen, the direct representation of sacrifice violence is found mostly in fiction films. Feature filmmaking allowed vast control over lighting, camera movement, and special effects, enabling filmmakers to aestheticize death. Furthermore, sacrifice violence requires heroes, and the melodrama of fiction film sets the stage for individuals to face death bravely with wonderful music and blazing special effects. But the control in documentary is limited, and the bodies it captures on film are all too real and vulnerable. Sacrifice violence in documentary involves looking nearby. It's represented metaphorically (with traditional images of death like cherry blossoms) or metonymically (with

Fig. 9.
(Credit: National Archives)

Fig. 10. *Sacred Soldiers of the Sky.*

graves, wooden urns, or shrines with possessions of the dead). Of all the war documentaries we examined for the Yamagata retrospective, only an early Fox-Movietone Japan production, *Kagayaku Nippon* (*Victorious Japan*, 1934), directly showed Japanese corpses. Kamei Fumio's supressed *Fighting Soldiers* (*Takakau heitai*, also *Soldiers at the Front*, 1939) reportedly contained a scene in which Japanese soldiers burning the bodies of their fallen friends, however, this footage is missing from the single print that surfaced after the war. Earlier documentaries from the war against the Chinese often show funerals and soldiers carrying boxes of their comrades' ashes. After Pearl Harbor, however, movie narrations and songs could call for citizens' beautiful, sacrificial deaths, but visual representations became exceedingly indirect.

The example of the hit *Sacred Soldiers of the Sky* (*Sora no shinpei*, also *Divine Soldiers of the Sky*, 1942) is instructive. It follows a group of boys through rigorous paratrooper training, topped off by a spectacular practice jump with a cast of hundreds. The thrilling flying sequences of this paratrooper film inspired many young Japanese boys to join the air force, but the reality of these jumps into enemy territory was disastrous. When they finally arrived at the front, many of these boys swept away by the beauty and thrill of the film were killed before they hit the ground. The ugly fact of death could not be represented directly, for bloody bodies are not a pretty sight. Instead, filmmakers referred to death in more indirect, more aesthetically pleasing ways. After their practice jump, the sacred soldiers of the sky march away from the camera down a road lined with cherry trees. Blossoms flutter through the air like parachutes, a seductive, traditional image of beautiful death standing in for, calling for, the real thing.

The comparison of life (to be specific, the end of life) to cherry blossoms was a typical way of representing death. Another example would be "Sakura of the Same Class," a popular wartime song that people sing to this day. The first verse goes:

> You and I are *sakura* of the same class
> We bloom in the same military school garden
> Our readiness is that of blooming flowers that will fall
> Let's fall gracefully for our country.[9]

In general, the Japanese vocabulary referring to death at war was far more aesthetic than the clinical terms of the English language, (such as "casualty"). Men killed on the battlefield were *sange*, which literally translates "fallen flower." The slaughter of masses of Japanese soldiers at Guadalcanal and Saipan was referred to as *gyokusai*, or literally "crushed jewels." Tsurumi Shunsuke has translated it more properly as "glorious self-destruction."[10] Now these fallen soldiers' *eirei* ("splendid spirits") or *sukō na rei* ("sublime souls") rest in shrines and temples all across Japan. These were some of the many methods media and popular culture used to seduce people to their deaths.

By the late 1930s, the conventions for sacrificial violence in documentary had become rigid enough to subvert. In his brilliant *Fighting Soldiers*, Kamei Fumio attempted to criticize the aestheticization of sacrificial violence *from within*. Alert viewers will recognize a subtle critique beneath the fascist spectacle of the film's surface. For example, it includes an obligatory victory march into a Chinese city;

Fig. 11. This dying horse stands in for all of the suffering humans — Chinese and Japanese alike— in *Fighting Soldiers*.
(Credit: Japan Film Library Council)

however, Kamei subverts the scene by showing grim Chinese faces, not the usual flag-waving Japanese audiences had come to expect. Elsewhere, an intertitle talks grandiloquently about Japanese soldiers carving a new page in history, yet the subsequent images are massive mountains that suggest that this is only one of many pages (most of which do not mention the Japanese). Another scene typical of wartime documentary shows a small shrine to a fallen soldier; less typically, the soundtrack features the voice-over of a letter from the soldier's wife, who doesn't know he's died. Kamei undercuts any sense of valor and sacrifice through irony and melodrama. The film's most famous scene features the protracted death of an abandoned horse. It's miserable death stands metaphorically for the suffering of everyone involved in the war. In this indirect manner, nearly every scene is subverted through clever, ironic editing. We may assume that the missing footage of a funeral pyre was excised because it threatened the spectacle of sacrifice violence too directly. Kamei was one of the few filmmakers to resist the militarization of Japanese documentary and his fight continued after the war. Below I will discuss how he deployed images of massacre violence in the post war era to critique the sacrifice violence of fascist spectacle.

THE GULF WAR: JUST VIOLENCE?

"I have resolved all moral questions in my mind. This is black and white, good versus evil."
— *George Bush*, Time, 21 January 1991.

Once more we must ask what can and can't be shown. The answer to this question is at once surprising and revealing. The Gulf War and its recent predecessors Panama and Greneda, were hailed as just — indeed, the war in Panama was named "Operation Just Cause." Partly to affirm this conviction, World War II images and rhetoric were ubiquitous. What set the Gulf War apart was its spectacle and its surface, the live images of reporters donning gas masks, sirens announcing the flight of Scuds, and luminescent fireworks over Baghdad. For all this surreal spectacle, image gatherers failed to show us the end results of our verdict. We never saw the war's violence.

It wasn't because television and newspapers couldn't show such things. After all, the very same media followed their war coverage with images of combat and dead bodies in the streets of South Africa's black townships (another issue to be sure). It wasn't for lack of images, for on the eve of the ground war, National Public Radio reported that helicopter crews were being trained for what to expect with videos of Iraqi soldiers being chased down by helicopters and ripped apart by machine gun fire (the Gulf War version of *Kill or Be Killed*). As superimposed titles like "cleared by military censors" constantly reminded us, these and other violent images were held from view by the military. While this tight censorship is no doubt an important issue, we can learn more by looking at the violence which managed to reach our television screens and how people reacted to it.

If you look at what violence was shown, it's clearly not the just violence we find in the documentaries of World War II. Armed with video cameras rather than Eyemos, journalists documented crews firing cannons and launching missiles. We saw silent, grainy black and white images of bombs hitting their targets far below; we saw war planes taking off at dawn (there were far more stunning sunrises than corpses in this war). When the ground war began, we saw oblique references to our violence: piles of Iraqi equipment, burned out husks of planes, tanks, and trucks, and the litter of the battlefield (helmets, maps, toothbrushes). The few dead bodies that inched their way onto our television screens were contained in fleeting glimpses of a foot or a hand, or veiled by body bags. When shown living, the enemy was in the pathetic position of POW, receiving our kind medical treatment, food or kisses (!). In one scene with symbolic weight, a group of Iraqis came across a CBS news team and surrendered to the media.

This is precisely the metaphoric and metonymic sleight of hand we saw in the Japanese films from World War II. Though the Gulf War was called just, its violence was not. It was massacre violence, and the few times it erupted into public view it caused a uproar. When CNN showed civilian victims of our military brutality, Peter Arnette was labeled a dupe of the Iraqis. *Time* raised a furor when it showed the traffic jam of thousands of burned vehicles left when we attacked Iraqis fleeing Kuwait. The magazine felt compelled to answer the controversy by printing the military justification for killing thousands of soldiers in retreat. Rather than deflecting the issue back onto the military, *Time's* response would have been more valuable had they asked basic, difficult questions about media's representation of violence.

The fact that we couldn't look 200,000 Iraqi's in their dead faces suggests that there is an underlying unease with the war lurking behind the more visible signs of patriotism and feverish support. Unities are never as pure as they seem, and so it goes with the Gulf War backing. A vast number of Americans didn't want war in late 1990. The people opposing it were inevitably shown as noisy (but ultimately voice-less) masses in quick cut-away shots. When the war began, these people virtually disappeared from the media overnight. Most Americans seemed to "sup-

Fig. 12. Japanese don't understand this comic. The famous flag raising on Iwo Jima is imprinted in all Americans' minds, but Japanese associate the end of the war with the image of a devastated Hiroshima and the sound of the Emperor's voice surrendering.
(Credit: Ed Stein)

port our troops so they can come home as soon as possible," and this is not the same as promoting the just extermination of Iraqis in the name of freedom and democracy for Kuwait. Historically, Americans simply tend to support the wars their presidents start for them.

Forty-five years ago, with the war-time restrictions on Japanese filmmaking lifted, Kamei Fumio's *A Japanese Tragedy* (*Nihon no higeki*, also *The Tragedy of Japan*, 1946) ruptured the beautiful violence of Japan's war with images of massacre from the Philippines. He showed U.S. Navy footage of (sacrificed) *kamikaze* pilots pathetically missing their targets. Other planes land in the water after their mother ship sank, all to the tune of the familiar Japanese Navy's theme song, "March of the Battleships" *(Gunkan maachi)*. He subverted the familiar images of soldiers' triumphant parade and *banzai* at Nanking with screams and shooting, the sounds of massacre. After years of "non-violent" war films, Kamei used massacre violence to rip away the beautiful veneer of the war and raise issues of morality and responsibility. Like the Japanese of half a century ago, we've "prosecuted" a war and looked the other way. However, I suspect that if we saw the reality of what a "smart" bomb does to the thinking human being, there would be a lot less flag-waving and tanks on Main Street. Americans, and their allies (including Japan), take their weapons and the deeds of their military frighteningly lightly. It takes a delicate sleight of hand to keep massacre violence safely veiled. Now is the time for filmmakers to fall into the steps of Kamei and let the dead speak of war.

NOTES

1. I adapt this term from Bill Nichols' discussion of the various gazes of documentary cinema. See Nichols, Bill. *Representing Reality* (Bloomington: Indiana University Press, 1991).
2. See Barnouw, Erik. "Hiroshima-Nagasaki: The Case of the A-Bomb Footage," in *New Challenges for Documentary*, ed. by Alan Rosenthal (Berkeley: University of California Press, 1988), 381-591.
3. Life (22 May 1944): 35
4. Lindbergh, Charles A. *Wartime Journals of Charles A. Lindbergh, The* (New York: Harcourt Brace Jovanovich, 1970), 797-923.
5. For more complete descriptions and references, see Dower, John W. *War Without Mercy: Race and Power in the Pacific War* (New York: Pantheon, 1986), 64-73.
6. Translation mine: *Umi yukaba/Mizuku kabane/Yama yukaba/Kusamusu kabane/Ōkimi no/Hen ni koso shiname/Kaerimihaseji.*
7. Todorov, Tzvetan. *Conquest of America: The Question of the Other, The* trans. Richard Howard (New York: Harper and Row, 1984), 143-145. Marsha Kinder also quotes this passage in her discussion of Spanish fascist cinema and violence in *Blood Cinema* (Berkeley: University of California, 1993). Her work inspired and informed much of my thinking here.
8. Shirai Shigeru. *Kamera to jinsei* [The Camera and Life] (Tokyo: Yuni Tsūshinsha, 1983), 132-140.
9. Translation mine: *Kisama to ore to wa dōki no sakura/Onaji kokutai no niwa ni saku/Saita hana nara chiru no wa kakugo/Migoto chirimashō /Kuni no tame.*
10. Tsurumi Shunsuke. *An Intellectual History of Wartime Japan 1931-1945* (London: KPI, 1986), 75.

PART V
WHEN THE HUMAN BEINGS ARE GONE...

Fig. 1. Kogawa Tetsuo and Tsurumi Shunsuke.
(Credit: Nakagawa Michio)

When the Human Beings Are Gone...

Tsurumi Shunsuke and Kogawa Tetsuo discuss
The Effects of the Atomic Bomb on Hiroshima and Nagasaki

> "Filmed in a manner reminiscent of 'police mug shots,' this film reduces human beings and their bodies to mere data."

> "A film which has lost the American habit of 'thinking from wounds.'"

Kogawa: It is my impression that the whole process leading from this film's conceptualization to its completion and present form was not unilinear and straightforward but filled with various twists and turns, conflicting intentions and chance events. In the beginning, Nichiei (Nihon Eigasha) laid plans for producing a documentary film of A-bomb casualties and damages with the help of the International Red Cross in Geneva, motivated by the desire to make the tragedy of Hiroshima and Nagasaki known to the entire world. While the project was in its planning stage, Monbushō (Ministry of Education) formed a Special Committee for the Investigation of A-bomb Damages, which was also supposed to examine the situation in Hiroshima and Nagasaki. I don't know any details about the interactions between the two groups, but it turned out that the plan worked out by members of Nichiei, such as Kanō Ryūichi (the producer of the film) and Itō Sueo (one of the directors), joined hands with the government's intentions, and the two groups decided to cooperate. The shooting of the film and the investigations by the Committee were both begun in September.

Fig. 2. Kogawa Tetsuo.
(Credit: Nakagawa Michio)

However, about the same time the United States Strategic Bombing Survey, set up by the American government intent on carrying out its own on-site investigations, also began its activities. When the United States became aware that the Japanese had already filmed at the scene and even taken shots of the epicenter [the bomb's explosion center], they decided they could use this footage for themselves.

Fig. 3. Dan McGovern, supervisor of *The Effects of Atomic Bomb*, photographing Urakami Cathedral.
(Credit: Daniel McGovern Collection)

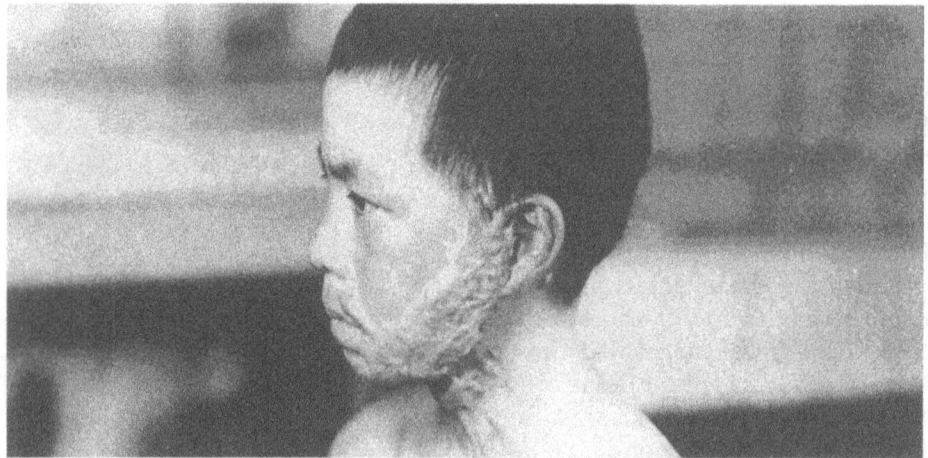

Fig. 4. "When I saw this movie I was reminded of the way in which 'Police Mug Shots' are taken."

Fig. 5. Nagasaki.
(Credit: Daniel McGovern Collection)

When one sees the film in video-form, this change in direction reveals itself in several ways.

The bulk of the movie is shot in the manner of the "scientific film" *(kagaku-eiga)* of the period. Perhaps this is going a bit too far, but when I saw this movie I was reminded of the way in which "police mug shots" are taken. The film is an accumulation and recording of scientific facts, and it eliminates the human factor altogether. This is a very inhumane way of treating this topic, and it seems clear that this film implicitly uses the tragedy wrought by war as just another kind of scientific "data."

I can't help thinking that the United States Strategic Bombing Survey made the 19-reel film that we are seeing now, primarily as a kind of supplement to the enormous mass of materials on A-bomb damages it had collected.

This tendency appears particularly clearly in the Hiroshima part where there is a veritable obsession with minute detail. For example, they tried to calculate the precise spot where the bomb exploded by examining the shadows cast by buildings, or the amount of heat generated by the bomb by examining physical evidence like melted glass or shrine stones which had swelled up from the heat. Or, by examining how many centimeters a stone had moved, it was possible to calculate the original weight of the stone, and so to assess the amount of energy that had been released in the explosion, and so on.

Moreover, this way of collecting materials was applied to human beings as well, so that human bodies were reduced to just another kind of data. For example, there is a scene of a sleeping child whose entire body is covered by burn wounds, with a doctor applying medicine to the wounds using a piece of absorbent cotton. In this case too, the child is simply an object for data collection.

There is also the image of a child who is clearly crying, but the child is filmed in a way that only the lower half of its face is shown and the viewer cannot see that it is actually crying. There are very few shots which show the children actually screaming or crying in this film. Certainly, there must have been many, many children who were crying out in pain and who were suffering, and surely some of them had also been filmed, but these images were not used; the children were taken to be mere scientific data.

As far as the intentions of the filmmakers are concerned, one can't help thinking that this "police mug shots"-attitude prevailed; when we see this film today, we are struck by the coolness and callousness of the depiction. On the other hand, it is also certain that this film powerfully reveals the sheer facts in all their monstrosity and tragedy.

In conclusion, in stark contrast to the melodramatic war movie, the film succeeds not so much in depicting the tragedy of war as in conveying a sense of total hopelessness and despair in which there is no way out.

Tsurumi: I must admit that I was shocked by the film. Initially, I was overwhelmed by its sheer length, and there were things I couldn't understand. Even after watching for quite a while, I still couldn't figure it out. There was this word that popped up many times, "epicenter." — "Epicenter" — "epicenter" — "epicenter"...It was like Kafka's *The Castle*. One could feel that one was gradually getting closer to the "center," and to knowing what this center actually represents.

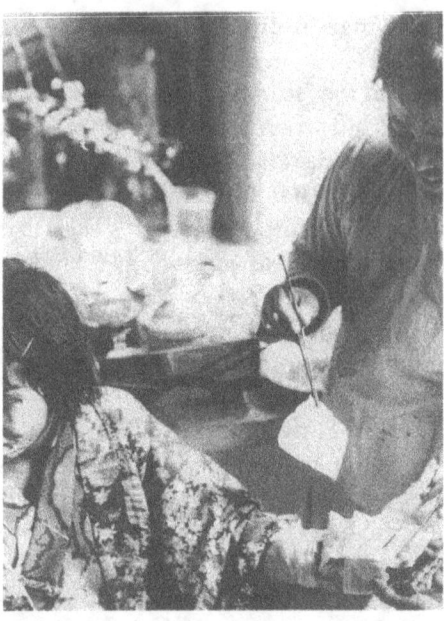

Fig. 6. "Certainly, there must have been many, many children who were crying out in pain and who were suffering, and surely some of them had also been filmed, but these images were not used; the children were taken to be mere scientific data."

Fig. 7. Tsurumi Shunsuke. (Credit: Nakagawa Michio)

You see, this movie was brought to the United States and treated as classified material because it could provide clues regarding the optimum height at which the bomb should be detonated; this was an extremely important strategic problem at that time.

Once I saw the whole film, it became clear to me that the documentary had been made expressively for this purpose. But when one looks at it with the eyes of a disinterested lay person, it is totally incomprehensible, like Kafka's *The Castle*. This word — "epicenter" — "epicenter" — popping up continuously.

Also, there are the "shadows" in the film. This again reminds me of Kafka, and also of Tolkien. In Tolkien, there is this black horseman, and the way in which the shadows are filmed reminds me of him.

The film shows not only the shadows of passers-by, but also those of mechanical objects like the handle of a machine. From the location of the shadows, you can tell from what direction the flash had come. I feel that these shadows, how should I put it, express a world "after human beings have gone" *(ningen ga satta ato ni)*. In the beginning, no human beings appear in this movie, and I couldn't help feeling that I was watching an extremely avant-garde film like Buñuel's *Andalusian Dog*.

Kogawa: Yes, I know what you mean.

Tsurumi: Now, it isn't long before there appear some Japanese people in the film. Probably it was Dr. Nishina Yoshio's research team.[1] They make a weird impression, in their shabby summer clothes and with this extremely neutral expression in their faces. Also, the background music for this scene is totally inappropriate. It's strange, strange music. It doesn't fit the devastation of the scene, and it doesn't fit the shabby summer shirts worn by the Japanese. It was probably chosen because classical music was very popular at that time, but in this context, it's very odd. Even if you deliberately wanted to create such a thing today, you probably couldn't. It's very difficult to create such an ill-fitting combination, you know. I think that this was a one-time happening.

Kogawa: In a certain sense, this movie is "too well done." This extremely scientific attitude, expressed by the calculation of shadows etc., might have been more natural if the film had been shot by the military, but one shouldn't forget that it was made by Japanese civilians.

Tsurumi: Right, right.

Kogawa: But this way of filming suited the Americans just fine. What I'm suggesting is that from the very beginning, the Americans requested that the film be made in this fashion, in the manner of a scientific record. What do you think really happened?

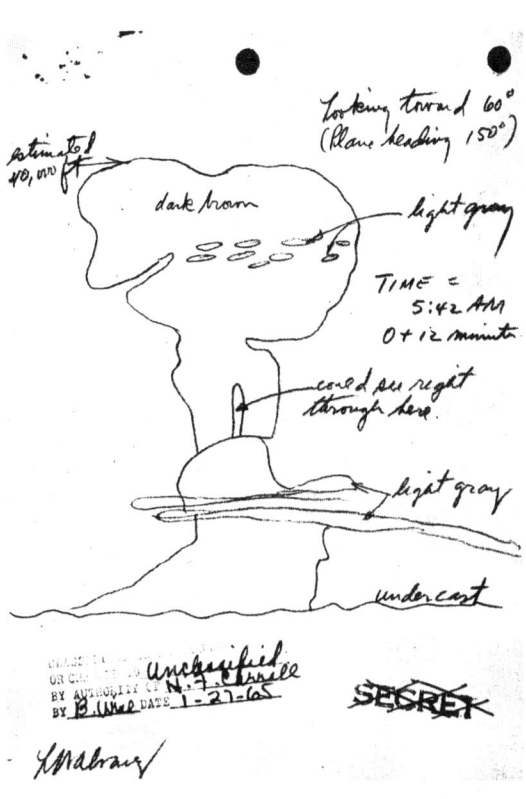

Fig. 8. The first representation of a shape etched in every mind on the planet. Manhattan Project scientist Luis Alvarez' sketch drawn at the explosion of the first bomb. (Credit: National Archives)

Tsurumi: The United States Strategic Bombing Survey's main task during the war was to take footage from the air. The General Headquarters were aware of the fact that Japan's entire industrial capacity was collapsing. The aerial footage was finished after a few months, and they wanted some ground footage to complement the data they already had. Therefore, it seems that plans for filming on the ground were made quite early on.

Kogawa: I see.

Tsurumi: Then, there are the telephone poles. Because they are quite resistant to downward pressure, there were many of them left in Hiroshima even after it was A-bombed. It was like looking at the city with X-rays, with only the poles standing in the emptiness. It made a terrific impression on me.

Fig. 9. The bridge to a new age: sun shadows on the right — atomic shadows on the left.
(Credit: Daniel McGovern Collection)

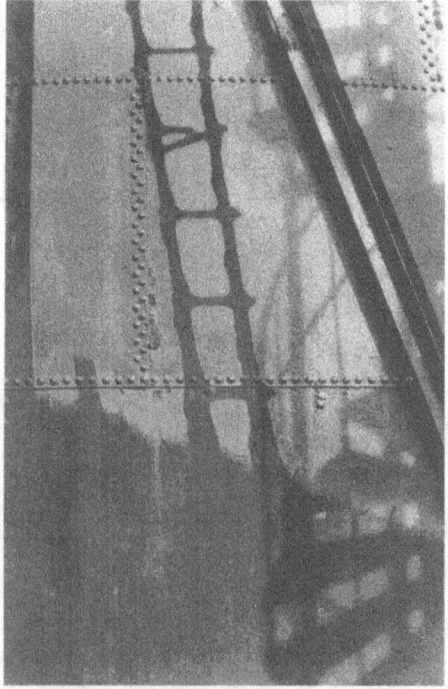

Fig. 10. Atomic Shadows.
(Credit: Daniel McGovern Collection)

Fig. 11. Atomic Shadows.
(Credit: Daniel McGovern Collection)

Fig. 12. *Torii* are gates to sacred places and the homes of gods.
(Credit: National Archives)

The Nagasaki part seemed less cold, more humane, don't you agree? For example, when seeing an image of the Urakami church, one knew immediately which church it was, with the icons of saints still standing there, though the statues' faces had been scarred. Those who know about Japanese history will know that ever since Xavier [a Spanish missionary from the 16th century] had come to Nagasaki, Catholic believers continued to flock to the city, and the statues' scarred faces seem to express just another martyrdom suffered by the Catholics. There is the strong feeling in this film that Nagasaki's experience was a kind of sacrificial offering made by the entire human race. In this sense too, it goes beyond the scientific film.

Kogawa: That's true. There are great differences between the Hiroshima and Nagasaki parts. When I saw the Nagasaki part, especially the images of the Urakami church and the statue of the Christ, I couldn't help thinking that the influence of the Americans had been particularly strong. It seems that the filmmakers expressed a feeling of anger and indignation in these images. This is certainly because of Nagasaki's relationship to Christianity. I felt that Nagasaki had been looked at through Western eyes.

In the case of Hiroshima, there should have been more images like these, but the scenes weren't filmed in this way, and the editing was done differently, too. I thought to myself that all things considered, this movie seems more American than Japanese.

But all in all, this is a difficult problem. We don't know what the rushes of this 19-reel film looked like; the film we're seeing now was thoroughly edited and revised by the Americans. Clearly, an enormous amount of footage was thrown away. In this sense, it can be said that the film is American rather than Japanese, though it had been made by Nichiei.

Fig. 13. Urakami Cathedral.
(Credit: Daniel McGovern Collection)

Tsurumi: When we take an overall view, it is true that the film was made by the Americans.

Now, when we consider the period between August and December 1945, it becomes clear that the Americans' lacked the way of "thinking from wounds" *(kizu kara kangaeru)*.[2]

I would not say it was impossible for Americans to "think from wounds." For example, the Civil War inflicted a heavy wound on the American mentality. Robert Pen Warren, in his *The Legacy of the Civil War*, suggests that "pragmatism" was born out of the ashes of the Civil War. Until then, you had absolute concepts of right and evil, and the notion of righteous Christian anger against all those who dared to disagree, as expressed in the writings of Puritan Jonathan Edwards. After the experience of the Civil War, it was no longer possible to live by such beliefs.[3] It was necessary to find some kind of compromise, to find a way in which the two contradictory philosophies of puritanism and legalism could coexist. This dilemma led to the birth of pragmatism. In this analysis, Warren demonstrates a historian's broad vision. Though the author is known as novelist as well as a poet, he was a very powerful historian as well.

Henry and William James were initially unable to depart for the front because of illness; the younger brothers were drafted and fought in the war. Both were injured and became lifelong cripples. This experience of "being wounded" had a deep effect on their thinking, which emphasized the importance of "human rights" as well as a practical approach to life. This was true in the case of Oliver Wendell Holmes, Jr. Thus, pragmatism was literally born out of a battle wound.

After that, a whole generation of young men that had just graduated from college was drafted for World War I; they received a terrible wound as well. Writers such as e.e. cummings, Faulkner, Dos Passos, Hemingway were all from this generation.

The next "wound" was the one inflicted by the panic following the 1929 New York stock market crash. The crash spawned a whole series of suicides; many people who had lost their homes leaped to their death from high-rise buildings. The fact that all the money one possessed suddenly turned to mere paper was a terrible shock. These multiple wounds thoroughly affected American thinking for many years.

This mentality had a great influence on the Japanese as well because the men who had grown up permeated by this way of thinking came to Japan as members of the Occupation army. Even the Japanese Constitution has its roots in this attitude. That is, even the lower ranks of the Occupation army — men who were born and raised during the New Deal era, had gone to graduate school and many of whom became lawyers — had vast influence on the Japanese polity because they had the power to carry out purges of Japan's military leaders. These men were born out of the "wound" of the 1929 panic. We Japanese owe these people a lot.

But this film is entirely different. There is no attempt in it to "think from within the wounds" and to apply the lessons of human suffering, even if there are many images of actual wounds. Thus the brightness of the final message of the film — an abstract brightness advocating the importance of "human rights." This message has no relationship to human suffering (to human "wounds"). That is, not only does it ignore the wounds of the Japanese A-bomb survivors, but it also refuses to acknowledge its own self-inflicted wound, the wound of those who have dropped the bomb.

Kogawa: It is only in the epilogue of this 19-reel film that one actually gets a glimpse of the lives of the people. There are images of reconstruction and rebuilding, of people eating rice balls. The film ends with the lines, "The day may come when atomic energy, used for the first time in the world for strategic military purposes, will be utilized towards the ends of peace and the happiness of all mankind. So it is desired, so it is hoped, and so it is believed." With these lines, the film suddenly changes into a very conventional movie.

Tsurumi: "So it is hoped, so it is believed." This way of talking has absolutely no relationship with "wounds." This is not the talk of people who have been wounded. It's quite unbearable to watch. Finally, that's the attitude which dominates the whole film. That's why I was struck vividly by the film's closing lines.

"A film with many meanings ('with many centers') in which the consciousness of both aggressor and victim connect."

Kogawa: The people who did on-site research and made this film immediately after the war ended were not simply a group of cameramen who ventured into the devastated areas on their own initiative and took some random footage; the whole affair was more systematized and organized. Because of this organizational aspect (and therefore its political implications), the film could not become an objective documentary made with the purpose of simply transmitting the tragedy to the world. Nor could it be made entirely from the point of view of Japan-as-victim despite the fact that the Japanese were the ones making the film. It was inevitable that the film should try to link up with the "consciousness of the aggressor" [i.e. try to reach some kind of compromise with the Americans].

Tsurumi: In this context, we should remember the remarkable courage of some cameramen who were filming on site and decided to hide their films when the Americans threatened to confiscate them. They were aware that if caught, they would get a 10-year prison term — they would have been sent to Okinawa and their fate would have been more than uncertain.

The fact that these men hid away their footage is of great significance even today. That is, when the film was returned to Monbushō in 1968, the latter eliminated the scenes with images of bodily destruction before releasing it.

Therefore, both countries, the one that had suffered the bomb and the one that had dropped it, colluded in their desire to camouflage the true extent of the damage. They were both silent. There was no opposition between aggressor and victim; rather, they both conspired to hide the truth.

In this context, these cameramen became important witnesses because they, as individuals, decided to protect the truth both victor and loser tried to hide, at the risk of 10 years of prison.

Kogawa: When countries conspire to hide the truth, there is the danger that wars are repeated over and over again. Only through the power of individuals and their protest can we prevent war from happening again.

Perhaps there is some overlap between the parts that have been censored and the 19-reel film that we are seeing now; it is difficult to say. I would like to know more.

Be it as it may, didn't Monbushō decide not to show those parts which depict autopsies, and other scenes which depict the effects of the bomb on the human body?

Fukushima: The Ministry did not choose the word *"kōka"* (effect) for the title. The film was released under the title *The Influence of the Atomic Bomb on Hiroshima and Nagasaki*, and even now, the Ministry uses the word *"eikyō"* (influence). This is certainly because there was a psychological barrier toward using the word "kōka," which had persisted ever since the film had been returned to the Japanese.

Tsurumi: There was a similar problem in the Japanese translation of the Potsdam Declaration; the government refused to translate the term "war criminal" directly. The same was also true for the translation of the secret agreement which would guarantee Okinawa's return to Japan. Nakano Yoshio[4] violently criticized this tendency in one of his essays.

Among the Japanese, the word "kōka" is usually associated with the feeling that they had been used as guinea pigs for a scientific experiment. Monbushō wanted to avoid controversy by not mentioning the word at all. So it was not the Americans but the Japanese government who did the cover-up. I think this mechanism is very interesting. These are Japan's "internationalists" *(kokusaijin)*. I guess I'm not too happy about this! (Laughter)

Kogawa: In this aspect, the Americans that worked on this project are entirely different. From the beginning, they openly used the word "kōka," and by choosing this title they had already decided that they were not going to depict human beings as human beings. As the title indicates, they are mere research material. Even if some Japanese happened to share this attitude, they would never have publicly expressed it.

Once the film was returned to the Japanese, the term "kōka" was seen as undesirable especially since the film had been made by a Japanese team.

What I find difficult to understand is that even though the Japanese had originally planned to make this documentary to convey the tragedy of Hiroshima and Nagasaki to the whole world, through the auspices of the Red Cross, at the time they actually began the shooting it was the Americans who completely dominated the entire process, as Professor Tsurumi has pointed out. Although the United States Strategic Bombing Survey participation was established later than the Monbushō's Special Committee for the Investigation of A-bomb Damages, it seemed that the intentions of the Americans had already been taken in consideration before that.

Tsurumi: It was extremely difficult to conduct direct negotiations after the end of the war. People were like the *"danmari"* (mimes) in the *kabuki* theater who could not speak but could only grope in the dark — you could only guess but not ask directly. People were afraid they would stir up trouble.

Moreover, at that time, there were not enough people in the various government ministries who knew how to read and speak English. That was a huge problem. Of course, you could absolutely not use military language. The situation was so bad that you actually had to send the Foreign Minister himself to the Grand Hotel [to conduct negotiations] because none of his inferiors could communicate in English.

That was the situation, and Monbushō, unable to carry out direct negotiations, tried to guess what the Americans had in mind and decided to proceed according to that.

So the Japanese were basically guessing. But it really sounds as though there was an American speaking [in what the Ministry was saying].

Kogawa: Even if they were guessing, there was certainly some overlap between them and the Americans.

Tsurumi: The film was bound to become an extremely important historical document, and there were still survivors; so a lot was at stake in the kind of footage on which it would be based.

Naturally, there is the problem of the revision and falsification of written historical documents, as was the case in the Nanking Massacre, or the massacre of Koreans which followed the Great Kantō Earthquake — people who were responsible attempting to "rewrite" and cover up history. We must be equally critical toward the documentary film with regard to the kind of reality it seeks to transmit. This documentary is an extremely important example.

Kogawa: That's true. But it seems that as yet, the government doesn't want to show the film to the public, right?

Fukushima: The Ministry has a 16mm version of the whole print, and we asked them if we could borrow it. But they said that according to internal regulations, they won't lend it to anyone except for medical research purposes. In the case of our Film Festival, the film would be shown to many different people from different backgrounds, so they refused.

Fig. 14. Nichei in Nagasaki.
(Credit: Daniel McGovern Collection)

Kogawa: But the ambiguity remains. Even if the Americans made this film, for whom did they actually make it? Of course, you could argue that they wanted to make it for the collection of data to be left behind for posterity, but even so.

For example, the epilogue is clearly destined to be seen and read by many people. But for whom is the rest of the film? Certainly, they wanted to show us details like where the epicenter was and at what height the bomb exploded, because these things were covered up before, and the film was supposed to be a scientific record — I understand that.

But not only did they put in this epilogue, they also intended to show the film to the general public — perhaps this was the desire of Nichiei. This aspect is really unclear. How about the voice-over narration, was it added later?

Tsurumi: Certainly it was Captain McGovern [project supervisor from the United States Strategic Bombing Survey] who was responsible for the voice-over and everything else. During the Occupation period, even a captain had a lot of power. For example, the Occupation army officers, even if they were not of high rank, had a free hand in deciding who was to be purged. Someone like MacArthur, for example, didn't know details of Japanese life. He couldn't speak Japanese at all.

Kogawa: The kind of unilinear narration we saw in the film could only have been possible with a plan, with a scenario that had to be there from the beginning.

It's the last scene that I really can't accept. This epilogue with the text that you mentioned before.

Tsurumi: That part. There is vegetation growing, there are people returning to their homes, cheerful-looking children and passersby strolling by. "(A)tomic energy...will be utilized towards the ends of peace and the happiness of all mankind. So it is desired, so it is hoped, and so it is believed." These final lines make you believe that the captain was responsible for the film and that he had made the film in good faith.

But when you see the whole film, you see that there was not just one motive for making it; actually, there was a multiplicity of perspectives. At the end of the film, you have this attitude of social morality, which was supposed to bring all these divergent perspectives together.

Another perspective is the scientific one, the one interested in the epicenter and the height at which the bomb exploded, and so on. This perspective is interested in using the A-bomb for strategic purposes, and is opposed to social morality.

And then, people like Dr. Nishina came in, who wanted to make an entirely scientific documentary on the bomb. And then, there was also the desire to make the tragedy known to the world, by appealing to the Red Cross.

So there were at least three conflicting perspectives which motivated this film. This is a very strange way of making a film. Normally, there is only one intention, one underlying motive behind a film because a commercial company has invested a lot of money in it. In this film, there is no unity of motive; it's a film "with many centers." (Laughter)

If you take this film as a symbol, then the very process by which it was made can also be seen as a symbol. You can almost "see" this process, the making of the film. The perspectives are constantly shifting and there are many centers...It was at the beginning of the Occupation period, and the American military's control over the Japanese was not very strict yet. That's why there was no unity of purpose but this multiplicity of perspectives.

"National 'Mechanical Images' which rely neither on the individual nor the citizenry."

Tsurumi: About the music [in the film] — what kind of music is it?

Kogawa: It's a very strange music. First, they use Richard Strauss' "Thus Spoke Zarathustra."

Abé-Nornes: As an American, when I look at this film, I feel that the choice of music was made by the Japanese. That's because much of the music they used over scenes of the A-bomb's destruction contains strong Christian connotations. It's an incredible mismatch, and so I suspect it's basically a Japanese movie.

Furthermore, the conceptualization seems very Japanese to me. In comparing Japanese and American documentaries, one sees that there is a tendency among the Japanese films to transmit detailed information as faithfully as possible. For example, the Japanese documentary *Bakufū to danpen (Bomb Blast and Shrapnel)* teaches us about the exact details of the damage done by explosions. It shows various sized bombs' effects on doors and windows, rabbits and dogs, in much too much detail — in the same manner as *The Effects of the Atomic Bomb*. American documentaries normally don't show such excessive detail. It's the melodrama that's more important. That's why I think that the concept underlying this film was Japanese...

Tsurumi: Do you think that it was the Japanese who chose the film music?

Abé-Nornes: Yes, I do.

Kogawa: That's an interesting point. As I said in the beginning, I felt this movie was like a "police mug shot." The Japanese are quite good at doing this kind of merciless technical "accumulation" of data. So the film was first begun in this spirit, and then the Americans came in; I wonder if the two perspectives really managed to converge.

In this context, Douglas Lummis [a professor at Tsuda College in Tokyo] claims that the Japanese owed their technological comeback to the A-bomb. He believes that because the Japanese had been A-bombed, they began nurturing an excessive belief in the power of technology. In this sense, he argues that it is because the Americans had dropped the bomb that the Japanese now have such immoderate expectations toward technology. I think there is some truth to that.

So, in the first scene, there is Strauss' "Thus Spoke Zarathustra." This is based on Nietzsche, and his belief in the birth of a new human being. It is used also in Stanley Kubrick's *2001: A Space Odyssey* and Hal Ashby's *Being There*.

Tsurumi: Really? It was used for *Being There*?

Kogawa: This is the music used for the scene when Chance comes out of the house for the first time.

Tsurumi: Is that right? That's really interesting...

Kogawa: So this music is used to express some kind of anticipation for the birth of a new world, a different world.

Tsurumi: When Hitler died, Wagner's "Twilight of the Gods" was played all over Germany. It was already in their heads. In this case, they didn't use Wagner but Strauss' Nietzsche.

Fukushima: In the *Greater East Asia News* that reported on Japan's successful surprise attack on Pearl Harbor, "Thus Spoke Zarathustra" was used for a scene in which a fighter plane takes off from an aircraft carrier.

Kogawa: The music is used both in America and Japan when there is the feeling that a new world will come, that the world will change fundamentally; they have this in common. It is a kind of "will to power," isn't it.

Tsurumi: But whose power? In "Zarathustra," it is sung in praise of one's own power. Suppose the Japanese chose the music, it's strange because they were the ones that had been crushed by defeat. It's totally inappropriate. (Laughter)

Kogawa: There's been an extremely masochistic attitude in Japan because it has been A-bombed...

Tsurumi: Doesn't that remind you of *Kachikujin–Yapū (Domestic People Yapoo* [a Japanese cult novel on the theme of sado-masochism])? (Laughter) These people [who had been A-bombed] thinking to themselves, "I'm finished, I'm finished," with faces expressionless like *Nō* masks. How strong and powerful they would seem to us if they started to sing "Zarathustra" spontaneously...It's inconceivable, it would be so strange.

Kogawa: Mr. Lummis is also saying that though the Japanese had been A-bombed, this experience did not lead to anti-American feelings. Rather, they put their hopes in technology.

Tsurumi: As for the Japanese scientists, they were embittered by the government's long standing lack of support for scientific thought and activities, and they

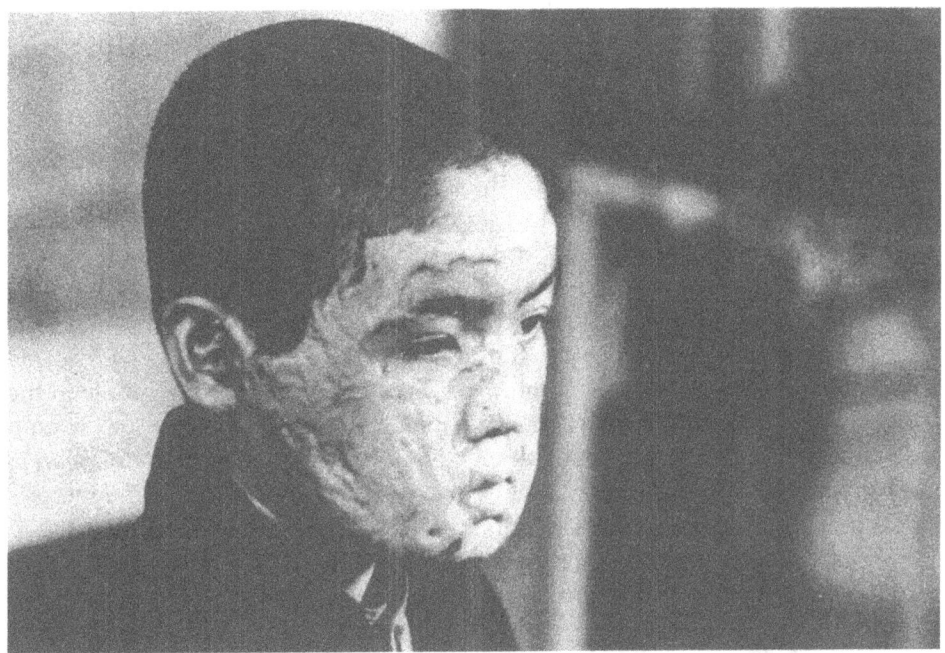

Fig. 15. "Filmed in a manner reminiscent of 'police mug shots' this film reduces human beings and their bodies to mere data."
(Credit: Daniel McGovern Collection)

didn't harbor any anti-American feelings. So if there were any people who actually were anti-American [among those who made the film], it was the cameramen.

Kogawa: Also, when faced with an experience of such complete destruction, a clear conception of who did what can become blurred.

Tsurumi: All the people who appear in this film, the patients and also the scientists who are doing their investigations so eagerly, seem completely expressionless, like Nō masks. When the Japanese are faced with extreme crisis the Nō pops up from somewhere. For example, when they go to funeral ceremonies, their expressions turn to stone and become Nō-like.

Kogawa: The children, especially, seem almost completely expressionless. Certainly, their senses must have been paralyzed by the shock they received in the bombing, and perhaps they were even unable to hear anything. The absence of expression in their faces must have been due to this state of blank amazement. But at the same time, their attitudes express a silent protest against the violation committed by the camera. In ordinary times, it is usually not possible to film patients in this manner, but for this film, these children were made to turn their faces toward the lens and to show their wounds, and to expose themselves to the bright lights of the cameras. This was certainly an extremely painful and humiliating experience for them. The fact that they were made to undergo it was an act of sheer power, even violence. I just couldn't help thinking this when I was watching these scenes.

When considered in this way, the expressionless faces of these children can be seen as a kind of wordless resistance, a silent protest against the fact of being filmed in this way. The terror, fear and defiance expressed in this silence were not only a consequence of their hellish experience in the bombing, but also an indictment against this new violation, the glare of the cameras which in some ways became the bomb's extension. At the same time, there is also resignation there, a despair so deep that these images cut right into your heart.

Tsurumi: When the Shōwa (Hirohito) was ill, there was this emphasis on "self-restriction."[5] Japanese television was shooting in the garden surrounding the Imperial Palace, which was filled with people who had come to ceremoniously present their well-wishes to the emperor. Because the quality of the television image has become so much better nowadays, when you looked closely you could see people in the background who didn't look solemn at all, but seemed rather playful, jumping up and down on the ground. They weren't Nō-like. Thus, after 1945, there were already many people who did not behave in a Nō-like fashion during the emperor's illness. In contrast, when the Meiji Emperor died, people were still Nō-like. When the Shōwa emperor's voice was broadcast over the radio [to announce the end of the war and Japan's defeat], some people who were sitting in the Palace garden in mourning were Nō-like.

Kogawa: That's true. When the emperor was ill, the media expected people to commit suicide at the Imperial Palace upon his death. I went to the Imperial Palace. I saw many groups of people from the countryside who had been mobilized (by various organizations) and who had come by bus to Tokyo. They came looking very cheerful, like tourists. I thought to myself, these people are not ones to commit suicide.

Tsurumi: Things have changed a lot in 45 years. To come back to an earlier point, the music used in the film is classical, which was popular in Japan at that time. They used it many times, didn't they.

Kogawa: Yes, they used it a lot. They used Beethoven, too.

Abé-Nornes: The U.S. government has apparently hired the National Football League to produce the official video of the Gulf War. Maybe they will use "Zarathustra" for the opening scene...(Laughter).

Kogawa: The filmmakers, by using "Zarathustra" for the film's beginning, completely annihilated their initial purpose of appealing to the International Red Cross.

Tsurumi: In a documentary, the background music is extremely important because it determines the attitude of the viewer.

Kogawa: The scene of the weeping children who are administered medicine is an image used in many subsequent films, such as Alain Resnais' *Hiroshima Mon Amour*. Because we are in the video-age, it is easy to substitute the sound for another, so this image can be used in many different ways. It has a tremendous potential for being appropriated in this fashion. In this sense too, this film goes beyond the category of "film."

Tsurumi: Is the Soviet Union making this kind of film on Chernobyl?

Kogawa: Certainly, they are recording the kinds of details we see in our A-bomb film, but normally they don't make such footage public.

Tsurumi: As yet, there is no place which does comparative research on the topic in the world.

Kogawa: In that regard, this film is an extremely unusual case.

Tsurumi: It also shows us what different nations are conspiring to hide.

Kogawa: This is true. I think that the reason why this film has weighed on people's minds for over 20 years is that the people who did the shooting, and those who created the concept for the film, were not directly involved in national politics. The situation is very different in the case of the Gulf War, where all shooting was completely controlled by the government. Of course, in the Vietnam War, the Korea War and World War II, the United States also sent professional film teams which recorded the events using particular methods and means; however, they still had to rely on the help of civilians.

By the time the Gulf War came, however, there was no more necessity whatsoever to rely on the people, to rely on individuals. Rather, the shooting was done by "mechanisms" which run all on their own. The video cameras contained in rocket missiles do the shooting, for example. So we are seeing a situation in which things are recorded in a way that the editors' intentions are transcended. Without a doubt, data about the present war are collected in a manner which represents a purified form of this very mechanistic way of filming human beings which we see in the film *The Effects of the Atomic Bomb on Hiroshima and Nagasaki*.

But we don't see any of this process. It is completely hidden from our view that this footage is used and analyzed. For example, the images taken from a spy satellite are stored and accumulated somewhere, and there are people who see these images, analyze the situation and try to assess the effects. This is a terribly frightening process, which makes the terror of *The Effects of the Atomic Bomb on Hiroshima and Nagasaki* pale in comparison. Now things are much more cruel and callous.

Tsurumi: Yes indeed, but this film is a first-grade historical record, of epochal significance, and with various international implications. It's a very strange film, made with conflicting methods and approaches. A very unusual film. I think that by the time of the Korea War, intentions and motivations had been unified, and it would no longer have been possible to make this kind of film. At the time this film was made, the Occupation army itself had no unified purpose.

Kogawa: The last scene begins with "The day may come." The word "may" sounds very vague. They are saying that even though nuclear energy has been used for war, it "will be utilized toward the ends of peace and happiness of all mankind." The first time I saw the film, I heard it wrong; I thought that "the end of peace" meant the "cessation of peace." But "end" means "goal," doesn't it.

Tsurumi: But you were right! Yours was indeed the right interpretation! (Laughter)

Again these lines seem incongruous with the rest. The sentence at the beginning, "For several days no information was available," expresses the point of view of the Japanese who had been bombed. But the ending lines, "So it is hoped, so it is believed," reveal the state of mind of the Americans, quite cheerful and not suffering from any "wounds." In this sense, this film is really strange; there is a gap between the beginning and the ending.

Kogawa: It is interesting that in the end, both the Japanese and American elements seem to disappear. If one stretches the term "many centers," suggested by Professor Tsurumi earlier, this same situation also existed in the Gulf War, where CNN played a big part as a kind of "war machine."

In reality, CNN, supposedly private television, became a media controlled by the Pentagon, a government-controlled channel which provided the sole coverage of the war for the entire world.

Certainly, the people who were on location and who were in charge of the coverage and reporting had their own, differing views on the war. If there were people who did just what the Pentagon had told them to do, there were also others who wanted to transmit the tragedy in a more realistic and objective way. So, within the images broadcast by CNN, you have "many centers" as well.

These things are not always noticeable but they exist. Images taken by missiles which parallel the scientifically filmed images in the A-bomb movie, images sponsored by the Pentagon, and many other images, come together and mingle.

In this sense, there are many similarities between the reporting done by CNN and our A-bomb film. Only, in the case of the Gulf War, the Pentagon didn't release classified footage. Certainly we must wait another 10 years before these images will be made public.

In the case of the A-bomb film, many images which could be considered "military secrets" are shown. That is, this film shows war in a total manner. It is a kind of "know-how" manual for soldiers, but it also expresses individual citizens' anger against war. The voice-over narration also contains elements of typically American democratic thinking. There are a lot of elements in this film. In doing so, the film expresses a total picture of war.

Tsurumi: The film also reveals the changing conditions in the beginning of the Occupation period — August, September, October 1945, all different — and it expresses the state of mind of the Japanese, that of the Americans, and so on. Precisely because it is so diffuse, it is an extremely interesting documentary. It is like a passageway which allows us to return to the past.

NOTES

1. Nishina was one of the first Japanese scientists to become involved in the Japanese government's nuclear weapons research program before the end of the war. He was thus able to recognize immediately that the bombs dropped on Hiroshima and Nagasaki were atomic bombs, and lead a scientific research team into the devastated areas [trans.].
2. The term "wound" is of course taken metaphorically though it can also imply physical suffering. By "kizu kara kangaeru," Tsurumi means a philosophy or set of attitudes that arise from painful past experience. In a broad sense, it connotes sensitivity to suffering [trans.].
3. Tsurumi means that during the Civil War, two absolute principles (both claiming the right to truth) clashed, resulting in much suffering, and thus making people suspicious toward dogmatic beliefs. "Kizu kara kangaeru" thus implies a distrust of ideological systems which, it is implied, caused the suffering in the first place, and a more "realistic," pragmatic approach to reality [trans.].
4. Nakano Yoshio was a liberal thinker and editor of the journal *Heiwa* (Peace) [trans.].
5. During the emperor's illness, many popular festivals and "frivolous" television programs were cancelled as a result of a kind of tacit agreement with Japanese authorities [trans.].

— Translated by *Maya Todeschini*

DISCUSSION AFTERWORD

The Effects of the Atomic Bomb on Hiroshima and Nagasaki and its subject matter could not be closer; in principle they are one and the same. That is to say, there is the fact of the atomic bombing and there is the fact of the film, and both are shrouded in a web of complicated politics, contradictory histories, cultural misunderstandings and misplaced assumptions. While watching the film can be a frustrating experience, it is not without some fascination (as plainly shown by Tsurumi and Kogawa's conversation, or Nibuya's "Cinema/Nihilism/Freedom" for that matter). Written accounts of this film's production history tend to concentrate on the film's "confiscation" and each tells a different story. They would seem to suggest that suspicion and distrust are a basic component of Japan-American relations to this very day.

In the course of preparing the retrospective from which this book arose, we came across information which suggests this suspicion is somewhat misplaced. After Kogawa and Tsurumi met to talk about this film, Fukushima Yukio and I discussed the film with Daniel McGovern (one of the American supervisors) and Itō Sueo (one of the Japanese directors). Their stories clear up many of the mysteries surrounding the film, and reveal that many of the written production histories are misleading or erroneous. While McGovern and Itō can ultimately only speak for themselves, their descriptions match on every point. For this reason, we decided to piece together what happened, based on our conversations as well as U.S. military memos provided by McGovern. It is unfortunate that we did not have this information before Kogawa and Tsurumi met, for it would have made for quite a different discussion. At the same time, as it stands their talk is an excellent example of the mysteries that have surrounded this puzzling film and the intense emotions it has stirred.

As a "discussion afterword," we structure this history by the questions and issues raised by Tsurumi and Kogawa:

THE FILM BEFORE THE AMERICANS: Initially, the project was a response to the International Red Cross' request for a two-reel film on the atomic bombings. Monbushō organized a research team to thoroughly describe the "effects of the bomb." Filmmakers from Nichiei were sent along with the scientists to make a visual document of the research. When the 2nd Marine Division occupied Nagasaki, they stopped the team from continuing their project. On a trip to Hiroshima and Nagasaki, McGovern (then a press liaison) met a Nichiei cameraman who informed him of their troubles, which were apparently with the Marine Radiological Team. McGovern contacted the officer in charge and "gave him some good reasons why the Japanese team should be permitted to continue their documentation." It was allowed, as long as McGovern took responsibility for them. Up to this point, 6,000 feet of film had been exposed about the medical aspects and 20,000 feet on everything else. According to U.S. military memorandum, on December 18, GHQ "confiscated" the film and delivered it to the Surgeon General's office.

THE FILM AND THE AMERICANS: The Surgeon General and Strategic Bombing Survey decided to return the negative to Nichiei so that they could finish the film. On December 27, the first projection of the work print took place and the Surgeon General's Office decided that they had adequate material for their purposes. They took the medical portion (approximately 8,000 feet) of the work print rather than wait for the finished product. Two days later, McGovern sent a memo to Lt. Commander Woodward of the USBS in which he pushed to let Nichiei complete their film:

> "In its present form this heterogeneous mass of photographic material is practically valueless, despite the fact that the conditions under which it was taken will not be duplicated, until another atomic bomb is released under combat conditions [sic]. Several weeks will be required [to finish]. The only individuals qualified to do this work are working in conjunction with Nippon Newsreels Co. [Nichiei]."

On January 3, it was decided that the 8,000 feet of film on the medical aspects would be copied and returned to Nichiei so they could finish what they had started.

"A FILM WITH MANY CENTERS": According to both Itō and McGovern, American supervision was loose. The Japanese filmmakers and scientists were free to do as they wished. The film's multiple points of view come from the unusual mode of production. Each section was produced by a different, relatively independent, crew consisting of filmmakers and scientists. Itō attributes the lack of unified direction and generally less than thrilling filmmaking to the fact that he and Okuyama were the only professional directors. Itō worked on the Nagasaki sections, as he was a native of the area; the rest of the film was made by assistant directors and scientists.

JAPANESE FILM OR AMERICAN FILM?: While it is certainly a co-production, Itō and McGovern feel that the film's nationality is properly Japanese. The Japanese were free to complete it as originally planned. As for the frigid, academic approach, Itō blames Monbushō and its initial conceptualization.

From a legal point of view, the rights situation is complicated. The U.S. government considers it a military production, and thus is naturally in the public domain and cannot be copyrighted. At the same time, Nichiei considers it their film and the Yamagata Festival required their permission to screen it. Nichiei readily granted permission, however, Monbushō and the Nishina Institute continue to suppress the film by placing their prints (which have been censored) off limits.

NARRATION: The script was written by the Japanese filmmakers and scientists, then translated into English with the help of SBS staff and an American professor who had taught at Kyōto University before the war.

PROLOGUE AND EPILOGUE: Both were written by Itō, who supervised the film's post-production and final edit. Itō was furious at the Americans for dropping the bombs, and attempted to subtly communicate those emotions in his sections through editing and narration. He tried to insert words in the narration that connoted his indignation. He also used many shots of the Urakami church, as well as a scene showing a factory that produced bombs for the attack on Pearl Harbor. As Tsurumi and Kogawa point out, the Nagasaki sections contain a much more humane tone; Itō successfully subverted the cold, scientific orientation of the film as a whole.

MUSIC: Japanese choice.

THE "CONFISCATION": Until now, all historians of cinema have considered this a "confiscated film." Some histories even suggest that the film was forcibly taken from the Japanese. While the word does pop up in government memos produced in 1945 (regarding the initial footage shot by Nichiei), calling the finished film "confiscated" is simply incorrect. When the film was returned to Nichiei in January, Iwasaki was instructed to return all production materials to the Strategic Bombing Survey. Furthermore, Nichiei was working under contract, and submitted a purchase order for 316,399 yen ($20,158.66) "for services rendered" on March 30, 1946 (procurement demand number SC-8TPD 200-46). According to Itō, the Japanese staff knew that the film would be returned to the Americans from the start. Thus the word confiscation, especially with its violent connotations, is erroneous.

THE HIDDEN PRINT: Although the Americans were funding this project, a significant amount of footage was shot before they entered the scene. Iwasaki Akira, Itō Sueo, Kanō Ryūichi and others felt this footage belonged to Japan, and made their own copy. Assuming that they would be arrested and sent to Okinawa if caught, they hid the footage in photographer Miki Shigeru's lab (without his knowledge). Ironically, McGovern knew that they had made their own copy, but said nothing and looked the other way; he simply felt it was a Japanese film, and that they were entitled to their own print.

CENSORSHIP: It has been assumed "the Americans" confiscated the film and locked it up until the 1960s. Actually, McGovern had every intention to release the film to the American public. He had intervened on behalf of Nichiei because he felt that it was important to show Americans what the bomb had done to Hiroshima, Nagasaki and the citizens of those cities, as well as make a cinematic record to pass down to future generations (McGovern himself was responsible for the color footage we occasionally see in documentaries about the atomic bombings). Certainly this bears some similarity to the intentions of the Japanese filmmakers. Far from hiding the film's existence, McGovern envisioned releasing the film through one of the Hollywood studios. He paved the way by feeding information to the press. Among the stories that were printed, one begins, "Seventy-two hours after the atomic bomb fell on Hiroshima picked Japanese scientists [sic] and cameramen began to record on film and charts an invaluable study of the effects of the bursting atoms on steel, stone and human flesh."[1] Upon his return to the States, McGovern talked with film studios and set a screening in Washington D.C. for officials from the Navy, Army Air Forces, the Manhattan Project, public relations officers and media representatives. The screening took place on 9 August 1946 at the U.S. Naval Scientific Laboratory in Anacostia. Unfortunately, the Japanese researchers and filmmakers were perhaps too enthusiastic in their accumulation of data, for they triangulated the atomic shadows, found the epicenter, and determined the point of detonation within 50 feet. The representatives of the Manhattan Project considered this classified information, and thus it was classified SECRET RD until, according to the National Archives' William Murphy, sometime in the 1950s (not 1968, which was when it came to Erik Barnouw's attention). The film became a victim of the Cold War.

In conclusion, we can see that the story behind this film is not as sensational as has been thought. However, the film is there, and it can inspire as fascinating a discussion as Kogawa and Tsurumi's. The film itself is something like an Other onto which many people have projected their internal feelings. We can see this rather clearly in Kogawa and Tsurumi's discussion of the title. As mentioned, Monbushō continues to use the word "influence" (eikyō) rather than "effect" (kōka), because "kōka" has an indifferent, *clinical,* feel to it. Its connotations suggest the people of Nagasaki and Hiroshima were guinea pigs in a dispassionate experiment, while "eikyō" is more vague, even metaphysical. Native speakers of English were most likely lost during this part of the discussion, for the phrase "influence of the bomb" is unnatural and nonsensical (if anything, it implies the political ramifications of its existence). One could also note that Erik Barnouw, who also found the film's scientific approach offensive, did not make an issue of the title's use of "effect." This is really a semantic problem for Japanese speakers, and has nothing to do with America or the English language. Therefore, it could be said that their discussion of the title's wording and the callous attitude it reveals is really the projection of their suspicions toward America. In the same way, Erik Barnouw projects his anger onto the film by writing about treacherous, *anonymous* American soldiers who confiscate and ban the Japanese filmmakers' film. While Monbushō and the American government have certainly acted irresponsibly, the relationship between the Americans and Japanese (at least according to Itō and McGovern) was cordial and professional. This certainly confirms Kogawa's distrust of governments and their will to war, and his faith in the power of individuals to make a difference.

NOTES

1. Gayn, Mark. "Jap Film of Atom Bomb Damage En Route Here," *Chicago Sun* (Monday, 13 May 1946): 8.

— *Abé Mark Nornes*

PART VI
THE FILMS:
FROM THE FIELDS OF
MUKDEN TO TOKYO BAY

Fig. 1. Torpedo squadrons move out for the attack on Pearl Harbor.
(Credit: National Archives)

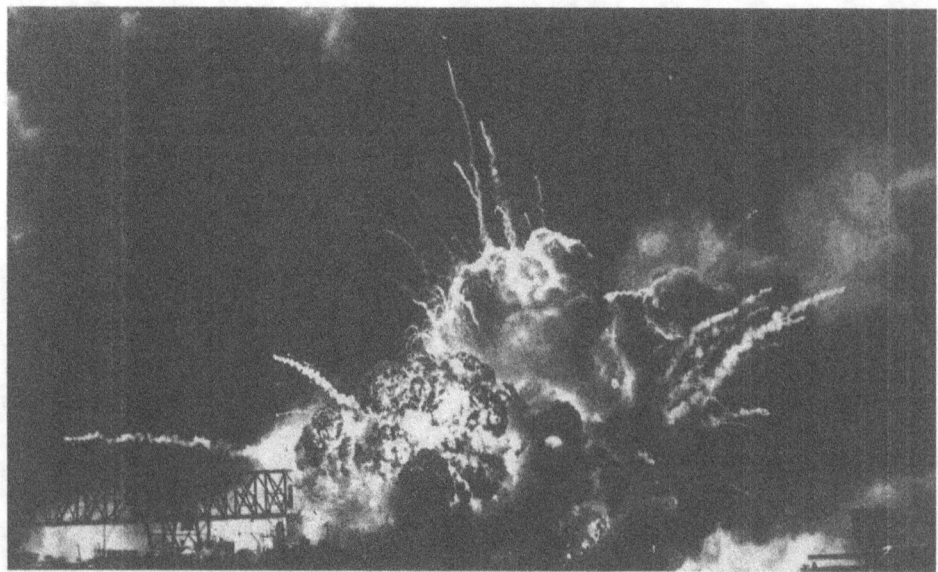

Fig. 2. The Arizona under fire.
(Credit: National Archives)

PEARL HARBOR

Greater East Asia News #1 — Air Attacks Over Hawaii
(Daitōa Nyūsu #1)

Japan *Production:* Nichiei, *Print:* 35mm, sd., English, b&w, 4 min., 1941.

During the Pacific War, *Greater East Asia News* was produced as propaganda for the occupied territories by the Overseas Department of Nichiei, which engaged in newsreel production in accordance with national policy. There were various editions available in a variety of languages, including a Philippines version (in English and Tagalog), a Celebese version, a Malaya version, and a Burma version. This newsreel reports the air raid on Pearl Harbor by the Imperial Naval Air Force. Of course, it was produced in December 1941, and is the Philippines edition, judging from its English narration.

This is a precious film for its recording of the Japanese perspective on Pearl Harbor, from deployment of the ships to the attack itself. Jittery shots and the narrator's agitated voice vividly describe the actual conditions that day. It's also extremely interesting to note the use of "Nippon" as opposed to "Japan" to refer to Japan, or the use of "March of the Battleships" as theme music. In several parts of *Nihon News* #62 and #82 (which is entitled, "Great Air Raid on Hawaii"), we can see the same shots which were probably picked up from this film.

— *Yamane Sadao*

December 7th

U.S.A. *Direction:* John Ford and Gregg Toland, *2nd Unit Direction:* James C. Havens, *Photography:* Gregg Toland, *Editing:* Robert Parrich, *Music:* Alfred Newman, *Production:* U.S. Navy, *Print:* 35mm, sd., English, b&w, 20 min./83 min., 1943.

Americans shot only a few minutes of film at Pearl Harbor, so when director Gregg Toland and John Ford set out to make a movie about the attack they built their film out of special effects and Hollywood intrigue. Besides commemorating the attack, the filmmakers intended to celebrate the impressive rebuilding of the Pacific fleet, destroy any vestiges of isolationism, and bring the loyalty of Japanese Americans into question. The resulting mess provides an example of how not to make a propaganda film. It was so unacceptable to so many people that its release was held up for a year and it was finally cut into several lengths, one of which won the Academy Award for best documentary short in 1942.

In 1940, John Ford created a "Field Photographic Unit" within the Office of Strategic Services (the OSS, what would be known later as the CIA). The idea was to create a film team that could go out and shoot the shooting, should the U.S. enter the war. When the head of the OSS, William Donovan, proposed a film about Pearl Harbor, Ford suggested Gregg Toland as director, the renown photographer for *Citizen Kane* and *Wuthering Heights*. Toland spent much of 1942 producing an 83-minute docu-drama on location in Hawaii and at the Hollywood lot of 20th Century Fox.

The unexpurgated version of *December 7th* is simply awful. Much of the running time is divided between a racist account of the imaginary Japanese American spy activities and a simplistic debate between Uncle Sam and Mr. C (his conscience). Uncle Sam (Walter Huston) is in Hawaii taking a break from the world's state of crisis. His conscience, Mr. C (Harry Davenport) won't leave him in peace. He chides Uncle Sam for his isolationist and relaxed attitudes; there are dangerous countries out there and their spies are paving the way for an attack. The film then shows Japanese American hairdressers, gardeners, and cabbies eavesdropping on white Americans, then reporting their findings to Japan by secret radios (a paranoia not unlike that in the Japanese film *Weapons of the Heart* (*Kokoro no busō*)). A subversive Shintō priest (played by a Korean American) exhorts Japanese Americans to pledge themselves to the emperor and the Japanese race. A token Nazi makes an appearance, but it's important to note he's an American of German ancestry.

After the spectacular battle scenes, the ghost of a victim of Pearl Harbor (Dana Andrews) meets a ghostly soldier from WWI in Arlington Cemetery. The latter predicts a third world war if American returns to isolationism, using a baseball metaphor straight from *Kill Or Be Killed:* "America decided they [sic] didn't want to play ball in the international league and left Wilson on third base." The Pearl Harbor ghost returns the metaphor, saying he's depending on the leaders of the free world to make the world safe:

> "Safe, period. Safe for us to continue our democracy; safe for any other nation to live under any book of rules whatever its name so long as they call a fair ball fair and a foul ball foul [sic]. This time Uncle Sam's going to be in there pitching. When this ball game is over, a lot of guys are coming back to home plate and they're going to ask a lot of questions."

Most of the scenes above were expurgated from the final film, leaving the battle and its aftermath. For filmmakers and military and civilian bureaucrats, the film's failure was not its attack on the Japanese American community. According to research by William Murphy and James Skinner, the reasons were multiple.[1] Secretary of Navy Frank Knox found the film too easy on Japanese Americans. Julian Johnson, Fox's head of production, liked the film but found the "graveyard stuff" anti-climactic, Harold Stark, commander of naval forces in the European theater, thought it portrayed the navy in a poor light:

> "It is true that every caution was being maintained to prevent internal sabotage, but it is not true that U.S. Navy task forces were not at sea, as they were; also, Navy PBYs were out on patrol work...As I reported to the President that afternoon, our striking forces were not impaired despite the destruction we suffered. The picture leaves the

distinct impression that the Navy was not on the job, and this is not true. Also, a goodly part of the damage was done by Jap torpedo planes and not enough of these are shown. I am not concerned with minor inaccuracies but great harm will be done and sleeping dogs awakened if the picture is released as it now stands, leaving the impression that the Navy was asleep."[2]

Toland was crushed by the criticism, and beat a retreat to Rio with the Field Photographic Unit. Ford turned his attention to the work print upon his return from India, where he worked on *Victory in Burma*. He gutted *December 7th*, except for the battle, and won an Academy Award for the effort.

Americans shot only five or six minutes of documentary footage at Pearl Harbor — mostly burning ships and medics tending to the wounded. According to a biographer of John Ford, 100 feet of 16mm black and white was shot by C. Daugherty, and Lt. Cmd. Edward Young shot another 100 feet on 8mm Kodachrome. A few of Daughtery's shots may be seen in *December 7th*, but by and large the entire sequence is special effects. In the last 40 years, these reconstructions have been recycled as reality by countless, naive documentary filmmakers, blurring the line between fiction and documentary in ways Toland and Ford couldn't have predicted.

— *Abé Mark Nornes*

NOTES

1. Murphy, William T. "John Ford and the Wartime Documentary," *Film and History* IV/1 (February 1976), and Skinner, James. *December 7th: Filmic Myth Masquerading as Historical Fact*," (unpublished manuscript). This essay relies heavily on the latter for historical material.
2. Murphy, op cit., p. 7.

Momotarō's Sea Eagle
(Momotarō no umiwashi)

Japan *Planning:* Navy Dept. of Information, *Photography:* Seo Mitsuyo, *Music:* Itō Noboru, *Engineering, Orchestration:* Mochinaga Tadahito, *Special Effects:* Kimura Hajime, *Script:* Kurihara Shigeru, *Assistance:* Tanabe Toshihiko, Hashimoto Tamako, Tsukamoto Shizuyo, *Production:* Geijutsu, *Executive Produce*r: Ōmura Einosuke, *Print:* 35mm, sd., Japanese, b&w, 37 min. (the extant print is 33 min.), 1943.

Story: Here is a press release from the time of the film's release:

"Momotarō, the hero of children's stories, makes a leap up onto the stage of the Greater East-Asia War! As the commander of the Sea-Eagles, he takes to the field in the greatest bombing of the century. Displaying their skill honed through rigorous daily training, his pheasant, canine and simian troops cleverly spread out freely, in all directions, and using bombs and torpedoes destroy the enemy airfield on Onigashima Military Harbor (Demon Island — Hawaii's Pearl Harbor), filling the screen with countless thrilling, unparalleled scenes. The spectacular shape of the mother ship, riding the wind and waves of the Pacific, heads east! While the attack signal steadily grows in volume, the stern, manly Commander Momotarō gives an address of instructions and sends the air assault division on their bombing run. As a rabbit ground crew member encourages them on, the large force takes off towards the enemy army's port! To crush the enemy fleet! To the tune of Hawaiian music, they rush into the enemy

Fig. 3. Magazine ad for *Momotarō's Sea Eagle*. "Annihilate American Cartoons! Those American gangsters Popeye and Roosevelt are nothing! This is how Momotarō's troops will blow them away!"

Fig. 4. Momotarō inspects the troops before the attack on Pearl Harbor. (Credit: Shochiku)

harbor at dawn, beginning an exciting bombing and torpedo attack. Fish riding on torpedoes, acting as living missiles, make a surprise attack on the enemy ships; using their unique prowess, monkeys land at the enemy airfield and destroy all the planes in a ball of fire; a triumphal song rises high. After watching the spectacle of the red and blue demons run about flustered over the near-instantaneous sinking of their ships, the air assault division, still singing their victory march, returns to the mother ship. Our surprise attack is a success. A triumphant cry goes up over the wireless and the whole ship begins celebrating."

Commentary: The press sheet above has the approval of Lt. Commander Hamada Shōichi of the Navy's Information Division. Here is a passage from his comments:

"I think that in the feature-length animation *Momotarō's Sea Eagle*, in which Momotarō subjugates Onigashima in a manner similar to the attack on Hawaii, Geijutsu Motion Picture Company is showing a prejudiced view. Regarding this type of film, the Navy has been careful from long before to try and take measure of its application. This time, we have again sponsored production...This is the first feature-length animated film in Japan, and more than that, it gives me great pleasure to think that here we have brought forth a superior work that rises above the average animated movie. Looking at the absurd animated films made before now, the flavor of *Momotarō's Sea Eagle* can enlighten people's conceptions of aviation. I believe that without a doubt, there is something of value in this movie that makes it worth seeing by all Japanese people, and on those grounds it has been approved."

Here is a representative film critique of the time:

"This animated film, using the spirit of Momotarō, raises the aggressiveness of the Japanese people, and with the intent of planting self-confidence in brave hearts...is a work that is possessed of the will of the war film (Tsumura Hideo, *Asahi Shinbun*, 3 December 1943)."

Even with the support of the army, to make a work during the war was very difficult. Seo Mitsuyo's recollections:

"As the time before the Battle of Midway was Japan's time of superiority, when I went to the Navy Department there was a very festive air, like a *matsuri* [fair or festival]. On desks here and there whiskey bottles were laid out. According to Lt. Commander Hamada, they were working with Tōhō on feature films, but as best as they could tell we were the only ones who could make an animated film for them. The Navy Department would pay all expenses, no matter how much. It was decided that once the film was completed, it would be screened in regular theaters. The animated movies we had made before hadn't been shown in everyday theaters because there was no distribution route. As we had a guarantee against narrow distribution and would be able to show the film to large numbers of people, both President Ōmura [Einosuke] and I were very pleased. But there was a problem with production time. A feature film shot by Tsuburaya Eiji, utilizing the entire staff of Tōhō, and with large amounts of cement and other supplies for SFX, was completed within the allotted six months. That was *The War at Sea from Hawaii to Malaya* [*Hawai, Marē okikaisen*, released in December 1942, directed by Yamamoto Kajirō]. They told us to make an animated film in three months. This is really too little time. Even if you increase the size of the staff, soon all they are doing is painting colors and tracing. As it turned out, Mochinaga and I ended up doing all the animation, backgrounds, and photography. I'm known as a fast drawer. I didn't keep track of how many drawings I made, but I kept drawing from morning to night. Today, I wonder just how much I did draw — if they were stacked up how high would the pile be? The drawings were soon sent to the tracers. At any rate, they were made in a reckless dash. Mochinaga is the opposite: the type who does things calmly and thoroughly. Even though our characters are opposite, we got along well. I suppose the production time took close to six or seven months. We worked without breaks, sleeping only a little each day. During the times I was waiting for Mochinaga to finish a picture, I took naps next to the camera. Because we didn't have time, we made the scenes of the ship-borne planes taking off and landing first, then filled in the middle. We didn't have a consistent scenario to follow from the start, so to fill up blank spaces we put in episodes of monkeys playing *tsume shōgi*, small carp streamers, monkey ladders, eagle parent and child couples... The B-17 bomber was drawn from pictures seen in *Life* magazine. Due to wartime shortages, it was difficult to find cels, but not just because they were expensive. At this time, cels were made from real celluloid. The raw material for it, cellulose, was also used as a raw material for gunpowder, so the military had priority rights to it. But since this was sponsored by the Navy Department, we received some provisions. Our film was cut to size from a base negative roll, but there really wasn't enough. Unavoidably, the cels that we had finished shooting on were washed until the color came off so we could use them again. We washed them five times and kept using them. When we would do that, the cels would get warped or otherwise damaged. When you put as many as three cels that have lost their transparency together, it becomes impossible to see the background. So we established a rule to only stack two cels together. The thickness of old cels is uneven, so the middle becomes depressed and warped. When held against a flat glass for shooting, the edges of the cel warp into waves. The people who see this film usually ask, 'The edge of the screen is a little whitish. What were you trying to do with that?' Nothing, really: that is halation resulting from the warping of the cel. On the deck of the sinking enemy ship, there is a small joke — the sailor running frantically looks just like Bluto from 'Popeye.' There was a problem: when that shot was lip-synched by a Japanese actor, the joke feeling just didn't come out. Eventually, we dubbed it from a 'Popeye' print we had taken from Paramount. That's why the same voice is heard two or three times in that shot. Even though at this time Geijutsu was having difficulties and paying low, they made unreasonable demands on the staff and pressed them to finish the film. Speaking for myself, I had been pushing myself too hard. It caught up with me, and I was laid up for awhile. I should probably talk about more than production background and plans. This film, in other words, was made during the Pacific War, by direct order and with the assistance of the military, whose direct aim was to raise the fighting spirit, aggressiveness, and perhaps help collect volunteers. At the same time, it was the first feature-length Japanese animated film. By today's standards, with respect to screening time it might be considered a semi-feature length film, but when you remember the conditions of the time when it was made, it was naturally an achievement to be proud about. At the preview, Prince Takamatsu was greatly pleased, and said 'This is good. We must show it to His Highness the Royal Prince.' Later on, I heard that they had screened it in the palace. That means that the current emperor, Akihito, has seen this movie. It was a big hit with the industrial sector as well, and on opening day, the area around Nippon Theater was surrounded by children three rows deep."

While it is a fact that this film does not tell much about the background of the time, when talking about the history of animation, this film is always listed up. Don't be affected by "formal" criticism; approach the work frankly and openly. You'll be surprised at the many interesting qualities. 1) The solemn preparations for the bombing attack at dawn give a sense of tension enough to make a person shudder. As a result of the depth of the multi-plane photography, the shots from the bridge have a strange power from the slowly cresting, out-of-focus waves beyond the empty deck. You feel that something is steadily advancing. This creates anticipation and tension in the viewers, keeping them alert. 2) Commander Momotarō's speech: the headbands of the men, motionless, standing at attention, are flapping in the strong wind. The motion in the midst of such stillness is oddly fitting. 3) The scenes of the ship-borne planes taking off are fully-animated — note the realism of the turning propellors. 4) The flight scenes are quite powerful, focusing on the roar of the engines and the rotating propellors of the large force Momotarō has sent to Onigashima. 5) The animators skillfully show the idle relaxed mood on Onigashima: the ships rocking in the waves as Hawaiian music plays. 6) At the end of the attack, when the planes return to the ship and land, the tires bulge, the planes taxi and stop. A plane that was hit by enemy fire is missing. "One plane missing, crew unhurt" comes the announcement by the rabbit ground crew member. His expression is the only one with an adult-like feeling to it. This character of the rabbit was so appealing that, after the war, Tezuka Osamu used him for one of his comics.

On the other hand, it is true that the vital air attack scenes are horribly confused. In this scene, we have a shot showing the interior of a cockpit after the plane has been hit, showing the small soldier spinning around as he begins to burn, but there is also a shot that breaks the laws of physics, showing a plane stop in mid-air and drop a bomb directly beneath it. There's the episode where the monkey pilot makes a monkey ladder and climbs down it to attack the base. It works as long as you suppose an airplane can stop in mid-flight. It's animation, so it doesn't have to be totally real, but there are also some pretty bad failures. For example, the scene where the grounded thousand-round plane (supposed to be a B-17) is burned and totally destroyed by one match usually gets a good laugh. If you have an enemy that you can't beat in an open fight, there is the idea that it's good to go after him in little ways. Actually, before the war ended, that is exactly the tactic used in Okinawa during the fighting there. This kind of unfair strategy may hold some appeal to Japanese feelings.

While this war movie suffers some weaknesses, it is also a monumental achievement in Japanese animation history. It is a work possessed of both light and shadows — good and bad aspects — and it is on that basis that it should be appraised.

In 1945, Seo Mitsuyo completed what could only be called a sequel to this work, called *Momotarō — Divine Troops of the Ocean (Momotarō — umi no shinpei)*. There is a well-known story that when, as a boy, Tezuka Osamu saw this animated film at the Onboro Theater (in the midst of an area ravaged by air attacks), he was to moved to tears and decided to become an animator himself. It was long believed that this film had been lost or destroyed in the confusion following the end of the war, but negatives were found in 1983 in the Shōchiku Ōfuna Studio warehouse. People probably remember the "Discovery of Famous Phantom Cartoon" *(maboroshi no meisaku anime hakken)* as the mass media community called it. According to Seo, "Fleisher moved on down to *Mr. Bug Goes to Town*, right? That's quite a step down from *Superman*. There's a big drop from my Momotarō of the war to my post war *Ōsama no shippo (The King's Tail)*. In the long run, I put all of my efforts into Momotarō, and that became the high-point of my animation career." Seo, who always remembers those (for a creator) fatal images, changed his style as he said above, and carries on to the present day.

Mochinaga Tadahito, who did the engineering and coordination on this film, emigrated to Manchuria right before the War ended, and lived through the Soviet intervention in the War and the Chinese Communist revolution. He helped to establish Shanghai Animation Studios, and was otherwise active in the revival of Chinese animation. After returning to Japan, he became accomplished as a doll animator. While working as a lecturer at the National Film College in Beijing, he contributed to Sino-Japanese film exchange. The producer, Ōmura Einosuke, became an ardent documentary producer after the war, and was also active as an executive of the Japanese Communist Party. He passed away in 1986 at the age of 80.

— *Komatsuzawa Hajime*

Japan in Time of Crisis

Lifeline of the Sea
(Umi no seimeisen)

Japan *Production:* Yokohama Cinema, *Sponsor:* Navy, *Instruction:* Commander Taketomi Kunishige, Commander Shibata Zenjirō, *Editing, Screenplay:* Aochi Chūzō, *Photography:* Saeki Eisuke, Ueno Yukikio, *Print:* 35mm, silent, Japanese intertitles, 32 min., 1933.

Shot in 1933, *Lifeline of the Sea* is a scrupulous record of the native features, products, and daily lives of the native peoples in Japan's trust territories, the Marianas, the Caroline Islands, Marshall Islands, Tinian and Saipan. At the same time, it emphasizes how important those tropical islands are to national defense. They had been the colonial territory of Germany until the outbreak of World War I, when the Japanese military began its colonization in October 1914. After the war, the islands became a trust territory of Japan.

According to Tanaka Jun'ichirō's *Nihon kyōiku eiga hattatsu shi* (History of the Development of the Japanese Educational Film, 1979), Yokohama Cinema Company received information from Commander Shibata (of the Navy's Military Promotion Department) regarding the gunboat Koshu's visit to the tropical islands to carry out land surveys starting in April 1933. The company sent two cameramen on board with orders to shoot throughout the islands. Obviously, this was influenced by the intentions of the Navy, and the results of the 1930 London Naval Disarmament Treaty. When the government accepted the treaty at the London Naval Conference, there was a great outcry from opponent cliques in the navy. The treaty specified a Japanese naval warship ratio of 70% against that of the United States. A debate on the chain of supreme command ensued, and the navy became sensitive to the warship construction competition with Britain and the States, which would presumably start after the invalidation of the treaty in 1936. Under such circumstances, the navy could support the production and distribution of this film to exaggerate the menace posed by Britain and the U.S. in the south seas, as well as stress the importance of these islands from the point of view of national security. The ad for *Lifeline of the Sea* in a magazine from the time of the film's release displayed a "letter of appreciation" to Yokohama Cinema Company from the Ministry of the Navy.

This film was produced by Yokohama Cinema Company, then sold to Mainichi Newspapers; nationwide distribution was conducted by Sanei Motion Picture Co. with a November 16 opening. The film found public favour and was a big hit throughout Japan. For example, on the morning of opening day, a long line of spectators stood before Tokyo's Teikoku Theater. The box office receipts never dropped for the following three weeks. Iida Shinmi admired its workmanship in the 1 December 1933 edition of *Kinema Junpō,* then added "in terms of box office, there has been no more successful Japanese documentary in history."

Even watching it now, we can see why it was such a hit with both audiences and critics. The film starts with a precise explanation of the history of the islands using skillful engravings. The screen openly and concretely talks about the climate and the native's daily lives, as if it were a precious ethnographic documentary. It is vividly real and never feels like a so-called national policy film. In the final minutes, the touch of the screen suddenly shifts with a message in the spirit of national defense: "Protect it! *Lifeline of the Sea!*" However, audiences at the time probably considered this simply tacked on. The film suggests Japan can never surrender these islands because of their tens of thousands of yen in potential profits from sugar cane and fish, but it's more than that. Beyond this national policy gesture, the scenes from these rich islands excited audiences, filling with them with dreamy expectations. In the same way, the staff probably turned the warm, inquisitive gaze of the documentarist toward the South Seas scenery and lifestyles.

Camera operator Saeki Eisuke represented Yokohama Cinema Co., which was established in 1913 (the present name of the company is Yokohama Cinema Laboratory). It received great public attention after the success of *Lifeline of the Sea,* and the Ministry of the Navy came to realize the power of cinema. This brought about the production of a companion film, *Japan Advancing to the North* (*Hokushin Nihon,* by the same staff). It involved a long location shoot focusing on the daily life and climate at Sakhalin and Chishima Islands, and, of course, stressed the importance of the "lifeline of the northern sea." The word "lifeline" was one of the phrases in vogue at the time. It originated from a quotation used in a speech given by the Seiyu Party's Matsuoka Yōsuke at a parliamentary plenary session in January 1931. Matsuoka declared, "Manchuria is the lifeline of our nation."

After this speech, people frequently used the phrase whenever they referred to national security subjects. It was also used in slogans like "lifeline of our home" and "lifeline of the skin."

— Yamane Sadao

Toybox Series #3: Picture Book 1936 (Momotarō vs. Mickey Mouse)
(Omochabako shiriizu daisanwa: Ehon 1936 nen)

Japan Art: Nakano Takao, Tanaka Yoshitsugu, Funaki Shun'ichi, Nagahisa Yoshirō, Nishiguchi Higuma, *Photography:* Taira Yasunobu, *Music:* J.O. Orchestra, *Production:* J.O. Studio Productions, *Print:* 16mm, sd., Japanese, b&w, 8 min., 1934.

Story: On a southern island, a black cat (who looks just like Felix) and some dolls are playing and sporting about. Suddenly, a large group of mice, looking very much like Mickey Mouse, ride up on bats and begin bombarding the island. From the sea, a crowd of huge snakes with machine guns instead of mouths lands on the island. In no time at all, the peaceful island is ablaze in war, and the peaceful inhabitants can do nothing but flee in confusion. The invaders kidnap a little girl doll and tie her to a post, and dance around her in a frenzy. The islanders who fled plead for help to folk tale characters in a picture book: "Please help us, we're in a terrible

Fig. 5. Murderous Mickey Mouse on his flying bat.
(Credit: Komatsuzawa Hajime)

situation." Momotarō, Kintarō, and other ancient Japanese folk heroes appear from the picture book, and dispatch "Mickey Mouse" and the other invaders. As could be expected, Hanasakuji also appears, and when he scatters the ashes, cherries blossoms pop open on the dead trees. Beneath the flowers, everybody celebrates, dancing and singing the "Tokyo Chorus."

Commentary: Please note that although this film was made in 1934, the title reads 1936. Three years before this film, the Manchurian Incident occurred. To call a spade a spade, the Japanese army started a war. The League of Nations determined that Japan was the aggressor. The year before the movie is set in 1933, Japan announced that it was going to leave the League of Nations, starting in 1935. As a result a problem arose over the jurisdiction of the South Seas Mandate, which was comprised of the Marshall Islands and so on, what was at the time called the Inner South Pacific. As the mandate had been formally received from the League of Nations, the basis for possession under international law disappeared upon withdrawal. Moreover, the next year (1936) was the year when the London and Washington Armament Limitation Treaties expired. This is when the right wing of the time began its dangerous opinion campaign of 1936. "America is going to attack the Imperial lands in the Pacific!" and "Better safe than sorry — expand the military!" became the slogans of the day.

Without this historical background, this animated short cannot really be understood.

On a southern island, animals lived a happy life, dancing and playing... This opening scene is meant to show the peaceful life of the "southern natives" under the benevolent rule of Japan. The background music, believe it or not, is "Chieftan's Daughter": "I am the daughter of Chief Rabu, I'm dark-colored, a south seas beauty..." those lyrics with their racist smell are absent, but the song is attacked by an army of mice who bear an uncanny resemblance to Mickey Mouse. This is basically an anti-foreign viewpoint showing America as a potential enemy. The islanders flee in panic. Then the *deus ex machina* of Momotarō, Kintarō, and friends appear from the picture book and save the day. This is nationalism (yeah, right!). As animation goes, one might defend the film if this were well-done, but this is nothing but loose, wobbly animation. Moreover, the number of repeated scenes is excessively large. In the final scene, all the characters dance to the "Tokyo Chorus." Were this scene to appear in a movie today it would be taken as a surrealistic gag.

It could be said that this is nothing more than an empty or meaningless attempt to satisfy those threatened by the fact that war could happen any time. But for this reason, it is important as historical material.

J.O. Studio Productions had a strange, abrupt and unusual existence in the annals of Japanese animation. First, it was originally an amateur film group called Hitomi M.P. Co., but they came out suddenly one day, and became engaged in epoch-making pre-scoring recordings with orchestras, and included on their register such future big-names such as Ichikawa Kon. None of their films were particularly impressive, and the animation division soon disappeared. The company was merged with PCL and became Tōhō Eiga, and began to concentrate on feature films. Although the PCL animation division was affiliated with Tōhō, it continued on, and during the war was called Tōhō Aviation Educational Material Productions. After the war, it became known as Tōhō Illustrated Pictures, and in the end continued on to today in the same stream as Tōhō Animation.

J.O. Cartoons could be called an experiment, a trial-and-error process with the aim of advancing animation, and serves as an example of failure.

But it is true that the staff tried to make good films, and they tried to make animated movies that would sell. That effort was meant to follow the current of the times, and as a result of that effort, this film has come down to us today.

— *Komatsuzawa Hajime*

Japan in Time of Crisis
(Hijōji Nippon, also Japan in Time of Emergency, The Critical Period of Japan)

Japan *Director:* Kondō Iyokichi, *Co-Director, Editor:* Nakajima Masatsugu, *Sound:* Sayato Tsuneo, *Photography:* Satake Mitsuo, Sumita Eisuke, *Credits and Graphics:* Murata Yasuji, *Prod:* Osaka Mainichi Shinbun, *Advisors:* Lt. Col. Honma (Ministry of War, Press Section), Lt. Col. Maeda (Adjunct to Minister of War), Maj. Matsui (Ministry of War, Press Section), Infantry School, Cavalry School, Artillery School, Engineering School, Tokorozawa Air Force Academy, Div. 4, Army Band of Toyama School, *General Manager:* Mizuno Shinkō, *Editing:* All Nippon Cinema Education Inst., *Print:* 35mm, sd., Japanese, b&w, 99 min., 1933.

Japan in Time of Emergency was released to the public in August 1933. Based on a speech by Minister of War Araki Sadao, the film utilizes various materials, such as documentary film, drama, and animation, to explain Japan's invasion of China and its historical importance, as well as the features of the Japanese State. The film was not considered a documentary for propaganda use; rather, it was released widely to the public at ordinary movie theaters, just like any ordinary feature film. Later, the film was submitted to the "Tokyo Trials" as material evidence, which may imply the film is endowed with high qualifications as documentary cinema.

The title's phrase, "Time of Crisis" had been popular from 1931 on, roughly corresponding with the outbreak of the Manchurian Incident. For example, Prime Minister Saitō Makoto (successor to Prime Minister Inukai Tsuyoshi, who was assassinated in the May 15 Incident of 1932) used the phrase "Time of Crisis" in speeches to describe the severe situation Japan found itself in. From this time on, the phrase increasingly entered the popular vernacular. Following Japan's withdrawal from the League of Nations in March 1933, the Ministry of Education (Monbushō) instigated a movement called, "Citizens' Movement in Time of Crisis." In April, a mass meeting was held under the name "Prayer to Overcome the Nation's Crisis." In July, Monbushō published 10,000 copies of a book entitled, *Hijōji to kokumin no go* (Crisis Time and the National Mind), and offered it to all schools and political youth parties. The words "Time of Crisis" prevailed throughout Japan in this period. Some people even joked about it, answering the question, "What time is it now?" with "It's Crisis Time."

It was under such circumstances that the film *Japan in Time of Crisis* was produced. Large numbers of documentary films were produced in Japan, particularly with the outbreak of the Manchurian Incident, and these film constantly used the words "Crisis Time." One of the representative films along these lines is *Lifeline of the Sea*, for which Murata Yasuji also produced the intertitles.

> "After long patience, it's now *Japan in Time of Crisis!!*"
>
> "Look at Japan in its time of crisis, and defend the sacred country of Japan!"
>
> "An 'active movie' *(katsuei)* for our times. This is it!"

These are advertisement slogans for the film from *Kinema Junpō*. These exaggerations give us a glimpse at the intentions with which this film was produced. As we see by looking at the production staff, this was a project crystalized with the might of the Japanese military. The neologism "katsuei" (literally: active/living movie) was used above to deliberately set this apart from the everyday film and emphasize its documentary value.

This film begins with Minister of War Araki Sadao's speech, in which he explains that the roots of Japan's "Time of Crisis" come from the Manchurian Incident. He continues to explain how "sacred Japan" *(shinkoku Nippon)*, and the "Yamato race" was destined to be the "sole guardian of the Oriental hemisphere." Therefore, the Manchurian Incident was entirely justified. At the same time, Araki says that a "warning from heaven" *(ten no keishō)*, a "revelation from heaven" *(ten no keiji)*, will strike those people who, because of their infatuation with Western customs, have forgotten "Japanese consciousness" *(Nihonjin no jikaku)*. He argues the defence of the nation is inextricably linked to the "Imperial Way," and that the "Imperial Way" is by nature "eternal" *(yūkyūeiensei)* and "ever-expanding" *(kakudai hattensei)*. The absolute mobilization of the nation is not simply for fighting, but for spreading the

Imperial Way. Araki continues to explain how "the soldiers of Japan act obediently according to the will of the Emperor." These examples show how the "Ideology of the Japanese Spirit" was one and the same as the "Ideology of Invasion." It's no wonder that this film proved useful as material evidence in the "Tokyo Trials." When Araki shouted the words "Sacred Japan" and "Yamato Race," the screen was decorated skillfully with scenes of cherry blossoms, pagodas, *torii*, and close-ups on the rising sun flag. These images contributed greatly to the effectiveness of the speech. It serves as excellent evidence of the extent to which the ideology of invasion spawned by the nation's leaders had penetrated the people's minds. We can also imagine the enthusiastic endeavor of the film's staff. However, watching it today, it's not terribly interesting. The drama was clumsy, and because it is basically an illustrated speech, no single section can stand on its own. One can only wonder how people found the film in those days.

— *Yamane Sadao*

China

Diary of Boys Reclaiming the Land
(Shōnen takushi no nikki)

Japan *Photography:* Yamaguchi Takezō, *Editing:* Akutagawa Mitsuzō, *Music:* Sugiyama Haseo, *Orchestra:* PCL Symphony Orchestra, *Sound:* Kanayama Kinjirō, *Production:* Manchurian Railway Corp. (Mantetsu), *Print:* 35mm, sd., Japanese, b&w, 29 min., 1941.

Although some references cite 1941 as the production year for *Diary of Boys Reclaiming the Land*, 1940 is more likely, since a message in the title credits informs us that this film was intended to participate in the festival celebrating the 2,600 year anniversary of the founding of Japan. From the beginning of this year, there were various kinds of commemorative events. The ones occurring throughout October and November bore the word "celebration" (*hōshuku*) in their names. This mood for celebration came to a peak when the government sponsored a massive ceremony for the 2,600th year of the Imperial Era, which took place on November 16. The film would have participated as a commemorative event, and was released to the public throughout Japan.

The formal name of the Manchurian Railway Studio (Mantetsu) was the Southern Manchurian Railway Co., Ltd., Public Relation Department, Movie Section, (Minami Manshū tetsudō kabushikigaisha kōhōbu eigahan) and was founded in 1928. The company experienced remarkable development from 1931 to 1932, which corresponds to the time of the Manchurian Incident and the inauguration of the Manchurian Empire. Akutagawa Mitsuzō was responsible for production at the company. His work in *Hikyō Nekka* (*Jehol — The Dreamland of Manchukuo*, 1936), *Sōgen Baruga* (*Barga Grasslands*, 1936) and *Nyan nyan miyao hoi* (also *Nyan Nyan Musume*; Japanese transliteration: *Roro byōkai*, 1940) won high praise as documentary films. Later, Akutagawa joined the Manchurian Movie Association in 1941. *Diary of Boys Reclaiming the Land* should be a film from the end of his Mantetsu period.

For this film, he shot the daily life of the Manchuria-Mongolia Brave Young Reclamation Corps (Man-Mō kaitaku shōnen giyūgen) on location in Manchuria and Mongolia. The first scene presents a map of the locations where the corps were training throughout China. The film then continues in the form of a diary, recording their daily routine from getting up to going to bed. It shows their obligatory daily work, including the care of livestock, farming, battle training, studying, and the like. The film describes the true feeling of corps members by presenting scenes of boys recollecting travel and their hometowns. The touch of this straightforward approach brings about a certain lyrical feeling. The scene showing pressed flowers discovered in a boy's parcel from home, or the boys delight in even simple food, leave a lasting impression. The film's intention, needless to say, was to appeal to young boys to be aggressive pioneers for the "Imperial Empire." However, this appeal was not exaggerated in the film, and the boy's simple life came out with a pure impression.

The Manchurian/Mongolian Brave Young Reclamation Corps were, in fact, young immigrants sent to the regions of North East China and its adjoining territory, Inner Mongolia. The plan for full-scale immigration to Manchuria was completed in 1935. The "Manchurian Immigrants Association" (Manshū imin kyōkai) was created in the same year, and in the next year formal immigration was initiated under the Kwantung Army's "Plan for Housing 1,000,000 Farmer Immigrants to Manchuria" (Manshū nōgyō imin hyakuman to keikaku). As far as the movie world was concerned, the Ministry of Reclamation produced mainly documentaries promoting farmers' immigration to Manchuria, such as *Hirake Manshū (Develop Manchuria)*, *Hokuman o hirake (Open North Manchuria)*, and *Manshū nōgyō imindan kinkyō (Recent Report on Farm Settlers in Manchuria)*. In this context, the "Corps of Young Volunteers Reclaiming Manchuria-Mongolia" was formed. Five-thousand young people were sent out as the first corps. This was in 1938. The corps consisted of volunteers consisting of boys aged 17 to 20. After completion of training, two months in Japan and three years in Manchuria, they were to be settled down in the regions along the Russian border, changing their corps name to "Volunteer Reclamation Group Corps." The scenes in this film are various aspects of daily life at their training center. According to the rules, the volunteer corps consisted entirely of free applicants; however, the allocation of spaces was distributed among all urban and rural prefectures, and some applicants were appointed by their teachers. Despite the fact that they were called "reclamation corps," they were apt to be converted into soldiers in many cases.

Plenty of boys were sent to Manchuria and Mongolia year by year. The exact number is uncertain. According to the records of the Ministry of Health and Welfare, the number of Japanese civilians (not counting soldiers and their civilian staff) amounted to 1,550,000 at the time of Japan's surrender in 1945. The civilian death toll was counted at 179,000. Among the survivors, it's estimated that 270,000 were members of the reclamation corps, but in truth of fact, not all survivors returned safely to Japan. Many lost their lives or disappeared in the mess caused by the surrender, and we all know the sad stories about the lasting problem of Japanese orphans displaced by the war in China. What was the fate of these innocent boys in this film?

Quite a few documentaries like *Diary of Boys Reclaiming the Land* were produced, however, none are extant. Drama films about immigrant farmers in Manchuria were produced, for example, *10,000 Ri of Fertile Land* (*Yokudo banri*, Nikkatsu, 1940) was shot on reclaimed land in Manchuria by director Kurata Bunjin; Toyoda Shirō's *Ohinata Village* (*Ohinata mura*, Tokyo Hassei, 1940) was a story about immigrants to Manchuria from Nagano Prefecture; other films are still available. There were quite a few films called "continental films" (*tairiku eiga*). Among them, the ones with the highest reputations are *Song of the White Orchid* (*Byakuran no uta*, 1939), *China Night*

(*Shina no yoru*) and *Vow in the Desert* (*Nessa no chikai*) (both 1940), which were presented as a series by Tōhō, featuring the co-stars Hasegawa Kazuo and Ri Kō-ran (Yoshiko Yamaguchi). Owing to the popularity of "Manei Star" Ri Kō-ran, these melodramas were big hits, and made audiences long for the Chinese continent simply because the films were set there. Other continental films include *Kokusenya gassen* (*Kokusenya Battle*, Shinkō, 1940) which was set in China, and *Jingisukan* (*Genghis Khan*, Daiei, 1943) which was shot in Mongolia.

— Yamane Sadao

China Incident
(Shina jihen)

Japan *Production:* Ministry of Education, *Sound:* Tōhō and Photo Chemical Research Lab, *Print:* 35mm, sd., Japanese, b&w, 29 min., circa 1938.

China Incident was produced as part of the Department of Education's (Monbushō) plan for uplifting the national fighting spirit. The film elaborates the roots of the incident between Japan and China, as well as important implications for the nation. The year of production remains uncertain, however, we can presume it's around 1938, because it covers events from the China Incident up the the invasion of Nanking. Furthermore, the footage itself apparently originates from the Yomiuri Newspaper Company's newsreels. The production of films at Monbushō began around 1923, initially subcontracting work. Their own filmmaking activities started in 1927, and regular production began from 1933 when the ministry moved to its new office building. However, they had no facilities for talkies, so all sound had to provided from outside. In this case, sound was completed by Tōhō. The films produced by Monbushō were primarily bought by local self-governing bodies. They used the films for social studies and education. They were also offered to the general public. Originally, the main subject matter the ministry dealt with involved the Imperial family, geography, child care, job training, and even dramatic subjects. During the war, however, the ministry devoted itself to producing films exalting the fighting spirit, spreading scientific knowledge, and describing the affairs of the Imperial family. This production continued until the end of the war.

In July 1937 with the Marco Polo Bridge Incident, the war in China completely changed. The government initially named the war the "North China Incident." The Second Shanghai Incident in August (the first occurred in 1932) spread the war further, making the government change the name of the war to the "China Incident" in September. Immediately after that, an official notice and instruction as to the overall exaltation of the nation's spirit followed. This meant that the authorities came to rigidly realize the true meaning and massive impact the on-going war was going to involve. Simultaneous with these events, Tōhō Motion Picture Co. Ltd. was established through the merging of four companies: Tokyo Hassei, Nan'o, Takarazuka and Daihō. Nanking was captured in December. During that time there was a slogan stating, "Luxurious life is the Enemy," rising-sun lunch boxes were popular, and permed hair was banned. The broadcasting of "people's songs" began in October 1937, the first of which was "If We Go To the Sea" ["Umi yukaba," see Abé-Nornes' article on violence for the lyrics. — ed.] The government invited people to write songs to promote the war, holding a contest in which "Patriot March" won first prize in December. This was one of the events for strengthening the national fighting spirit. It could be said that the authorities were attempting to dye the whole of Japan with only a wartime color.

China Incident was produced in this stream of events in order to stir up the fighting spirit. The atrocities in Nanking following its occupation, which the world now knows, were not reported to the Japanese public. Quite the contrary, the Japanese people celebrated the capture of Nanking with processions of flags in the daytime and lanterns at night. The first scene begins with a firm declaration of friendship between Japan and China, followed by a portrait of Japan's industrial strength and China's raw materials. It continues with an explanation on the one hand of 4,000,000 Chinese' misery under the anti-Japanese policies of the Chinese Communist Party and the China National Party, and on the other hand, how the Japanese army did their best to rid China of these powers. Looking at it today, the film dumbfounds us for it's crude rationalization for a war of invasion. Beyond that, it vividly shows how cinema may be utilized to the ends of war, and in that sense it can send shivers down the spine.

— Yamane Sadao

The Battle of China

U.S.A. *Direction:* Frank Capra and Anatole Litvak, *Editing:* William Hornbeck, *Screenplay:* Leonard Spigelgass, William L. Shirer, James Hilton, Robert Heller, *Music:* Dmitri Tiomkin and Alfred Newman, *Animation:* Walt Disney Productions, *Narration:* Walter Huston and Anthony Veiller, *Production:* Special Service Division, Army Service Forces, U.S. War Department, *Print:* 35mm, sd., English, b&w, 65 min., 1944.

In 1991, Frank Capra died at the age of 96, leaving behind a body of work resolutely American in character. In addition to his classic feature films, Capra will always be remembered for supervising the definitive propaganda documentary, the *Why We Fight* series. *Battle of China* was the fifth installment of the series, and in many ways the weakest. For this reason, it's also one of the most interesting, because it reveals the pressure reality exerts on the simplistic world of propaganda.

The *Why We Fight* series grew out of 15 lectures on foreign policy prepared by the Bureau of Public Relations. The idea was to use these canned speeches to ensure that American men in uniform were aware of the past 20 years of foreign affairs, but the results were a disaster. They decided that film was a better medium to capture young soldiers' attention and introduce them to the fundamental ideas underlying their war. For this job, they (literally) enlisted the help of Capra and other Hollywood talent.

Capra had joined the reserves before the war, and the day after Pearl Harbor two officers from the Signal Corps visited him on the set to recruit his help. He readily joined, despite being at the height of his career (with a string of recent hits including *It Happened One Night* (1934), *Mr. Deeds Goes to Town* (1936), *Lost Horizon* (1937), *You Can't Take it With You* (1938), *Mr. Smith Goes to Washington* (1939), and *Meet John Doe* (1941)). Capra set up shop in the Department of Interior, and began watching and accumulating footage for compilation. The military, Hollywood, and the Museum of Modern Art (MOMA) all helped the project. MOMA showed Capra their German films, including *Triumph of the Will* (1935) which had recently been translated by Siegfried Kracauer and other German ex-pats. Capra also gathered around him a powerhouse of Hollywood talent, including Anatole Litvak (for direction), Walter Huston (narration), Joris Ivens (writing), Dmitri Tiomkin (music), Irving Wallace (writing), William Hornbeck (editing), Theodor "Dr. Seuss" Geisel (writing), Disney Studios (animation), Anthony Veiller (writing), and Eric Knight (writing).

In the summer of 1942, Capra, Knight, Litvak and Veiller worked hard on outlines and scenarios, although in truth of fact the films were written by committee, with countless advisors and government agencies checking the scripts. By November 1942 the first film, *Prelude to War*, was released, and won the Oscar for Best Documentary that year. This and the subsequent installments were seen by millions of GIs as mandatory viewing before they set out for the war. Three of the films were distributed commercially, and foreign-language versions were produced in French, Spanish, Chinese, and Russian. Studies have questioned the practical effectiveness of the series, but no one can fail to be impressed by the filmmaking. Had Japanese seen it and compared it to their own films, they might have realized they were doomed to lose.

Writer Eric Knight summed up the approach of the filmmakers, stating that "positive assertion of your beliefs and aims" was more effective that "refutation of enemy assertions."[1] When we consider propaganda, we often imagine a film form free from any responsibilities save asserting one's aims and beliefs. As Knight put it, cinema is "particularly adept at expressing most glibly one of the subtlest tricks of the propagandists: to state a well-known truth, and bracket it with a new truth, or a half-truth or a patent lie."[2] However, *The Battle of China* suggests that reality exerts pressure upon the propagandist, and that propaganda that strays too far from the truth ultimately fails.

Like other films in the *Why We Fight* series, *The Battle of China* divides the earth into two pure spheres: the free world and the slave world. China is a site of contestation between the two, and the first step for the slave world of Japan to take over the free and democratic peoples of North America and Europe. The Chinese race becomes a projection of American ideals with the help of experts like Joseph Grew (the pre-Pearl Harbor ambassador to Japan who is widely admired as a moderating force by today's Japanese). Grew characterizes the Japanese as a "closely disciplined and conformist people — a veritable human bee hive or ant hill" in contrast to the "independent and individualistic" Chinese.

The insect metaphors for the Japanese were old, worn stereotypes, but thinking of China as a bastion of freedom and democracy was relatively new. Chungking is called the capital of "Free China" or "New China" — a dubious description no matter how you look at it — but what really got the film in trouble was the fact that the filmmakers left out Mao and the Communists, disavowing the political turmoil *among Chinese*. Over images of Japanese atrocity, the narrator cries, "In their last bloody blow [Nanking] the Japanese had accomplished what 4,000 years had failed to bring into being...a united China, an aroused China." The discrepancy was too much, and the film was shelved. In the end, however, the film was released anyway, and nearly 4 million soldiers saw it before the end of the war. Today, the film's hyperbole and racism (both latent and blatant) is as striking as the skill with which it was made. Like *Triumph of the Will*, the series Capra left behind has defined "good" propaganda. We need to think about the relationship of these films to today's documentaries, especially those made in times of war, for World War II films like these solidified an array of documentary conventions that are with us to this day.

NOTES

1. Culbert, David. "Why We Fight: Social Engineering for a Democratic Society at War," in K.R.M. Short, ed., *Film and Radio Propaganda in World War II* (Tennessee: University of Tennessee Press, 1983), 181. Much of the historical background here comes from Culbert's essay. See also Murphy, William T. "The Method of Why We Fight." *Journal of Popular Film* I (1972): 185-196.
2. Culbert, p. 181.

— *Abé Mark Nornes*

The Homefront

Women of Steel

U.S.A. *Production:* War Manpower Commission, *Print:* 35mm, sd., English, b&w, 10 min., 1943.

Presented, ironically enough, by the War Manpower Commission, *Women of Steel* is a Rosie the Riviter classic documenting life in a wartime steel mill. With most of the men off at war, women have taken their places, easily debunking the myth that each sex has appropriate work. In this film, women pour molten steel into molds, perform chemical tests, weld materials, machine parts, and move large slabs of glowing steel around the factory floor. They are obviously happy and proud of the work they do, yet the film sets this satisfaction within a framework that reveals much about society's sexist attitudes toward women.

Though clearly proving they are fit for any work, the film tells us women are performing "a man's work and they can draw a man's pay." In a patronizing manner, they are complimented for their "adaptability to small tools." Women often compare tasks like pouring molten steel to housework, and one woman assures the audience that "this job belongs to some soldier, and when he comes back he can have it." The gains women made in the early forties were swiftly lost after the war, when the possibility of work outside the home was foreclosed. This is foreshadowed in several places in *Women of Steel,* especially the interviews:

(Male) **INTERVIEWER:**	Edith Stoner's husband is in Alaska. She took this job for the duration. How do you like your job Mrs. Stoner?
EDITH:	I love it.
INTERVIEWER:	How about after the war? Are you going to keep on working?
EDITH:	I should say not. When my husband comes back, I'm gonna be busy back home.
INTERVIEWER:	Good for you!

At the much more subtle level of cinematic narration, we can find an apparent sexism that raises questions about power relationships in documentary cinema. A useful conceptual tool here is what Bill Nichols has called "documentary voice." To consider the "voice" of documentary is to ask from where the film speaks. Rather than looking to the director for the source of meaning, one looks inside the film itself. Where is the origin of the film's storytelling? In the case of most WWII documentary, it's centered near the voice-over narration. This narration works hard to control the disparate bits of information contained in images, sounds, and

Fig. 6. Rosie the Riveter propaganda poster.
(Credit: National Archives)

Fig. 7. Women of steel.
(Credit: National Archive)

interview, making the film coherent and meaningful. Positioned omnipotently off-screen, the narrator wields considerable power over the film, to the degree that he is often called the "voice of God." Perhaps it's not surprising that this voice is almost always male. Woman's voice is usually restricted from this potent point of origin and enunciation, especially in American films

Not only is the narrator male, but the intended audience seems to be as well. The narrator of *Women of Steel* addresses a male "we" about a female "them." In a condescending attempt at praise, the narrator says, "Of course, *we* had long since accepted *their* aptitude in fabrication, the swift, sure dexterity of their fingers [emphasis mine]." This kind of comment reveals that at the deepest level of documentary voice, the film is organized around a masculine point of view. Thus the women of steel are objects of speech and of looks; though we hear them talk, their interviews are within the domain of the documentary's main, masculine voice.

— *Abé Mark Nornes*

We Are Working So So Hard
(Watashitachi wa konna ni hataraite iru)

Japan *Direction:* Mizuki Sōya, *Production:* Asahi, *Photography:* Konishi Shōzō, *Print:* 16mm, sd., b&w, 18 min., 1945.

Produced in the final months of the war, the title of this film is a complaint about working conditions, and the film itself is the government's stern answer: work harder. The setting is a clothing factory, where women churn out piles of uniforms in furious fast motion. In retrospect, the film's urgent tone appears desperate, and within six weeks of its release, Hiroshima lay in ruins. Seen together with its American counterpart, *Women of Steel*, we can compare attitudes toward working women and their relative position in each society.

The first clear difference is the nature of the work and how it's represented cinematically. Instead of pouring molten steel, these women are performing the most domestic of chores: sewing. This "women's work" is, indeed, performed. The mundane task of sewing endless uniforms is transformed into dance-like spectacle through fast and slow motion. The fast motion creates a sense of urgency and the slow motion turns the work into a thing of beauty.

In the *Women of Steel* essay above, I discussed the power relations evident in the film's organization, particularly the narration. Narrators, particularly those that remain off-screen, are a site of power to the extent that they orient the film in a variety of ways. Off-screen female narrators in American films are extremely rare, but not in Japanese films. Many Japanese films, features and documentaries alike, use women's voices for narration. *We Are Working So So Hard* uses an off-screen, female narrator, but as a site of power this narration is weakened by the grammatical inflection of the text itself. As in the film's title, the narrator uses the first person plural "we" *(watashitachi)*. While her voice is singled out above all others, the narrator places herself within the group that's working so hard on-screen. This position has little of the objectifying, controlling power of *Woman of Steel's* omnipotent male narrator.

The fact that the narrator herself is included in the on-screen group strengthens the emphasis on group work and submerged or diffused subjectivity. This is common to most Japanese films of the war period. While the American women of steel are individualized by interviews and are introduced by name, the women of this uniform factory work as a harmonic mass. Virtually the only time a woman worker is singled out for individual attention is when one gives a sewing demonstration. However, as soon as the lecture is over, she quietly melts back into the crowd.

Generally, the documentary form places much less emphasis on individuals than fiction filmmaking. Documentaries encourage us to identify with the film as a member of society or humanity. In comparing Japanese and American war documentary, however, we can see how the American films still rely heavily on characters as hooks for our indentification. Examples from this volume would include *Jap Zero*, *The Fleet That Came to Stay*, *Let There Be Light*, and *Women of Steel*. *We Are Working So So Hard* is typical of Japanese war documentary in that audiences are encouraged to identify with an on-screen group, and by extension the *kokutai* (national structure or body politic). This is one reason for the obligatory exercise scenes that may puzzle foreign viewers of Japanese war films. There could be no better example of group unity than rows upon rows of healthy, young bodies moving in synch. Furthermore, these are group activities (exercises, factory work, singing) that the audience itself was undoubtedly performing on a daily basis.

There is one individualized figure in *We Are Working So So Hard*, and this is the key to the film's sexual politics. While women fade in and out of their group, the male supervisor remains apart. He barely tilts in the face of the women's deep bows. He drills them on the correct way to march, and leads their exercises. He is geographically separated from the group, giving speeches to them from a platform. At lunch, he sits at his own table and accepts tea from one of the workers. While he supervises their every move, they are infantilized by being shown skipping ropes and playing on swings. As Father/Manager/Superior Officer, he takes the place of a substitute patriarch. Together with his factory workers, he functions as a microcosm of the emperor and his subjects. By contrast, *Women of Steel* presents a much more positive image of women and their potential.

— *Abé Mark Nones*

Justice

U.S.A. *Production:* Signal Corps, *Print:* 35mm, sd., English, b&w, 3 min., 1945.

Placed before feature films, *Justice* was a trailer designed to attract people to war jobs. It opens in a factory with the narrator calling out to the workers (and the theater's audience): "Hold on to your seats folks, have you killed a Jap soldier today?" The film continues by cataloging the horrors Chinese suffered under the Greater East-Asia Co-Prosperity Sphere, using footage of Japanese massacres that were recycled in countless films, including *Let's Have a Drink* and most episodes of the *Why We Fight* series. The ending cross cuts between shots of factories and scores of Japanese corpses with the voice of God narration booming, "Every forging...Kills a Jap. Every tank...Kills a Jap. Every truck...Kills a Jap. Every plane...Kills a Jap. Every shell...Kills a Jap. Every gun...Kills a Jap." Simply stated; no subtlety here.

There's a decisiveness of will here that hasn't been seen in any of America's subsequent wars. The hysteria and severity of the violence in this film beg us to reexamine our assumptions about the role of media in both Vietnam and the Gulf wars. Many people assume that the violence TV brought from Vietnam to American homes contributed to the lack of support for the war and the chaos in society. This in turn led to the restriction of media coverage in the Persian Gulf. However, any number of films from this sidebar plainly show that there was no shortage of graphic violence served up for middle America during World War II. And despite the support for the Gulf War, when faced with corpses, Americans showed none of the unflinching confidence exuding from *Justice*.

— Abé Mark Nornes

Introduction to Our Weaponry Series: The Fighting Homefront
(Warera no heikishū — johen — tatakau jūgo)

Japan *Direction:* Azumi Kōji, *Production:* Riken Kagaku, *Inspection:* Ministry of War, Press Section, *Print:* 16mm, sd., Japanese, b&w, 12 min., 1941.

The Fighting Homefront was the introductory issue of a long series produced from 1941 to 1942. The *Our Weaponry* series was made under the supervision of the Army Weaponry Headquarters. Oya Sōichi and Azumi Kōji acted as producer and director, respectively. It consists of sections covering ammunition, cannons, bullets, bombs, guns, swords, machine guns, optical arms, electrical arms, and the like. In each edition, the production process and the features of each weapon is introduced. This introductory episode entitled *The Fighting Homefront* attempts to show how the production of arms requires the participation and contribution of the entire nation.

In the very first scene, the movie camera itself appears on-screen with narration pledging that, "The camera speaks nothing but the truth." Then it captures the figures of women, students, and children working at the production sites. The on-screen camera returns at the end, with the narration stressing, "We must always win," and "That's what the camera screams." On a movie screen containing a record of reality, showing the camera shooting through the eye of the record leaves a strong impression. This is the fruit of labor of excellent documentarists. We imagine that, by offering such peculiar scenes in the film, the staff tried to express the spirit of true workmanship as true documentarists.

However, when we examine the scenes of housewives and children polishing and assembling bombs in surprisingly orderly steps, we must assume that they had to be deliberately arranged. Consequently, by taking advantage of the rhythmic and delicate handiwork, the film succeeds in capturing our interest till the end. Meanwhile, even the bar hostesses and *geisha* have been chased out for the war effort on the homefront, which, we are told, has become the battlefield itself.

The word "homefront" (*jūgo*: literally behind the guns) became popular during the Russo-Japanese War, and meant behind the front lines. With the outbreak of the Sino-Japanese War, the term was immediately revived, signifying the whole of Japan as opposed to the front on the continent. For example, after the outbreak of the so-called Manchurian Incident, a fundraising campaign for the soldiers immediately followed; newspaper coverage used the headline, "Jūgobidan" ("Admirable Story on the Homefront"). Moreover, when the battle in China became a full-scale war in 1937, there were many women standing on street corners collecting *senninbari* (thousand-stitch belts). These women also made the papers: "The Sincerity of the Homefront Revealed by Senninbari." It was at that time that phrases such as "Duty at the Homefront," and "Defense at the Homefront," became popular throughout Japan. In terms of cinema, slogans like "National Unity" and "Keep Defense Firm at the Homefront" were obligatory titles at the beginning of all film screenings starting 1 August 1937. *Devotion on the Homefront (Jūgo no sekisei,* also *Sincerity on the Homefront)* was released by Nikkatsu the same month. In October 1938, "Strengthening the Support from the Homefront Week" was established, which was closely linked to the "Movement for Mobilizing National Spirit." After that, the same week-long celebration was repeated every year. In 1939, Army Support Groups in all cities and villages across Japan were merged under a single organization, "The Association of Devotion from the Homefront."

The Fighting Homefront was produced in this climate. When we think about this title today, the fact that the modifier for "homefront" changed from "defend" *(mamore)* to "fight" *(tatakau)* is deeply meaningful. The motive for the change was the outbreak of the Japan-America War in 1941.

— *Yamane Sadao*

Topaz 1942-1945

U.S.A. *Production:* Dave M. Tatsuno, *Print:* 8mm and color corrected VHS video, silent, color, 48 min., 1942-1945.

> With the help of a sympathetic government employee, Dave Tatsuno smuggled an 8mm movie camera into the Topaz Relocation Authority Center. Around 8,000 Japanese Americans lived in the center, which was located in the desert near Delta, Utah (156 miles south of Salt Lake City). Under the guards' collective noses, he filmed his friends and family for the duration. The form is the home movie; the setting is not home. In the bleak context of the camps, they mug for the camera, show off their kids, and make mochi between the barracks. Mr. Tatsuno regards this film a living memorial to Walter Honderick, the kindly government administrator who slipped the camera into the camp. Below, he tells the story behind the film.

These movies were taken secretly as no cameras were allowed in Topaz, which was within the Western Defense Command Zone. Immediately after Pearl Harbor, all contraband articles such as cameras, swords, guns, shortwave radios and transmitters had to be turned into the police station. However, in our case, we loaned the cameras (both movie and still) to a very good Caucasian friend living in Oakland.

How did the movie camera get to Topaz? I worked as manager of the Dry Goods Division of the Co-op. One day my Co-op Supervisor from the War Relocation Authority (WRA), a grad of the University of Washington and a YMCA man, was taking a shot with his 8mm movie camera. I made a chance remark: "Gosh, I would give my right arm to have my camera here now." His reply was, "Where is it?" So,

Fig. 8. Mugging for the camera in *Topaz*.

Fig. 9. Making *mochi* (New Year's rice cakes) in an American concentration camp — *Topaz*.

I told him that it was loaned to a friend in Oakland for the duration of the war. Instead of ending the matter there, he said, "Why don't you have your friend mail it to me?" Here is where this WRA friend was a key help. Since all packages mailed into the centers for the evacuees were opened and inspected, it would have been impossible for me to get my camera without the help of this friend. When the camera arrived, he brought it to my barrack and said, "Dave, here's your camera...just be careful where you take your shots... I wouldn't get too close to the (barbed-wire) fence."

So I had my camera, but how about movie film, and color film at that...when film was so scarce because of the wartime shortages. As a buyer for the Topaz Co-op, I made three buying trips back East. When I was in Chicago, I would go to Bass', the largest camera store there, and buy several rolls of Kodachrome film. However, once I got the rolls into camp, processing was a problem. I couldn't just drop the developed film in a mail box since films were processed in Los Angeles (within the Western Defense Command Zone). So, instead, I had the films mailed outside the camp in Salt Lake City and returned to my brother who was a student at the University of Utah. He would then give the processed films to someone coming into camp. So, that is how I was able to get these now-priceless shots of camp life in Topaz. It was sheer luck.

When viewing these home movies, there are several things to keep in mind:

1. These films were taken secretly. Since I was afraid of being discovered, you will not see scenes of the guards and sentries at the gate, the barbed wire fences, sentry watchtowers, etc.

2. These films are in color. They tend to make the scene more colorful than the bleak, dusty and arid wasteland it actually was.

3. These are home movies. As I was merely a hobbyist who enjoyed taking home movies, these films were taken without the intent of being documentaries. As a result, I focused on family and friends. Most of the shots look peaceful and almost happy because whenever I took shots of evacuees, they would "ham it up" and smile...as you might do today. I did not get candid shots of evacuees in a pensive and dejected mood.

Thus, the camera shots do not fathom the emotions hidden within the evacuees...the fear, the loneliness, the despair and the bitterness that we felt.

Despite these shortcomings, I hope my home movies share with you one aspect of the camp experience that we older folks would like to leave with the *sansei*...that is the spirit of the Japanese American community. Despite the loneliness and despair that enveloped us, we made the best we could with the situation. I hope when you will look at the scenes of *mochizuki*, pipe repairing, dining hall duty and church service, you look at the spirit of the people. You will see a people trying to reconstruct a community despite overwhelming obstacles. That, I feel, is the essence of these home movies. All in all, what were just some homemovie shots made as a hobby are now, with the passing of almost half a century, a movie of historical interest. I am glad that because of one chance remark made to a kindly and understanding WRA friend, these scenes are preserved for the sanseis and other generations to follow. Sometimes I wonder whether it was just sheer luck or not.

— Dave M. Tatsuno

Japanese Relocation

U.S.A. *Narration:* Milton S. Eisenhower, *Music:* Adapted from *The Plow That Broke the Plains*, *Production:* Office of War Information, *Distribution:* War Activities Committee of the Motion Picture Industry, *Print:* 16mm, sd., English, b&w, 11 min., 1943.

The day after Pearl Harbor, the *New York Times* reported that police forces across the nation acted to "control Japanese nationals," and that "a nation-wide round-up of Japanese nationals was ordered by Attorney General Biddle through cooperation

Fig. 10. Americans.
(Credit: Rea Tajiri)

by the FBI and local police forces." Americans of Japanese descent were subsequently harassed and gradually stripped of their rights until President Roosevelt signed Executive Order 9066 making it all official. This directed the government to remove nearly 120,000 Japanese Americans from their homes in California, Oregon and Washington and imprison them in 10 hastily built camps in the interior. *Japanese Relocation* is the government's explanation and justification for this betrayal of its own citizens.

The setting is California, where Japanese Americans are assembled at Los Angeles' Santa Anita race track before incarceration at Manzanar, deep in the California deserts. Milton Eisenhower, the director of the War Relocation Authority, narrates the film using specious euphemisms and suspicious adjectives. As they pack their belongings, he assures us that "the evacuees cooperated wholeheartedly. The many loyal among them felt this was a sacrifice they could make on behalf of America's war effort." Upon arrival at Santa Anita, "the Japanese themselves cheerfully handled the enormous paper work involved in the enormous migration," and "the Army provided housing and plenty of healthy, nourishing food for all." A more credible account would point out that the first Americans arrived at Santa Anita only four days after the horses were evacuated. Their only bathing facilities were the horse showers, and the smell of horse shit lingered for the duration. These Americans were treated like animals in other states as well, placed initially in converted horse, cattle and pig pens before being moved to the camps.

Japanese Relocation characterizes Executive Order 9066 as either a war-time sacrifice or (more curiously) a frontier experience. These Americans "migrated" to "pioneer communities." Deep in the interior, they found "land that was raw, untamed, and full of opportunity. Here they would build schools, educate their children, reclaim the desert." Though more appropriately compared to Native Americans, the Japanese Americans take the place of white settlers in this documentary western scenario. As for the role of the democracy that put them there, the film ends by announcing, "we are setting a standard for the rest of the world in the treatment of people who may have loyalties to an enemy nation. We are protecting ourselves without violating the principles of Christian decency." Words to make every Christian and democrat wince.

— *Abé Mark Nornes*

Fighting Young Citizens — Winter
(Tatakau shōkokumin — Fuyuhen)

Japan *Production:* Dentsū, *Sponsor:* Bureau of Military Preservation, *Print:* 16mm, sd/silent, Japanese, b&w, 23 min. (incomplete), 1944.

Fighting Young Citizens was completed in April 1944, and was one of a series of films designed to introduce children throughout the country as "supporters at the homefront." This "Total Uprising Edition" *(sōkekkihen)* features the children of Yamagata Prefecture's Ōsone Primary School. Dentsū M.P. Co., formally called Nippon Electric Communication Co., was engaged in the production of newsreels from 1928. They began larger scale independent productions in 1941, then became Dentsū M.P. Co. with the absorption of several companies in 1943.

The film begins with study at school, followed by scenes of the children helping at farm houses, mail delivery, and clearing snow. Watching the film today, the most impressive scenes are the posters next to school room doors declaring, "Class Devoted to Dead Soldiers *(eirei)*," or "Class Devoted Families Who Have Lost Relatives at War," or the figures of little girls visiting shrines with banners reading, "Annihilate America and Britain." The snow boats used to transport heavy items though the snow create a beautiful, lyrical atmosphere. The children look healthy enough, and we sense their purity in a raucous snowball fight. For all these pleasant scenes, we cannot avoid feeling painful sadness watching half-naked kids attacking mounds of snow with bamboo spears, then attacking the flag of the United States. The film's depiction is simple, and somewhat indifferent. In this manner, the film suggests a state of affairs where even these "young citizens" are chased to the battlefield.

The words "young citizens" *(shōkokumin)* indicate not only little boys and girls, but also popularly designated the "Emperor's citizens" *(kōkokushinmin)* from as early as the outbreak of the Sino-Japanese War. It was in February of 1942 that "young citizens" became an official term. Such measures took place after the establishment of an association named "Japan Little Citizens Cultural Association," whose purpose was the promotion of hard training among the new generation of young male citizens. In the same month, Shogakukan, a publisher of magazines aimed at school children, combined their magazines called *National Primary School Grade 3, Grade 4, Grade 5,* and *Grade 6* into a single volume under the new title, *Young Citizens' Friend*.

Japan experienced its first American air raid in April 1942, and perhaps this contributed to the spread of the term "young citizens." The Battle of Midway was in June of the same year, the withdrawal from Guadalcanal in February 1943, and subsequently students were mobilized through emergency enlistment, and Japan's defeat seemed inevitable. *Fighting Young Citizens* was produced under such circumstances and this special "Total Uprising Edition" is haunted by the tension of the war situation. The scenes of children singing, "If We Go to the Sea" ("Umi yukaba") and praying for victory at a shrine were depicted in a quiet atmosphere, but one senses their desperate hearts more than their will to fight.

—Yamane Sadao

Sending Off Our Students (Never to Return)
(Gakuto shutsujin[1])

Japan *Production:* Ministry of Education, *Print:* 16mm, sd., Japanese, b&w, 15 min., 1943.

Sending Off Our Students was the official record of the "send-off ceremony for the student soldiers" sponsored by the Headquarters of the National Patriot Organization of the Ministry of Education (Monbushō). It took place at the athletic field of the Outer Gardens in the Meiji Shrine (presently called the National Athletic Stadium) on 21 October 1943. Photographers included Hayashida Shigeo and about 10 other camera operators from Nikkatsu. The same footage was used in Nichiei's

Nihon News No. 177, however, the piece edited by Monbushō was more detailed and longer than that of *Nihon News*.

Nichiei was established in 1940 to monopolize the production of news films, expanding the scope of their operation to include cultural film production and distribution in 1941. In those days, there was a heavy shortage of film stock, however, Nichiei's activities were united with the government's interests, so it was favored with a sufficient supply of film. This is the explanation for the use of the same footage for both Monbushō's *Sending Off Our Students* and Nichiei's *Nihon News No. 177*.

The screen first displays Tokyo Imperial University's famous Yasuda Hall, avenue of ginko trees, and Red Gate *(akamon)*, followed by Waseda University's campus. The narration states the students' resolution to go to the front. In an autumn rain, the film continues with scenes of the orderly marching of student warriors wearing school caps and uniforms, puttees, and rifles with bayonets. School girls and middle school boys gathered to see off the students with enthusiastic cheers and applause from the packed stands. Of course, these boys and girls stayed there with neither caps nor umbrellas. According to several references, the number of spectators was from 65 to 70,000; there was no official announcement concerning the number of students being deployed to the war front.

Needless to say, "sending off the students" was necessary to reinforce Japanese armed forces which had been weakened considerably. As a consequence of Japan's ultimate doom, as made evident by the sea battle around Midway in June 1942 and the landing of U.S. forces in Guadalcanal in August, a nationwide movement called "Shoot to Stop" unfolded nationwide in February 1943. The Students Mobilization Order was proclaimed in June, and a conscription system for those still in school was announced on on 2 October 1943. Through this law, the exemption from conscription for students studying in liberal arts departments was overturned. The law did not apply to those in science courses or to teachers in training courses. *Sending Off Our Students* was produced under these conditions. The ceremony took place not only in Tokyo, but also throughout Japan. After the second seeing off ceremony in 1944, no further ceremonies were offered. The number of students going to the front was regarded as a military secret and never disclosed. It is estimated at approximately 130,000 people. Because of the mobilization and deployment of students, all universities and colleges ended up empty those days.

When we watch the film now, we cannot help feeling bitter grief in our hearts. The scene describes precisely the tension and enthusiasm at the site, the upsurging of a kind of solemn air. Deep emotion wells gradually with a stirring chorus of "If We Go the Sea" ["Umi yukaba," see Abé-Nornes' article for lyrics — ed.] The shot showing the students' calm, orderly marching upside down in a puddle of water, the closeups on students' faces, the famous head to toe tilt down a student's mud-splattered back all testify to the power of cinematic expression. Send off messages offered by Prime Minister Tōjō Hideki and Minister of Education Okabe Chōkei were responded to by a speech from Ebashi Kinshirō, who represented the drafted students of Imperial University. He concluded by saying, "We do not expect to return alive." With the declaration of this determination, the entire film becomes shrouded in an atmosphere of death. With its vivid description, the film probably inspired profound feelings through this atmosphere. The film's final scene shows the students marching in front of the Imperial Palace crying "banzai."

After this, each of the students returned to their hometowns to receive physical examinations for conscription. In December, they entered the military and headed for the battlefields. How many among them could return? After the war in 1949, diaries written by the students were published under the title *Listen to the Voice of the Sea (Kike wadatsumi no koe)*, and the fate of the students finally became acknowledged.

NOTES

1. More than any other film of the period, this one (quite unwittingly) communicates the tragedy of war. It never fails to leave today's audiences devastated. For this reason, we've crafted a title that expresses the meanings implied by *"gakuto shutujin."* Literally, it simply translates "students deployed," but Japanese read this title and think not about the deployment, but the sad fact that most these young boys never returned—ed.

— *Yamane Sadao*

Manufacturing the Enemy

The Educational System of Japan
U.S.A. *Production:* Signal Corps, *Print:* 35mm, sd., English, b&w, 32 min., 1945.

It's obvious that whoever wrote *The Educational System of Japan* loved Japan. Unlike the better-known films which attempt to explain away the enemy (for example, *Japanese Behavior, The Enemy Japan — Dream of Empire, The Battle of China, Our Enemy — The Japanese,* and especially *Know Your Enemy — Japan*) this film makes a sincere attempt to separate the military from the culture. It emphasizes the beauty of the latter rather than conflating and condemning the two. Significantly, it is one of the few American films of the period that does not use the word "Jap." Japanese civilization's appreciation of nature and its artistic achievements are called "remarkable," but government-controlled education is equated with "inculcation" and "indoctrination."

This was produced for use in Civil Affairs Training Schools, along with two companion pieces, *The Government of Japan* and *The Geography of Japan*. Like the two other editions, *The Educational System of Japan* was edited from found footage, including a travelogue, an unidentifiable Japanese propaganda film and even Ozu's *I Graduated, But... (Daigaku wa deta keredo)*. The narration's tone is straight to the point of being comical. It's difficult not to snicker when the deadpan voice of the not-so-skilled narrator recites poetry ("Blooming Blooming, Cherry Blossoms are Blooming") or attempts a limp joke ("When the weather permits, much of the teaching is done out of doors, under the sun which they hope will never set").

From this material, the film crafts a thesis that viewers may find convincing, despite the thick American rhetoric: "In recent years there has been an increasing trend toward regimentation of the Japanese youth [Over typical Japanese images of group exercises]. This is all a part of the government's plan to destroy any individuality or free thought by the people. It is another of the methods for ensuring future power by teaching the emperor's young subjects from the very beginning that they do not exist as individuals but they exist only as a part of the State. They are never to realize what it means to be a free citizen of a democratic nation." The film establishes a clear difference between the current "totalitarian regime" and Japan's rich civilization. For every scene offering evidence of inculcation and anti-individualism, there are two about tea ceremony or poetry. The importance of this separation is discussed elsewhere in this volume (see *Let's Have a Drink*).

Viewers will be as ambivalent about the narration as the narration is about Japanese culture, for among the cogent critiques of Japanese education is the latent racism of war-time rhetoric. Stereotypes abound (stereotypes, it should be pointed out, that are as strong today as ever): the Japanese are "small people," and lack individuality and creativity (the film never passes a chance to point out Western influence or "imitation"). This orientation is partly due to a second difference introduced by the film, that of class. The beautiful aspects of Japanese civilization are associated with "elites," while the lower classes are "natives." The latter's crafts are referred to as "crude" and "primitive." At the same time, *The Educational System of Japan* is refreshing for its sincerity and will to stress the positive aspects of Japanese culture in an era of rampant race hatred.

— Abé Mark Nornes

Superman: Japateurs

U.S.A. *Producer:* Seymour Kneltel, *Animation:* Myron Wildon, Nicolas Tafaly, *Story:* Bill Turner, Carl Mayor, *Voices:* Bud Collier, Joan Alexander, *Production:* Famous Productions, *Print:* 16mm, sd., English, color, 8 min., 1942.

Story: The familiar dialogue of "What's that?! — It's a bird! — It's a plane! — No, it's Superman!" is followed by scenes explaining Superman's origin. In the far reaches of space, a scientist on the planet Krypton places his beloved son in a rocket and launches him into space shortly before the planet's destruction. After drifting to Earth, the child is found by the childless Kent couple and raised as their own. Before long, he begins to exhibit strange superhuman powers, a result of his alien origin. Under the name Clark Kent, he works as a reporter for the *Daily Planet* newspaper. But when danger threatens or an emergency arises, he changes into Superman and fights for truth and justice. "Faster than a speeding bullet...More powerful than a locomotive...Able to leap tall buildings in a single bound..."

The opening narration above is standard with this series. This time, Kent, along with fellow reporter Lois Lane, is sent to cover the maiden flight of a new military airplane and gets involved in the hijacking of the plane by a Japanese spy. The fighter planes sent out to intercept the hijacked plane are themselves shot down and destroyed. Kent, deciding that "This is a job for Superman," hides himself and changes into his costume — a scene we see as a silhouette through a glass door. Lois, who has been taken hostage, is in danger of being thrown from the bomb bay. Just in the nick of time, Superman flies up and defeats the villains. The plane and the crew land safely in a happy ending. This is the tenth episode in the 17-episode series.

Commentary: During the War, the Fleisher brothers (who also created Popeye and Betty Boop) were involved in the creation of the animated version of this popular comic character. This is essentially the last work of the brothers, who split up in the middle of production and faded without a sound into animation history afterwards. This work was made after the Fleishers broke up. The producer, Seymour Kneltel, was the son-in-law of Max Fleisher (the older of the two brothers). The title is a play on words, combining the words "saboteur" and "Japan" to make a beautiful patriotic story where the alien Superman captures the Japanese spy! This episode was made when the staff Fleisher had trained was still in the studio, which accounts for the excellent, forceful animation.

The Films 223

Fig. 11. Clark Kent and Lois Lane in a quiet moment before their encounter with the Japateur. (Credit: Komatsuza Hajime)

Fig. 12. Evil Japanese in *Superman: Japateurs* (Credit: Komatsuza Hajime)

We are shown a scene of a room in a building where an Oriental man sits typing at a desk. But wait! Something strange is happening: the picture of the Statue of Liberty hung on the wall transforms into the rising-sun flag. The man bows deeply. It's the Jap spy! This scene, even while being seriously presented, has a rather racist stench about it. Moreover, this spy has buck teeth, wears glasses, has a small moustache, is ill-mannered and cruel — in other words, is drawn in the typical one-pattern manner (here drawn literally as well as figuratively) that Americans thought of Japanese. It's not known if the fact that the number of rays on the rising-sun flag is incorrect was meant to be a parody or if it is simply ignorance on the staff's part.

What the spy is after is a just-completed large bomber. This jumbo plane can also be called a carrier or mother ship, as it is capable of launching smaller planes from its belly while still in flight. This type of plane is one of the "Dream Planes" that was imagined in the 1930's, and in the end it was nothing more than a dream, non-existent in reality. There would probably be financial infeasibilities, not to mention engineering ones. Now, on to the group of spies. After tying the crew up and taking over the cockpit, they announce, "We're taking this plane to Tokyo!" It seems that this plane is capable of crossing the Pacific without refueling! This is where Superman makes his appearance. While the familiar pattern of Superman saving the day by beating up the villains is a bit tried, there is a moment at the end which should bring some laughs. Superman catches a New York National Guard plane in midflight and lowers it to a gentle landing in the street below. The camera trucks back and...I won't let the cat out of the bag. You'll have to see for yourself!

What I think is more meaningful for us to consider now, more than the racism is the way women are portrayed here, to be specific, the character of Kent's girlfriend/rival Lois Lane. She's a beauty with outstanding style, a hip career woman whose only flaw is that she tends to try and make a fool out of Kent. She's always trying to get a scoop and rise to fame, but usually ends up failing. When she gets into trouble, she undergoes a sudden transformation into a helpless princess heroine who simply waits for Superman to come and rescue her. This kind of conservative, traditional view of male-female relationships remains surprisingly strong, and modern examples can be found in computer games.

In episodes of the Superman series following this, Superman appears in Yokohama and demolishes the Japanese army (*Superman in the Eleventh Hour*, 1942), and cleans up the German Nazis (*Superman and the Jungle Drums*, 1943). At any rate, he gets around a lot. But after Famous Productions moved under Paramount's control, the quality steadily dropped. One of Fleisher's other big stars, Popeye, gets his licks in on the Japanese Navy in *You're a Sap, Mr. Jap* (1942). The rival Disney also produced a wartime series showing Donald Duck fighting for his country. In this manner, even the world of American animation was sucked into the War.

— *Komatsuzawa Hajime*

Private Snafu: Censored

U.S.A. *Created by:* Theodor "Dr. Suess" Guisel, *Voice:* Mel Blanc, *Animation:* Warner Brothers, *Production:* Army Pictorial Services, Signal Corps, U.S. War Department, *Print:* 35mm, sd., English, b&w, 5 min., circa 1943.

SNAFU: *"Situation Normal, All Fouled Up."*

That's the basic theme and tone of Warner Brothers' animation series featuring the mishaps of Private Snafu. Each delightful episode contains a moral aimed at teaching soldiers important lessons for life at the front. In *Censored*, Private Snafu is shipped out to Bingo Bango Island in the South Pacific. His attempts to tell his girlfriend, Sally Lou, his destination are frustrated at every step by the military censors. When he finally gets through, word spreads quickly to the Japanese who destroy him in animated chaos, until next week when Snafu meets up with Anopheles Annie or some other enemy.

Private Snafu was a regular feature of the *Army-Navy Screen Magazine*, a newsreel produced by Leonard Spigelgass specifically for American troops. Each bi-weekly newsreel kept soldiers in touch with international events, as well as the homefront. The filmmakers attempted to be responsive to their audiences' desires, and would regularly answer soldiers' requests. For example, if some homesick soldier wrote in and asked to see his tiny hometown, the crew would pack up their cameras and shoot street scenes there. Responding to letters from steamy Southeast Asia, they showed a Chicago blizzard. *Private Snafu* was also designed to please. He was created by Dr. Seuss, and his voice contains shades of Mel Blanc's other characters, like Bugs Bunny, Daffy Duck, and Porky Pig.

Fig. 13. No rubber no good time for American boys — Philippines.

This was not, however, the stuff of children. This particular episode depicts Snafu's unlikely girfriend as a (tastefully) topless, buxom brunette. The descriptions of the Japanese enemy were more typical. Like many cartoon caricatures, Snafu's Japanese are modeled after Tōjō. Special attention is given to their different eyes. They are likened to insects with their ant farm-like tunneling under the ground (who minds smashing a bug?). However, the most prominent feature of this caricature is the mouth. Films from the war period constantly refer to The Grin, which was a convenient sign of their supposed insincerity. Though the buck-teeth stereotype predates the war, it was a convenient hook for the Japanese's "treacherousness" as exemplified by Pearl Harbor. For example, *Life's* 15 December 1941 report on Pearl Harbor describes Ambassador Nomura Saburō and Envoy Kurusu Kichisaburō's last minute visit to Secretary of State Cordell Hull, who flings sharp words "into the teeth of the two Japanese, who for once did not smile." When the Japanese soldier in *Censored* overhears a phone conversation about the troop movement to Bingo Bango Island, he rushes across the room to a radio to inform Tokyo. With the fluid magic of animation, his buck teeth actually detach and fly to the microphone ahead of the rest of his body.

This is more than a simple distortion of physical features. The constant evocation of The Grin suggested to Americans that the Japanese were by nature dangerously duplicitous. The sometimes dopey buck teeth also fed a Western sense of racial superiority, and it was also compatible with comparisons of Japanese to vermin. The blatant racism of The Grin is recognized and condemned today, however, the image of Japanese' "duplicity" runs deeper. It's a wartime stereotype that Americans regularly reproduce in today's so-called "Trade War."

— *Abé Mark Nornes*

Princess Iron Fan
(Saiyūki)

China *Executive Producer:* Zhiang Shan-ku, *Editing:* Wang Jin-yi, *Photography:* Liu Guang-xing, Chen Zheng-fa, Zhou Jia-pand, Shi Feng-gi, Sun Tioa-xia, *Script:* Wan Gan-bai, *Sound:* Liu En-ze, *Music:* Lu Zhong-pen, *Stills:* Wan Lai-ming, Wan Ku-chan, *Production:* China Joint Film Company, *Distribution:* China Film Co. (Chuka Den'ei), *Print:* 16mm, sd., Japanese, 90 min. (extant print: 70 min.), 1941.

Story: First, the title: "Originally, the *Hsi Yu Chi* was wholesome, enjoyable literature, but it has come to generally be seen as a thriller or mystery. Working on this film, we tried to remove ourselves from the mystery and show that what protected Priest San Cang's party at Mount Huo Yan was like the difficulties in life — if people work together, they can overcome troubles."

The story starts with Priest San Cang's party, who, during their arduous journey to India to get the revered scriptures of Buddhism, have arrived at the raging fire mountain, Mount Inferno. The villagers tell them that the mountain is surrounded for hundreds of miles by a sea of flame, and that the only way to put out the flames is to use the large Banana Fan kept by Princess Iron Fan, who lives in the Banana Cave. Sung Wu-kong goes on a reconnaissance flight but is chased about by fireballs. Princess Iron Fan, her son having been killed in the past by Sung Wu-kong, comes out and gives chase to Sung. Zhu Ba-Jie steals the chariot belonging to Princess Iron Fan's husband, takes his form, and tricks his way into the Banana Cave. Princess Iron Fan, not realizing the imposter, welcomes her husband home.

Fig. 14. *Princess Iron Fan.*
(Credit: Komatsuzawa Hajime)

Ba Jie tricks the princess and steals the fan. On the way back, the husband, disguised as Sung Wu-kong, has been waiting for them and steals back the fan.

San Cang teaches his three disciples that the reason they have been failing is because they are not working together. The three, with the cooperation of the villagers, rise up and overcome the husband, who has changed into the form of a massive bull. The villagers split a large tree into two and use it to him. Princess Iron Fan, distraught at her husband's transformation and capture, offer the banana fan in exchange for her husband's life. With the first wave of the fan, Sung Wu-kong puts out the roaring flames on Mount Inferno, with second he causes a cool breeze to blow, and with the third he brings down a fertile rain. In this manner, peace returns to the area, and the villagers see off the party, which continues on its trip towards India.

Commentary: This is at once the first Chinese and the first Oriental full-length animated film. When one remembers that until then, the only full-length animated films had been Disney's *Snow White and the Seven Dwarves* (1937) and the Fleisher brother's *Gulliver's Travels* (1939), I think the historical significance of this film can be understood. Based on the popular *Hsi Yu Chi* (*Saiyūki*), and showing the fantastical shape-changing abilities of the characters, this movie was a big hit. For details, I quote from the 21 March 1942 issue of *Kinema Junpō*:

> "The China Joint Film Company of Shanghai spent three years and 350,000 yuan to produce the first Oriental full-length animated film, Princess Iron Fan. This film played for 30 days at the Greater Shanghai Daigekiin Theater — establishing a record for popularity — and became immensely popular everywhere. Based on those results, the movie was released in a Japanese theater (the Shanghai International Theater) for six days beginning February 13, and as was expected, the movie was greeted with favorable comments from the Japanese people, and became a hit, selling out for several days in a row. Zhang Shan Kun, the godfather of the Chinese film industry, personally took command of the production, and the animators, brothers Wan Lai-Ming and Wan Ku-Chan, had as many as 9,000 sketch cards and a staff comprised of 237 Chinese artists. For a major film coming from the Chinese film industry, it has a surprising value."

This is a comparatively early introductory article; continuing on, in the April 1 issue: "[*Princess Iron Fan*] completely overwhelmed an American full-length animated film that opened in Shanghai. Here is another victory for Asian films!"

Fig. 15. *Princess Iron Fan.*
(Credit: Komatsuzawa Hajime)

This film was also a hit when released during the war (September 1942) in Japan. The version released at that time was the one dubbed into Japanese by Tokugawa Musei, Yamano Ichirō, Makino Shūichi, and Maruyama Shōji, and shortened as a result of police censorship cuts. The version left remaining in Japan is this one. In *Nihon eiga hattatsu-shi* (The History of the Development of Japanese Film) by Tanaka Jun'ichirō, it says "The strange, mystical material is drawn in an unrestrained, unfettered manner and represented perfectly, and the attempt at inserting Japanese dubbing was also successful."

Tezuka Osamu, then 16 years old, was impressed by this film when he saw it, a fact that was to have a great affect on the Japanese animation world. Beginning in 1952, Tezuka's comic *Boku no Songokū (Son-goku the Monkey)* began to appear in a magazine. The influence of *Princess Iron Fan* can be seen at every turn in this comic, which shows the struggles of Sung Wu-kong at Mount Inferno, his injuries from the husband's bladed chariot, and the aerial battle between Sung Wu-kong and the massive bull. Furthermore, this comic was used as the basis for Tōei Animation's feature-length animated film *Princes Iron Fan* (*Saiyūki*, co-produced by Yabushita Taiji, Tezuka Osamu, and Shirakawa Taisaku in 1960). The teasing suffered by the character of Sha Wu Jing because of his stutter, the process by which the three pupils end their quarrels and combine their strength to win, and the aerial battle of the climax — especially the airbrushed clouds on their feet — without a doubt, all these show the influence of the original *Princess Iron Fan*. This is the reason why all young Japanese get a sense of déja vu when they first see *Princess Iron Fan*.

Now, important facts. Please think of the historical backdrop of this film. It was produced during the Sino-Japanese War period. It appears that within the movie there are hidden signs of resistance towards Japan. For example, the husband — the villain of the film — has a rising-sun symbol drawn on his hip buckle. He is clearly meant to represent the Japanese army. There is probably more, but all we can see now is the censored version, which means we regrettably cannot confirm any of that. But one of the film's makers tells us this in his autobiography:

> "Later, even the Japanese people became aware of the anti-Japanese theme of *Princess Iron Fan*. When shown in Japan in Tokyo at that time, many people came to see it, but the military later prevented it from being shown. In 1979, I was able to see the article by Komatsuzawa Hajime that had been published in 1976 in a Japanese magazine, and [I saw] that the Japanese had fully grasped this theme. There he quotes Tezuka Osamu as saying that, 'The people who, while sneering at Chinese animation, went to see this film were so surprised at the quality and humor of it they were speechless. I also hoped for an opportunity to get ahold of a set of this film, but when I watch it know I clearly understand that this is a work of resistance. It is clearly a satire, saying that if the Chinese people work together they can overcome the Japanese Army which has invaded and attacked their country' (Tezuka Osamu, *Firumu wa ikite iru* [Film Lives], Suzuki Shuppansha, 1959). Tezuka Osamu is not unknown to me. He is the creator of the Japanese animated work *Astro Boy*. Last month, when we met in Shanghai, together we drew a picture of Sung Wu Kong and Astro Boy standing next to each other..." (*Boku no Songuku* [Son-goku the Monkey], Hokugaku Bungei Shuppansha, 1986). Mr. Wan's memory seems to be a little faulty in his recollections. Because the version shown in Japan was the censored version, it was not prohibited and was screened.

When we view this film, we should put aside its historical significance and look at it as any other film. The result of this is usually great disillusionment. Looking at this film from a modern perspective, the style is extremely inexperienced and underdeveloped.

Fig. 15. The Wan brothers.
(Credit: Komatsuzawa Hajime)

For a start, no matter how one thinks of them, the characters' images cannot be called refined. The trace lines are not clear and are loose, making it difficult to grab the features and characteristics. There is full movement throughout the film, but sometimes their feet do not seem to be touching the ground, giving a queer, unstable quality to their movements. Outrageous shots using "wall-painting" photography are calmly, continuously shown, tiring the viewer. (Wall-painting photography is a method where the camera's field of vision is needlessly moved from left to right and back again, like painting a wall.) Then and now, animation is supposed to be shot in frames. Why they were even able to do wall-painting photography is difficult to understand in the first place. But if one looks closely, it is a live action shot. A poor photographer took a picture of a bad actor, and an unskilled animator drew it as it was on rotoscope. If you only see it once, the story is difficult to understand. The Japanese dubbing is also poorly engineered, and there is still more to complain about. However, on the screen, it is true that an odd energy, an unusual spirit flows out, and this causes the strange appeal of this film.

The makers of this film, the Wan brothers, were twins born in January 1900 (Kosho 25, December 18 by the lunar calender) in Nanking. They did most of their work after the Revolution, becoming known for works like *Ōabare Songokū (The Rage of Sung Wu-kong)*, *Ninjin-chan (Mr. Carrot* also *The Spirit of Ginger)*, and *Kin'iro no horagai (The Golden Trumpet Shell)*, which were made at the National Shanghai Animation Studios. Their younger brother, Wan Chao Chen, also became famous as an animator, and although they have retired due to their advanced age, the "Chinese Wan brothers" are still well-known.

— *Komatsuzawa Hajime*

Weapons of the Heart
(Kokoro no busō)

Japan *Print*: 16mm, sd., Japanese b&w, 52 min., circa 1942.

Through a kaleidoscope of drama, *Weapons of the Heart* was a warning alarm to the Japanese people that the eyes and ears of foreign spies are everywhere. It literally described the "weapons of the heart." The year of its production remains uncertain, however, we may presume that it might have been produced in the latter half of 1941, or in 1942 at the latest. This assumption derives from the fact that during this period, the government leadership encouraged a nationwide anti-espionage movement.

The National Defence and Security Law went into force on 10 May 1941. This law aimed at reinforcing the protection of national secrets, and relentlessly stipulated capital punishment for crimes against the state. The anti-espionage movement took off from there. During "Defence Against Espionage Week," May 12 through 18, many events were staged. For example, the Japan Paper Picture-Story Show Association went around primary schools in Tokyo and presented a show called *Beware of Spies*. In the "Sorge Spying Incident" of October 1941, Ozaki Hozumi and his comrades were arrested for violating the national defence and security law. Needless to say, these movements implied a preparation for imminent war against the United States, and *Weapons of the Heart* was clearly produced in the same spirit.

Incidentally, after the outbreak of the war with the US, even regular features films promoting an anti-espionage mentality (or an "armed heart") were produced one after the other. In the year 1942, for example, Nikkatsu's April releases included *Fifth Column Fear* (*Daigoretsu no kyōfu*, produced by Yamamoto Hiroyuki) and Shōchiku's *The Spy Isn't Dead Yet* (*Kanchō imada shisezu*, Yoshimura Kimisaburō); *You're Being Aimed At* (*Anata wa nerawarete iru*, Yamamoto Hiroyuki) was shown by Daiei in November. Many entertainment films based on spy stories were released thereafter, such as *On the Eve of War* (*Kaisen no zenya*, Shōchiku, Yoshimura Kimisaburō 1943) and *The Spy Named Rose of the Sea* (*Kanchō umi no bara*, Tōhō, Kinugasa Teinosuke, 1945).

In one sense, *Weapons of the Heart* could be regarded as a sort of entertainment film. As if describing the proverb, "The walls have ears, and the *shōji* have eyes." The film dramatizes daily life as a battlefield in the intelligence war. The film's fierce pressure stirred up suspicion and fear in the spectators. Looking at it today, the storytelling is not terribly good, yet the seriousness of the telling creates a humorous feeling. It makes one wonder how was it received at the time. The fictional period scenes describing a battle at Osaka Castle, as well as the transferring of enemy codes by cigarettes (of which much of the film consists), were undoubtedly taken from Japanese and foreign feature films of the time. Director Ozawa Tokuji produced feature films at Shōchiku's Kamata Studio and Teikōku Cinema. He also worked at Kawai and Daitō under an exclusive contract in the 1930s. According to *Kinema Junpō's Nihon eiga terebi kantoku zenshū* (Japanese Movie and Television Directors Guide), he was reported to have stopped working after his last film, the documentary *Mongolia Rising* (*Tachiagaru Mō-Ko*), in 1938. However, *Weapons of the Heart* is, no doubt, a later production than that.

— Yamane Sadao

Nippon Banzai

Japan *Production:* Asahi, *Original Story:* Yoneyama Tadao, *Plot:* Mikami Ryōji, Nagatomi Eijirō, *Shadow Pictures:* Arai Kazugorō, Tobiishi Nakaya, *Animation:* Maeda Hajime, Kimura Ichirō, Asano Takumi, *Line Drawings:* Shiga Tomoyasu, *Editing:* Arimatsu Yoshimasa, *Narration:* Sekiya Ieji, *Print:* 16mm, sd., Japanese, b&w, 10 min., 1943.

Story: An introductory article published in the *Asahi Gurafu* (*Asahi Graph*) at the time of the release, describes the film like this:

> "Fully utilizing animation, line drawings, and shadow photography, here is the birth of a new style of anti-British/American PR war film. The Great Western Colonial Powers — our ABCD enemies — who have committed acts of aggression against the various people of Southeast Asia are conspiring to surround and lay siege to Japan. Unable to stand by any longer, Japan begins a war, and in the wink of an eye, liberates Asia to the exaltation of the native peoples. But the enemy is preparing for a counter-offensive with the strength of his production power. We must be able to beat him not only in a military war but in a war of production..."

This is a fairly emotional explanation of the meaning of the war as seen from Japan's eyes.

Commentary: During a war, all countries have movies made that make claims to the legitimacy of their cause. Among those, it is probably this film, combining real photography with animation, which represents Japan's definite agitation and high level of technology.

The first thing that is surprising is probably the clear pro-war theme. "The peaceful Southeast Asian countries have been trampled underfoot for many years, their inhabitants made to suffer by the devilish British, Americans, and Dutch. In the midst of this hardship, in their hearts they (the inhabitants) have waited and hoped for a ray of light, a strong soul. That light, that soul was Japan." Swaggering troops, using whips, overwork the natives, exploiting them, tying them up. They have prominent noses under their flat helmets and are wearing knee breeches. No matter how you look at them, they must be British soldiers. The local inhabitants, seeking salvation, stretch their arms up to the sky, beseeching the sun. Then, the bright white sun shining in the southern skies is overlapped by the rising-sun flag. While this montage is a very simple image, it probably ticked the self-conceit of the Japanese at the time. Of course, the Japanese themselves kept mum about the fact that they too were committing acts of aggression against Korea and China. The local inhabitants in this film fervently worship Japan, revering the Japanese as liberators and regarding Japan as Heaven. There is not much footage showing them working for their own liberation. In other words, they are really being looked down upon as "natives."

Abruptly, there is a sequence of actual war footage: "December 8, 1941. Our patience, which had been tested until the breaking point, finally exploded." A return to silhouette animation showing the burning flags of enemy countries. If you look carefully, you will see that France's flag is not among them. Please remember that the Vichy government of Petan, which was the legitimate government of France, was allowing Japanese advancement into French Indochina. Even such clear agitation required the viewers to have no small amount of mental armament when they saw it.

Continuing with animation: "Now, the poor Prince of Wales, on which Roosevelt and Churchill had their meeting, is also at the bottom of the sea, nothing more than

Fig. 17. Churchill in *Nippon Banzai*.
(Credit: Komatsuzawa Hajime)

Fig. 18. FDR impeached in *Nippon Banzai*.
(Credit: Komatsuzawa Hajime)

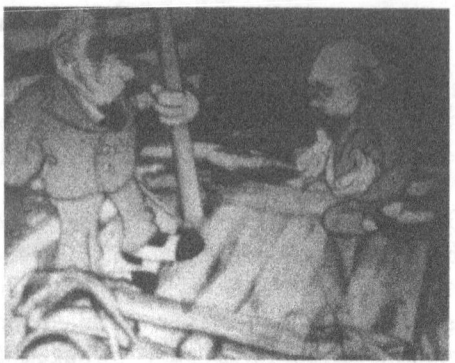

Fig. 19. Infantilized Churchill begs for a toy boat
— *Nippon Banzai*.
(Credit: Komatsuzawa Hajime)

a fish hotel." A cartoonish scene which shows whales diving and swimming around a sunken warship on the sea floor. The tongue-in-cheek quality of the movie is really quite excellent. Chiang Kai-shek and Madam Chiang, like marionettes, fall under the thumbs of British and American military advisors, and in the end themselves set adrift in a raft on the ocean. They are helped by fellow castaways Roosevelt and Churchill. The scene where Chiang joyfully receives a toy plane from Roosevelt is probably meant to be a parody of the Flying Tigers. At any rate, at that time Chungking was receiving large quantities of strategic goods and aid via the Burma Road, and it is a fact that this was a cause of offence to Japan.

Return to silhouette animation. Churchill's trademark cigar falls with a thud from his downcast face, and Roosevelt is impeached in Congress. The staff, as well as Japanese people of the past, did not understand that, in systems where military strategy may be freely criticized, public motivation could be aroused if an effort was made. Well, it's best if we don't read so deeply. It's enough if we, who know the results of the war, laugh at the humor of these anachronisms.

The last scene is real footage once more. Title insert: "Postwar Navy Anniversary Day" In a sonorous voice, the narration sings out: "We will not treat our enemies with contempt, nor will we make fools of them." It's very fun to hear a pledge like this coming in the middle of a movie that has been making fun of the enemy all along! "Young people. Go to the sea. It is your duty to push onward and seek your individual glory on this road of battle." The shot of the Japanese fleet advancing on a turbulent sea is taking from the last shot of the film *The War at Sea from Hawaii to Malaya (Hawai, Marē okikaisen)*. This is probably due to the sponsorship of the Navy Department.

About two-thirds of this film is animated, and the animation is split more or less equally between cells and silhouettes. Maeda Hajime's cartoon caricatures are well-done, and while there is movement all across the screen, the reason for all this movement cannot be really fathomed. Without a doubt, the strong impact of the silhouette portions can be felt.

Silhouette animation, a method basically no longer used today, was developed in Germany in the 1920's. The representational backlight photography, with light rays of a highly transparent nature, has an almost mystically beautiful appeal to it. But although those who later used this method were raised in Japan and China, the first to use it were Arai Kazugorō and Tobi'ishi Nakaya. After the war-time death of Tobi'ishi, Arai continued to tenaciously use silhouette photography on his own, but by this time, only this technique's faults — inability to move up or diagonally — were obvious. As this production can be called the last flash of glory for a special type of technique, this film is important from a historical perspective.

On the staff list, the strange name of Asano Takumi can be seen. This is the pen name of Asano Megumi. Sekiya Ieji, the narrator, had been an NHK announcer, and after the war worked for many years on a Christian program, *Rūteru awaa (The Lutheran Hour)* on public broadcasting, and became endeared to children in Japan with his *"Sekiya no ojisan."* Such an image gap is rather interesting.

— *Komatsuzawa Hajime*

Let's Have a Drink

U.S.A. *Production:* Office of War Information and Army Air Forces, *Distribution:* War Activities Committee of the Motion Picture Industry, *Print:* 35mm, sd., English, b&w, 2 min., 1945.

Read between the lines, *Let's Have a Drink* is a call to genocide. Made in the final days of the war as a theatrical trailer, it celebrated the surrender of Germany while warning Americans that the war wasn't over yet. Simply put, it's the biography of a corpse. It begins by displaying a dead Japanese man lying on a ravaged battlefield. Then the film begins a mini-narrative, flashing back over scenes from his life beginning with childhood, continuing with his participation in the Nanking Massacre, and ending with the moment he's shot by American troops on a Pacific Island. The film's finale uses Japanese propaganda footage of thousands of marching troops to point out that "there are still 4,000,000 Japanese soldiers left alive." The two-minute short ends with the sure command, "Get the Jap and get it over!"

This last phrase deserves close attention. More than most representations of the Japanese, "Jap" reveals a crucial attitude of Americans toward their enemy to the East. The Japanese, as Americans frequently claimed, were barbaric and uncivilized *by nature*. Americans' search for new "others" in the immediate post-Cold War period has focused renewed attention on Japan. While many of the issues around which tensions pivot could be directed at any number of our trading partners, Japanese' racial difference and our violent WWII confrontation has singled out Japan. In the context of what has been occasionally (and unproductively) called our "Trade War" with Japan, I have been shocked to hear "Jap" used occassionally by Americans. While today's stereotypes of Japan are not necessarily racist, they are similar to wartime stereotypes to the extent that they exclude plurality. Our descriptions of Japan rarely stray from the worn clichés of traditional art and postmodern super cities — the dance of the kabuki actor and salaryman. In reality, Japan is a raucous mix of fishing, farming, industrial, commercial, rural and urban cultures. Every region features different food, arts, language, and all manner of regional pride (try telling anyone from Kansai that Tokyo and Osaka are basically the same). Americans rarely see this wealth of difference, even when they travel there, as tourists rarely stray from Kansai and *Kantō*. Our images of Japan have grown with the times, but they are as monolithic as ever. These representations can make a dangerous difference, as we saw in the Pacific War.

The monolithic term "The Jap" allows for no difference and plurality; it condemns the entire race. Unlike the war in Europe, no distinction was made between the enemy government in Japan and its people. "Nazis" left room for the possibility of "good Germans," but as the popular phrase of the war put it, the only good "Jap" was a dead one. By the end of the war attacking "The Jap" enemy meant attacking the military *and* civilians.

Although the U.S. vehemently condemned the bombing of China's civilians by the Japanese military (in films as late as *The Battle of China* (1944) and *Justice* (1945)), the American government was preparing new technology for this very same practice. Both the incendiary bomb and the atomic bomb were designed for the hateful slaughter of civilians. Most Americans have forgotten the first large-scale test of the incendiary bomb on Tokyo's *shitamachi* on 9 March 1945. Home to upwards of a million people in an area four miles by three, it was the most populated place on earth. With only 2,000 tons of payload, the Army Air Force made them all homeless within hours. Between 70,000 and 140,000 people died, making it comparable to the un-"conventional" attacks on Nagasaki and Hiroshima.[1] Young Americans do not know that by the end of the war most other urban populations met the same fate, nor do they know that the last raid over Tokyo (though it already lay in ruins) involved 1,014 planes. Staged as a "finale" to the war, the raid occurred two days after Nagasaki and only hours before the end of the war. Some planes did not touch earth before Truman announced Japan's complete surrender.[2] To put a human face on these vast numbers, I might tell you about my mother-in-law, who was in her 20s during the war. She came from a fairly wealthy family, and lived in a beautiful, large home in Tokushima. A month before the end of the war — on the Fourth of July — American planes appeared in the sky, and when they disappeared 70% of the city was rubble. Their house, with its generations of *kimono* and furniture, was completely destroyed. She fled the burning city, carrying her mother on her back, and was lucky to survive the attack.

These atrocities against civilians were made possible in part by the lack of distinction between Japanese people and their government. Popular culture, and it's documents such as *Justice* and *Let's Have a Drink*, constantly reinforced these attitudes through image and word. The fact that the killing of Iraqi civilians was considered a crime against humanity during the Gulf War can be partly attributed to the comparison of Hussein to Hitler. Politicians and journalists alike were careful to separate an evil Hussein and the unfortunate populace that happened to live under him.

When the Gulf War allies officially apologized for the civilian casualties shown on world-wide television, the famous Japanese cartoon *Fujisantarō* featured a Japanese grandmother watching CNN and wondering what happened to their apology for the targeting of civilians in her youth. *Let's Have a Drink* affords a glimpse at the prevalent exterminationist attitudes that made the dropping of the atomic bomb the logical extension of the policy of bombing civilians.

NOTES

1. Calvoressi, Peter, Guy Wint, and John Pritchard. *Total War: The Causes and Course of the Second World War*, (New York: Pantheon, 1989), 1175-1176.
2. Dower, John W. *War Without Mercy: Race & Power in the Pacific War* (New York: Pantheon Books, 1986), 301.

— *Abé Mark Nornes*

Dawn of Freedom
(Ano hata o ute, also Fire on that Flag!)

Philippines/Japan *Direction:* Abe Yutaka, *Assistant Director:* Gerardo de Leon *Photography:* Miyajima Yoshio, *Cast:* Ōkochi Denjirō, Nakamura Tetsu, Fernando Poe Sr., Leopoldo G. Salcedo, Angel Esmeralda, Ricardo Passion, Norma Blancaflor, Ōkawa Heihachirō, *Production:* Tōhō and Sampaguita, *Print:* 35mm, sd., English, Tagalog, Japanese, b&w, 76 min. (incomplete), 1943.

As American troops converged on Japan after the surrender, the skies of Japan were filled with the smoke of burning documents. Contributing to this haze was the smouldering negative of *Dawn of Freedom*, which cameraman Miyajima Yoshio torched with a sigh of relief. We can only imagine what fears haunted him. Beyond being one of the slickest fascist productions of the war period, the film has documentary value for its (ab)use of POWs as non-actors and its cloak and dagger production history. It also reveals many attitudes the Japanese held towards both their enemies and supposed friends.

Despite Miyajima's attempt to destroy the film, Tōhō Studios still has a single master positive of the Japanese version (thus, it cannot be screened), and the Film Center holds on reel. Of the Philippines version prints, only one survived the war; the others were lost or destroyed. At least one copy was even attacked by Filipino guerillas, who vented their anger towards Japan by taking it out on the film. We can thank MacArthur himself for the surviving print.[1] In early 1943, he received intelligence reports about an anti-American propaganda film and ordered the Filipino resistance to kidnap a print. At the end of a run at a provincial theater, the resistance fighters presented fake receipts to the theater staff and made off with the print. Hiding their cargo in everything from mangos and horse feed, they smuggled the print to Australia by Japanese truck, push-cart, boat and submarine. Eventually the print wound up in the National Archives waiting to be found.

Dawn of Freedom represents the first Japan-Philippines co-production of the war. Though considered a co-production to this day, it would be best to en-

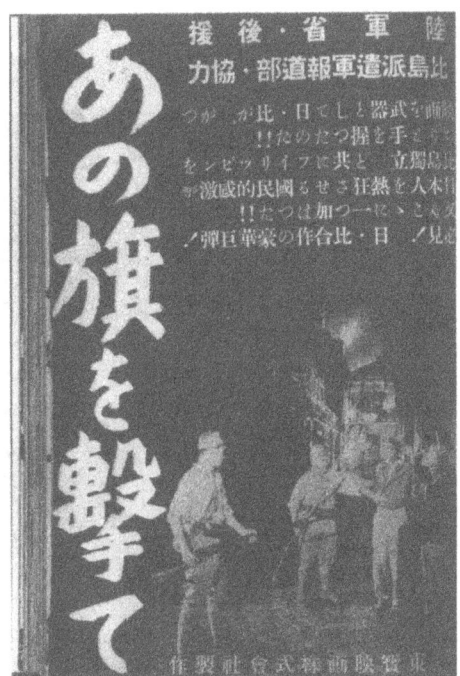

Fig. 20. Magazine ad for *Dawn of Freedom*. The subversive irony of Japanese soldiers holding Filipino civilians at gun point is such that it's difficult to believe it was unintentional. Text: "Japan and Philippines join hands to use films as a weapon!! ...Together, the Philippines and Japan rage with patriotic fervor, and here join as one!! It's a must see! The Japan/Philippines co-produced, magnificent, massive bullet"

Fig. 21. Japanese photograph captured by U.S. troops: Americans surrender at Bataan, one of the scenes later recreated by POWs for *Dawn of Freedom*.
(Credit: National Archives)

Fig. 22. Bataan Death March — captured Japanese photograph.
(Credit: National Archives)

close "co-production" in ironic quotes, for at least half of the staff was working under the gun (figuratively and literally). Contemporary reviews and publicity for the film made much of the pan-Asian cooperation. An ad in the 11 November 1943 issue of *Eiga Junpō* proclaims, "Japan and the Philippines join hands to use film as a weapon!!... Together, the Philippines and Japan rage with patriotic fervor, and here join as one!! It's a must see! The Japan/Philippines co-produced, magnificent, massive bullet!" Ironically, the still accompanying this ad copy features two Japanese soldiers holding two Filipino civilians at bayonet point. In the film, these Filipinos are thieves the soldiers captured, but the ad does not explain this crucial plot point. Rather, it unwittingly sums up the terms of the "co-production". Today, Japanese critics still refer to this film as a co-production, but what exactly this means under the terms of military colonization should be examined closely.

After the Japanese invasion, the Philippines' film industry was at a standstill.[2] Most of the actors and technicians had moved to the theater, where short plays were still being produced. When the Japanese moved to revive the film industry for propaganda purposes, they went to the theaters and rounded up the nation's best professionals and coerced them into work. Under these conditions, the Japanese producers formed an all star cast and crew for *Dawn of Freedom*. Though early in his career, Gerardo de Leon was already a major director. Ricardo Pasion and the other children were well-known child actors. Norma Blancaflor, Leopoldo Salcedo, and Fernando Poe were all stars before and after the war. Poe held particularly strong propaganda value for the Japanese because he had been a captain in the American military. For this reason, he was perfect to fill the role of Capt. Gomez, who realizes the Japanese' benevolence and switches sides. Salcedo was apparently caught spying for the Americans. His co-conspirators were executed, but he himself was spared when his captors discovered he was the star of *Dawn of Freedom*. Despite these conditions, some Filipino and Japanese crew members (including Abe and De Leon) struck up close friendships and kept in touch long after the end of the war.

The two American leads were, in fact, Filipino-Americans that worked in the pre-war industry. Frankie Gordon, the mustachiod American officer, dubbed songs for actors who couldn't sing in the early sound ear. Burt Leroy, *Dawn of Freedom's* despicable Capt. Adams, was known for playing heavies. In 1992 critic Teddie Co screened a video tape of the film for some old film hands, who pointed out that the man playing Capt. Adams was not Burt Leroy. They identified the actor as Johnny Arville, a radio personality that cooperated with the Japanese as an announcer for the "Neighborhood Hour" and the "Republic Hour". Further digging produced post-occupation intelligence reports confirming Arville's role in the film.[3] These interrogation summaries by the US 457th Counter Intelligence Corps Detachment and the Philippines Department of Justice illustrate the difficult position media workers found themselves in. After Manila fell, Arville was asked to work for the Japanese, and consented because he felt he had no choice. He admitted to his interrogators that the meager pay did help him support his family through difficult time. Apparently caught sabotaging radio equipment, he claimed he was imprisoned, interrogated and tortured. His co-workers were believed to have been executed. After the occupation, American and Filipino intelligence officers subjected him to more interrogation, comparing his answers to those of his colleagues. While the agents ominously note inconsistencies in their stories, Arville was fortunate. His Filipino inquisitor finally determined he was a "victim of circumstance". Bert Leroy was nowhere near as lucky. No one knows why he was taken off the *Dawn of Freedom* production, and according to film lore he was castrated by the Japanese.

By the way of contrast, a surprisingly pleasant aspect of this "co-production" was the on-screen appearance of hundreds of Allied prisoners of war. In the context of the fiction film, they are particularly bad non-actors. However, their presence pushes the film from the realm of fiction to that of documentary. *Dawn of Freedom* features extraordinary documentary scenes of POWs reenacting their own surrender at Corregidor. I have been able to find a few former prisoners of war who participated in the filming of *Dawn of Freedom*. E.S. (Ted) Lockard was one of the American extras for the opening scenes of Americans fleeing Manila. He had never told anyone about this wartime experiences as a POW, but after the string of 50th WWII anniversaries in 1991-2 convinced him it was valuable to share his story:

> "One day, I think it was in early 1943, they gave us new everything — trousers, belts, shirts, helmets, and guns (without, of course, the important stuff). They took us into the city, and we drove down the streets in these big trucks past big movie cameras. And you know the funny thing was, word about the filming had spread among the Filipinos, and they came out and just bombarded all our trucks with fruit and food. I think it was just a sign of the Filipinos' hope. It exasperated the Japanese.
>
> "The guards told us they wanted all the new stuff returned. The next day, we were supposed to put everything in a pile. Well, what they found was every gun, every helmet, and the biggest pile of ragged, dirty clothing. For a few days, the guards gave us a hard time for keeping the uniforms, but all of a sudden they just quit."[4]

Weldon Hamilton acted in the Bataan surrender scene:

> "We had no idea what they wanted, they gathered us and sent us out with a bunch of food. We drove into the mountains to this open, hilly area. There were awfully tough looking troops around the outside of the area, but inside they were nice. They had us go over a ridge with all these explosions going off; I think they were just duds, you know. Then we had to walk over this hill in a line, throw our weapons in a hugh pile and act like we were surrendering. We were treated really nicely that day. It was a real outing... like a picnic."[5]

Burton C. Galde was a sailor before being captured. He also reenacted the surrender at Bataan:

> "I did a bit part in a Nip movie... The Americans in charge sent out a different detail every day, so we could steal whatever we could. I stole the sling from the rifle I was to carry and used it for a belt, and the helmet for a wash basin. We were made to do a surrender act as we came over a knoll. We had the rifles over our heads as we marched by the cameras we threw the weapons in a pile. Oh! There were no bolts in them. The Japs in charge spoke good English, and told us they had been trained in Hollywood by Americans. They treated us pretty good. They weren't mean and we did fare somewhat better than we had back at camp. I am glad that some of us survived so we could live to tell the tale of our life as guest of the emperor."[6]

There's a bizarre contrast between these (real) American soldiers woodenly delivering their lines before Japanese (actors) playing soldiers. The Americans look pathetic and uncomfortable before the cameras, while their Japanese actors are artfully arranged in heroic poses. Presumably, the political implications of this all-around bad acting led Miyajima to fear reprisals from the Occupation forces.

Dawn of Freedom is one of the finest Japanese war films in terms of production values. Some critics might attribute the film's effectiveness to Abe's pre-war experience in Hollywood, however, I would be more inclined to give a measure of credit to the great Filipino director Gerardo de Leon. In terms of style, *Dawn of Freedom* is schizoid; it shifts between two apparent styles from scene to scene. One style features the melodrama de Leon was known for; the other, which we can safely attribute to Abe, is archetypally fascist. Because both can be seen in the same film, *Dawn of Freedom* is instructive example of fascist cinematic conventions.

According to Ricardo Pasion, de Leon directed all the scenes involving Tagalog dialog. The camerawork in these scenes is fluid, as is the mise-en-scene. Actors appear natural, especially the kids. The scenes among family members are reminiscent of de Leon's other work. They are notable for their melodramatic excess, particularly in regard to sexuality. Those familiar with Japanese war films may be surprised to see one of *Dawn of Freedom's* Filipino soldiers with a girlfriend. Romantic sexuality between Japanese men and women is, as a rule, disavowed in fascist films.

This, and other conventions of fascist style, may be clearly seen in *Dawn of Freedom's* English and Japanese-language scenes. In regard to sexuality, most Japanese war films focus on the relationship of soldier and mother. Fathers (whose potential to upset this relationship is threatening) have usually died in other wars, from inexplicable natural deaths, or they are simply out of the picture. Soldiers have sisters, but they don't have lovers. Thus, the main focus is the love between soldiers, funnelling sexual energy into the war effort. Films like *Five Scouts (Gonin no sekkōhei)* and *Young Soldiers of the Sky (Sora no shōnenhei)* emphasize the comradarie of the group and the beauty of the male body, while at the same time disavowing homosexual connotations through violence and action. However, *Dawn of Freedom* comes close to bringing the latent to light. The scene in which Gomez says goodbye to his Japanese friend is shot like a love scene with Ingrid Bergman. The two stare lovingly at each other and spout absolutely amazing lines:

JAPANESE SOLDIER: (IN JAPANESE)	Now we must part company. You may not understand me now, but you must feel the mutual sympathies between us. That's all.
GOMEZ: (IN ENGLISH)	I know you are going to Corregidor and saying goodbye to me now, but I'm sorry I cannot understand what you are saying.
JAPANESE SOLDER:	Capt. Gomez, please understand just this. Nippon and Philippines are not enemies.
GOMEZ:	Nippon ... Philippines.
JAPANESE SOLDER:	Nippon ... Philippines. [They hold hands and stare dreamily into each other's eyes in a pretty, backlit CU.]
GOMEZ:	Nippon ... Philippines ... Peace.

Outside of this remarkable love scene, the other parts directed by Abe feature typical fascist conventions. The scenario often screeches to a halt for long speeches and pep talks. Actors tend to deliver lines at a shouting pitch, and appear de-humanized or robot-like. Mise-en-scene is wooden, unmoving, statue-like. If anything, the actors look simply arranged in the frame, like human *ikebana*. They are shot from below, turned slightly away for a heroic line, and they rarely move. In fascist films, the chain of command is made spectacle, usually mapped out physically by the set with the officers inside and the enlisted men outside. In *Dawn of Freedom*, the officers give speeches from positions above their assembled soldiers. They strike stiff, heroic poses as their subordinates go off to battle. Deaths at the front are always aesthetically pleasing, and accompanied by pretty songs like "Umi yukaba" ("If We Go to the Sea").

Critics also praised this kind of filmmaking, and a short quote from *Eiga Hyōron* reveals how the fascist beautiful deaths in *Dawn of Freedom* were received in 1942. Tsumura Hideo compliments the film for the "quality of [Leonardo Salcedo] being slaughtered in the mountains by an [American] plot," and the "spectacle of Filipino soldiers being annihilated by sweeping machine gun fire." The critic continues, "I said there are at least four magnificently intense and convincing depictions in *Dawn of Freedom*. Except for the latter one, three describe the beauty of cruelty. Not only do they pursue the beauty of cruelty, but they attempted to create a new *sublime beauty* which can only be derived through the beauty of cruelty [original emphasis]."[7] Audiences today may wonder if this writer saw the same film. At least the quote suggests that film criticism as an institution is deeply implicated in encouraging and interpreting proper responses to fascist filmmaking.

Documentaries never showed the beautiful death directly, but all of the other conventions are common to both. The primary difference between the two is the melodrama of feature film. *Young Soldiers of the Sky* and *The War at Sea from Hawaii to Malaya* (*Hawai, Marē okikaisen*, 1942) are basically carbon copies of each other, save the latter's individualized boy and his family. The narrative of *Dawn of Freedom* is far more complex, with the splitting of Filipino loyalties across the front line, as well as nice narrative touches like Ōkawa's donation of blood for little Tony. Outside of story, however, there are few differences between documentary and fiction filmmaking in terms of the manner in which they represent warfare.

One final point relates to this film's presence in our program of "Enemy Images". It has been widely assumed that the enemy rarely appears in Japanese war films. I would argue that, while Japan never made a "Know Your Enemy — The United States," nearly every film features enemies, and that the assumption they don't partially comes from the traditional privileging of image over soundtrack. Even if *images* of an enemy never reach the screen, the narrator and on-screen Japanese constantly *talk* about the *"teki"*. This is an appearance of the enemy, and we need to look closely at how the enemy is portrayed through the soundtrack, as well as the screen.

Generally, the sonic energy is hateful and amorphous. It's out there and it's hateful *(nikui)*, but is nationality or race is vague at best. The films are quick to point out that the enemy hates Japan and threatens Japan's future prosperity, but it's often unclear who exactly they're talking about. The reason for the ambiguity is debatable (see the essay by Ueno), but the constant talk about the "the enemy" is not.

Furthermore, as the films of this retrospective show, the argument that the enemy never (visually) appears is tentative at best. In feature films like *Five Scouts, General, Staff and Soldiers* (*Shōgun to sanbō to hei*), *General Katō's Falcon Fighters* (*Katō hayabusa sentotai*) and *Mud and Soldiers* (*Tsuchi to heitai*), Anglo or Chinese enemies make brief appearances, often in the distance. *Dawn of Freedom* and *The Tiger of Malaya* (*Marai no tora*) have full-blown caricaturizations of Asian and American enemies. Documentaries give more detailed attention to dangerous foreigners.

They often focus on Westerner's white faces, mustaches and round eyes, as in *Weapons of the Heart (Kokoro no busō)* and *Oriental Song of Victory (Tōyō no gaika)*. In the latter, as well as *Malayan War Front (Marē senki)* and *Yaburetaru shōguntachi (Officers Who've Lost — Life of POWs)*, hundreds (even thousands) of captured Westerners are put on display and roundly denigrated. Ueno Toshiya's essay amply proves that to simply state that the enemy rarely appears in Japanese film is to miss a valuable opportunity to understand Japan's actions during the war.

Dawn of Freedom is particularly rich with images of self and other. The Japanese portray themselves as ethical, benevolent liberators, while the Americans are vicious and bloodthirsty. These bald stereotypes are to be expected in times of war, but what's really fascinating are the Filipinos caught in the middle. The plot separates friends and family across the front line. Divided loyalties provide an opportunity for Filipinos to "discover" the true nature of friend and enemy. Little Tony asks his brother to bring back an enemy (ie., Japanese) helmet, but both come to realize they were wrong. Tony receives kindness and a blood transfusion (!) from a Japanese soldier, and his brother is murdered by an American officer. Before he dies, he scratches a message to Tony on his own (American) helmet, telling Tony the real enemies are the Americans. All Japanese war films are rich in terms of (aural and visual) images of the enemy. Rather than stating the enemy is rarely seen in Japanese films, it's much more valuable to look at where, when, and how the enemy appears, and attempt to discover the work of these images of the other.

— *Abé Mark Nornes*

NOTES

1. Barrano, Vic. "They Smuggled the Dawn of Freedom." *Examiner Newsmagazine* [Manila], (April 1976): 6, 27.
2. Teddie Co has provided me with the background of the film from the perspective of the Philippines. His invaluable research included interviews with Leopoldo Salcedo and Ricardo Pasion, private screenings of the film, and the articles in notes 1 and 3.
3. Smith, Jr., Capt. T.D. Headquarters, 457th Counter Intelligence Corps Detachment (area), United States Armed Forces, Pacific (APO 75, File No. 53-1091, 11 June 1945), 5 pages. Agent No. 2, Commonwealth of the Philippines, Department of Justice, Division of Investigation, Manila (File No. 65, 10 December 1945), 2 pages.
4. E.S. Lockard, extra in *Dawn of Freedom*. Interviewed by telephone, 17 May 1992.
5. Weldon Hamilton, extra in *Dawn of Freedom*. Interviewed by telephone, 10 May 1992.
6. Burton C. Galde, extra in *Dawn of Freedom*. Letter to Abé Mark Nornes dated 10 May 1992.
7. Tsumura Hideo, "Sūko no bi to tekkishin no kōyō" [Sublime Beauty and Promoting Hostility Toward the Enemy], *Eiga Hyōron* 10 (October 1943): 24.

Violence

Combat Film Report — No. 722

U.S.A. *Production:* Signal Corps, Army Air Forces, *Print:* 35mm, silent, b&w, 8 min., 1944.

This is one of the more curious cinematic artifacts of the war period; it could be described as a film memo circulated only at the highest levels of the military. This particular report describes the activities of a field hospital somewhere in the Pacific.

The Signal Corps cameramen were shooting the war at every front, and their footage constantly converged on New York. Of the estimated 200,000 feet of film that arrived weekly, selections were edited into *Staff Film Reports*, and their less classified counterparts, *Combat Film Reports*. Prints were distributed to service commands, training schools, and commanding officers in both theaters. These are documents from the front, and are as close to objective as one could imagine. On the other hand, as this sample shows, the reports are clearly structured and infused with a discernible point of view.

Combat Film Report — No. 722 begins with a line of ox carts on a country road; the passengers are wounded Americans being evacuated from the front. Upon their arrival at a field hospital, the staff unloads them and chooses who goes to surgery first. Inside the surgery tents, instruments are arranged and bodies are prepped. Surgery is performed on a head and a leg with bullet wounds. Some of the soldiers are evacuated by plane. Another is read his last rites as a hole is dug and a cross is constructed of bamboo. The body is lowered into the hole, and after a funeral, covered with dirt.

Watching this silent film memo, one has the feeling of watching unedited rushes. There are extraneous shots of grimacing faces and planes flying overhead. Poor lighting and details like the soldiers' dirty, ragged clothing contrast with the well-worked images of films like *Jap Zero*. Upon closer examination, however, a clear structure follows the processing of wounded soldiers and their two options after surgery: evacuation or death. Furthermore, the latter half of the report is packed with religious images. Posture slightly bent, a priest reads a man his last rites. Soldiers pray during his funeral, and the last shot of the film is a close-up of a make-shift bamboo cross. This imagery conjures a religious voice within the film, and envelops the fact of this death in an aura of Christian sacrifice, a trope typical of the American war documentary.

— *Abé Mark Nornes*

Jap Zero

U.S.A. *Production:* First Motion Picture Unit, Army Air Forces, *Distribution:* Office of War Information, *Print:* 16mm, sd., English, b&w, 20 min., circa 1943.

> *"Dedicated to the fliers who are helping to make the total number of zeros...zero."*

The "training film" for Japanese meant endless scenes of exercises at boot camp. On the American side of the lines, it meant thinking of film as a *means of training.* *Jap Zero* teaches pilots how to identify enemy planes. Ronald Reagan makes an appearance as a cocky flier who, despite his confidence, has a tough time distinguishing between the American P-40 and the Japanese Zero. If spectators enjoy the irony of Reagan shooting — and missing — his own man, they'll groan when, after being chewed out by his commander, he tells his commander (with a painfully familiar smugness) about downing a real zero. Needless to say, he is promptly forgiven.

A few training films were shot during World War I, but nowhere near as many as World War II. The military was producing training films at all levels and branches of the service. The larger units, such as the Army Air Force's First Motion Picture Unit and the Signal Corps, were bureaucratic rivals, and most units cooperated with Hollywood in one way or another. They farmed out work to established studios. Marine Corps and Navy recruits assigned to camera-duty were trained by *March of Time* staff; Louis de Rochemont swapped know-how for war footage. The Signal Corps and the First Motion Picture Unit both bought out and moved into old Hollywood lots. The latter, for example, moved their production facilities from Ohio to Hollywood and took over the facilities of the old Hal Roach Studios in Culver City. Among their 228 films, the most noteworthy are William Wyler's *Memphis Belle* and *Jap Zero.*

The premise of *Jap Zero* hinges upon a practice new to cinema: taking footage from planes for surveillance, bombing surveys, training, checking accuracy, and even propaganda. During the war, new cameras were designed which could be fitted into airplanes. Sometimes, entire planes were modified into flying cameras, such as the Lockheed Lighting F-5 (a stripped down P-38). This plane's pilots were known as "Focus Cats" and Gen. Arnold, the chief of the Army Air Forces, once remarked, "Our photo-reconnaissance pilots are instructed to fly on the theory that fighter planes win battles, while camera planes win wars."[1]

More interesting is the story of the camera machine gun, which starts with Wallace Beery's 1932 film *Hell Divers*. Beery used an early version of the Navy's camera machine gun, shooting mostly sea gulls by mistake (at least they weren't his fellow countrymen). When the film played in Brazil, officials were so impressed that they hired Fairchild, a Los Angeles camera maker, to design a new one (the Navy camera was classified). The resulting 16mm camera looked like a machine gun, ran at the same rate as a machine gun (16 shots per second), and even left crosshairs on each frame of film. Soon most Western air forces were using the Fairchild cameras. By the time *Jap Zero* was filmed, they abandoned the machine gun look for a rugged camera the size of a cigar box, its shutter connected to the real gun's trigger.[2]

At a more metaphorical level, the camera was often likened to the gun. Bell & Howell's ads for the Eyemo camera used catchy phrases like, "The camera is a weapon," and "We're shooting Japanazi's." Ironically, Japanese cameramen also packed Eyemos when they went to the battlefield. In *Jap Zero*, Reagan returns to base after mistakenly attacking an American plane, and his officer roughly commands him to "develop his film." We are then offered spectacular footage of dog fights from the point of view of his machine gun.

Fig. 22. Ronald Reagan hunting his own in *Jap Zero*.

Violence is glamorized by every aspect of filmmaking here. Besides the unusually star studded cast, this is a training film with impeccable costumes, chiaroscuro lighting, and a rousing musical score. The battle scenes are a cleverly edited mixture of Hollywood special effects and camera-gun documentary footage. Patrol is likened to hunting, a frequently deployed metaphor in films and writing about the Pacific front. The hunt evokes images of the Old West and good, rural life. It directly or implicitly compares the enemy to an animal, and most people find it easier to kill animals (especially predatory ones) than sentient men and women.[3] *Jap Zero* further dehumanizes the enemy by only obliquely referring to the human being piloting the plane. Narrator and characters usually talk about "knocking down" the machine. In one of the few references to the pilot, the narrator asks (in a disturbingly light tone), "See that plane, climbing to heaven like a skyrocket? Heaven's the wrong destination for that baby. That's a zero, the real McCoy. It was shot down over Alaska, and as luck would have it, the only thing that got really damaged was the pilot. Swell, eh?" For all its animated detail teaching the features of the Japanese Zero, this film also trains its viewers to adopt a necessarily casual attitude about killing (a way of thinking that Ronald Reagan learned all too well).

NOTES

1. Camera Planes Win Wars," *American Cinematographer* (December 1941): 115.
2. Bailey, R. H. "Movies of Bullets," *American Cinematographer* (April 1944): 114.
3. For a discussion of the hunting metaphor, see Dower, John W. *War Without Mercy: Race & Power in the Pacific War* (New York: Pantheon Books, 1986), 89-93.

— *Abé Mark Nornes*

Sacred Soldiers of the Sky
(Sora no shinpei, also *Divine Soldiers of the Sky)*

Japan *Production:* Nippon Eigasha, *Supervision:* Army Air Forces, Producer, *Script:* Watanabe Yoshio, *Photography:* Kawaguchi Kazuo, Fukuda Saburō, *Music:* Takagi Tōroku, *Sound:* Shikama Sumio, *Print:* 16mm, sd., Japanese, b&w, 30 min., 1942.

Sacred Soldiers of the Sky premiered on 10 September 1942. The film featured scenes taken on maneuvers with the Army Paratrooper Corps at Nittabara, Miyazaki Prefecture, which faces the sea of Hyūga. The film begins with the enlistment ceremony, then various on-ground training, their first descent exercises in the air, and finally combat practise after landing.

At the time, the Paratrooper Corps received earnest hopes from the nation. People paid them great attention because just before this, the Naval Paratrooper Corps achieved their first successful war results at Menado in the Celebes through surprise raids in January, as did the Army Paratrooper Corps at Palembang of Sumatra in February. Nichiei's *Nihon News #88* triggered the boom. This newsreel, entitled *Surprise Attack Operation at Celebes,* celebrated the successful operations achieved by the Naval Paratroopers using extensive documentary footage. It made a lasting impression on audiences, and received many awards including the Prize of the Ministry of Education. The film used Wagner's "Ride of the Valkyrie" to great effect as background music for a scene depicting countless parachutes spitting from planes into the sky, like floating bits of cotton. Of course, Francis Coppola later used the same music impressively in *Apocalypse Now* (1979). It is quite fascinating to discover a strange relationship between war and music, because the same music was chosen for the war in Japan and the war in Vietnam.

Apparently, the splash *Nippon News #88* made paved the way for the production of *Sacred Soldiers of the Sky*, as both films were made by Nichiei. The film was a big hit immediately after being released, which is not surprising since it followed the great success of *Malayan War Front (Marē senki,* 1942), which showed the vigorous power of the Japanese Army as it landed and fought its way down the entire Malaya Peninsula to Singapore. For example, Shimizu Chiyota recorded his thoughts about the popularity of documentary films in the 1 October 1942 issue of *Eiga Hyōron:* "There is no record in our movie industry of films like *Malayan War Front* and *Sacred Soldiers of the Sky* overwhelming fiction films. This is a phenomenon that should elate us. At the same time, it must be said this is the saddest of records for Japanese fiction filmmaking."

But were documentaries that popular in reality? In *Eiga Junpō,* 11 April 1943, we can find the box office results for films made in the first half of 1943 (*Sacred Soldiers of the Sky* was a double bill with the animated feature *Princess Iron Fan (Saiyūki)*):

(A) RANKING ACCORDING TO BOX OFFICE:

1) *Malayan War Front;*
2) *The Man Who Waits (Matte ita otoko);*
3) *Mother-and-Child Grass (Hahako-gusa);*
4) *Her Hidden Past (Onna keizu);*
5) *Her Hidden Past — Part 2 (Zoku — Onna keizu);*

6) *Fifth Column Fear (Daigoretsu no kyōfu)*;
7) *Sacred Soldiers of the Sky/Princess Iron Fan*.

(B) RANKING ACCORDING TO AUDIENCE NUMBERS:

1) *Malayan War Front*;
2) *Mother-and-Child Grass*;
3) *Sacred Soldiers of the Sky/Princess Iron Fan*;
4) *Fifth Column Fear*;
5) *The Man Who Waits*;
6) *Her Hidden Past*;
7) *Her Hidden Past* — *Part 2*.

This clearly shows the high reputation documentary cinema attained. For reference, *The Man Who Waits* and both parts of *Her Hidden Past* co-starred Hasegawa Kazuo and Yamada Isuzu under the direction of Makino Masahiro. *Mother-and-Child Grass* was a melodrama director for Shōchiku by Tasaka Tomotaka, and *Fifth Column Fear* was a spy movie by Yamamoto Hiroyuki.

Movie reviewers highly praised *Sacred Soldiers of the Sky* as well. For instance, Tsumura Hideo wrote, "My heart was moved by *Sacred Soldiers of the Sky*. This is, for the most part, an unusual experience for Japanese culture films...It's not only the power of the footage itself, for this is an eminant film, even considering the expressive powers of Japanese documentary cinema." He continues, "This film's greatest value lies in the way it depicts the "sacred soldiers." Simply stated, one can really feel how bitter and how scrupulous the preparations were for the welling power of present-day Japan in the Greater East Asia War." Tsumura closes his comments by writing, "In the very least, this is not the kind of film that simply shows the knowledge of the paratroopers. If a series were provisionally made to express the spiritual history of post-Taishō Japan through cinema (although this is probably impossible), it would by no means be possible to pass by this film as the single edition that represents the Shōwa Era. That is how extremely important this film is." (Tsumura Hideo. "'Sora no shinpei' o mite" [Watching 'Sacred Soldiers of the Sky'], in *Zoku — Eiga to kanshō* [Cinema and Appreciation — Part 2] (Tokyo: Sōgensha, 1943)).

Sacred Soldiers of the Sky is an interesting film even today. The sincerity of instructors and trainees was caught precisely and concretely. Audiences were deeply impressed when, before jumping, the tense soldiers stuck their heads out of the plane and the wind warped their faces. The spectacle of parachutes spreading across the sky like flower blossoms was particularly thrilling. Speaking somewhat hypothetically, if they hadn't shown the combat scene at the end, it could be enjoyed as a sports film. We can see that the zeal of the audiences' appreciation for the film proves the close adhesion of filmic expression and war.

After participation in the production of this film, Watanabe Yoshio, who was in charge of the script and production, won a great reputation with *Attack to Sink* (*Gochin*, 1944, also *Sunk Instantly*), the documentary describing the battle of Submarine No. 10 in the Indian Ocean. In October 1944, he departed to shoot his third combat film at the battle of Leyte. He never returned. We may say that his life journey symbolized the fate of documentarists during the war.

The theme song, which gives the film its subtitle, was written by Umeki Saburō and composed by Takagi Tōroku. The song made a big contribution to the film's success. The disc of the song issued by Victor Co., Ltd. spread all over the country immediately, and the words "sacred soldier" came to mean paratroopers.

Following the film on December 3, Tōhō's feature film titled, *The War at Sea from Hawaii to Malaya* (*Hawai Marē okikaisen*, 1942, under the direction of Yamamoto Kajirō) was released on the occasion of the first anniversary of the outbreak of the Japan-America War. It did record breaking business, which may have been influenced by the success of *Sacred Soldiers of the Sky* and *Malayan War Front*.

At any rate, almost all movie companies then rushed to make warfare films. Those concerned paid great attention to the influence cinema affected over young people and actually produced a number of such films aimed at stirring up their dreams. The success of *Sacred Soldiers of the Sky* confirms such influence. The documentary on cadets in the Naval Air Force, *Young Soldiers of the Sky* (*Sora no shōnenhei*, 1942) had strong repercussions among young people. After that, there were many drama films classified in the same category, such as *Toward the Decisive Battle in the Sky* (*Kessen no ōzora e*, 1943) which is about trainees in the Naval Air Force, and *Suiheisan* (*Marines*, 1944), which is about the recruitment of sailors. In order to recruit new Air Force cadets in 1944 two other films were produced: *Teki wa ikuman aritotemo* (*The Enemy Will Be Legion, But We Will Fight*) and *Kimikoso tsugi no arawashi da* (*You Are The Next Wild Eagle*).

— Yamane Sadao

Kill or Be Killed

U.S.A. *Production:* Signal Corps, Army Ground Forces, *Print:* 35mm, sd., English, b&w, 10 min., circa 1944.

The lesson to be learned in this training film is stated baldly in the title, *Kill or Be Killed*. The narration contains the ostensive theme, "use the weapon that fits the job," but the more likely training this film performed was to prepare green soldiers for the violence of the battlefield. In scene after scene, the spectators' faces are shoved into images of throats slit, heads bludgeoned, testicles kicked, and bodies shot and bayoneted. This is hand to hand combat and it's nothing pretty. Most of the scenes consist of one or two medium shots, but the violent impact is accomplished through slick editing as well. The last image of the film is a composite of three shots: the close-up of a Japanese soldier, the overlap of an American GI thrusting a rifle butt into the camera, and an enormous explosion. Because *Kill or Be Killed* was not designed for public consumption, it could be free of any beautifying rhetoric about honor and glory, and is thus one of the straightest films about the essential brutality of war.

The American military began using films for troop orientation before the war started. Pre-war subjects include *Personal Hygiene, Military Courtesy, Safeguarding Military Information,* and *Sex Hygiene*. All of these films were produced in Hollywood. *Sex Hygiene*, for example, was directed by John Ford and contrives an onscreen audience of soldiers grimacing at images of diseased penises in a training film within Ford's training film. (Needless to say, people looking for Fordian touches would be frustrated by *Sex Hygiene*.) Initially, the studios made the training films on a non-profit basis, but once the war was underway the demands became too high and the Signal Corps began farming out work by contract. This was how Darryl Zanuck (then the vice-president in charge of production at Twentieth Century Fox) became a lieutenant colonel in the reserve. The participation of Hollywood filmmakers increased when the War Department bought the old Paramount studios in Astoria, Long Island (originally built by Famous Players-Laskey), and converted it into the new Signal Corps Photographic Center. By the end of 1942, all production of training films was centered there.[1]

Kill or Be Killed is one episode from the *Fighting Men* series, which was initiated shortly after the establishment of the Signal Corps Photographic Center. Other examples from the series include *Crack That Tank, On Your Toes, Wise Guy* and *How to Get Killed — In One Easy Lesson*. In official correspondence, one general promised the *Fighting Men* series would be "short, highly dramatized, and hard hitting. Presentation will in general be by a soldier speaking typical soldier language."[2]

Japanese viewers are always impressed by the informal tone of American documentaries' voice-over narration. Films released to the public were couched in the casual speech of middle America, as though Uncle Sam were shooting the bull over the back yard fence of American movie screens. It stands in stark contrast to the stiff formality and patriarchal tone of Japanese narration and on-screen speeches. The *Fighting Men* series uses the rough language of wartime buddies. This "soldier language" is fascinating for its use of worn clichés and their variations as necessitated by war, and is worth an extended quote from *Kill or Be Killed*:

> "You're seeing more than a half-back going for a touchdown, a south paw burning a strike down the inside corner, a sharp shooter nailing the basket from midcourt. [Over images of football, basketball, tennis, boxing, and hockey.] You're seeing more than a cannon ball serve and a neat right cross to the jaw. You're looking at the spirit of America. This is the way we like it: fast and hard-hitting and clean. Instinctively, Americans love fair play. It's built up from childhood; give the guy an even break, play the game on the level, don't hit a man when he's down. There's a 15-yard penalty for clipping, and a fighter that hits below the belt gets tossed out of the ring. We like it fast and hard hitting, and we like it clean. [Dissolve to combat scenes.] When you step from the gridiron to no-man's land, the rule book is buried and forgotten except the one for losing. And it's not measured in yards; it's measured in life and death. War is the law of the jungle: kill or be killed. It's played to win. *Any way*. The goal is destruction, pure and simple. Your mind must be tuned to a new pitch. To go for your enemy all out — no holds barred — to hurt, to cripple, to kill. This is war."

In this spirit, *Kill or Be Killed* deploys countless clichés to draw a comparison between war and sports, a connection that is implicit in much war documentary (including television coverage of the Gulf War). After all, most sports are essentially organized violence. They channel and control humans' most violent impulses, regulating them with rules and abstract concepts of "fair play," thereby making violence a socially acceptable spectacle. Here the comparison serves to assure soldiers that "playing by the rules" is the essence of the American spirit. But the enemies are not American. They're a "gang of bandits with as much sense of fair play as a scorpion." There are no rules on the battlefield except the frightening axiom pronounced loudly in the title and on every front of the war.

NOTES

1. MacCann, Richard Dyer. *The People's Films: A Political History of U.S. Government Motion Pictures,* (New York: Hastings House, 1973), 153-155. MacCann's book is a rich history of U.S. government filmmaking and provides much of the historical background of this essay.
2. Commanding General, Army Ground Forces to Chief Signal Office, Attention Army Pictorial Service, 10 September 1942, quoted in MacCann, p. 155.

— Abé Mark Nornes

The Fleet That Came to Stay

U.S.A. *Production:* Depts. of Navy, Marine Corps, and the Coast Guard, *Print:* 35mm, sd., English, b&w, 24 min., 1945.

"It was weird; it was savage."

The fleet of the title is Task Force 58, and the film documents the battle for Okinawa and the fleet's three month defense against *kamikaze* flying from the mainland. Along with *The Battle of San Pietro, With the Marines at Tarawa,* and *To the Shores of Iwo Jima,* this is one of the great American combat films. Neither their Japanese or Hollywood counterparts can compare to the visceral impact of these documentaries. Even with the help of special effects, Hollywood war epics rarely achieve the sense of scale found in the American combat documentaries. For their part, Japanese filmmakers remained far from the real action as a rule.

Fig. 24. Kamikaze attack.
(Credit: National Archives)

Of course, the Japanese military was on the other side of the firing lines in these battles, though one would not have guessed looking at their documentaries. Japanese filmmakers made many "war records" *(senki)* of this combat, but none of them are as effective as the American documentaries. By the 1940s, Japanese documentary had already become entrenched in restrictive conventions. They largely set out to show how something worked or an event unfolded...and little else. Elsewhere in this book, I discuss some of the reasons Japanese filmmakers didn't move closer to the war's violence. By way of contrast, *The Fleet That Came to Stay* shows how the American filmmakers plunged right into the combat and, trained as they were in Hollywood, could turn the vio-

Fig. 25. Approaching Tokyo — A sacred icon and the fleet that came to stay. (Credit: National Archives)

lent spectacle of war to their advantage.

Perhaps the most crucial element of the Americans' success (in terms of filmmaking) was their command of narrative, and their ability to seamlessly marry it to documentary. When American filmmakers donned uniforms to make documentaries, they didn't leave the lessons of Hollywood behind them. They knew the importance of guiding audiences through story telling and the manipulation of desires and fears. For this reason, their films are incomparably more pleasurable to watch, if not vastly more effective in terms of propaganda value.

We can easily see the role narrative plays in the American combat documentary by examining *The Fleet That Came to Stay*. If a Japanese wartime documentarist were to make this film, it would certainly be a rather dry diary with a predictable structure: preparation, attack, banzai, and triumphant march down main street. While Japanese filmmakers relied primarily on external events to structure their films, American filmmakers attempted to strike a balance between history and its (fictionalized) telling. *The Fleet That Came to Stay* begins with sailors (actors) enjoying a peaceful night under the moonlight. They discuss how close they are to "the Jap home office" in terms of the distances between cities back home. In the next scene, the narration introduces a problem to be interrogated and resolved, the most basic device of narrative: in the past, distance has been against the Japanese, but now this huge American fleet was within reach of land-based enemy aircraft that threaten U.S. ships. Put simply (as such narrative is always at pains to do), "With Okinawa in our hands we could control the China coast, send swarms of planes to smother Japan; we were reaching for the throat of an empire. The risk must be taken." Having introduced the problem and its stakes, the film then proceeds to resolve the tension it's created with battle scenes of the Okinawa invasion.

The Fleet That Came to Stay gives a sense for the exasperation of the Americans in the face of the suicide bombers. It was "weird" and "savage" and "maniacal" and they didn't understand it. Watching the fireworks of anti-aircraft fire (at times strangely reminiscent of that over Baghdad), one can sympathize. Despite their bafflement, they did realize an essential difference between the two sides: "It was a struggle between men who want to die and men who fight to live."

— *Abé Mark Nornes*

Civilian Victims of Military Brutality

U.S.A. *Production:* Rev. John Magee and George Fitch, *Photography:* Rev. John Magee et al, *Editing:* George Fitch, *Print:* 16mm, silent, English, b&w, 20 min., 1938.

Civilian Victims of Military Brutality is a bed-to-bed tour of a hospital in China. A doctor simply points out wounds on the bodies of Chinese peasants, with plain, grey intertitles explaining how they were inflicted by Japanese soldiers. It is not a pleasant experience to watch, however, the film's violence is a fact of war and we are morally obligated *not* to look the other way. The film confronts us with crucial issues about the relationship between documentary and history. At the same time, *Civilian Victims of Military Brutality* naturally raises other questions (and blood pressures) because of the fact of its (probable/possible/apparent) location: Nanking.

In August of 1991, Kyōdō News Service announced it had found 10 minutes of Rev. John Magee's 20-minute *maboroshi* Nanking film. "Maboroshi" is a favorite word of the media, for it means those things which are known to exist but whose locations are uncertain. They are phantom-like things, and thus are the subject of intense fascination, desire, and media attention. Magee was a member of the American Church Mission and Chair of the "International Red Cross Committee of Nanking," which was set up to manage the hospitals within the Red Cross' Safety Zone. This was a demilitarized zone (whose sanctity the Japanese soldiers largely ignored) that contained 25 refugee camps housing some 60,000 people, depending on the stage of the occupation. George Fitch, who eventually smuggled the film to Shanghai, was with the YMCA and helped the committee organize food relief for the refugees. The letters generated by this committee pleading to Japanese officials to control their men are collected in *Documents of the Nanking Safety Zone*. Interspersed among memos concerning the running of the camps are lists of hundreds of incidents involving looting, rapes, and shootings. This running log was sent regularly to the Japanese Embassy in Nanking, and it provides a feel for how the city's Westerners desperately attempted to intervene in the mischief of Japan's occupation forces. As we will see, this list's narrative style forms an important backdrop for the intertitles of *Civilian Victims*, and for this reason it's worth an extended quote. A typical excerpt:

"25. On December 16 Japanese soldiers took two cows and two men from the Hsu Dairy at Yin Yang Ying. (Fitch)

26. On December 16 Japanese soldiers turned 40 volunteer workers with our armbands out of their residence at 9 Chih Pi Lu and would not allow them to take their bedding or baggage with them. Two of our trucks were taken at the same time. (Fitch)

27. On December 16 Japanese soldiers entered the residence of our chief sanitary inspector at 21 Kuling Road and took several motor-cycles, one garbage bucket and five bicycles. (Fitch)

28. At 4 p.m. on December 16 Japanese soldiers entered the residence at 11 Mokan Road and raped the woman there. (Fitch)

29. On December 16 Japanese soldiers tried to take the ambulance from the University Hospital and were only prevented by prompt arrival of an American member of the Committee, Rev. John Magee. (Magee)

30. On December 16 Dr. Smythe's house at 25 Hankow Road was entered five times by stray soldiers looking for *hao kuniang* (literally: good girls). (Riggs)"[1]

There are over 400 of these short, dry descriptions, which start out polite, gradually adopt a snide irony and a touch of rage, and then eventually peter out as their memos were obviously being ignored by Japanese officials. Unlike a long-narrative account or an academic description, they conjure a patchwork of events, unrelated except for their common context: a scene of loose, disorderly misconduct ranging from petty thievery to massacre.

This film was shot with an amateur 16mm movie camera at one (or several) of the hospitals within the Zone, with some additional footage from Shanghai, Nanking, and environs. Magee remained in Nanking, however, Fitch made several attempts to leave and finally succeeded:

"I was crowded in with about as unsavory a crowd of soldiers as one could imagine in a third class coach, a bit nervous because sewed into the lining of my camel's-hair great-coat were eight reels of 16mm negative movie film of atrocity cases, most of which were taken in the University Hospital. My baggage would undoubtedly be carefully examined by the military when we got to Shanghai. What might happen if they discovered these films?! Fortunately they weren't discovered, and as soon as I could after my arrival I took them to the Kodak office for processing. Most of the exposures were made by John Magee, of the American Episcopal Mission, later Dean of St. John's Episcopal Church in Washington. They were so terrible that they had to be seen to be believed. The Kodak representative rushed through four sets for me, and of course I was asked to show the film at the American Community Church and one or two other places.

"Miss Murial Lester, of the Fellowship of Reconciliation (British) happened to see one of the showings and expressed the thought that if some of the Christian and political leaders in Japan could see the film they would work for an immediate cessation of hostilities. She offered to go to Japan and show it there to selected groups if we would supply her with a copy. I didn't have much faith in the success of her plan but nevertheless gave her one of the copies which I then had. Some weeks later she reported that she had shown it before a small group of leading Christians in Tokyo but that they felt only harm could come from an effort to show it further so she finally abandoned her plan."[2]

Fitch sent another print to Germany and brought the others to America. This first version was hastily edited. He simply strung the hospital scenes together, followed by an assemblage of unrelated shots from around Nanking and Shanghai. Finally, Fitch supplemented the images of the hospital tour with plain, grey intertitles that duplicated the "objective," matter-of-fact style Fitch used in his many Red Cross entries. Once in America, he re-edited the footage into a film specifically to use for fundraising on lecture tours. This new version, entitled *China Invaded*, has a much more passionate tone. The intertitles look clean and professional. They're infused with an offended rage and a touch of melodrama ("The dead are dead."), and the final title is a call for relief donations. The images may be identical, but these are two very different films. *Civilian Victims* is a simple record of military brutality; *China Invaded* borders, in a sense, on a call for military brutality. The film itself asks only for relief money for China, however, in the context America in the late 30s and early 40s, the film certainly fueled troubling thoughts about Japan. It demonstrates how editing and writing can *push* images between professional and just violence.

Fitch writes that audiences were always shocked, sometimes physically ill, when they watched his film. *Life* magazine devoted an entire page to nine frame enlargements, with the overly hopeful headline, "These Atrocities Explain Jap Defeat."[3] Fitch took it to Washington D.C. and screened it for the House of Representatives Foreign Affairs Committee and the Office of War Information. The latter probably made their own copy, for the footage was worked into Capra's *The Battle of China*. Fitch screened it all across America and in parts of Asia. Then it disappeared.

...Sort of. The U.S. Government copy eventually ended up in the National Archives.[4] Fitch's prints and outtakes were handed down to his granddaughter, who deposited them at Visual Communications in Los Angeles. For Japanese the film became maboroshi. Its existence was known; its whereabouts was not. Then, in 1991 Mainichi Broadcasting's Katō Hidetoshi heard about the film, sensed a hot story, and began searching for it. Just as he was closing in on Fitch's old prints, Kyōdō New Service (Japan's largest) was following their own leads concerning a Chinese women's group in New York which supposedly held a copy. Ironically, while these communication giants spent the summer fighting to claim credit for this high-profile discovery, Fukushima Yukio and I had already stumbled upon the National Archives print earlier in the year and had programmed it for the Yamagata retrospective. After Mainichi found Fitch's grand-daughter and his prints, they kept their video copy under lock and key. Ironically enough, anyone could have dropped in the National Archives and bought a copy. When the story broke and swept through Japan, we could look with some amusement at the media war between Mainichi and Kyōdō over the "Maboroshi Nanking Massacre Film."

The discovery once again brought the question of the Nanking occupation to the media foreground. Every network showed photographs — Mainichi managed a coup by reserving the right to show moving images. Every newspaper carried stories (including Japanese American newspapers). Debates ensued about the film's veracity, Fitch and Magee's trustworthiness, and every other conceivable point. Typical articles are Tanaka Masaaki's "There Was No Massacre or Anything Else at Nanking" and Ara Ken'ichi's "The Ability of the 'Maboroshi Film' as Evidence."[5] In the end, Katō probably won his media war. He eventually went to Nanking with a crew and a video tape of Fitch and Magee's film. He actually found the victim described in *Civilian Victims*' first intertitle. Now an old woman, she showed the scars of the bayonet wounds that Magee filmed, and led Katō to the cellar where she had been raped, bayonetted, and left to die 50 years before.

At the height of the media fervor, Katō invited a distinguished group of historians (including an aid to Ishihara Shintarō, the outspoken politician who remained surprisingly quiet and polite about the entire matter), to Mainichi's Tokyo office across from the Imperial Palace in Kudanshita. After introducing ourselves, Katō screened a video tape of *Civilian Victims* shot-by-shot. Never has film been used so intensely and exclusively for its *documentary value*, as an object of history. These historians (most of them hostile to Katō's intentions) poured over every shot to verify the film's location and determine whether it stands up as evidence of a massacre. They stopped the motion of the picture and scrutinized the very depths of the screen. They squinted through the grain to read signs and wonder at the objects suspended in cinematic space. And there are countless things to wonder about.

Fig. 26. This French man makes an appearance in both Kamei Fumio's *Shanghai* and *Civilian Victims of Military Brutality*.

The original edit consists of two reels. The first seems largely shot in Shanghai. French troops mill around crowds of Chinese refugees. Japanese soldiers pose for (Magee's?) camera on a large gun (is that a Caucasian at the edge of the screen?). A French man wearing a beret smiles for the camera. The same man also makes an appearance in Miki Shigeru and Kamei Fumio's *Shanghai* (1937), in which he compliments the Japanese military for their kindness towards the Chinese people. Why he's in a Japanese propaganda film and Magee's film is difficult to imagine. According to the historians, Magee did not go to Shanghai, and they wonder who shot this section. The National Archives catalog card calls *some* of the same images, "captured footage," but we will probably never be certain. The final sequence consists of other unrelated shots: Japanese tanks drive down a snowy road; a woman kneels, pleading for mercy before Japanese soldiers rounding up Chinese men; a procession of men (are they tied to together?) are led down a distant, country road. These images are shot through trees and dark windows. The image trembles, suggesting the camera operator's nervousness...perhaps.

The second reel begins with the title *Civilian Victims of Military Brutality*. Explanatory titles are intercut with a Western doctor pointing out wounds on Chinese peasants (both dead and alive). The title describing the woman Katō found — one of the *least* horrific — reads, "Pregnant with her first child, this 19-year old woman was bayonetted when she sought to resist raping at the hands of a Japanese soldier. When admitted to a refugee hospital she was found to have no less than 29 wounds." This tone is supremely banal, literal, leaving everything to the imagination. One can't help wondering *why* and *for whom* this film was created. These are more of the unanswerable questions that the film begs us to ponder.

Looking closely at *Civilian Victims of Military Brutality*, only three things are beyond doubt.

1) The fact of Shanghai.
2) The fact of Nanking.
3) The fact of hateful violence.

Like the Magee film, the Nanking Massacre itself is maboroshi. This is an event, as Rea Tajiri puts it in *History and Memory*, for which there were no cameras present. The (apparent) fact that this is an event for which there are no images bothers us as much, or more, than the violence itself. This itself is troubling, for it reveals the depth of history's dependence upon the photographic image. The problem is that the photographic image is always a messy text. It's always con-

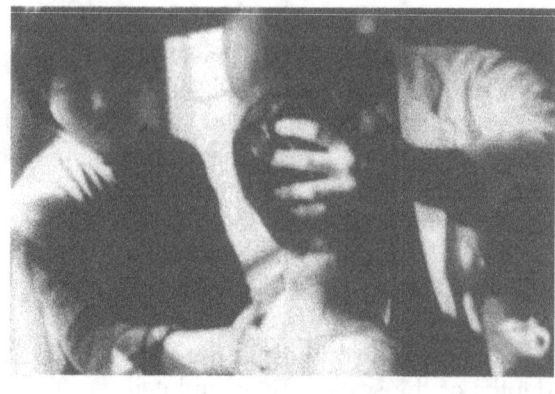

Fig. 27. *Civilian Victims of Military Brutality*'s banal inter title: "Two Japanese soldiers tried to decapitate this woman, severing the neck muscles to the vertebral column."

textualized by editing, written and spoken language and countless other factors (including the shifting, fickle relationship to a historical viewer). Katō didn't inform his hostile historians that he possessed two versions of the film. They would have dismissed the images based on the apparent anti-Japanese attitude of *China Invaded*. The two films also describe the incidents contained in images with occassionally conflicting "facts." Even without this knowledge, some of the historians seemed smugly delighted that the film features only the bodily *traces* of Japanese military brutality, violence in the past tense. They pointed out that the film shows only a handful of bodies, and argued about the number of victims, as if it were important.

I dare say that too much energy is put into such debates, and perhaps we can escape this wheel-spinning by drawing a distinction between "atrocity" and "massacre." There is violence which is sanctioned by society for its political expediency and less obvious psychological reasons (see the essays in this catalog by Renov and myself). At the same time, some violence crosses the line of acceptability, transforming as if by magic into atrocity. The line demarcating sanctioned and atrocious violence is constantly shifting, as we've clearly seen concerning violence against civilians in the last five decades. Massacre, on the other hand, is an accumulation of atrocity. It involves severe violence against many, if not countless, "improper" victims. The atrocities of World War II (on both sides) are beyond doubt, as is the violence (barely) contained in these images. It happened everywhere the Japanese went, not just Nanking. We need to stop arguing about names and numbers, and start asking, "Why?" If we refuse to look away and confront the question squarely and honestly, when faced with the option of fighting our only available choice is peace.

NOTES

1. *Documents of the Nanking Safely Zone*, ed. by Hsü Shuhsi (Shanghai, Hong Kong, Singapore: Kelly & Walsh, Ltd., 1939).
2. Fitch, George A. *My Eighty Years in China* (Taipei: Mei Ya, 1974).
3. "These Atrocities Explain Jap Defeat," *Life* IV/20 (16 May 1938): 14.
4. The National Archives holds two prints of *Civilian Victims* under the same call number (242.307). One has the original dull, grey intertitles; the other has recently restored intertitles using a slick,

unserifed typeface. The new titles are also tinted blood-red, which certainly covers the film with a new layer of meaning.
5. Tanaka Masaaki. "Nankin ni daigyakusatsu nado nakatta — 'maboroshi no firumu' wa maboroshi ni arazu" [There Was No Great Massacre in Nanking — The 'Maboroshi Film' is not Moboroshi], *Seiron* 229 (September 1991): 140-146. Ara Ken'ichi. "'Maboroshi no firumu' no shōkonōryoku" [The Ability of the 'Maboroshi Film' as Evidence], *Shokun!* XXIII/9 (September 1991): 104-111. Also see "How Bad Was the 'Rape of Nanking?'" *Asiaweek* (9 August 1991): 43.

— Abé Mark Nornes

INTERTITLES FROM CIVILIAN VICTIMS OF MILITARY BRUTALITY

1. Pregnant with her first child, this 19-year old woman was bayoneted when she sought to resist raping at the hands of a Japanese soldier. When admitted to a refugee hospital, she was found to have no less than 29 wounds.
2. This 11-year old girl was standing with her parents near a dugout in the international refugee zone as the Japanese entered. The soldiers bayoneted her father to death, shot her mother, and gave the girl herself a horrible slash in the elbow with a bayonet.
3. Bayoneted five times in the abdomen, this 7-year old youngster died three days after admission to the hospital.
4. Sole survivor of 80 men taken from their houses in the international refugee zone and shot, this man escaped by feigning death, making his way to a refugee hospital with wounds in the neck, cheek and arm.
5. This stretcher-bearer was taken to the river bank with several thousand others, and there machine-gunned. He was one of a score to escape death.
6. This man owned a small saipan on the Yangtze River. He was shot through the jaw by a Japanese soldier, then soaked in gasoline and set afire. The upper and lower parts of his body were horribly burned and quite black. He died after two days in hospital.
7. After having been beaten by Japanese soldiers with an iron bar, this 13-year old boy was bayoneted in the head.
8. Two Japanese soldiers tried to decapitate this woman, severing the neck muscles to the vertebral column.
9. This entire family was massacred by the Japanese when they entered the city. Two of the women were raped, and then put to death, one of them in a particularly horrible fashion.

INTERTITLES FROM CHINA INVADED

1. Peaceful pacifist China at work and play.
2. A war-ridden nation as seen by an amateur's camera.
3. Hundreds of thousands of civilians deceived by the invader's promises of goodwill remained in Nanking after the retreat of the Chinese troops.
4. Instead of goodwill — Invaders march the menfolk to execution grounds in batches of 20 to 30.
5. Women beg for the lives of their menfolk who were seized on suspicion of being ex-soldiers.
6. Country people were ruthlessly slaughtered by the invading army.

7. The dead are dead.
8. A grandmother returns home, her entire family massacred. Eye witnesses report her two daughters raped, mutilated and horribly killed.
9. Hands tied behind their backs, shot or bayoneted, civilians were thrown into the many ponds in and near the city.
10. Civilians transport victims of military brutality for hospitalization.
11. Hospitals overflowing with the injured, mutilated and dying.
12. Sadistic, war-crazed invaders burned, mutilated, pillaged, raped in the most terrible war orgy of modern military history.
13. Bayonetted five times in the abdomen, this 7-year old youngster died three days after admission to the hospital.
14. A 13-year old boy, who was mercilessly beaten and bayonetted after being forced to work more than a month for the Japanese army.
15. Eleven years old, she was forced to witness the murder of her parents. She herself received a horrible bayonet wound.
16. Kept for 28 days, raped ten to twenty times daily, this 18-year old girl contracted every form of venerial disease and was then discarded.
17. Pregnant, this 19-year old woman was bayoneted when she resisted rape, receiving 29 wounds on her head and body.
18. Another woman, with head nearly severed by soldiers who had raped her repeatedly.
19. A similar case, this woman was found in a pool of blood, taken to the hospital and recovered later.
20. Unable to meet soldiers demands for women, this man was shot through his hand — a typical retribution.
21. Shot through the jaw then soaked in gasoline and set afire, this man died after two days in the hospital.
22. A similar case of burning, this man had no other wounds on his body.
23. A group of refugees moving from one camp to another in search of greater safety.
24. Farmers, their homes burned, seek protection in refugee camps, building their own straw huts.
25. Millions are facing starvation, epidemic, plague.
26. The need for relief is urgent! $1 will maintain one adult for a month. $20 will keep a child for a year.
27. The End.

Banned Classics

Let There Be Light

U.S.A. *Direction:* John Huston, *Script:* John Huston and Charles Kaufman, *Photography:* Stanley Cortez, George Smith, Lloyd Fromm, John Doran, and Joseph Jackman, *Editing:* Gene Fowler, Jr., *Music:* Dmitri Tiomkin, *Narration:* Walter Huston, *Production:* Signal Corps, *Print:* 35mm, sd., English, b&w, 58 min., 1946.

Because WWII has the unfortunate moniker "The Good War," we've come to associate wartime psychological dysfunction with only Vietnam. *Let There Be Light* is John Huston's famous documentary about a hospital treating shell-shocked soldiers. Of all the films Americans produced during the war, only *Let There Be Light* (and Huston's *Battle of San Pietro* (1945)) have endured as something more than an exercise in propaganda and thought policing. Huston's other wartime documentaries were basically combat films, but *Let There Be Light* stands above all other war films for a simple reason. It treats human beings as something other than killing machines or vermin. The men here are vulnerable; they show the human face of war, which has more to do with stress and suffering than battlefield heroics.

When Huston entered the Signal Corps, he was riding high on the success of *The Maltese Falcon* (1941) and his highly praised screenplays for *Sergeant York* (1941) and *High Sierra* (1941). Many of Huston's best films, from *Treasure of the Sierra Madre* (1948) to *Prizzi's Honor* (1985), are infused with an irony that undercuts what would be macho heroics in another director's films. Considering Huston's wartime work, this irony takes on a more serious weight because of documentary's real events and real people. *The Battle of San Pietro* ends with liberated Italians, but much more memorable are the violent battle scenes and Huston's grim narration. In the ending of *Let There Be Light*, the dysfunctional soldiers all appear to be cured and play a game of baseball before jumping on a bus for the real world. But this ending seems almost surreal after watching soldiers who can barely function because of their horrifying experiences at the front. These endings seem tacked on...as if appended to fit into the wartime documentary mold or to please someone higher up.

What Huston himself thought is unclear, however, the releases of both films were held up, *The Battle of San Pietro* for a year, and *Let There Be Light* for several decades. The government's justification for withholding *Let There Be Light* was to protect the identity of the film's subjects. When the film was finally released, all the names were changed. Most people have assumed that the devastating effects of wartime horrors on fragile GI minds was not an image the military wanted to make public. However, according to Bill Murphy, the film's files suggest no reason other than the identity problem.

Despite the upbeat tone of the title, *Let There Be Light* is all shades of grey. Propaganda depends on black and white, on polarization, on sure divisions between us and them, good and evil, kill or be killed. It tries hard to leave no room for doubt, and this requires the imposition of this yes/no structure upon the world. Sometimes the maddening chaos of reality defies the propagandist's efforts at categorization, as we see in *The Battle of China*. Huston on the other hand, gave voice to the middle ground. Though he brings his material into a structure bearing both narrative and argument, his approach remains self-effacing. He allows the pain of war's reality to overpower the happy endings that attempt to keep the tragedy at bay. These two approaches, between films that reify the world and those that leave room for wonder and doubt, suggest the difference between propaganda and the finest kind of documentary.

— *Abé Mark Nornes*

Soldiers at the Front
(Tatakau heitai, also *Fighting Soldiers)*

Japan *Production:* Culture Films Section, Tōhō, *Sponsor:* Intelligence Dept., Ministry of War, *Producer:* Matsuzaki Keiji, *Director:* Kamei Fumio, *Photography*: Miki Shigeru, *Sound:* Fujii Shin'ichi, *Music:* Koseki Yūji, *Print:* 16mm, sd., Japanese, English subtitles, 60 min., 1939.

Soldiers at the Front is the feature length documentary film produced by filmmakers participating in the Bukan operation for four months in the summer of 1938. Completed in March 1939 and due for release in April, the official comment from the headquarters of the Army General Staff was, "This film is not likely to be open to the public in consideration of the present situation," preventing the film from being released.

In point of fact, the film was suppressed. Such measures reveal the tightening control over movies by authorities. Soon after this episode, more decisive measures were taken through the "Motion Picture Law" *(Eigahō)* in October of the same year.

Kamei Fumio, in his autobiography titled *Tatakau eiga — dokyumentarisuto no Shōwa-shi* (Fighting Movies — A Documentarist's Shōwa History, Iwanami Shinsho, 1989), wrote that, "I did not necessarily have any intention of making anti-war film. However, my film, not being favorable to the military, probably gave them an unusual impression. I myself didn't expect the suppression. A little while ago, an audience watching the film at a Tōhō preview room shook hands with me expressing their sympathy...I anticipated a sooner cease-fire

Fig. 28. A lifeless face from *Soldiers at the Front*.
(Credit: Japan Film Library Council)

from the bottom of my heart. I could hold no hostility or resentment toward the Chinese, even at the battlefield. My greatest concern was thoroughly describing the pain of the land and the sadness of all people, including soldiers, farmers, and all living things like horses. Even a plant, all these things suffered from the war."

His thoughts about the film, written just after its completion, can be found in *Kinema Junpō* (April 1939). According to the original plan, the film was supposed to be a grand war spectacle. However, having witnessing the severe situation on the Chinese continent, "we threw away the spectacular plan to describe the groups of 'fighting soldiers' and became determined to depict the humanity of the 'fighting soldiers'... I had no intention of describing the war as the ultimate tempest created by humankind, but only the people under this active power... We were all greatly moved finding scenes lacking egoism, just the self-sacrificing spirit of the soldiers at the front. Always at the risk of death, the honest life of the soldiers fully showed the most beautiful humanity with a pure and simple consciousness."

Kamei's intentions were probably what the authorities hated and controlled. Needless to say, the authorities judged the film as less than useful for exalting the fighting spirit, indeed, it inspires quite the opposite reaction. An episode from that time has the chief of the Metropolitan Police Board's *tokkō* ("thought" police) becoming angry when he watched the film and shouting, "These aren't fighting soldiers, they're broken soldiers!"

Before this, the film's staff, Kamei Fumio, Miki Shigeru, and Fujii Shin'ichi, made *Shanghai*. This film was, of course, produced by the Culture Film Section of Tōhō (in February 1938). They recorded aspects of Shanghai and it's suburbs and the propaganda of the Japanese Army just after the Shanghai Incident. Once again, they pretended to praise the "Holy War" while at the same time revealing the tragedy of war with substantially real images. *Soldiers at the Front* was made with the same attitude, but the film made enraged the authorities in this case. Actually, no vigorous, "fighting soldiers" appear in this film. It starts with fire, the miserable figures of Chinese farmers losing their houses because of the war, and a flood of displaced people driven from their villages. Chinese war prisoners tell of their desires to return home; soldiers sick with malaria take meals in the fields. The images continue, with an abandoned, sick horse, the cremation of dead soldiers, vehicle corps struggling in the mud, soldiers taking rest at the destination towns, and the like. We can find precise impressions of exhausted soldiers anywhere in this film. Sound was done by location recording and music, using no narration. Twenty-nine intertitles describe plainly the feeling and situation of the soldiers. Sometimes they match the image, other times they collide. This technique was quite effective. Undoubtedly, this is the very basis of documentary cinema and its relation to the world.

They realized this through the formidable dramaturgy of this film. Even though the film does not appear to be anti-war (indeed because of this fact) the film concretely showed the reality of war. This kind of cinematic attitude collided with the government.

The film contains a scene that showed the commander of an infantry company issuing successive orders after receiving reports from scouts. Kamei later confessed that this was staged (see *"Sengo eiga no tenkai"* [Development of Postwar Cinema] in *Kōza Nihon eiga* [Lecture on Japanese Cinema] Vol. 5, (Tōkyō: Iwanami Shoten, 1987)). This scene lasted 20-minutes long, and was the only direct battle scene in the film. It described precisely the strained atmosphere on the battlefield.

Later on, Kamei Fumio was arrested under suspicion of violating the Safety Defence Law and jailed in October 1941, just preceding outbreak of the Pacific War. *Soldiers at the Front* was one of the reasons for this punishment. One year later, he was set free provisionally, but did not have any opportunity to produce films until after the war.

Soldiers at the Front disappeared because of its suppression. Several parts of the film were reused in *War and Peace (Sensō to heiwa)*, a feature film co-directed by Kamei Fumio and Yamamoto Satsuo, and a nearly complete print of the film was discovered in 1975.

— *Yamane Sadao*

In The Wake of Hiroshima & Nagasaki

"Atomic Bombing" Interviews with Crews of "Enola Gay" and "The Great Artiste"

U.S.A. *Production:* Army Air Forces 2nd CCU, *Print:* 35mm, sd., English, b&w, 886 ft., 15 August 1945.

Standing before the Enola Gay, the crews that dropped the atomic bombs on Nagasaki and Hiroshima talk about their experiences on what one calls a "great, fantastic fairy-land project." The interviews are unedited, each beginning with a clap board and ending with a "cut." The tone of their descriptions is unexceptional;

Fig. 29. Paul Tibbetts and his machine.
(Credit: National Archives)

most of them express a shared relief at the explosion's flash of light — it worked. Paul Tibbetts' (the pilot of the Enola Gay) matter-of-fact comments exemplify the lofty point of view of the crews: "The sight that greeted our eyes was quite beyond what we had expected because we saw the cloud of boiling dust and debris below

Fig. 30 The man-made cloud from America's "fairyland project" — Nagasaki.
(Credit: National Archives)

us with this tremendous mushroom on top. Beneath that was hidden the ruins of the city of Hiroshima." In this tone, these raw interviews sweep us from atomic fairy-land to the deadly banality of war.

— Abé Mark Nornes

The Effects of the Atomic Bomb on Hiroshima and Nagasaki

U.S.A./Japan *Production:* GHQ, Strategic Bombing Survey, Motion Picture Project, Naval Technical Mission to Japan, Nihon Eigasha, *Producer:* Iwasaki Akira, *Assistant Producer:* Kanō Ryūichi, Aihara Hideji, *Direction:* Itō Sueo, Obata Chozō, Okuyama Dairokurō, Yamanaka Masao, *Supervision:* 1st Lt. Daniel A. McGovern, Dan Dyer, *Narration:* Shimauchi Toshirō, *Photography:* Yamanaka Masao, Miki Shigeru, Suzuki Kiyoji, Mitano Kimio, Sakazai Koichiro, Fujinami Jirō, Kannō Kei'ichi, Print: 35mm, sd., English, 165 min., 1946.

A Japanese Tragedy
(Nihon no higeki, also *The Tragedy of Japan)*

Japan *Direction:* Kamei Fumio, *Producer:* Iwasaki Akira, *Editing:* Kamei Fumio, *Production:* Nippon Eigasha, *Print:* 16mm, sd., Japanese, b&w, 39 min., 1946.

Japanese Tragedy is a compilation film drawing on wartime footage from Nichiei. It was completed in May 1946, and received permission for public showing after initially being censored. There was no company to handle it's release, although it was shown in several local theaters. After this, it was screened independently in one location within Tokyo. The following August, the Occupation censored the film a second time, and both the positive and negative were confiscated.

Producer of the film (and then head of production at Nichiei) Iwasaki Akira wrote in *Eiga-shi* (Film History, Tōyō Keizai Shinpō, 1961) that, "*A Japanese Tragedy* is a four reel documentary film that should be considered a history of the 20 stormy years of the Shōwa Era. Primarily through a montage of the period's newsreels, it

Fig. 31 & 32. Images of the end from both sides of the line: the flag raising on Iwo Jima and Japanese POWs listening to the Emperor surrender on radio.

traces the development of Japanese capitalism, the rise of fascism, the imperialist invasions, the Manchurian Incident, the Shanghai Incident, the May 15 Incident, and the February 26th Incident. Finally, it describes the appearance of the Tōjō Cabinet and the outbreak of the Pacific War and Japan's ultimate defeat. This is a cinematic trial to encourage we Japanese, who have been greatly deceived through untrue and forged information during the war years, to gaze introspectively at the truth." Mark Gayn, correspondent for the *Chicago Sun* at the time and author of *Japan Diary*, sent the following article to his home office: "The Prime Minister offered a private cinema party to show this film, inviting high ranking American officers on August 2. Among them, there were officers from G2 (Intelligence Office of the GHQ for the Occupation army). The film was presented to members of the house of noblemen on August 6, and Akira Iwasaki, producer of the film, received a suspension order of approval for presenting to the public from the U.S. Army Censorship section on August 13."

Apparently, *Japanese Tragedy* aroused the anger of Prime Minister Yoshida Shigeru. In Kamei Fumio's biography, *Tatakau eiga — dokyumentarisuto no Shōwa-shi* (Fighting Movies — A Documentarist's Shōwa History, Iwanami Shoten, 1989), he writes, "There was an officer in the propaganda section of the Occupation Army by the name of Conde, a liberalist of the New Deal school, who asked Iwasaki and myself to make an appropriate film in order to appeal to the Japanese people to ask themselves 'why did the war occur and how should we act in the future to prevent it from happening again?' I knew it would take a lot of money and time to make a

Fig. 33. Surrender.
(Credit: Daniel McGovern Collection)

Fig. 34.
(Credit: Daniel McGovern Collection)

new film, so we thought it would be a good idea to utilize the newsreels taken during wartime." Considering this production background, the policy of the U.S. Army was drastically reversed after completion of the film.

David Conde, as Cinema and Drama Section Chief of the Civil Information and Education Department in GHQ, set up the rules for film production which included the suspension of *samurai* pictures. He gave his utmost effort to inspire democracy in Japanese cinema, and at the same time support labor unions in the film companies. Kamei Fumio's story proved his attitude toward democracy. In the end, Conde was expelled from his position in July 1946 over the *Japanese Tragedy* debacle, namely, its public release, re-examination, and suppression. This meant that all New Deal staff in GHQ were swept away, followed by a change in policy in the occupation of Japan. This was the start of the so-called "backlash period" (*gyaku kōsu no jidai*), which apparently triggered suppression of the film.

Of this film, Iwasaki Akira has written that it reconstructed the development of Japanese capitalism and the progress of war with concrete evidence. We can clearly see that the film was made based on Marxist ideology. This probably contributed to the changing attitude of the Occupation army. Furthermore, the Occupation army decided to maintain the emperor system in Japan, therefore, the montage scene of Emperor Hirohito wearing civilian suits after abandoning military uniform, which implied he was responsible for the war, would obviously be points to be checked. We can highly appreciate its reticent attitude toward authority. However, giving present thought to the matter, because the film devoutly followed the ideology of the Japan Communist Party, it featured only a loud voice criticizing opponents. Stretching the point, such production methods designed to stress a specific ideology might be closely connected to that applied to the production of films "exalting the fighting spirit" during the war. At the very least, here one cannot find the subtle touch of Kamei's *Soldiers at the Front*. He obviously took a step back as a documentarist.

After completing *Soldiers in the Front*, Kamei Fumio was arrested in 1941. One year later, he was released, quit Tōhō and joined Nichiei. After the war, his first production was *A Japanese Tragedy*, which was eventually censored. He then quit Nichiei and returned to Tōhō, shooting *War and Peace (Sensō to heiwa)* with Yamamoto Satsuo in 1947. Kamei made films under "War" and the Occupation, which was supposed to be "Peace"; under both, his films were censored. In this sense, the history of Kamei's film career reveals the relationship between power and cinema.

— Yamane Sadao

History and Memory

U.S.A. *Direction:* Rea Tajiri, *Tape:* Akiko Productions, 125 Withers St. #2, Brooklyn, NY 11211, video, stereo sd., English, color/b&w, 32 min., 1991.

Rea Tajiri's *History and Memory* sums up the conceptualization behind this book in a variety of ways. Her tape deals with the relationship of historical events to their filmed record. As a Japanese American, the schism between the two is obvious and painful. *History and Memory* is both a personal quest and a re-writing of the history of World War II.

Tajiri reveals the extent to which history is dependent upon the photographic image. Near the beginning of her tape, she reconstructs the decisive historical event in this story, Pearl Harbor. Although edited from a variety of cinematic sources, the montage faithfully follows the battle's temporal sequence of events. The attack begins with American newsreel footage of exploding ships; then jiggling Japanese documentary images taken from planes provide establishing shots of Pearl Harbor under siege; we hear the first radio reports (the first writing of this history) courtesy of *From Here to Eternity*, and see the U.S. Navy's counter attack taken from John Ford's *December 7th*; *The War at Sea from Hawaii to Malaya (Hawai, Marē okikaisen*, 1942) provides dramatic close-ups of Japanese pilots; finally, *Universal News* shows documentary scenes of the aftermath. This hodgepodge of imagery is re-edited into a continuous flow, a reconstruction of history common to documentary. More than an impressive assemblage, this sequence attempts to break down distinctions between the fiction of feature film and the historical truth of documentary.

Tajiri is interested in analyzing the implications of documentary's "historical writing." She identifies several types of events: events that took place before cameras, events staged before cameras when none were originally present, and events for which there are no images. Images of the first two kinds of events are used by filmmakers to write histories, a prime example being the dramatic attack of Pearl Harbor. Events for which there are no images are recorded only by personal memories. Tajiri's example is her father's story about how, while their family was incarcerated, the government literally picked up their house and stole it away. No one was there to record this event on film, and they didn't even know about it until after the fact. Tajiri's father describes this event over a black, empty screen. Without having been imaged, this kind of history survives only if people release it from their memories.

Tajiri explains how this private memory continues to affect subsequent generations, even if it is never placed in public narrative. She recreates an image of her mother filling a canteen with water which recurs throughout the tape. The setting

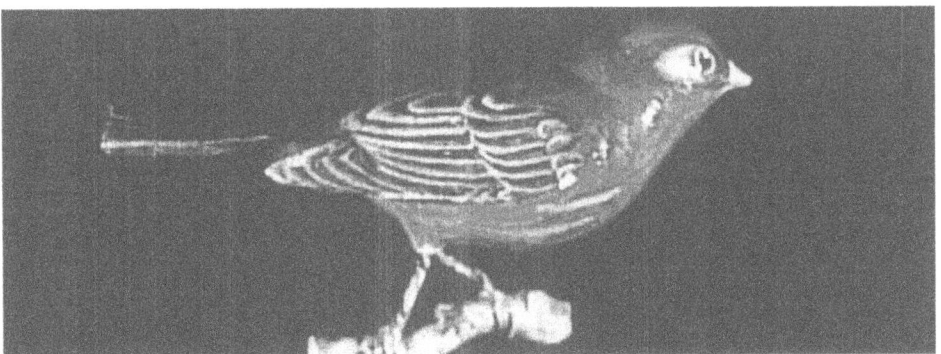

Fig. 35. *History and Memory*. A memento from the camps.
(Credit: Rea Tajiri)

is a desert place, where her mother splashes cool water on her face. Tajiri retained this potent image from childhood, when her mother told her a story about the camps. The story is long forgotten, but the mental image remains. She recreates the fragmented image and *History and Memory* is Tajiri's attempt to re-write the missing story.

The story of the Japanese American experience during World War II begs for images, and nearly all the photographic images available are inadequate, being Hollywood melodramas or government apologies. Tajiri uses these, but intervenes by manipulating the images and recording new soundtracks. For example, she places the verbal recollections of her own family over the official images from *Japanese Relocation*; sometimes her parents question the veracity of the documentary images. She also uses outtakes from the film, scenes where the uncontrolled reality before the camera spoiled the image for the writing of official history.

Hollywood's images are no less suspect. Tajiri's nephew reads his own ironic review of Alan Parker's *Come See the Paradise* over Hollywood's images of romance during "relocation." Tajiri uses other Hollywood images, ironically identifying with Spencer Tracy in *Bad Day at Black Rock* (1954). Tracy travels to a small desert town to investigate the murder of a Japanese American man after Pearl Harbor. Despite being the center of the film, the murdered man never appears on screen. Tajiri comments, "Komoko's disappearance from Black Rock was like our disappearance from history. His absence is his presence. Somehow, I could identify with this search. This search for an ever absent image and the desire to create an image where there are so few." Where there are no images, history is committed to the memories of those present, where it usually remains silent. Tajiri's mother refused to remember for her daughters. She was left only with the image of her mother filling a canteen in the desert, an image without a story. By re-creating both, she comes to understand her mother's silence and the relationship between history and memory.

— *Abé Mark Nornes*

Translators: *Abé Mark Nornes (Yamane Sadao)*
Ronald Foster (Komatsuzawa Hajime).

Selected Bibliography

Amakasu Masahiko. "Kessenka no Manei" [The Manchurian Film Association During the Decisive Stage of the War], *Eiga Junpō* (1 March 1943): 24.

Amakasu Masahiko. "Manjin no tame ni eiga o tsukuru" [Making Films for Manchurians], *Eiga Junpō (1 August 1942):89.*

Ara Ken'ichi. "'Maboroshi no firumu' no Shōkonōryoku" [The Ability of the "Maboroshi Film" as Evidence], *Shokun!* XXIII/9 (September 1991): 104-111.

Bailey, R. H. "Movies of Bullets," *American Cinematographer* (April 1944): 114.

Barnouw, Erik. "Hiroshima-Nagasaki: The Case of the A-Bomb Footage," in *New Challenges for Documentary*, ed. by Alan Rosenthal (Berkeley: University of California Press, 1988), 381-591.

Barsam, Richard Meran. *Nonfiction Film: A Critical History* (New York: Dutton, 1973).

Benedict, Ruth. *The Chrysanthemum and the Sword, Patters of Japanese Culture* (London: Rutledge, 1967).

Bhabha, Homi K. "The Other Question — the Stereotype and Colonial Discourse," *Screen* XXIV/6 (November-December 1983): 27.

Blum, John Morton. *V Was For Victory: Politics and American Culture During World War II* (New York: Harcourt Brace Jovanovich, 1976), 159.

Calvocoressi, Peter, Guy Wint, and John Pritchard. *Total War: The Causes and Course of the Second World War* (New York: Pantheon, 1989).

"Camera Planes Win Wars," *American Cinematographer* (December 1941): 115, 126.

Capra, Frank. *The Name Above the Title* (New York: The Macmillan Company, 1971).

Clausewitz, Karl von. *Living Thoughts of Clausewitz* (New York: Longmans, Green and Co., 1943).

Culbert, David. "Why We Fight: Social Engineering for a Democratic Society at War," in K.R.M. Short, ed., *Film and Radio Propaganda in World War II* (Tennessee: University of Tennessee Press, 1983).

Documents of the Nanking Safety Zone, ed. by Hsü Shuhsi (Shanghai, Hong Kong, Singapore: Kelly & Walsh, Ltd., 1939).

Dower, John W. *War Without Mercy: Race & Power in the Pacific War* (New York: Pantheon Books, 1986).

"Eigajin no kakushin" [A Revolution Among Cinematographers], *Eiga Junpō* (21 January 1943):12-15.

Fitch, George A. *My Eighty Years in China* (Taipei: Mei Ya, 1974).

Gayn, Mark. "Jap Film of Atom Bomb Damage En Route Here," *Chicago Sun* (Monday, 13 May 1946): 8.

Gayn, Mark. *Japan Diary* (Rutland: Tuttle, 1981).

Gilman, Sander L. *Difference and Pathology: Stereotypes of Sexuality, Race and Madness* (Ithaca: Cornell University Press, 1985).

Herr, Michael. *Dispatches* (New York: Knopf, 1977)

High, Peter. "The War Cinema of Imperial Japan," *Wide Angle* I/4 (1977): 19-21.

"How Bad Was the 'Rape of Nanking?'" *Asiaweek* (9 August 1991): 43.

Imamura Taihei. *Sensō to eiga* [War and Film] (Tokyo: Yumoni Shobō, 1991).

Iwasaki Akira. *Eiga-shi* [Film History] (Tokyo: Toyo Keizai Shinpō, 1961).

Iwasaki Akira. "Jizen kenetsu no hei" [The Corrupt Practice of Preproduction Censorship], *Asahi Shinbun* (4 April 1939).

Iwasaki Akira. *Nihon eiga shishi* [A Private History of Japanese Cinema] (Tokyo: Asahi Shinbunsha, 1977).

Jacob, Heinrich Edvard. *Blood and Celluloid* (New York: R. R. Smith, 1930).

Kamei Fumio. *Tatakau eiga - dokyumentarisuto no Shōwa-shi* [Fighting Movies - A Documentarist's Shōwa History] (Tokyo: Iwanami Shoten, 1989).

Kamei Fumio and Tsuchimoto Noriaki. "Dokyumentari no seishin" [The Spirit of Documentary], in *Sengo eiga no tenkai* [Development of Postwar Cinema] from *Kōza Nihon eiga* [Lectures on Japanese Cinema], Vol. 5, (Tokyo: Iwanami Shoten, 1987), 342-361.

Kindai Nihon sōgō nenpyō [Chronology of Modern Japan] (Tokyo: Iwanami Shoten, 1989).

Koppes, Clayton and Gregory Black. *Hollywood Goes to War: How Politics, Profits and Propaganda Shaped World War II Movies* (New York: Collier Macmillan, 1987).

Leyda, Jay. *Dianying: Electric Shadows: An Account of Films and the Film Audience in China* (Cambridge: MIT Press, 1972).

Lindbergh, Charles A. *Wartime Journals of Charles A. Lindbergh, The* (New York: Harcourt Brace Jovanovich, 1970).

MacCann, Richard Dyer. *The People's Films: A Political History of U.S. Government Motion Pictures* (New York: Hastings House Pub., 1973).

Meltzer, Newton E. "The War and the Training Film," *American Cinematographer* (July 1945): 230.

Murphy, William T. "John Ford and the Wartime Documentary," *Film and History* IV/1 (February 1976).

Murphy, William T. "The Method of Why We Fight." *Journal of Popular Film I* (1972): 185-196.

Nakai Masakazu. *Eiga no motsu bunpō* [The Grammar of Film] in *Nakai Masakazu zenshū* [The Complete Works of Nakai Masakazu], (Tokyo: Bijutsu Shuppan, 1964)

Nakai Masakazu. *Kikai no me* [The Eye of the Machine] in *Nakai Masakazu zenshū* [The Complete Works of Nakai Masakazu], (Tokyo: Bijutsu Shuppan, 1964).

Nakai Masakazu. *Shisōteki kiki ni okeru geijutsu narabi ni sono dōko* [Arts and Their Tendencies in Ideological Crisis] in *Nakai Masakazu zenshū* [The Complete Works of Nakai Masakazu], (Tokyo: Bijutsu Shuppan, 1964).

Nichols, Bill. *Representing Reality* (Bloomington: Indiana University Press, 1991).

Nihon eiga terebi kantoku zenshū [Complete Guide to Japanese Film and Television Directors] (Tokyo: Kinema Junpō, 1988).

"Picture of the Week," *Life* XVI/21 (22 May 1944): 34-35.

"Rakkasan butai no satsueisha" [Photographers of the Airborne Infantry], *Eiga Junpō* (11 July 1942): 3.

Renov, Michael. "Imaging the Other: Representations of Vietnam in Sixties Political Documentary" in *From Hanoi to Hollywood*, Linda Dittmar and Gene Machaud, ed. (New Brunswick, NJ: Rutgers University Press, 1990), 255-268.

Renov, Michael. "Re-Thinking Documentary: Toward a Taxonomy of Mediation," *Wide Angle* VIII/3 & 4 (1986): 71-77.

Renov, Michael. "Towards a Documentary Poetics" in *Theorizing Documentary*, Michael Renov, ed. (New York: Routledge), 1993.

Rohde, Jr., Alfred. "How the Marine Corps Makes Training Films," *American Cinematographer* (December 1941): 566.

Rohde, Jr., Alfred and Edward R. Butterly. "How the Navy Makes its Training Films," *American Cinematographer* (December 1942): 513, 536-538.

Said, Edward. *Orientalism* (New York: Pantheon, 1978).

Satō Tadao. "War as a Spiritual Exercise: Japan's 'National Policy Films,'" trans. by Peter High, *Wide Angle* I/4 (1977): 22-24.

Shibata Yoshio. *Sekai eigasensō* [World Film Wars] (Tokyo: Tokyo Shapan, 1944).

Shirai Shigeru. *Kamera to jinsei* [The Camera and Life] (Tokyo: Yuni Tsūshinsha, 1983).

Shōwashi zenkiroku [Complete Record of the Shōwa Era] (Tokyo: Mainichi Shinbunsha, 1989).

Skinner, James. "*December 7th*: Filmic Myth Masquerading as Historical Fact," (unpublished manuscript).

"Speaking of Pictures," *Life* (1 March 1943): 12.

Squiers, Carol. "Screening the War: Filmmakers & Critics on the Images that Made History," *International Documentary: The Journal of Non-Fiction Film and Video* 8 (Spring 1991): 21.

Tada Re'ikichi. "Kessen-ka eigakai no shinro" [The Path of the Film World During the Decisive Stage of the War], *Eiga Junpō* (21 March 1943): 14.

Tanaka Jun'ichirō. *Nihon Kyōiku eiga hattatsu shi* [History of the Development of the Japanese Educational Film] (Tokyo: Katatsumurisha, 1979).

Tanaka Jun'ichirō. *Nihon eiga hattatsu-shi* [The History of the Development of Japanese Film] (Tokyo: Chuō Kōron, 1980).

Tanaka Masaaki. "Nankin ni daigyakusatsu nado nakatta - 'maboroshi no firumu' wa maboroshi ni arazu" [There Was No Great Massacre in Nanking - The "Maboroshi Film" is not Moboroshi], *Seiron 229* (September 1991): 140-146.

Terkel, Studs. *The Good War: An Oral History of World War II* (New York: Pantheon, 1984).

Tezuka Osamu. *Boku no Songokū* [My Sun Wu-kong] (Tokyo: Hokugaku Bungei Shuppansha, 1986)

Tezuka Osamu, *Firumu wa ikite iru* [Film Lives] (Tokyo: Suzuki Shuppansha, 1959).

"These Atrocities Explain Jap Defeat," *Life* IV/20 (16 May 1938): 14.

Todorov, Tzvetan. *Conquest of America: The Question of the Other, The* trans. Richard Howard (New York: Harper and Row, 1984).

Togawa Naosuke. "Eigahō no yobikentō" [Preliminary Examination of the Motion Picture Law], *Eiga Hyōron* (1 October 1939), 36–54

Tsuchimoto Noriaki. "Kamei Fumio - 'Shanhai' kara 'Tatakau heitai' made" [Kamei Fumio - From "Shanghai" to "Fighting Soldiers"] in *Sengo eiga no tenkai* [Development of Postwar Cinema) from *Kōza Nihon eiga* [Lectures on Japanese Cinema], Vol. 5, (Tokyo: Iwanami Shoten, 1987), 322-341.

Tsumura Hideo. *Eigasen* [Film War] (Tokyo:Asahi Shinbunsha, 1942).

Tsumura Hideo. "'Sora no shinpei' o mite" [Watching *Sacred Soldiers of the Sky*], in *Zoku - eiga to kanshō* [Cinema and Appreciation - Part 2] (Tokyo: Sōgensha, 1943).

Tsumura Hideo, "Sūkō no bi to tekkishin no kōyō" [Sublime Beauty and Promoting Hostility Toward the Enemy], *Eiga Hyōron 10* (October 1943): 24.

Tsurumi Shunsuke. *An Intellectual History of Wartime Japan 1931-1945* (London: KPI, 1986).

Virilio, Paul. *War and Cinema: The Logistics of Perception*, trans. by Patrick Camiller (New York: Verso, 1989).

Waller, Gregory A. "Historicizing, a Test Cast: Japan on American Screens, 1909-1915," an unpublished paper delivered at the Society for Cinema Studies conference, Los Angeles, CA May 1991.

Žižek, Slavoj. *Looking Awry: An Introduction to Jaques Lacan Through Popular Culture* (Cambridge: MIT Press, 1991).

Sources

Sources for most of the films cited in this book are listed below. Titles in the index are followed by abbreviations of these addresses. This listing is by no means complete. In the case of well-known American films like *The Way We Fight* series, many distributors hold prints. The best place for further information is James Limbacher's *Feature Films: A Directory of Feature Films on 16mm and Videotape for Rental, Sale and Lease* (New York: R.R. Bowker, 1985). Films available on videotape are noted only with a "V;" for specific sources see *The Video Sourcebook*, ed. by Julia C. Furtaw (Detroit: Gale Research, 1992). Both books are available in most libraries. Videotapes of some of the Japanese films have been released in Japan (without subtitles, of course).

A	Akiko Productions 125 Withers St.#2 Brooklyn, NY 11211
B	Budget Films 4590 Santa Monica Blvd. Los Angeles, CA 90029 (213) 660-0187
BC	Biblioteca del Cinema "Umberto Barbaro" Piazza del Caprottari, 7000186 Rome, Italy
DD	Deep Dish Satellite Network 339 Lafayette Street New York, NY 10012 (212) 473-8933; Fax: (212) 420-8223
F	Films Inc. 733 Wilmette Ave., Suite 202 Wilmette, IL 60091 (312) 256-6000

FC	National Film Center, National Museum of Modern Art, Tokyo 3-1-4 Takane, Sagamihara-shi Kanagawa-ken 229 (0427) 58-0128; Fax (0427) 57-4449 * = Fragment
FR	First Run/Icarus 153 Waverly Place/6th Floor New York, NY 10014 (212) 727-1711
I	Images Film Archive 300 Philips Park Road Mamoroneck, NY 10543 (914) 381-2993
K	Japan Film Library Council Kawakita Memorial Film Institute Ginza-Hata Bldg.4-5, 4-chome, Ginza, Chūo-ku, Tokyo (03) 3561-6719; Fax: (03) 3561-6676
KA	Kawasaki City Museum 3049-1 Todoroki, Nakahara Kawasaki 211 (044) 754-4531; Fax: (044) 754-4533
KH	Komatsuzawa Hajime Nichiban Co., Iwata Bldg. 4-4 Nihonbashi, Kofune-chō Chūo-ku, Tokyo 103
KP	Kit Parker Films Carmel Valley, CA 93974 (800) 538-5838
LOC	Library of Congress Motion Picture, Broadcasting, and Recorded Sound Div. Washington, DC 20540 (202) 707-2371; Fax: (202) 707-5840
MGM	MGM/United Artists Entertainment 1350 Ave. of the Americas New York, NY 10019 (800) 223-0933
N	National AudioVisual Center General Services Administration Washington, DC 20409 (310) 763-1896

NA	U.S. National Archives Motion Picture, Sound and Video Branch Washington, DC 20408 (202) 501-5446; Fax: (202) 501-5778 * = Fragment; = †Print condition prohibits projection.
NC	New Cinema, Ltd. 35 Britain Street Toronto, Ontario M5A 1R7 Canada
NHK	NHK 2-2-1 Jinnan Shibuya-ku, Tokyo 150-1 Japan (03) 3465-1111
NY	New Yorker Films 16 W. 61st Street, New York, NY 10023 (212) 247-6110
O	Ōsone Primary School c/o International Relations Office Yamagata City Office 2-3-25 Hatago-machi Yamagata City 990 (0236) 41-12120; Fax: (0236) 24-9618
P	Planet Film Library 203 Umeda-Nakatō Blg. 15-2 Dōyama-chō, Kita-ku, Osaka 530 (06) 364-2165; Fax: (06) 312-8232 * = Fragment; †= Print condition prohibits projection.
PT	Paper Tiger Television 339 Lafayette Street New York, NY 10012 (212) 473-8933; Fax: (212) 420-8223
V	Available on videotape
VC	Academy Visual Communications Southern California Asian American Studies Central, Inc. 263 S. Los Angeles Street, Room 307 Los Angeles, CA 90012 (213) 476-0248; Fax: (213) 687-4848

Index

A

ABCD enemies, 38, *38*, 230
Abe Yutaka, 22, 44, 235
Academy Awards, 3, 61, 62, 66, 189, 191
Advancing on French Indo-China (Futsuin shinchū), 25
Aiki minami e tobu (see *Flying South in His Plane*)
Air Attacks Over Hawaii (see *Greater East-Asia News*)
Akihito, Emperor, 194
Akimoto Ken, 24
Akutagawa Mitsuzō (Kōzō), 203
Alexander, Joan, 222
All Orientals Look the Same (V), 107
All-out Attack on Singapore (Shingaporu sokogeki), 41
Amakasu Masahiko, 84, 85
America's Answer (NA), 60
Anata wa nerawarete iru (see *You're Being Aimed At*)
Andalusian Dog, The (V), 168
Andrews, Dana, 190
Angry Sea, The (Ikari no umi)
Angst, Richard, 24
animation, 102, 195, 200, 207, 231
Ano hata o ute (see *Dawn of Freedom*)
Ant Farm, 115
Aochi Chūzō, 23, 25, 197
Apocalypse Now (MGM, V), 246
Ara Ken'ichi, 254
Arai Kazugorō, 230, 232
Araki Sadao, 14, 200, 201, 202
Arimatsu Yoshimasa, 230
Army (Rikugun; FC, K), 47
Army-Navy Screen Magazine, series (N, NA, V), 224
Arnette, Peter, 159
Arrest of dissidents
    Kamei Fumio, 35
    Iwasaki Akira, 31, 35

Arts and Their Tendencies in Ideological Crisis (Shisōteki kiki ni okeru geijutsu narabi ni sono doko), 78
Aru hi no higata (see *The Beach at Ebb Tide on One Day*)
Aru hobo no kiroku (see *Record of a Nursery*)
Arville, Johnny, 237
Asahi Graph (Asahi gurafu), magazine, 230
Asahi Home Graph (Asahi hōmu gurafu), magazine, 35
Asahi M.P. Co., 19, 36, 40, 57
Asahi Shinbun (Asahi Newspaper), 31, 36, 46, 47, 193
Asahi World News (Asahi sekai nyūsu; FC), 36
Asano Takumi, 230, 233
Ashby, Hal, 178
Asia Calling (Sakebu Ajia), 15
Asian American Media Reference Guide, 108
Asian CineVision, 118
Asiaweek magazine, 257
Astro Boy, 228
Ato ni tsuzuku o shinzu (see *They Will Continue After Me*),
"Atomic Bombing" Interviews with the Crews of "Enola Gay" and "The Great Artiste" (NA), 263
Atsumi Teruo, 35
Attack to Sink (Gochin, also *Sunk Instantly)*, 46, 247
Attendance in a Torpedo Squad (Raigekitai Shutsudo, also *Torpedo Squadrons Move Out;* V), 47, 80, *81*, 83
Autobiography of a Jeep, The (N, NA, V), 67
Azumi Kōji, 213

B

Bad Day at Black Rock (V), 114, 269
Bakufu to danpen (see *Bomb Blast and Shrapnel*)
Barga Grasslands (Sogen Baruga; FC, KA), 203
Barnouw, Erik, 148, 149, 161, 185, 186
Basics of Victory, The (Shōri no kiso, also *The Foundation of Victory,* V), 48
Battle for the Marianas, The (NA), 63

279

Battle of Britain, The (BI, I, N, NA, V), 63
Battle of China, The (B, I, N, NA, V), 63, 102, 107, 109, 151, 206, 207, 221, 234, 254, 260
Battle of Midway, The (NA, V), 61, 193
Battle of Russia, The (B, I, N, NA, V)
Battle of San Pietro, The (N, NA, V), 65, 250, 259
Battleship Potemkin, The (V), 72, 130, 131
Bauhaus movement, 77
Bazin, André, 101
Beach at Ebb Tide on One Day, The (*Aru hi no higata*; FC, P), 34, 34
Beckett, Samuel, 121,145
Beery, Wallace, 244
Before Dawn (*Remei izen*),13
Being There (MGM, V), 178
Benjamin, Walter, 75
Bergson, Henri, 142
Berlin Wall, fall of, 89, 90
Bhabha, Homi K., 98, 99, 117
Birds at the Foot of Mount Fuji, The (*Fujisanroku no tori*), 34
Biruma senki (see *War Report from Burma*)
Bitter Memory: America's Concentration Camps, The, 118
Blanc, Mel, 224
Blancaflor, Norma, 235, 237
Blood and Celluloid, 74
Blume, John Morton, 118
Boku no Songokū (see *Son-goku the Monkey*)
Bomb Blast and Shrapnel (*Bakufū to danpen*; FC), 177
Bosshū sareta genbaku firumu (see *Confiscated Atomic Bomb Film*),
Brian Winston Reads the TV News (PT), 116
Bresson, Robert, 132, 137, *137*, 139, 144,145
Bucher, Jules, 67
Bugs Bunny, 224
Bujin no seika — Kuga Shōsa (see *The Essence of the Warrior Spirit: Lieutenant-Commander Kuga*)
Buñuel, Luis, 168
Burden of Representation, The, 101
Byakuran no uta (see *Song of the White Orchid*)

C

Cabinet Information Board, 38, 39, 40, 41, 42, 49, 52, 53, 56
Camera and Life (*Kamera to jinsei*), 126, 161
Campaign in Poland (NA, V), 59
Caniff, Milton, 107
Capra, Frank, 4, *62*, 63, 64, 65, 96, 101, 102, 107, 109, 118, 151, 206, 207, 208, 254
Castle, The, 167, 168
Censored (NA), 224, 225
censorship, 61
Challenge to Democracy (NA, V), 67
Chen Zheng-fa, 225

Chi no tsume moji (see *Written With Bloody Nails*)
Chiba Yasuki, 51
Chicago Sun newspaper, 186, 266
Chichi ariki (see *There Was a Father*)
Chicken Little (NA), 61
China Incident,16, 17, 18, 24, 37, 38, 42, 43, 48, 205, 206
China Incident (*Shina jihen*; FC, NA*), 205
China Invaded (VC), 253, 254, 256
China Night (*Shina no yoru*), 27, 204
Chūka Den'ei (China Film Co.), 45
Chukon nikudan Sanyushi (see *The Faithful Spirits of the Three Soldiers That Became Human Bullets*),
Churchill, Winston, 231, 232
Cinema and Appreciation — Part 2 (*Zoku — Eiga to kansho*), 247
Civil War (U.S.), 149
Civilian Victims of Military Brutality (NA), 148, 149, 252, 254, 255, 256
Co, Teddie, 237, 241
Color of Honor, The (V), 111, 118
Collyer, Bud, 222
Combat Film Reports (NA), 149, 243
Come See the Paradise (V), 114, 269
Committee on Public Information, 60
Complete Thailand, The (*Taikoku no zenbō*), 35,
Conde, David, 266, 267
Confiscated Atomic Bomb Film (*Bosshū sareta genbaku firumu*), 148, *148*
Concentrated Americans (V), 118
Connally, Senator, 150
Conquest of America, The
continental films (*tairiku eiga*), 161
Conversations: Before the War/After the War (V), 118
Coppola, Francis, 246
Cortez, Stanley, 259
Cowboy (NA), 66
CNN, 95, 115, 159, 182, 234,
Crack That Tank (NA), 249
Cronkite, Walter, 115
Cuckoo, The (*Jihi shincho*), 34
Culbert, David, 208, 271
cummings, e.e., 172
Cummington Story, The (NA), 66

D

Daffy Duck, 224
Daigaku wa deta keredo (see *I Graduated, But...*)
Daigoretsu no kyōfu (see *Fifth Column Fear*)
Daiho M.P. Co., 39, 41, 205
Daimai-tōnichi (Film Dept. of Osaka Mainichi Shinbun and Tokyo Nichinichi Shinbun), 19, 24, 25, 35, 36, 40
Dai-Nihon Eiga Kyōkai (Greater Japan Film Association), 40, 42, 52, 53, 56
Dai-Nihon Eiga Seisaku Co. (Daiei), 44, 51

Daitō M.P. Co., 39, 230
Daitoa nyusu (see *Greater East-Asia News*)
Danjurō san-dai (see *Three Generations of Danjurō*)
Daugherty, C., 191
Davenport, Harry, 190
Dawn (Sikuang, FC), 24
Dawn of Freedom (*Ano hata o ute*, also *Fire on That Flag!* NA), 44, 235, 236, 237, 238, 239, 240, 241
Dawn of the Founding of Manchukuo and Mongolia, The (*Man-Mō kenkoku no reimei*), 15, 16
Day England Fell, The (*Eikōku kuzururu no hi*), 44
Days of Waiting (V), 112, 118
de Leon, Gerardo, 235, 237, 238
de Rochemont, Louis, 4, 62, 244
De Witt, John L., 101
December 7th (N, NA, V), 62, 114, 170, 191, 268
Decisive Battle (*Kessen*), 49, 50
Deep Dish Satellite Network, 115, 116
Deleuze, Gilles, 132
Dentsū M.P. Co., 40, 217
Der Fuehrer's Face (NA), 61
Develop Manchuria (*Hirake Manshū*), 204
Devotion on the Homefront (*Jugo no sekisei*, also *Sincerity on the Homefront*), 214
Diary of Boys Reclaiming the Land (*Shōnen takushi no nikki*; FC), 203, 204
Dietrich, Marlene, 133
Difference and Pathology, 95, 117
Ding, Loni, 111, 118
Disney Studios, 61, 102, 207
Dispatches, 88
Dittmar, Linda, 117
Divide and Conquer (B, I, N, NA, V), 63
Divine Soldiers of the Sky (see *Sacred Soldiers of the Sky*)
Documentary Film: Essays Critical and Theoretical, 118
Documents of the Nanking Safety Zone, 252, 256, 271
Dōmei Tsūshin Co., 19, 24, 36
Domestic People Yapoo (*Kachikujin—Yapū*), 178
Donald Duck, 224
Donald Duck in Nutzi Land (see *Der Fuehrer's Face*)
Donovan, William B., 62, 190
Doolittle Fliers, 106
Doran, John, 259
Dos Passos, John, 172
Dotō o kette (see *In the Face of the High Seas*)
Dower, John, 96, 97, 98, 99, 100, 106, 117, 161, 234, 245
Dr. Suess (see Theodor Geisel)
Dyer, Dan, 265

E

Eastern Conference (*Tōyō kaigi*), 7
Ebashi Kinshirō, 219
Education for Death (NA), 61

Educational System of Japan, The (NA, V), 221, 222
Edwards, Jonathan, 172
Effects of the Atomic Bomb on Hiroshima and Nagasaki, The (M, N, NA, PM), 147, 148, *148*, 149, 166, 177, 181, 183, 265
Eiga Hyōron, 31, 240, 246
Eiga Kōsha, 56
Eiga Junpō, 74, 75, 79, 84, 85, 236, 246
Eiga no motsu bunpō (see *The Grammar of Film*),
Eigasen (see *Film War*)
Eigashi (see *Film History*)
Eikoku kuzururu no hi (see *The Day England Fell*)
Eisenhower, Dwight, 66
Eisenhower, Milton, 109, 216, 217
Eisenstein, Sergei, 72, 129, 132, 136, 137
Emi (V), 118
Emperor's Naked Army Marches On, The (*Yuki yukite shingun;* NY), 155, *155*
Enemy Japan — Dream of Empire, The (NA), 221
Enemy Will Be Legion, But We Will Fight, The (*Teki wa ikuman ari totemo*), 248
Esmeralda, Angel, 235
Essence of the Warrior Spirit: Lieutenant — Commander Kuga, The (*Bujin no seika — Kuga Shōsa*), 14
Eye of the Machine, The (*Kikai no me*), 77

F

Faithful Spirits of the Three Soldiers That Became Human Bullets, The (*Chūkon nikudan sanyushi*), 13
Family Gathering, A (V), 118
Famous Players-Laskey, 249
Famous Productions, 222, 224
Faulkner, Robert, 172
February 26th Incident, 266
Fifth Column Fear (*Daigoretsu no kyōfu*), 230, 247
Fighting Homefront, The (*Tatakau jūgo;* FC), 213, 214
Fighting Lady, The (NA), 62
Fighting Men, series (NA), 249
Fighting Movies — A Documentarist's Showa History (*Tatakau eiga — dokyumentarisuto no Shōwa-shi*), 260, 266
Fighting Soldiers (*Tatakau heitai* also *Soldiers on the Front;* BC), 25, 35, 157, *158*, 260, *260*, 261, 262
Fighting Young Citizens (*Tatakau shokokumin;* FC), series, 217
Fighting Young Citizens — Winter (*Tatakau shokokumin — fuyu;* O), 218
Film History (*Eigashi*), 265
Film War (*Eigasen*), 71, 74, 75, 76, 78, 80, 82, 84, 85, 87, 89, 91
Fire on That Flag! (see *Dawn of Freedom*)
Fires Were Started (I), 103
First Motion Picture Unit, 244
Fitch, George, 252, 253, 254, 256

Five Scouts (*Gonin no sekko-hei;* FC), 19, 239, 240
Flaming Sky (*Moyuru ōzora;* FC), 22
Flavor of Green Tea Over Rice, The (*Ochazuke no aji;* FC, NC, NY, V), 31
Fleet on the Yangtze River (*Yōsukō kantai*), 24
Fleet That Came to Stay, The (NA, V), 63, 154, 212, 250, 251
Fleisher Brothers, 222, 224, 226
Flying South in His Plane (*Aiki minami e tobu,* FC), 41, 49
Ford, John, 4, 61, *61*, 62, 189, 190, 191, 249, 268
Foreman, Carl, 65
Foundation of Victory, The (see *The Basics of Victory*)
Four Hundred Million, The, 64
Four More Years (V), 115
Fowler, Jr., Gene, 259
Fox-Movietone Japan, 157
Framed, 108, 118
Franco, Francisco, 153
From Hanoi to Hollywood, 117
From Here to Eternity (I, V), 114, 268
Fromm, Lloyd, 259
FRONT, 72
Fuchinkan gekichin (see *Sinking the Unsinkable Warship*)
Fujii Sei, 24
Fujii Shin'ichi, 260, 261
Fuji Studio Co., 40
Fujinami Jirō, 265
Fujisanroku no tori (see *The Birds at the Foot of Mount Fuji*)
Fujiwara Keita (aka. Kamatari), 30
Fujiwara Yoshie, 15
Fukuda Saburō, 246
Funaki Shun'ichi (Toshikazu), 198
Fury in the Pacific (NA, V), 63
Fushimizu Osamu, 27
Futsuin shinchū (see *Advancing on French Indo-China*)
Fuwa Suketoshi, 79

G

Gakuto shutsujin (see *Sending Off Our Students*)
Galde, Burton, 238, 241
Garcia, John, 95
Gayn, Mark, 266, 186
Geijutsu M.P. Co., 34, 40, 46, 191
Geisel, Theodor (Dr. Suess), 65, 207
Gendai seishin ni kan suru oboegaki (see *A Memorandum on Today's Spirit*)
General Katō's Falcon Fighters (*Katō hayabusa sentotai*), 48, 240
General, Staff, and Soldiers (*Shogun to sanbo to hei;* FC), 22, 41, 240
Genghis Khan (*Jingisukan;* FC), 205
Gekiryu (see *Torrent*),

Geography of Japan, The (NA), 62, 221
Gilman, Sander L., 95, 98, 99, 100, 117
Global Village, 115
Glory of the Colours! (*Gunkanki ni eikō are,* also *Glory to the Warship's Flag*), 24
Godard, Jean-Luc, 135, *135*, 138, 143
Godzilla (V), 80
Gochin (see *Attack to Sink*)
Golden Shell, The (*Kin'iro no horagai*), 229
Gone With the Wind (MGM, V), 74
Gonin no sekkō-hei (see *Five Scouts*)
Good War: An Oral History of World War II, The, 95
Gordon, Frankie, 237
Government of Japan, The (NA), 221
Grammar of Film, The (*Eiga no motsu bunpō*), 93
Grapes of Wrath (F, V), 62
Greater East-Asia News (*Dai tōa nyūsu;* NA), 189
Greater Japan Film Association (see Dai-Nihon Eiga Kyōkai)
Greneda War, 158
Grew, Joseph, 207
Grierson, John, 3
Griffith, D.W., 60, 132
Guadalcanal Diary (F, V), 105, 106
Gulf Crisis TV Project (DD), 95, 96, 98, 115, 116
Gulf War, 71, 73, 89, 90, 91, 92, 95, 115, 121, 122, 152, 158, 159, 180, 181, 182, 213, 234, 249
Gulliver's Travels, 226
"*Gunkan maachi*" (see "*March of the Battleships*")
Gunkanki ni eikō are (see *Glory of the Colours!*)

H

Hackenschmied (Hammid), Alexander, 67
Hagiyama Teruo, 50
Hahako-gusa (see *Mother-and-Child Grass*)
Hal Roach M. P. Co., 244
Hall, Arsenio, 116
Hamilton, Weldon, 238, 241
Hara Kazuo, 155
Hara Setsuko, 133, 134, *134*, 135
Hasegawa Kazuo, 26, 27, 205, 247
Hashimoto Tamako, 191
Havens, James, 189
Hawai Marē okikaisen (see *The War at Sea from Hawaii to Malaya*)
Hayashi Fusao, 89
Hayashida Shigeo, 218
Heidegger, Martin, 78, 132
Heisler, Stuart, 64
Heiwa (see *Peace*)
Hell Divers (MGM), 244
Heller, Robert, 206
Hemingway, Ernest, 172
Her Hidden Past (*Onna keizu;* FC), 246
Her Hidden Past — Part 2 (*Zoku — Onna keizu*), 246, 247
Here is Germany (N, NA, V), 64

Herr, Michael, 88
Hidden Preparedness (Himetaru kakugo), 41
High Sierra (MGM, V), 259
Hijōji Nippon (see *Japan in Time of Crisis*)
Hikyō Nekka (see *Jehol — The Dreamland of Manchukuo*)
Hilton, James, 206
Himetaru kakugo (see *Hidden Preparedness*)
Hinawashi no haha (see *Mother of Little Eagle, The*)
Hino Ashihei, 21, 47
Hiraga Yuzuru, 48
Hirake Manshu (see *Develop Manchuria*)
Hirakida Sei'ichi, 35
Hirohito, 55, 180, 267,
Hiroshima Mon Amour (F, I, V), 118, 180
History and Memory (A), 108, 112, 113, 256, 268, 269, 269
History of the Development of the Japanese Cinema (Nihon eiga hattatsu shi), 227
History of the Development of the Japanese Educational Film (Nihon kyōiku eiga hattatsu shi), 227
History of the Development of the Newsreel — Traces of Rapid Progress (Nyūsu eiga hattatsushi — yakushin no ato, also *History of the Newsreel*; FC), 36
Hitomi M.P. Co., 200
Hitler, Adolf, 28, 64, 104, 178
Hokuman o hirake (see *Open North Manchuria*)
Hokushin Nihon (see *Japan Advancing to the North*)
Hollywood, 59, 66, 95, 105, 114, 137, 189, 190, 206, 238, 244, 245, 248, 249, 251, 269
Holmes, Jr., Oliver Wendell, 172
Holy War (Seisen; FC), 24, 43
Honderick, Walter, 214
Honma Kinsuke, 75, 200
Hornbeck, William, 206, 207
Hot Wind (Neppū), 41, 49, 50, 50
Howard, Richard, 161
How to Get Killed — In One Easy Lesson (NA), 249
Hozumi Toshimasa, 49
Hsi Yu-chi, 225, 226
Hsü Shuhsi, 256, 271
Hull, Cordell, 225
Huston, John, 65, 259, 260
Huston, Walter, 63, 190, 206, 207, 259

I

I Graduated, But... (Daigaku wa deta keredo; FC), 11, 12, 221
Ichiban utsukushiku (see *Most Beautiful, The*)
Ichikawa Kon, 200
Ieki Miyoji, 51
"If We Go to the Sea" ("Umi yukaba"), 205, 218, 219, 240
Iida Shinmi, 45, 198
Ijiichi Susumu, 22

Ikari no umi (see *Angry Sea, The*)
Ikeda Tadao, 31
Ikeru ningyō (see *A Living Doll*)
Imai Tadashi, 48
Imamura Taihei, 74, 79
In the Face of the High Seas (Dotō o kette, also *Over the High Seas*; NA), 23
Imperial Rule Assistance Association, 37
Indonesia (Ranryō Indo), 35
Inochi no minato (see *Port of Life*),
Inoue Kan, 34
International Military Tribunal for the Far East (Tokyo Trials), 7, 201
International Red Cross, 175, 177, 180, 252
Introduction to Our Weaponry Series (see *The Fighting Homefront*)
Inukai Tsuyoshi, 201
Invisible Citizens: Japanese Americans (V), 118
Irie Takako, 15
Ishigo, Estelle and Arthur, 112
Ishimoto Tōkichi, 34
Ishizuka, Karen, 118
Issatsu tashoken (see *The Sword Saving Many by Killing One*)
It Happened One Night (I, V), 206
Itō Daisuke, 13
Itō Noboru, 191
Itō Sueo, 165, 184, 185, 265
Ivens, Joris, 4, 64, 207
Iwasaki Akira, 30, 31, 185, 265, 267
Iwata Tōyō, 46

J

J.O. Studio Co., 198, 200
Jackman, Joseph, 259
Jacob, Heinrich Edvard, 74
James, William and Henry, 172
Jap Zero (NA, V), 212, 243, 244, 245, 245
Japan Advancing to the North (Hokushin Nihon), 23, 198
Japan in Time of Crisis (Hijōji Nippon; FC, LOC, NA), 200, 201
Japan in Time of Emergency (see *Japan in Time of Crisis*)
Japanese Americans in Concentration Camps (Boston) (V, VC), 118
Japanese Americans in Concentration Camps (L.A.) (V, VC), 118
Japanese Behavior (NA), 62, 221
Japanese Coast Line (NA), 62
Japanese Film (see *Nihon Eiga*)
Japanese Relocation (N, NA, V), 67, 109, 109, 114, 217, 269
Japanese Tragedy, A (Nihon no higeki, also *The Tragedy of Japan*; J, FC), 7, 160, 265, 266, 267, 268

Jehol — The Dreamland of Manchukuo (Hikyō Nekka), 203
Jennings, Humphrey, 103
Jihi shinchō (see *Cuckoo, The*)
Jingisukan (see *Genghis Khan*)
Joan Does Dynasty (PT), 116
Johnson, Julian, 190
Jūgo no sekisei (see *Devotion on the Homefront*)
Jūjiya M.P. Co., 40
Justice (NA), 97, 150, 151, 154, 212, 213, 234

K

Kachikujin — Yapū, (see *Domestic People Yapoo*)
Kaigun (see *Navy*)
Kafka, Franz, 167, 168
Kagayaku Nippon (see *Victorious Japan*)
Kaisen no zenya (see *On the Eve of War*)
Kamei Fumio, 24, 25, 35, 157, 158, 160, 225, 260, 262, 265, 266, 267
Kamei Katsuichirō, 89
Kamera to jinsei (see *Camera and Life*)
kamikaze, 13, 49, 125, 160
Kanayama Kinjirō, 203
Kanchō umi no bara (see *The Spy Named Rose of the Sea*)
Kanchō imada shisezu (see *The Spy Isn't Dead Yet*)
Kanin, Garson, 65
Kannō Keiichi, 265
Kanō Ryūichi, 165, 185, 265
Kant, Immanuel, 86, 90
Kasahari kenpō (see *An Umbrellamaker's Sword*)
Katō hayabusa sentōtai (see *General Katō's Falcon Fighters*)
Katō Hidetoshi, 254, 256
Katō Tateo, 48
Kaufman, Charles, 259
Kaufmann, Nikolas, 33
Kawai M.P. Co., 13, 230
Kawaguchi Kazuo, 246
Kawaguchi Sei'ichi, 24
Kawakita Nagamasa, 19, 33
Kessen (see *Decisive Battle*)
Kessen no ōzora e (see *Toward the Decisive Battle in the Sky; FC*)
Kikai no me (see *The Eye of the Machine*)
Kike wadatsumi no koe (see *Listen to the Voice of the Sea*)
Kill or Be Killed (NA), 151, 154, 159, 190, 248, 249
Kimi koso tsugi no arawashi da (see *You Are the Next Wild Eagle*)
Kimura Hajime, 191
Kimura Ichirō, 230
Kimura Sotoji, 24
Kindai no chōkoku (see *Overcoming the Modern*)
Kinder, Marsha, 153, 161
King, Rodney, 149
King's Tail, The (*ōsama no shippo*), 195

Kinema Junpō, 24, 26, 31, 206, 226, 230, 261
Kin'iro no horagai (see *The Golden Shell*)
Kinoshita Keisuke, 47
Kinugasa Teinosuke, 13, 230
Kitabayashi Atsushi, 25
Knelter, Seymour, 222
Knight, Eric, 207
Know Your Ally, series (NA), 64
Know Your Ally: Britain (NA), 64
Know Your Enemy, series (NA), 64, 83
Know Your Enemy: Japan (NA), 64, 76, 221
Knox, Frank, 190
Kōa M.P. Co., 39, 41
Kobayashi Hideo, 89
Kobayashi Issa, 35, 36
Kojima no haru (see *Spring on Leper's Island*)
Kokoro no busō (see *Weapons of the Heart*)
Kōkū kichi (see *Navy Base*)
Kokusenya Battle (*Kokusenya gassen*), 205
Konishi Shōzō, 211
Koseki Yūji, 260
Kōsugi Isamu, 19
Kracauer, Siegfried, 206
Krumgold, Joseph, 67
Kubrick, Stanley, 178
Kuga Noboru, 14
kulturfilm, 33, 34
Kumagai Hisatora, 21
Kurata Bunjin, 28, 204
Kurosawa Akira, 42, 51
Kurusu kichisaburō, 225
Kwantung Army, 84
Kyōdo News Service, 252, 254

L

Last Day of Nikōlaevsk, The (*Nikō saigo no hi*), 10
Last Emperor, The, 155
Lea, Homer, 117
League of Nations, 199, 201
Lee, Dick, 82
Legacy of the Civil War, The, 172
Lenin, V.I., 103
Lerner, Irving, 67
Leroy, Burt, 237
Let There Be Light (B, I, N, NA, V), 65, 212, 259, 260
Let's Have a Drink (NA), 97, 148, 151, 212, 221, 233, 234
Li Hsiang-lan (see *Yamaguchi Yoshiko*)
Liang Hung-chih, 19
Liberty magazine, 105, 106, *106*
Life magazine, 104, 118, 152, 193, 225, 254
Lifeline of the Sea (*Umi no seimeisen,* also *Lifeline of the Ocean; FC*), 23, 197, 198, 201
Lindberg, Charles, 152, 161
Listen to Britain (KP, V), 103
Listen to the Voice of the Sea (*Kike wadatsumi no koe*), 220

Litvak, Anatole, 63, 206, 207
Liu En-ze, 225
Liu Guang-xing, 225
Living by the Earth (Tsuchi ni ikiru), 34
Living Doll, A (Ikeru ningyō), 13
Lockard, E.S. (Ted), 238, 241
London Can Take It, , 4, 103
Lorentz, Pare, 61
Lost Horizon (V), 206
Lu Zhang-pen, 225
Lumière Brothers, 129, 136, 142
Lummis, Douglas, 178

M

Mabalot, Linda, 117
MacArthur, Douglas, 176, 235
Maeda Hajime, 200, 230, 232
Magee, Rev. John, 151, 252, 253, 254, 255
Mainichi Broadcasting Co., 254
Mainichi newspaper, 197
Makino Masahiro, 50, 247
Makino Shūichi, 227
Malayan War Front — A Record of the March Onward (Maré senki — shingeki no kiroku, also *Malayan War Record;* FC, P), 45, 84, 154
Malayan War Front — The Birth of Shōnan Island (Maré senki — Shōnan-tō tanjō; FC), 241, 246, 247, 248
Maltese Falcon, The (V), 259
Man-Slashing, Horse-Piercing Sword (Zanjin zanbaken, also *Man-Slashing, Horse-Slashing Sword)*, 13
Man Who Waits, The (Matte ita otoko), 246, 247
Manchurian Incident, 10, 11, 15, 18, 199, 201, 266
Manchurian Motion Picture Association (Manshū Eiga Kyōkai [Man'ei]), 27
Manhattan Project, 169, 185
Man-Mō kenkoku no reimei (see *The Dawn of the Founding of Manchukuo and Mongolia*)
Manshū nōgyō imindan kinkyo (see *Recent Report on Farm Settlers in Manchuria*)
Manufacturing the Enemy (DD), 95-96, 98, 116
Manyōshū, 153
Manzanar, 108, 110, 113, 118
Mao Tse-tung, 207
Maple Viewing (Momijigari), 36
Marai no tora (see *The Tiger of Malaya*)
"March of the Battleships" ("Gunkan maachi"), 160, 189
March of Time, 244
Maré senki — shingeki no kiroku (see *Malayan War Front — A Record of the March Onward*)
Maré senki — Shōnan-tō no tanjō (see *Malayan War Front — The Birth of Shōnan Island*)
Maréy, Etienne Jules, 71
Marines (Suiheisan), 248
Marshall, George C., 63, 101

Maruyama Shōji, 227
Marxism, 267
Matano Kimio, 265
Matsuishi Osamu, 14
Matsuoka Yōsuke, 198
Matsuzaki Keiji, 260
Matte ita otoko (see *The Man Who Waits*)
May 15 Incident, 266
Mayor, Carl, 222
McGovern, Dan, 127, 166, 170, 172, 176, 179, 183, 184, 185, 265, 266, 267
Meet John Doe (V), 206
Mekas, Jonas, 136
Memorandum on Today's Spirit, A (Gendai seishin ni kan suru oboegaki), 89
Metropolitan Symphony (Tokai kōkyōgaku), 12, 13
Michaud, Gene, 117
Mickey Mouse, 198, 200
Mikami Ryoji, 230
Miki Shigeru, 24, 34, 45, 185, 225, 260, 261, 265
Milestone, Lewis, 106
Military Courtesy (NA), 248
Military Musical Band and the Front (Yasen Gungakutai; FC, P†), 42
Millner, Sherry, 115
Minami jūjisei wa maneku (see *The Southern Cross Beckons*)
Ministry of Education (Monbushō), 128, 165, 174, 201, 205
Mission to Yenan (NA), 62
Miyajima Yoshio, 22, 235, 238
Mizoguchi Kenji, 13, 15, 54
Mizuki Sōya, 34, 57, 211
Mizuno Shinkō, 200
Mochinaga Tadahito, 191, 193, 195
Momijigari (see *Maple Viewing*)
Momotarō, 46, 85, 86, 193, 194, 195, 199, 200
Momotarō — Divine Troops of the Ocean (Momotarō — umi no shinpei; FC, LOC, V), 85, 195
Momotaro's Sea Eagle (Momotarō no umiwashi; FC, LOC, P*), 46, 191, 192, 192
Momotarō vs. Mickey Mouse (see *Picture Book 1936*)
Monbushō (see Ministry of Education)
Mongolia Rising (Tachiagaru Mō-Ko), 174, 175, 184, 186, 201, 205, 219
Morozumi, Jenni, 118
Moss, Carlton, 64
Most Beautiful, The (Ichiban utsukushiku, also *Most Beautifully;* FC, V), 51
Mother-and-Child Grass (Hahako-gusa), 42, 246, 247
Mother of Little Eagle, The (Hinawashi no haha), 49
Motion Picture Law *(Eigahō)*, 28, 29, 30, 31, 32, 33, 35, 39, 40, 260
Moyuru ōzora (see *Flaming Sky*)
Mr. Bug Goes to Town, 195
Mr. Carrot (Ninjin-chan also *The Spirit of Ginger)*, 229
Mr. Deeds Goes to Town (F, I, V), 206

Mr. Smith Goes to Washington (F, I, V), 206
Mud and Soldiers (Tsuchi to heitai; FC, NA*), 21, 240
Murata Yasuji, 200, 201
Murphy, William, 185, 190, 208, 259
Museum of Modern Art (MOMA), 104, 207

N

Nagahisa Yoshirō, 198
Nagatomi Eijirō, 230
Nakai Masakazu, 77, 78, 92, 93
Nakagawa Norio, 48
Nakajima Masatsugu, 200
Nakamura Robert, 110, 113, 118
Nakamura Tetsu, 235
Nakano Takao, 198
Nakano Yoshio, 174
Name Above the Title, The, 101, 118
Nani ga kanojo o sō saseta ka (see *What Made Her Do It?*), 13
Nan'o M.P. Co., 39, 41, 205
Nanking (Nankin), 24, 154
Nanking Massacre, 16, 151, 153, 155, 175, 233
National Archives (U.S.), 2, 60, 67, 127, 128, 144, 146, 150, 154, 156, 169, 171, 185, 188, 195, 210, 235, 250, 251, 254, 255, 264
National Film Board of Canada, 3
Natural Resources of Japan (NA), 62
Navy (Kaigun; FC), 41, 47
Navy Base (Kōkū kichi), 25
Nazis Strike, The (B, I, N, NA, V), 63
Negro Sailor, The (NA), 64
Negro Soldier, The (NA), 64
Negishi Toichirō, 13
Neppū (see *Hot Wind*)
Nessa no chikai (see *Vow in the Desert*)
New Battlefield on the Continent (Tairiku shinsenjō), 45
Newman, Alfred, 189, 206,
Newsreels
    Army-Navy Screen Magazine (N, NA, V), 224
    Asahi sekai (FC, NA, LOC), 19, 36
    Daimai-tōnichi (LOC), 19, 36
    Daitōa Nyusu, 189
    Dōmei (LOC, NA, P), 19
    March of Time, 244
    Shinbun dōmei, 36
    Shinbun renmei, 19
    Yomiuri (LOC, NA), 19
Nichols, Bill, 209, 161
Nietzsche, Friedrich, 129, 132, 142, 143, ,178
Nihon eiga (Japanese Film), 47
Nihon eiga hattatsu shi (see *History of the Development of Japanese Cinema*)
Nihon Eigasha (Nichiei), 45, 48, 78, 165, 171, 184, 185, 189, 218, 219, 265, 267

Nihon Kyōiku eiga hattatsu shi (see *History of the Development of the Japanese Educational Film*)
Nihon News (Nihon nyūsu; NHK, LOC, NA) , 49, 189, 219, 246
Nihon no higeki (see *A Japanese Tragedy*)
Nikkatsu (Nippon Katsudō Shashin Co.) 19, 22, 28, 39, 41, 214, 218
Nikō Incident, 10
Nikō saigo no hi (see *The Last Day of Nikōlaevsk*)
Ninjin-chan (see *Mr. Carrot*)
Nippon Banzai (KH, P*), 231, 232
Nisei Soldier: Standard Bearer for an Exiled People, 111, 118
Nishiguchi Higuma, 198
Nishina Yoshio, 177
Nishitani Keiji, 89
Nishizumi Senshachō-den (see *The Story of Tank Commander Nishizumi*)
Nomura Hiromasa, 51
Nomura Kichisaburō, 225
Northwest USA (NA), 66
Nyan nyan myao hoe (also *Nyan nyan musume;* Japanese pronunciation: *Roro Byōkai;* FC, KA), 203
Nyūsu eiga hattatsushi — yakushin no ato (see *History of the Development of the Newsreel — Traces of Rapid Progress*)

O

Oabare Songokū (see *The Rage of Sung Wu-kong*)
Obata Chozō, 265
Obinata Den (Ohinata), 21
Ochazuke no aji (see *Flavor of Green Tea Over Rice, The*)
Office of Strategic Services (OSS), 61, 62, 190
Office of War Information (OWI), 61, 66, 216, 233, 244
Officers Who've Lost — Life of POWs (Yaburetaru shōguntachi; FC*), 241
Ohinata Village (Ohinata mura), 28
Okabe Chōhei, 219
Ōkawa Heihachiro, 235
Okazaki, Steven, 111, 112, 118
Okochi Denjirō, 235
Okuyama Dairokurō, 265
Omochabako shiriizu (see *Toy Box Series*)
Ōmura Einosuke, 191, 193, 195
On the Eve of War (Kaisen no zenya), 230
On To Tokyo (NA), 64
On War, 88
On Your Toes (NA), 249
Onna keizu (see *Her Hidden Past*)
Open North Manchuria (Hokuman o hirake), 204
Oriental Song of Victory (Tōyō no gaika, also *Victory Song of the Orient;* FC*, LOC*, NA), 45, 46, 47, 82, 84, 154, 241

Orientalism, 100
Ōsama no shippo (see *The King's Tail*)
Ōtomono Yakamochi, 153
Our Enemy — The Japanese (NA), 221
Our Job in Japan (NA), 65
Our Weaponry series (FC), 213
Overcoming the Modern (*Kindai no chōkoku*), symposium, 89
Ōya Sōichi, 213
Oyama Isao, 16
Ozaki Hozumi, 229
Ozawa Tokuji, 230
Ozu Yasujirō, 11, 31, 41, 133, 134, 139

P

Panama War, 158
Paper Tiger Television, 115, 116
Parker, Alan, 269
Parrich, Robert, 189
Pasion, Ricardo, 235, 237, 239, 241
Peace (*Heiwa*), 182
Pearl Harbor, 43, 44, 46, 111, 157, 184, 214, 216, 268, 269
Peking (*Pekin*), 24
Perceptions: Japanese American Redress, 118
Pershing's Crusaders (NA), 60
Philippines Special Information Group, 45
Picture Book 1936 (*Momotarō vs. Mickey Mouse*) (*Ehon 1936 nen*; KH), 198
Platoon (V), 105
Plow That Broke the Plains, The (N, NA), 61, 216
Poe, Sr., Fernando, 235, 237
Popeye, 192, 194, 222, 224
Port of Life (*Inochi no minato*), 57
Porky Pig, 224
Prelude to War (B, I, N, NA, V), 63, 207
Princess Iron Fan (*Saiyūki*, 1941; K, KH), 225, 226, 226, 227, 227, 228,
Princess Iron Fan (*Saiyūki*, 1960), 246, 247
Private Snafu (N, NA, V), 224
Prizzi's Honor (V), 259
Proust, 121, 145
Purple Heart, The (F, V), 105, 106

R

Rage of Sun Wu-kong (*Oabari Songokū*), 229
Raigekitai Shutsudō (see *Attendance in a Torpedo Squad*)
Ran'in tanbōki (see *Report on Indonesia*)
Rankin, John, 96
Ranryō Indo (see *Indonesia*)
Rather, Dan, 115
Reagan, Ronald, 244, 245
Reason and Emotion (NA), 61
Recent Report on Farm Settlers in Manchuria (*Manshū nōgyō imindan kinkyo*), 84, 204

Record of a Nursery (*Aru hobo no kiroku*; FC), 34, 35
Record of the Construction of a New Continent (*Shintairiku kensetsu no kiroku*; FC), 24
Reed, Carol, 65
Remei izen (see *Before Dawn*)
religion, 144, 171
Renais, Alain, 180
Report from the Aleutians (B, N, NA, V), 65
Report on Indonesia (*Ran'in tanbōki*), 35
Representing Reality, 161
Ri Kō-ran (see Yamaguchi Yoshiko)
"Ride of the Valkerie", 246
Riefenstahl, Leni, 101
Riken Kagaku M.P. Co., 34, 40, 48, 213
Rikugun (see *Army*)
River, The (N, NA), 61
Road to Peace in the Orient, The (*Tōyō heiwa no michi*; FC), 19, 21
Roosevelt, Franklin D., 66, 192, 217, 231, 232
Roro Byōkai (see *Nyan nyan miyao hoe*)
"Rusa Sayan", 82
Russo-Japanese War, 9, 47, 213
Ryū Chishū, 132, 133

S

Sacred Soldiers of the Sky (*Sora no shinpei*, also *Divine Soldiers of the Sky*; FC, LOC, P), 48, 156, 157, 246, 247, 248
Saeki Eisuke, 23, 197, 198
Safeguarding Military Information (NA), 248
Sagimiya Fumihiko, 35
Said, Edward, 100
Saiyūki (see *Princess Iron Fan*)
Sakata Shigenori, 10
Sakasai Koichirō, 265
Sakebu Ajia (see *Asia Calling*)
Saitō Makoto, 201
Salcedo, Leopoldo G., 235, 237, 241
Sanei Co., 197
Santarō Giving His Best (*Santarō ganbaru*), 51
Sasaki Yasushi, 49
Satake Mitsuo, 200
Satō Hirokazu, 35
Satō Tadao, 273
Sawamura Tsutomu, 45
Sayato Tsuneo, 200
Sekai eiga sensō (see *World Film Wars*)
Sekiguchi Noriko, 155
Send Your Tin Cans to War (NA), 66
Sending Off Our Students (Never to Return) (*Gakuto shutsujin*, also *Students Going to the Battle*; FC, NHK), 49, 218, 219
Senjō no onnatachi (see *Senso Daughters*)
Senso Daughters (*Senjō no onnatachi*; FR), 155
Sensō to heiwa (see *War and Peace*)
Senyū no uta (see *Song for a War Comrade*)

Seo Mitsuyo, 46, 191, 193, 195
Sergeant York (MGM, V), 259
Sex Hygiene (NA), 248, 249
Shanghai (*Shanhai;* FC), 24, 255, 261
Shanghai Incident, First, 13, 16, 18, 19, 266
Shanghai Incident, Second, 16, 21, 205, 266
Shanghai Navy Brigades (*Shanhai rikusentai;* FC), 21
Shi Feng-gi, 225
Shibata Yoshio, 74
Shibuya Minoru, 51
Shiga Tomayasu, 230
Shigeno Tatsuhiko, 26
Shikama Sumio, 246
Shima Kōji, 41, 44
Shimauchi Toshir, 265
Shimizu Chiyota, 246
Shimomura Kenji, 34
Shina no yoru (see *China Night*)
Shinbun dōmei News (*Shinbun Dōmei nyūsu*), 36
Shinbun Renmei News (*Shinbun renmei nyūsu*), 19
Shindō Kaneto, 42
Shingaporu sōkōgeki (see *All-out Attack on Singapore*)
Shinkō Kinema Co., 14, 39, 41, 205
Shinseki M.P. Co., 25
Shintairiku kensetsu no kiroku (see *Record of the Construction of a New Continent*)
Shirai Shigeru, 23, 24, 154, 161
Shirakawa Taisaku, 227
Shirer, William, 206
Shisōteki kiki ni okeru geijutsu narabi ni sono dōko (see *The Arts and Their Tendencies in Ideological Crisis*)
Shōchiku Co., 22, 39, 40, 41, 47, 49, 50, 51, 230, 247
Shōgun to sanbō to hei (see *General, Staff, and Soldiers*)
Shōkokumin no tomo (see *Young Citizens' Friend*)
Shokun!, 271
Shōnen takushi no nikki (see *Diary of Boys Reclaiming the Land*)
Shōri no kiso (see *The Basics of Victory*)
Shussei mae jūnijikan (see *Twelve Hours Before Going to the Front*)
Signal Corps, 60, 63, 64, 65, 67, 206, 221, 224, 243, 244, 249, 259
Sikuang (see *Dawn*)
Sinking of the Unsinkable Warship (*Fuchinkan gekichin,* also *An Unsinkable Warship Sunk*), 50
Skinner, James, 190
Smith, George, 259
Snow Country (*Yukiguni, 1939;* FC), 34
Snow White and the Seven Dwarves (MGM, V), 226
Soe, Valerie, 107
Sōgen Baruga (see *Barga Grasslands*)
Soldiers at the Front (see *Fighting Soldiers*)
Son-goku the Monkey (*Boku no Songoku*), 227, 228
Song for a War Comrade (*Senyū no uta;* FC), 24

Song of the White Orchid (*Byakuran no uta*), 26, 26
Sora no shinpei (see *Sacred Soldiers of the Sky*)
Sora no Shōnenhei (see *Young Soldiers of the Sky*)
Sorge Spying Incident, 229
Southern Cross Beckons, The (*Minami jūjisei wa Maneku*), 23
Soviet Union coup d'état (1991), 89, 91
Spigelgass, Leonard, 206, 224
Spring on Leper's Island (*Kojima no haru,* also *Spring on a Small Island;* FC), 39
Spy Isn't Dead Yet, The (*Kanchō imada shisezu*), 230
Spy Named Rose of the Sea, The (*Kanchō umi no bara*), 230
Squiers, Carol, 115, 118
Staff Film Reports (NA, V), 243
Stark, Harold, 62, 190
Steichen, Edward, 63, 71
stereotype, 222
Stilwell, Joseph, 64
Stilwell Road, The (B, I, N, NA, V), 64
Story of Tank Commander Nishizumi, The (*Nishizumi Senshachō-den;* FC), 22, 48
Strategic Bombing Survey (U.S.), 67, 127, 165, 167, 169, 175, 176, 183, 185, 265
Strauss, Richard, 177, 178
Struggle of the Departments, The, 90
Suda Shōta, 85
Sugiyama Haseo, 203
Suiheisan (see *Marines*)
Sun Tioa-xia, 225
Sunk Instantly (see *Attack to Sink*)
Superman: Japoteurs (P), 223
Superman and the Jungle Drums, 224
Superman in the Eleventh Hour, 224
Suzuki Jūkichi, 13, 19
Suzuki Kiyoji, 265
Swedes in America (NA), 66

T

Tabata Tsuneo, 42
Tachiagaru Mō-Kō (see *Mongolia Rising*)
Tachiagaru Tai (see *Thailand Rising*)
Tada Reikichi, 84
Tafaly, Nicolas, 222
Tagg, John, 101, 102
Taguchi Satoshi, 22, 41
Taikoku no zenbō (see *The Complete Thailand*)
Taira Yasunobu, 198
tairiku eiga (see *continental films*)
Tairiku shinsenjō (see *New Battlefield on the Continent*)
Tajiri, Rea, 108, 113, 114, 118, 216, 256, 268, 269
Takagi Toshirō, 25, 78, 79
Takarazuka Eiga Seisakusho (Takarazuka M.P. Production), 39, 41, 205
Taketomi Kunishige, 197
Tanabe Toshihiko, 191

Tanaka Gi'ichi, 3
Tanaka Jun'ichirō, 197, 227
Tanaka Masaki, 254
Tanaka Memorial, 7
Tanaka, Rudy, 111
Tanaka Shigeo, 44
Tanaka Yoshitsugu, 24, 198
Tasaka Tomotaka, 19, 21, 247
Tatakau eiga — dokyumentarisuto no Shōwashi (see *Fighting Movies*)
Tatakau heitai (see *Fighting Soldiers*)
Tatakau shōkokumin (see *Fighting Young Citizens*)
Tatsuno, David, 214
Tegnell, Ann, 118
television, 9, 115–118, 116, 117, 118, 122, 135, 136, 138, 140, 142, 159, 180, 182, 230, 234, 239, 273, 277
tendency films, 11
10,000 Ri of Fertile Land (*Yokudo banri*; FC), 27, 28, 204
Terkel, Studs, 95
Tezuka Osamu, 194, 195, 227, 228
Thailand Rising (*Tachiagaru Tai*), 35
There Was a Father (*Chichi ariki*; F, FC, V), 41
They Will Continue After Me (*Ato ni tsuzuku o shinzu*), 48
Three Generations of Danjurō (*Danjurō san-dai*), 54
"Thus Spoke Zarathustra", 177, 178
Tibbetts, Paul, 263
Tienanmen Square Incident, 89, 91
Tiger of Malaya, The (*Marai no tora*; V), 80, 82, 240
Time magazine, 53, 159
Tiomkin, Dimitri, 206, 207, 259
To the Shores of Iwo Jima (NA, V), 63, 250
Tōa Hassei Nyusu Eiga Seisakusho (Tōa Sound News Co), 40
Todorov, Tzvetan, 153, 161
Togawa Naosuke (Naoki), 30, 31
Tōhō Film Co., 21, 22, 24, 33, 34, 39, 40, 41, 44, 47, 48, 49, 50, 51, 205, 235, 267
Tōjō Hideki, 219
Tokai kōkyōgaku (see *Metropolitan Symphony*)
Tokugawa Musei, 227
Tokyo Bunka Eiga Seisakusho (Tokyo Cultural Film Production), 40
Tōkyō Chorus (*Tōkyō no gasshō* also *Tōkyō no kōrasu*; FC, K), 11
Tokyo Hassei Eiga Seisakusho (Tokyo Sound Picture Production), 28, 39, 205
Tōkyō Story (*Tōkyō monogatari*; B, FC, NY, V), 133, 133, 134, 138
Toland, Gregg, 62, 189, 190, 191
Torpedo Squads Move Out (see *Attendance in a Torpedo Squad*)
Top Value Television, 115
Topaz 1942-1945 (A), 214, 215
Toscanini, Arturo, 67
Toscanini: Hymn of the Nations (N, NA), 67
Tōwa Shōji Goshigaisha (Towa Film Corp.), 19, 33
Toward the Decisive Battle in the Sky (*Kessen no ōzora'e*), 41, 248
Town, The (NA), 66
Tōyō no gaika (see *Oriental Song of Victory*)
Tōyō heiwa no michi (see *Road to Peace in the Orient, The*)
Toyoda Shirō, 28, 39, 204
Tragedy of Japan, The (see *A Japanese Tragedy*)
Treasure of the Sierra Madre, The (MGM, V), 259
Trial of Joan of Arc, The (F, V), 144
Triumph of the Will (*Triumph des Willens*; B, I, V), 101, 206, 208
True Glory, The (B, I, F, N, NA), 65
Tsubaraya Eiji, 22, 44, 80, 193
Tsuchi ni ikiru (see *Living by the Earth*)
Tsuchi to heitai (see *Mud and Soldiers*)
Tsuchimoto Noriaki, 272, 274
Tsuji Kichirō, 13
Tsukamoto Shizuyo, 191
Tsumura Hideo, 73, 193, 241, 247
Tsuno Keiko, 118
Tunisian Victory (B, NA, V), 64
Turner, Bill, 222
Turner, Ted, 116
TV Tōkyō, 148
Twelve Hours Before Going to the Front (*Shussei mae jūnijikan*), 41
Twentieth-Century Fox, 107, 190, 249
"Twilight of the Gods", 178
Two Down and One To Go (NA, V), 64
2001: A Space Odyssey (MGM, V), 178

U

UFA, 33
Uchida Tomu, 11, 15
Uehara Ken, 22
Ueno Yukikio, 23, 197
Ultraman, 80
Umbrellamaker's Sword, An (*Kasahari kenpō*), 13
Umeki Saburō, 248
"Umi yukaba" (see "If We Go to the Sea")
Umi no seimeisen (see *Lifeline of the Sea*)
Unfinished Business: The Japanese American Internment Cases (V), 11, 118
Unsinkable Warship Sunk (see *Sinking of the Unsinkable Warship*)
United States Film Service, 61

V

V Was for Victory: Politics and American Culture During World War II, 118
Valor of Ignorance, The (V), 117
Van Dyke, Willard, 61, 66
Veiller, Anthony, 63, 207
Vertov, Dziga, 129
Victorious Japan (*Kagayaku Nippon*; FC), 157

Victory in Burma (NA), 191
video, 121, 122
Video, Freex, 115
Vietnam War, 88, 89, 91, 181, 213
violence, 147–159, 239, 250, 255
Virilio, Paul, 71, 88
von Clausewitz, Karl, 88
von Sternberg, Josef, 66
Vow in the Desert (*Nessa no chikai*), 27, 205

W

Wagner, Richard, 178, 246
Wakai hito (see *Young People*)
Wallace, Irving, 207
Wallace, Mike, 115
Waller, Gregory, 117
Wan Brothers, 228, 229
Wan Ganbai, 225
Wan Ku-chan, 225, 226
Wan Lai-ming, 225, 226
Wang Chaomin (Chinwei), 18-19, 26, 42
Wang Jinyi, 225
War and Peace (*Senso to heiwa*; FC), 26, 262, 268
War at Sea from Hawaii to Malaya, The (*Hawai Maré okikaisen*; FC, NA*), 41, 44, 46, 47, 76, 77, 80, 83, 193, 232, 240, 248, 268
War Comes to America (B, I, N, NA, V), 63
War Relocation Authority (WRA), 67, 214, 217
War Report from Burma (*Biruma senki*; FC), 45, 154
War Without Mercy: Race and Power in the Pacific War, 96, 97, 106, 117, 161, 234
Warren, Robert Penn, 172
Wartime Journals of Charles A. Lindberg, 161
Washington Armament Limitation Treaties, 199
Watanabe Kunio, 26, 48, 49, 51
Watanabe Yoshimi, 45, 48, 246, 247
Watashitachi wa konna ni hataraite iru (see *We Are Working So So Hard*)
We Are Working So So Hard (*Watashitachi wa konna ni hataraite iru*; FC), 57, 211, 212
Weapons of the Heart (*Kokoro no busō*; FC), 190, 229, 230, 241
What Made Her Do It? (*Nani ga kanojo o sō saseta ka*, also *What Made Her Do That?*), 13
Why We Fight, series (B, I, N, NA, V), 63, 101, 151, 206, 207, 212
Wildon, Myron, 222
Window Cleaner, The (NA), 67
Wise Guy (NA), 249
With the Marines at Tarawa (NA, V), 63, 154, 250
Women of Steel (NA), 209, 210, 211, 212
Women Wanted (NA), 66
World Film Wars (*Sekai eiga sensō*), 74
World War I, 71, 244
Written With Bloody Nails (*Chi no tsume moji*), 51
Wyler, Willie, 244

X

Xavier, Francis, 171

Y

Yaburetaru shōguntachi (see *Officers Who've Lost — Life of POWs*)
Yabushita Taiji, 227
Yamada Isuzu, 247
Yamagata International Documentary Film Festival, 184
Yamaguchi Yoshiko (aka. Shirley Yamaguchi, Li Xiaglan, Li Hsiang-lan, Ri Ko-ran), 26, 27, 205
Yamamoto Kajirō, 41, 44, 47, 48, 193
Yamamoto Satsuo, 26, 50, 262, 268
Yamanaka Masao, 265
Yamano Ichirō, 227
Yangtze (*Yōsukō*), 25
Yasen gungakutai (see *Military Musical Band and the Front*)
Yasui, Lise, 118
yellow peril, 98
Yeltsin, Boris, 91
Yep, Sandra, 118
YMCA, 214, 252
Yokohama Cinema Shokai, 23, 24, 25, 40, 197, 198
Yokudo banri (see *10,000 Ri of Fertile Land*)
Yomiuri News (*Yomiuri nyūsu*; LOC, NA), 19, 35, 36, 40
Yomiuri Newspaper (*Yomiuri shinbun*), 205
Yonemoto, Bruce and Norman, 108, 118
Yoneyama Tadao, 230
Yoshida, Michael, 118
Yoshida Shigeru, 266
Yoshimura Kimisaburō (Kōzaburō), 22, 50, 230
Yoshimura Ren, 49
Yōsukō (see *Yangtze*)
Yōsukō kantai (see *Fleet on the Yangtze River*)
You're Being Aimed At (*Anata wa nerawarete iru*, also *You Are the Target*), 230
You Can't Take It With You (B, F, V), 206
You Are the Next Wild Eagle (*Kimi koso tsugi no arawashi da*; FC), 49, 248
Young, Edward, 191
Young People (*Wakai hito*; FC), 39
Young Soldiers of the Sky (*Sora no shōnenhei*; FC, LOC, V), 34, 76, 79, 239, 240, 248
You're a Sap, Mr. Jap, 224
Your Job in Germany (NA), 64
Yukiguni (see *Snow Country*)
Yuki yukite shingun (see *Emperor's Naked Army Marches On*)

Z

Zanjin zanbaken (see Man-Slashing, Horse-Piercing Sword)
Zanuck, Darryl, 4, 249
Zhiang Shanku, 225
Zhou Jiapand, 225
Žižek, Slavoj, 86, 87
Zoku — Eiga to kanshō (see Cinema and Appreciation — Part 2), 247

Contributors

Abé Mark Nornes is a graduate student of the University of Southern California's School of Cinema-Television. As a coordinator for the Yamagata International Documentary Film Festival, he co-programmed the retrospective of World War II documentary from which this book arose. He is currently writing about the history of documentary film in Japan.

Komatsuzawa Hiroshi was born just days before the end of the war. He studied economics at Ibaraki National University, and currently works in Tōkyō. Komatsuzawa devotes himself to studying the history of animation, particularly that produced during the war and recent foreign animation which Japanese have co-produced. His work includes The World of Independent Animation Film (Jishuseisaku animeshon no sekai, 1983) and The Footprints of Mochinaga Tadahito, Creator of Japan's Puppet Animation (Mochinaga Tadahito no sokuseki — renmei o kirihiraita animeshon sakka, 1985).

Shimizu Akira graduated from the Department of Literature of Tōkyō Imperial University in 1941, though his career as a film critic began several years before as a staff member of Eiga Hyōron (The Film Review). He lived in Shanghai from 1942 to 1943, where he worked at China Film Company (Chukadenei) under Kawakita Nagamasa. In the following years, he served as Chief Editor for Eiga Hyōron and Motion Picture Library, then entered Tōwa Film in 1951. There he was appointed to Head of Publicity then Chief of the Subtitling Department. Starting in 1960, Shimizu became General Secretary of the Japan Film Library Council, which is now known as the Kawakita Memorial Film Institute. Film critics and programmers from outside Japan have relied on him as a conduit to the Japanese film world. His works include The Situation of the Japanese Film World Under the Occupation by Allied Forces (1972), Half a Century of Tōwa (1977), The Life of Kawakita Nagamasa (1982) and 100 Faces Supporting Japanese Movie History (1991).

Tsurumi Shunsuke graduated from Harvard College about the same time America and Japan went to war. As a Japanese national, he was repatriated to Japan in 1942, and served with the Japanese Navy until 1945. Tsurumi is a critic in the broadest sense; his critical interests range from traditional literature to mythology and cartooning. In books like The Right to Misunderstand (Tokyo: Chikowashobo, 1960), he was one of the first writers anywhere to break down the oppositions between high art and low art, between an advanced West and a backward Japan. In the West he is best know for An Intellectual History of Wartime Japan 1931-1945 (London: KPI, 1986) and A Cultural History of Postwar Japan 1945-1980 (London:KPI, 1987). Chikowashobo has also published twelve volumes of his Collected Works.

For Product Safety Concerns and Information please contact our EU
representative GPSR@taylorandfrancis.com
Taylor & Francis Verlag GmbH, Kaufingerstraße 24, 80331 München, Germany

www.ingramcontent.com/pod-product-compliance
Lightning Source LLC
Chambersburg PA
CBHW071157300426
44113CB00009B/1235